THE BEST OF
NO B.S.

THE ULTIMATE
NO-HOLDS-BARRED ANTHOLOGY

DAN S. KENNEDY

Entrepreneur Books®

Entrepreneur Books, Publisher
Cover Design: Andrew Welyczko
Production and Composition: Eliot House Productions

Library of Congress Cataloging-in-Publication Data

Names: Kennedy, Dan S., 1954- author.

Title: The best of no BS : the ultimate no-holds-barred anthology / Dan S. Kennedy.

Description: Irvine, CA : Entrepreneur Press, [2021] | Includes index. | Summary: "Anthology of marketing expert Dan Kennedy's best writing from the No BS series. Focuses on the customer-getting, sales-boosting, classic marketing strategies that made him famous. Shares marketing knowledge applicable to print, digital, sales, and events"-- Provided by publisher.

Identifiers: LCCN 2021043832 (print) | LCCN 2021043833 (ebook) | ISBN 9781642011456 (trade paperback) | ISBN 9781613084588 (epub)

Subjects: LCSH: Selling. | Marketing--Management. | Customer relations.

Classification: LCC HF5438.25 .K4726 2021 (print) | LCC HF5438.25 (ebook) | DDC 658.85--dc23/eng/20211007

LC record available at https://lccn.loc.gov/2021043832

LC ebook record available at https://lccn.loc.gov/2021043833

Printed in the United States of America

25 24 23 22   10 9 8 7 6 5 4 3 2 1

Contents

P A R T   I
DIRECT MARKETING

P A R T   I I
BRANDING AND LOCAL MARKETING

PART III
PERSONALIZED MARKETING

PART IV
WEALTH BUILDING

PART V
PRODUCTIVITY AND MANAGEMENT

P A R T   V I
PRICING

IMPORTANT NOTICE

Because this Anthology is made up of selected chapters
from many previously published No B.S. books, there
are references throughout to entities identified as "KIC"
and "GKIC," for Inner Circle. These have been replaced
by NO BS INNER CIRCLE / MAGNETIC MARKETING,
and all Dan Kennedy resources, Inner Circle
membership, and other information can be
found at: MagneticMarketing.com or
via the Special Offer on Page 578.

Foreword

by Ken McCarthy,
TheSystemClub.com

I t's been a long time since I've had stage fright and I can't even remember the last time I had writer's block. That said, writing this foreword has been a real challenge. How on earth do I convey the value of this book and its author to you without sounding like I'm wildly exaggerating?

My job is made a little bit easier by the fact that many people who are reading this already know Dan and his work. They know from experience—and looking at their own "Before" and "After" Kennedy bank accounts—that the real challenge in introducing Dan Kennedy accurately is not overstating, but understating what he has to offer business owners, entrepreneurs, and anyone else who is sincerely striving to accomplish positive things in the world as it is.

Before I met Dan, I'd devoured everything I could get my hands on about the subject of accountable, results-driven, direct-response advertising from the pioneering work of Walter Dill Scott in the early 20th century to firsthand accounts by grand masters like Claude Hopkins, Maxwell Sackheim, John Caples, and Victor Schwab to contemporary masters like Eugene Schwartz, Gary Halbert, Gary Bencivenga, Robert Cialdini, Al Ries, and Jack Trout.

It's a big body of literature—many shelves of books, not just a stack or two—and it's all useful. I recommend you make it a life goal to read as much of it as you can. It will pay dividends way out of proportion to your investment of time.

That said, if you're looking for a comprehensive, "one-stop shop" of reality-tested and immediately actionable advice on a wide range of subjects in the direct-response arena, there's one body of work that stands out from all the rest and the book you're holding represents just the tip of the iceberg.

I once tried to make a list of all the areas of business, marketing, and advertising where Dan objectively has world-class experience and expertise. Here's what I came up with:

- Personal selling
- Copywriting
- Direct mail
- Space ads
- Infomercials
- Radio advertising
- Internet marketing
- Selling from the podium
- Book authoring
- Book promotion
- Event promotion
- Managing people

- Managing time
- Community building

I believe this list is comprehensive, but I have a nagging feeling I've left some important things out.

How one person accumulated all this expertise in a single lifetime is one of the mysteries of the ages, but what is not a mystery is the high level of esteem Dan is held in by leaders in the industries I've listed.

Just to pick two . . .

Dan has continuously been a trusted advisor to Guthy-Renker, the $1 billion+ a year giant in the infomercial space, since the day they launched their first product in 1988.

On the internet marketing side of things—an area where Dan's skills and expertise are not fully appreciated—he's had his hand on the pulse of things since 1993. Yes, 1993. August to be exact. That was the year he gave me a chance to share my "crazy" ideas about the potential of online marketing with his clients.

From that beginning, I went on to write the first article on email marketing, organize and sponsor the first conference devoted exclusively to the subject of marketing on the web (November 5, 1994, San Francisco), publish the first article on internet video, and, according to *Time* magazine, was the first person to recognize the importance of the clickthrough rate.

My own students went on to do great things: sell the first banner ads (Rick Boyce), write the first book on Google advertising (Perry Marshall), write the first book on direct-response-oriented web design (Ben Hunt), and write the first book on mobile marketing (Kim Dushinski).

That said, if someone were to ask me what was more important to my success, being early on the internet or meeting Dan Kennedy, it would be a tough call, but I'd have to say meeting

Dan. You see, I wasn't the only person who was early to the internet party, and while it's true some became wealthy (some fabulously so), most did not.

The insight that the internet had potential was mine, but the specific "nuts and bolts" understanding of how to exploit that insight and profit from it—the thing that made all the difference—came largely from Dan.

You'll find the tools and insights you need to achieve your own vision in this book.

Strangely, there's a fundamental fact of the entrepreneur's life that's missing from most discussions of business. It's this: There are a lot of moving parts involved in creating, growing, and maintaining a successful business. And they're ALL important.

By way of comparison, even a car with a world-class engine won't get you very far if it has a flat tire, a missing carburetor, or a gas tank running on empty.

The truth is while there are many credible experts who can help "fill your tank" on specific subjects, I don't know of anyone, past or present, who not only has first-rate operational expertise in all the essential moving parts of business, but who also understands how to weave them together in such a way that the whole is exponentially greater than the parts.

No one does real-world "where the rubber meets the road" advice like Dan. No one. And given the unique, irreproducible times he came up in—when direct mail was king and "audio" meant LPs and cassettes, to the very first infomercials, to the dawning of the Internet Age—we are not likely to ever see his like again.

If you're already a Dan Kennedy fan and client, you know all this. My apologies for stating the obvious.

However, if you're an ambitious person and Dan's work is new to you or you only know one or two dimensions of it, consider the book you're now holding in your hands nothing less than your gateway to a new—and bigger—life.

—Ken McCarthy
TheSystemClub.com

Introduction

A NOTHER book on how-to-succeed-in-business?
"Business Literature," if there can be such a term, has long been overloaded with academic theory from tweedy professors who wouldn't survive a week running a Dairy Queen®, retired or fired CEOs of Big, Dumb Corporations as far distanced from the entrepreneur or small-business owner as a martian, self-appointed, self-anointed expert consultants and professional advisors who know 365 different sexual positions but can't get a date—ever, and, finally, pure motivational performers who'll have you chanting mantras and walking on hot coals—but then what? Their books are their seminars, absent the circus excitement.

When I started my No B.S. book series back in the early 2000s, it was as a combative response to this entire collection of peddlers of stuff actually dangerous to your wealth. I set out to be a fact-based, *experience-based truth-teller*, at the cost of being shunned by many peers, media, and others. These books have earned a lot of praise, made bestseller lists, a "best business books" list, but they have also—for reasons that will shortly become obvious—been banned in corporate America and garnered a good-sized quantity of shocked and appalled reactions. I get mail. Even to my editors' distress, I am of the Jack Nicholson school of thought. Jack said: "What YOU think of me is none of MY business." I am only interested in syncing with "my people," who I see in two groups. **One, the small-business owner and entrepreneur** who rises each day with renewed optimism and determination, sallying forth against a conspiracy of dunces and small thinkers and slow movers, unintentional and intentional saboteurs, to dare to invent, innovate, make, grow, and expand, to make his own economy, to defy odds and others' skepticism and criticism, *to build.*

In addition to my own successful enterprises, I have, as consultant/advisor and marketing strategist, helped thousands and thousands of entrepreneurs make ordinary businesses extraordinary, create ideal lifestyle businesses, and grow from small to big—to millions, to tens of millions, even to over a billion dollars a year. You will find *that* in these pages.

Two, the sales professional, often unjustly discounted and looked down on, underappreciated as THE most vital energy of the entire economy. My famous speaking colleague and friend, the late Zig Ziglar, used to end speeches to sales groups with the plea: "Go sell *something* today. *America* needs the business." Fact is *nothing* happens unless and until *somebody* sells *something*—idea, strategy, tools, products, services. A life is *not* saved by cutting-edge medical technology if that new, expensive equipment isn't sold to the hospital, with a sales pro navigating the CEO, CFO, COO, doctors, committees, budgets, and winning against other priorities competing for the same dollars. A family's home is *not* safe and kids' college educations assured if the chief breadwinner suddenly dies in a tragedy, and the life insurance salesman failed to get that selling opportunity and ultimately close that sale. It used to be said "clothing makes the man," and maybe so, but not without a knowledgeable, professional menswear salesman. Men, after all, do *not* know what goes best with what.

I have led salespeople out of the grimy, primitive work of "cold prospecting" and random selling, provided the means to position and present themselves as "NOT Another Salesman," and quite literally changed the entire experience, effectiveness, and efficiency of being a sales pro. You will find *that* in these pages.

"My people" are NOT in need of coddling. NOT "sensitive" to impolitic, blunt, straightforward expression. NOT so cemented in "how IT has always been done around here" as to preclude improvement or replacement of methods. They recognize that conforming to their industry norms and common practices can only yield, at best, normal (i.e., average) results, and they want more. They want to stand apart from and above the clutter of a "me too" marketplace. They ARE interested in "What Works," and do NOT require it laden with spoonfuls of sugar to make its medicine palatable—they *want* the medicine.

I wrote all the No B.S. books for them, from my actual experience, telling my "No B.S." truth about what it *really* takes to be an outstanding success in a world of mediocrity, what it *really* takes to be independent in a groupthink, intimidated, conformist world. How to be an always-welcome-guest and never an annoying pest when selling. How to use smart advertising and marketing to discriminate and attract the absolutely ideal customers, clients, or patients for you and your business, who will pay, stay, and zealously refer.

If you are the right reader, the selections here from all the books will "ring true" to your experience, and you will think: "FINALLY, someone really understands what I'm doing, what I wrestle each day, what I need to figure out. FINALLY, someone is giving me the straight scoop."

You may still find some things here hard to swallow or, certainly, contrary to everything you've been told, in conflict with popular, common ideas, maybe even offensive if you are touchy. These "rough spots" may be the most important for you to force yourself to consider most carefully. You will, I promise, find OPPORTUNITIES.

These books are also meant as Permission Slips. In thousands of consulting sessions and ongoing relationships with clients I often find people who essentially know what they don't want, know what isn't working as it should, and even know what needs to be done—to assert their authority and sovereignty, to price more aggressively, to differentiate, to win, but they hold back and feel unsure about their own instincts and ideas, their own diagnoses and prescriptions. They benefit greatly from having a trustworthy advisor tell them "you ARE right about that" and urge them into action.

My end goal is for you to *attack* your goals' achievement with greater clarity, confidence, and capability by the information, examples, and the "permission" you draw from this book.

—DAN S. KENNEDY

List of Books Appearing in This Compilation

Part I: Direct Marketing,

featuring selections from:

No B.S. Direct Marketing

No B.S. Guide to Direct Response Social Media Marketing

Part II: Branding and Local Marketing,

featuring selections from:

No B.S. Guide to Brand-Building by Direct Response

No B.S. Grassroots Marketing

Part III: Personalized Marketing,

featuring selections from:

No B.S. Trust-Based Marketing

No B.S. Guide to Marketing to Leading-Edge Boomers and Seniors

No B.S. Guide to Maximum Referrals and Customer Retention

Part IV: Wealth Building,

featuring selections from:

No B.S. Wealth Attraction in the New Economy

No B.S. Business Success in the New Economy

Part V: Productivity and Management,

featuring selections from:

No B.S. Time Management for Entrepreneurs

No B.S. Ruthless Management of People and Profits

Part VI: Pricing,

featuring selections from:

No B.S. Price Strategy

PART I

DIRECT MARKETING

with selections from

No B.S. Direct Marketing

*No B.S. Guide to Direct Response
Social Media Marketing*

DIRECT MARKETING

DIRECT Marketing is derived from "mail order," with set-in-cement success principles dating to the turn of the century. You see it alive and thriving on TV now with the My Pillow guy, but also with Fisher Investments, aimed at a different demographic. Still, *why* would *you* ever think of applying *that* to your local brick-and-mortar retail business, or service business, or professional practice?

This gets a little less radical, outlier, and odd with each passing year, as more business owners get disgusted enough with traditional advertising and its often mysteriously hard-to-assess return on investment and look around for a different, more accountable, more intelligently manageable approach. Many find their way to Direct Marketing. Yet it is still a best-kept secret in many categories of business, particularly at the local, brick-and-mortar level. It offers you real competitive advantage because of that.

Crazy Like a Fox

Let me give you an example. The day I wrote this I had monthly tele-consulting sessions, including one with a dentist and his wife running a high-end restorative and cosmetic dental practice in the Midwest. With patients going through exams, diagnoses, and case presentations, but not proceeding with treatment, they had, over recent months, expanded their follow-up from one cursory letter and one phone call to, by my recommendations, a series of 17 letters, including several with specific offers, altered fee or terms options, and deadlines following the "rules" of Direct Marketing and Direct Response Marketing in the chapters of this book included here. Several of these letters ran a number of pages long, including patient testimonials and stories plus P.S.'s driving people online to see specific videos. I know: 17 sounds like a lot. *Crazy.* Enough to irritate. Something *no* dentist does. However, it has brought in new patients who would have, before, been chalked up to un-gettable. Its results are factually known. The net Return on Investment is, over a year, an extra six figures. Enough to pay for an offspring's college education or nicely fund a retirement account.

"Normal" retail businesses and professional practices do little or no follow-up to unconverted leads, and if they do, it's by email only, most never opened let alone read. DIRECT Marketing businesses have a very different "normal." It's called: *follow up until they buy or die.* And a lot of it is done offline, by real mail arriving at homes or offices. This aggressive strategy produces very useful testimonials; patients who say "NO ONE has ever cared so much about me to be as persistent and patient as you've been, and I'm grateful you were."

Here is the essence: in these excerpts from the book NO B.S. DIRECT MARKETING FOR NON-DIRECT MARKETING BUSINESSES you will be presented with an entirely different business model for attracting prospective customers, for converting them, for following up on those who don't immediately convert, and, overall, for extracting a great deal more return on your invested dollars. Nothing about this is new. Not at all. It is "transplanted" from a century of consistent success to your business. It is comprehensive—it is about whom you advertise for and market to, what you advertise, how you organize your marketing, and a "system" for managing the newly interested, prospective customer. This does literally change *everything*.

There are also selections here from the book NO B.S. GUIDE TO DIRECT RESPONSE SOCIAL MEDIA MARKETING. This is radical all over again, because it transplants and applies an "old" methodology to a "new" media. Most experts involved with social media reject the ideas of direct response and of direct accountability, telling you to measure its usefulness in new metrics like Likes or views or going viral. At the bank, though, the only thing you are allowed to deposit is dollars. So make a note: there has never been, is not now, and never will be a new media that should be allowed to eat your money or time while evading direct accountability in dollars.

From all this, you will see a thoroughly systematic, success principles-driven, accountable, and definitively unordinary approach to attracting, converting, monetizing, satisfying, and multiplying customers, clients, or patients.

The Big Switch

Why Direct Marketing for NON-Direct Marketing Businesses?

Originally appearing as Chapter 1
from *No B.S. Direct Marketing*

I *t is an odd sort of title, isn't it?*

If you picked it up hoping for huge breakthroughs in your business, you bought the right book. But first, I have to get these definitions out of the way.

By non-direct marketing business, I mean anything but a mail order, catalog, or online marketer who *directly* solicits orders for merchandise. It could be a local dental practice, carpet cleaning business, brick-and-mortar retailer, B2B–IT consultant, CPA firm, or industrial equipment manufacturer. The owners of such businesses do not think of themselves as direct marketers engaged in direct-response advertising, until I get ahold of them!

Examples of pure direct-marketing businesses just about everybody knows are the TV home shopping channels, QVC and HSN; catalogers like J. Peterman or Hammacher Schlemmer; contemporary catalog and online catalog/ecommerce companies like Amazon and Zappos; businesses like the Fruit of the Month Club; and mass users of direct mail to sell things, like Publishers Clearing House.

There are thousands of true direct-marketing businesses. Some are familiar to the general public; many, many more are familiar only to the niche or special interest they serve. For example, at any given moment, I have over 50 direct marketers as clients, each selling books, audio CDs, home study courses, and seminars and services by mail, internet and print media, teleseminars, and webinars, which market only to a specific industry or profession—one to carpet cleaners, another to restaurant owners, another to chiropractors, etc. If you are not a chiropractor, you don't know the name Dr. Chris Tomshack and his company HealthSource. If you are a chiropractor, it would be hard not to know of him, thanks to his full-page ads in the industry trade journals, massive amounts of direct mail, and other direct marketing. There are also direct marketers unknown by name but known by their products or brands, like a longtime client of mine, Guthy-Renker Corporation, the billion-dollar business behind TV infomercials for Proactiv® acne creams and many other products made into brands. What all these have in common is their fundamental process of selling direct via media to consumers, with no brick-and-mortar locations or face-to-face contact required.

These are not the folks this book is for, even if they are the kinds of entrepreneurs I work personally with a lot. They already know everything in this book, and live and prosper by it.

This book is for the owner of a brick-and-mortar business—a business with a store, showroom, or office; a restaurant; a dental practice; an accounting practice; or a funeral home—that is some kind of ordinary business, one most likely local and serving a local market. These are the entrepreneurs who have populated my audiences for four decades, subscribe to my newsletters, and use my systems to **transform those "ordinary" businesses into extraordinary money machines that far, far outperform their industry norms, peers, competitors, and their own wildest imaginations. How do they do it? The big switch is a simple one to state (if more complex to do): they switch from traditional advertising to** *direct-response* **advertising. They stop emulating ordinary and traditional marketing and instead emulate** *direct* **marketing.**

Most "ordinary" businesses advertise and market like much bigger brand-name companies, so they spend (waste) a lot of money on image, brand, and presence. But copycatting these big brand-name companies is like a rabbit behaving like the lion. It makes *no* sense. The big companies have all sorts of reasons for the way they advertise and market that have nothing to do with getting a customer or making sales! Because your agenda is much simpler, you should find successful businesses with similar agendas to copycat. Those are direct marketers. You and they share the same basic ideas:

1. Spend $1.00 on marketing, get back $2.00 or $20.00, fast, that can be accurately tracked to the $1.00 spent.
2. Do NOT spend $1.00 that does not directly and quickly bring back $2.00 or $20.00.

Please stop and be sure you get this life-changing principle. Be careful who you copy. Be careful who you act like. Be careful who you study. If their purpose, objectives, agenda, reasons for doing what they do the way they do it don't match up with your purpose, objectives, agenda, then you should NOT study or emulate or copy them!

Please stop and be sure you get this life-changing corollary principle. Find somebody who is successful, who shares your

Big Company's Agenda for Advertising and Marketing

1. Please/appease its board of directors (most of whom know zip about advertising and marketing but have lots of opinions)

2. Please/appease its stockholders

3. Look good and appropriate to Wall Street

4. Look good and appropriate to the media

5. Build brand identity

6. Win awards for advertising

7. Sell something

Your Agenda

1. Sell something. Now.

purpose, objectives, agenda, and pay great attention to what he does and how he does it.

I believe some call this sort of thing "a blinding flash of the obvious." Well, you can call it obvious if you like—but then how do you explain the fact that 99% of all businesspeople are operating as if ignorant of this obvious logic?

I might add this principle has power in places other than marketing. You *can* eventually get south by going due north,

each other,
incestuous,
Everybody

l deliberately
ent—not just

nd business more profitable,
rection that leads directly to
g inappropriate examples is
et to the North Pole. Odds
a giant iguana long before

rs, clueless as
ive marketing,
services. That's
for non-direct
esses is really
nal advertising
all. It is simply
multiplied in
actually already
rip on one-third
EDY RESULTS
at you'll master
. You know the
you do have this

, Unproductive,
nd Marketing
iy?

are just about clueless
g. They are, therefore,
media salespeople, ad
wizards, and others
actually produce a
ytime you are being
not *fact* based, and
s, and monkey-see-
d. Direct marketers

ely tell you where
to get a customer
ically come from
nsequently, he's
louldn't be, but

rketing for
esses

itself!) Please copy
em often until you
on track, save you a
marketing.

lnerability to
keting Incest.
you probably
ousiness was
it better, but
erybody in

an industry standing in a circle looking inward at
ignoring anyone or anything outside the circle. It's
and it works just like real generational incest:
slowly gets dumber and dumber and dumber.

This book dares you to turn back on the circle and
go far afield from your peers in search of differ
incrementally better—*different* ways of marketing.

Yes, Salvation Is within Reach

Now, here's the good news: most business owne
they may be about profitable advertising or effect
do know a lot about how to sell their products or s
very good news because DIRECT marketing

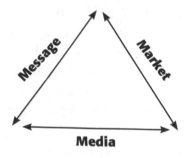

marketing busin
not about traditic
or marketing at
"salesmanship
media." So you
do have a firm g
of the KENN
TRIANGLE th
with this book

Media

Message. It'll get tweaked, as I'll explain. But
component part.

The Ten No B.S. Rules of Direct Ma
Non-Direct Marketing Busin
(My Ten Commandments)

I'll lay our foundation first. (A radical idea
these and post them somewhere you'll see th
get them memorized. Doing so will keep you
lot of money, and dramatically improve your

From now on, every ad you run, every flier you distribute, every postcard or letter you mail, every website you put up, every/anything you do to advertise or market your business MUST adhere to these rules. To be fair, they are simplistic and dogmatic, and there are reasons to violate them in certain situations. But for now, sticking to them as a rigid diet will work. You can experiment later, after you've first cleansed your business of toxins.

I once wrote an entire book about breaking rules, and generally speaking, I think rules are for other, ordinary mortals—certainly not for me, and not for you either if you are a true entrepreneur. So you'll chafe at rules here just as I would. However, when you are attempting to undo bad habits and replace them with new ones, some hard and fast rules are necessary, temporarily. Once you fully understand these and have lived with them for a reasonable

Rule #1.   There Will Always Be an Offer or Offer(s)

Rule #2.   There Will Be a Reason to Respond Right Now

Rule #3.   You Will Give Clear Instructions

Rule #4.   There Will Be Tracking, Measurement, and Accountability

Rule #5.   Only No-Cost Brand-Building

Rule #6.   There Will Be Follow-Up

Rule #7.   There Will Be Strong Copy

Rule #8.   It Will Look Like Mail-Order Advertising

Rule #9.   Results Rule. Period.

Rule #10. You Will Be a Tough-Minded Disciplinarian and Put Your Business on a Strict Direct-Marketing Diet length of time, then feel free to experiment if you wish. But get good at coloring inside the lines before ignoring them altogether.

Finally, a word about these aged rules and the newest of the new media and its promoters of new metrics. Try putting views or likes on a bank deposit slip. You will be told that no old rules—the time-tested, time-proven ones—apply to new media like Facebook or Snapchat or etc., etc., but be certain to take into account who makes that argument. It will come from young people on your staff or in agencies spending your money, not theirs, unable if pressed to prove profitable return on investment from their chosen media and made-up metrics. When pressed on this point, they won't argue facts, because they can't; they will only stigmatize and label you as a dummy and a primitive stuck in the past's old ways. It will come from people caught up in a dumb cattle stampede. You have to do it and throw harsh reality accountability aside because everybody else is doing it and ignoring financial accountability. It will come from peddlers of it for profit. Of course, the bald man should never ask the hungry barber if he needs a haircut. When all you have to sell are haircuts, everyone needs them.

If a media can't be used with these ten rules applied to it, my advice is: skip it.

CHAPTER 2

An OFFER They
Can't Refuse

Originally appearing as Chapter 2
from *No B.S. Direct Marketing*

here is a certain mindset in direct-marketing folks. We are result oriented. We find it difficult to just go out for a drive for the sake of going for a drive. We want a definite destination, an estimated time of arrival, and a purpose for the trip. Most direct marketers have trouble watching a sports telecast unless they've wagered on the game. We want to KNOW if we have won or lost, succeeded or failed, achieved something definitive or just wandered around. While this tendency gets in the way of a friendly family game night, it is extremely useful in avoiding the vagueness and lack of accountability that permeates most business owners' marketing activities.

It is this habit of thought that informs.

Rule #1
There Will ALWAYS Be an Offer or Offers

A key distinguishing characteristic of direct marketing and Direct-Response Advertising from all other marketing and advertising is the presentation of a very specific offer or offers. Ideally, yours is a Godfather's Offer—an offer that the appropriate prospect or customer for you *can't* refuse! We'll get to the architecture of offers in a few minutes, but first the overarching ideas: one, to make your *every* communication actually ask somebody to do something, and two, to inject new disciplines of selling and accountability into *all* your communication with prospects, customers, and the marketplace at large.

If you begin paying attention to advertising and marketing, you'll see that most of it merely shows up and talks about the marketers and advertisers, but does not directly offer something specific to be had by immediately and directly responding. A lot of print ads and TV commercials and brochures now include websites or Facebook sites where you can go like 'em, etc., but present no Offer as a compelling reason to go there. All this is undisciplined. It is sending money out to play a backyard game with no rules, and worse, no score-keeping, no clear means of judging victory or defeat. A chaotic mess. When you take this undisciplined approach and simply spend and hope and guess, you're at the mercy of opinion about your marketing—do you like it? Does your mother-in-law like it? Do your customers say nice things about it? Try paying any of your bills with that sort of feedback.

This all changes with direct marketing.

Direct marketing imposes discipline. That discipline may be as important and valuable as the benefit of direct response itself. For some mysterious reason, business owners are willing to let advertising and marketing off the hook, but tend to hold everything else accountable for results and return on investment.

If they tie up money in certain product inventory, they expect it to sell—or they refuse to restock it. If they employ a sales representative, they expect him to make sales. If they buy a delivery van, they expect it to start and run so it can make deliveries. If they pay a laborer by the hour, they expect him to clock in, be there, and work for the hour. Yet investments made for marketing are permitted to skate. Only direct marketing imposes discipline, by always making an offer or offers, so response to those offers can be tracked and measured, injecting factual accountability.

My old speaking colleague, one of the all-time greats, Zig Ziglar, always described salespeople who wimped out at closing sales and directly demanding orders as "professional visitors," not professional salespeople. Since you will be doing selling in print, online, with media, you rarely want to let it be a professional visitor on your behalf. Fire all the wimps. Demand real performance. So your task is to incorporate a direct offer each and every time you put out a message, of any kind, by any means.

I mean of *any* kind. By *any* means. We teach most business owners to use Thanksgiving greeting cards and/or New Year's greeting cards, with past and lost as well as active customers, clients, or patients, and, often, with unconverted leads, too. We also teach no greeting card should arrive without being accompanied by an offer. Typically, the offer will be a gift with visit to showroom or store, gift with purchase, gift for referral, etc., placed in a printed piece inside a separate envelope, inside the greeting card itself, to preserve some separation between the thank you or new year sentiment and selling. But we are not shy about our purpose in life either, and it is not merely being professional visitors.

In short, you have a fundamental governance decision to make. Will you let yourself be persuaded or bullied into wasting money on marketing that cannot be *directly* held accountable for results and return on investment? Or will you insist on accountability?

"Shined Shoes Save Lives"

My speaking colleague of some 40 events or so, the late General Norman Schwarzkopf, famous for Desert Storm, said, "Shined shoes save lives." He meant that establishing and adhering absolutely to minor disciplines ensured soldiers could and would adhere to vital battlefield disciplines. Norm believed that a person can't be undisciplined about some things but disciplined about others any more than an alcoholic person committed to sobriety can occasionally have a few drinks. You either are or you aren't. Your business is either run in a disciplined way, or it isn't.

Discipline is a central theme of all business success. Last year, 2017, was the 80th anniversary of widespread embrace by successful entrepreneurs of Napoleon Hill's works *The Laws of Success* and *Think and Grow Rich*, the summary of findings from his 30-year investigation into key commonalities of over 500 of the industrialists, inventors, entrepreneurs, and financiers who built America. In *Laws*, he detailed 17 such principles; in *Think and Grow Rich*, 13. Two of these are: accurate thinking and organized effort. Of a more contemporary nature, you might be familiar with Michael Gerber his book, *The E-Myth*, which is all about organized systems in business. One of the most successful of all buyers of and investors in businesses, Warren Buffett, has an absolute discipline for evaluating companies, and he has stuck to it with religious conviction. Top-performing athletes in every sport always exhibit a far greater level of discipline for everything from study to practice to actual playing of their game than the mediocre majority. The most successful authors

Resource Alert!

THE book entirely devoted to comprehensive imposition of success disciplines to a business is *No B.S. RUTHLESS Management of People & Profits, 2nd Edition.* The book entirely devoted to comprehensive imposition of success disciplines to an individual is *No B.S. Time Management for Entrepreneurs, 3rd Edition.*

past and present do not write whenever they're in the mood — they have a self-imposed discipline mandating a set number of hours or completed pages every day. Anywhere you find significant success, you will find imposed absolute discipline. Undisciplined, unorganized advertising and marketing "effort" is not going to defy this fact of success.

Two Types of Offers

There are basically two types of offers. There is an offer requesting purchase. There is also the lead-generation offer, asking only for a person to, in effect, raise their hand, to identify and register themselves as having interest in certain subject matter and information or goods or services, and to invite further communication from you. Often, although not always, the lead-generation offer is free. There are times and places for both kinds of offers, but no communication should be devoid of some offer.

The Direct Purchase Offer

Online media like Groupon or hybrid offline+online media like Valpak coupons deliver some of the simplest, most straightforward direct purchase offers, like "Buy One, Get the 2nd One Free"— used by everybody from pizza shops to window replacement companies. I am not a champion of discounting as strategy, and a co-author, Jason Marrs, and I provide much more sophisticated approaches in our book *No B.S. Price Strategy.* But for illustration purposes, this is a direct purchase offer you're very familiar with and may be using now in your business. Another common direct purchase offer, in place of or combined with discounting, is gift with purchase. These were birthed by direct marketers but have migrated to retail, service, professionals, and B2B, so they are commonplace. They should be and usually are married to a hard deadline. They certainly provide easy opportunity to accurately measure their effectiveness and production, although out of ignorance or sloth, many business owners fail to measure.

Direct Purchase Offers have several significant disadvantages. One is that they tend to sacrifice price integrity and profitability, and if relied on too frequently, train customers to only respond when a "great deal" is offered. Two, they can only be responded to by people ready and able to buy right this minute—they fail to identify people likely to buy in your category in the near future. Third, they can be easily and quickly comparison shopped, especially if you are conveying the offer online. Still, business does revolve around Direct Purchase Offers.

The Lead-Generation Offer

This is a more interesting kind of offer, because it can substantially reduce the waste factor in advertising, convert a sales culture to a marketing culture, and provide opportunity to build trust and create a relationship.

You see lead generation done by direct marketers routinely

and regularly. You may not have given them much thought, but now you will. They are commonly used by national direct marketers, but rarely used by local, small businesses—even though the national and local firms may be in the same product or service categories. For example, a company like Premier Bathtubs, which sells walk-in bathtubs that are safer for elderly people, advertises just about everywhere, offering a free information kit with brochures and a DVD. Once somebody raises their hand and registers themselves as interested in making a home's bathroom safe for themselves or an elderly parent, the company has a marketing opportunity. Oddly, you will almost never catch a local remodeling company duplicating this strategy. Instead, they tend to leap to offering an in-home estimate for work to be done. This is often A Bridge Too Far.

The Important Concept of Threshold Resistance

Alfred Taubman, one of America's most successful mall developers, spoke and wrote at length about the concept of Threshold Resistance as it applies to entrances to retail stores and window displays of retail stores. I find it applies even more broadly to direct marketing (see Figure 2.1 on page 20). All offers fall somewhere on a continuum between Low-Threshold Offer and High-Threshold Offer.

Here are examples of offers that would fall to the right of the middle, toward High Threshold:

Chiropractor	Free Exam
Financial Advisor	Free Seminar
Remodeler	Free Estimate
Restaurant	Out for a Meal and Experience That May Not Prove Pleasurable

These score toward High Threshold because they can be

FIGURE 2.1: Threshold Resistance

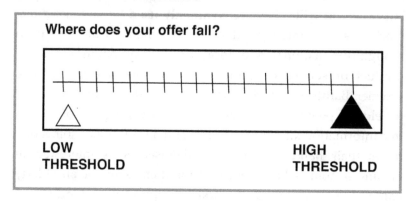

scary and intimidating to the consumer. They require people to put themselves in uncomfortable positions. They require a decision nearly made, to get care, to find an advisor, to get remodeling done. A great many people with evolving interest or interest that can be stimulated will still not be prepared to take this big of a step forward.

Examples of offers that fall at the High Threshold are:

Chiropractor $29 Exam

Financial Advisor   Free Private Appointment

Examples of Low-Threshold Offers

The lowest threshold offer is for free information, to be sent by mail or FedEx, or accessed online. This is *the* staple item of direct-response advertising, in virtually every category of business. The largest wealth management firm, Fisher Investments, on TV and radio, in *Forbes* and other magazines; one of the most successful home improvement product manufacturers, SunSetter Awnings, by direct mail and blow-in inserts in magazines and newspapers; one of the biggest health insurers, Humana, in TV commercials; virtually all of the retirement communities advertising in the *Where to Retire* magazine; my client, High Point University; my client, www.ExcellenceInOrthodontics.org—all offer low-threshold, information items like books, free reports, DVDs. If this is their number-one strategy, why shouldn't it be yours? Keep in mind, these are big, national direct-response advertisers who have plenty of opportunity to run split tests often, and do, and keep returning to the tried-and-true, low-threshold, free information offer.

I have coined the term "Information <u>First</u> Marketing" for this. Really savvy local business operators are embracing it, modeling the national advertisers. This is a wave of change, not just in the way businesses advertise to attract new customers, but in what they advertise. The karate school *doesn't* advertise itself, its lessons, or a free lesson. Instead, it advertises a free report by its owner: *The Parents' Guide to Cyber-Bullying and Bullying: Raising Emotionally Strong Kids.* The mattress store *doesn't* advertise itself, its mattresses, or some sale of the century. It advertises its free guidebook: *Why You Can't Seem to Get a Good Night's Sleep.* The IT consultant *doesn't* advertise his services. He advertises a free book: *You Are the Target: Cybersecurity Before It's Too Late.*

Consider a very ordinary business—a funeral home. Most funeral home advertising is very basic: name, location, years in the community, list of services. The only offer is implied: when you need us, we'll bury you. But even a funeral home can create and put forward a low-threshold, information-based, lead-generation offer that begins a relationship, builds trust, and establishes preference in advance of need, like this:

For a free "Pre-Need Planning Kit" and Audio CD:
"19 Financial and Estate Planning Tips for Responsible
Family Leaders," call our free
recorded message anytime at 000-000-0000.
It will be sent by mail, no cost, no obligation.

The Hybrid Approach

There is no law that says you must choose just one of these approaches.

Most advertising dramatically suppresses possible response by presenting only a single reason for a response. Typically, this is a High-Threshold Offer that requires somebody to be 99.9% ready to buy now. Nobody's coming in for a $59.00 exam unless they are 99% ready to put a chiropractic physician to work on their back pain today. But a lot of people suffering with nagging or episodically reoccurring back pain, who are having evolving thoughts about doing something about it, would respond to a Low-Threshold Offer of information about "True Causes and Best Ways to Relieve Nagging Back Pain—Without Surgery or Drugs." You don't have to be dead or have a dead family member in the parlor to respond to a High + Medium + Low Threshold, i.e., three reasons to respond ad for the funeral parlor. It can present the usual stuff—here we are, here's what we do; if you have an immediate need, call this number anytime 24 hours a day, 7 days a week, and one of our professionals will be immediately available to assist you—but also present the previously shown Low-Threshold Offer, and a Medium-High Threshold Offer, too, as shown here:

For a free "Pre-Need Planning Kit" and Audio CD,
"19 Financial and Estate Planning Tips for Responsible
Family Leaders," call our free
recorded message anytime at 000-000-0000.
It will be sent by mail, no cost, no obligation.

Tour our new Lakeside Eternal Rest Gardens, get
answers to any questions you have about pre-need
planning, by appointment, Monday–Saturday. Call
William Tourguide at 000-000-0000. Free Thank-You
Gift when you visit: complimentary dinner for two
at The Golden Corral Steakhouse.

To be clear, here's what I've introduced you to here:

1. The use of offers
2. The difference between Low and High-Threshold Offers
3. The use of Lead-Generation Offers
4. Single Reason to Respond vs. Multiple Reasons to Respond

Once a business owner understands these things, his objection is often about a possible trade-down of response. The fear is that somebody who might call or come in or otherwise respond to a High-Threshold Offer and make an immediate purchase will trade down to a Low-Threshold Offer and delay his purchase or be scooped up by a competitor. While this does happen, it usually affects far fewer people than a business owner fears, and the improved total response and value of leads captured for development more than makes up for what little trade-down occurs. After all, the person who fell off a ladder and has to crawl to the phone isn't going to trade down from making an appointment with the doctor to requesting a free report or DVD delivered days later by mail. The person with a dead body is unlikely to trade down from immediate assistance at the funeral parlor to booking a tour next Thursday. In most cases, you can safely add Low-Threshold Offers without significantly compromising response to a High-Threshold Offer designed for the person ready to buy right this minute.

Ultimately, your decisions about the nature of your offer(s), where they fall on the Low- to High-Threshold continuum, whether or not they feature information, whether they are for lead generation or immediate purchase activity or a hybrid of the two are situational. Different media, different markets, different timing will color those decisions. You should realize you have choices and you can make your marketing dollars work harder for you by offering people more than one reason and more than one means of responding to you. But no matter what you make of these choices each time you must make them in putting forward marketing, your pledge of honor to Rule #1 must be: there will *always* be an offer or offers.

Rule #2
There Will Be a Reason to Respond Right Now

Hesitation and procrastination are amongst the most common of all human behaviors.

If you are a mail-order catalog shopper, you have—more than once—browsed, folded down corners of pages from which you intended to buy items, set the catalogs aside, and never placed the orders. This happens with every marketing media. People watching a TV infomercial almost buy, but put it off, to do the next time they see it, or jot down the 800-number, to do it later, but later never comes. A shopper enters the mall, sees an outfit she likes, but tells herself she'll stop and look at it and probably get it on her way out. By the time she has walked the mall, had lunch, bought other items, and is headed back to the end of the mall she entered at, she is focused on getting to her car and getting home. The dress spotted on arrival is left behind.

We must be sharply, painfully aware of all the potential response lost to such hesitation. The hidden cost and failure in all advertising and marketing is with the Almost-Persuaded. They were tempted to respond. They nearly responded. They got right up to the edge of response, but then set it aside to take care of later or to mull over or to Google the next time they were at their computer. When they get to that edge, we must reach across and pull them past it. There must be good reason for them not to stop short or delay or ponder. There must be *urgency*.

At Disney World, at the parks' closing times, they need to get everybody out quickly, for they have much work to do during the night, to be clean, fresh, restocked, and ready to reopen on time the next morning. If they offered transportation from the parks to the hotels, resorts, and parking lots until everyone was accommodated, people would stroll, loiter, find a bench to sit on until the crowd thinned. But there are posted and announced times for the last bus and the last boat. Thus there is urgency. (Further, they switch from gentle to up-tempo music, dim lights first in the back sections of the park, and have cast members with flashlights waving people along toward the exits.) They undoubtedly empty a park faster by at least an hour than if they created no urgency and let everybody meander out at their own chosen pace. Southwest Airlines figured out how to get their planes boarded much faster than other airlines by issuing colored boarding cards but not assigning seats, so each group is in a hurry—sometimes a stampede—to board, to get the best remaining seat. They create urgency. No, these are not marketing examples, but they are excellent demonstrations of the role that success or failure at creating urgency has in every kind of business.

Direct marketing can often *contextually* provide opportunity to create urgency of immediate response. This can be done with limited supply, limit per household or buyer, the countdown clock you see on a direct-response TV commercial or a webinar. If the product itself cannot be limited in supply, some bonus or premium attached to it certainly can be. In the seminar business, a place I live and work, we use the obvious devices like "early bird discounts" and extend-a-pay monthly installments tied to a deadline to motivate early registrations. But we also use bonuses, entries into prize drawings, backstage-pass opportunities, preferred seating, closed-door, limited-number luncheon tickets available only to the first 50 or first 100 to beat the deadline in order to create even more urgency. Retail mimics this with the "doorbuster sales" starting at 5 A.M., 6 A.M., or 7 A.M., and can increase that urgency with a gift for the first x-number to be there with noses pressed against the glass. Disney creates false limited supply by bringing a product like a movie DVD, in their language, "out of the Disney vault just until Halloween—then it goes back in the vault and can't be had." They periodically bring the same product out of the vault, run the same short promotion, return it to the vault, wait until consumers have forgotten about the promotion, and then trot it out again. All these examples are about creating *a context for urgency of response.*

Direct marketing can also *structurally* provide opportunity for urgency of response. Anytime a group dynamic can be applied, a stampede effect seen, an "act now or lose out forever" reality displayed, a higher percentage of people presented with an offer will act than will under any other circumstances. People are motivated to buy what they will not be able to get if they don't buy now, even when they would not buy now if relieved of that threat of loss. An auction is a prime example of this, and it has successfully been moved to online media—with live auctions and with timed auctions on sites like eBay. Putting people "live" into a seminar room where a persuasive speaker makes an offer from the stage, citing limited supply or discount or gift only for the first x-number, and *having people see the stampede* of earliest responders rushing to the product table at the back of the room is hard to trump by any other means and impossible to perfectly replicate by any other means; however, we've learned to come close with live online webinars, where viewers can see the earliest buyers' comments, the "ticker" recording the purchase, the countdown clock for the closing of the shopping cart ticking away, and in live webinars, we can recognize by name the fast buyers. A direct mail, fax, and/or email sequence that begins by announcing that only 47 of the whatever-product will be sold (at this price, in this color, with this bonus, etc.) can, in its second piece, list the names of the first 18 buyers and show that only 29 remain, and in its third piece list the names of the 34 buyers and show that only 13 remain available.

The most powerful urgency by exclusivity is having only one available. Neiman Marcus does this every year, in the pages of its big Christmas catalog, with unique gift items and experiences that there are only one of. For example, in one year's Christmas book, they offered a backstage experience and actual walk-on part one night in the Broadway musical *Annie*, for just $30,000.00; a Woody Trailer reconfigured as an elaborate portable bar, as the ultimate tailgate party vehicle, for $150,000.00; a private dinner for a party of ten with a gaggle of great celebrity chefs, for $250,000.00; and a trip for two to Paris and Geneva, including a visit to the Van Cleef & Arpels boutique and watchmaking shop, and unique his and her watches, for $1,090,000.00. Will someone buy each of these one-of-a-kind gifts? Based on historical precedent with NM's annual one-of-a-kind gifts, that answer is almost certainly yes. But, really, anybody can create one-of-a-kind gifts and experiences, or very limited availability equivalents. NM also garners an enormous amount of media attention and free publicity each year because of these extraordinary gift offers—something a local business could do at a local level just as easily.

In B2B, in the advertising, consulting, and coaching fields, this is often done with geographic area exclusivity. A collection of licensed print ads and radio and TV commercials, a seat in a mastermind group, access to various resources becomes more desirable (and can be sold for a much higher price) when only one CPA in Pittsburgh can have it; thus the race is on and any delay may put it in the hands of your arch-competitor with you forever locked out than when it is available to any and all comers. A very successful program like this I helped a client, Burleson Seminars, develop is www.ExcellenceInOrthodontics.org. Only one orthodontist per geo-area gets the certification, use of the identity and logo, use of exclusive patient education books and videos, and holds a position in an online directory promoted to consumers by online and magazine advertising. They went from zero to a multimillion-dollar licensing business almost overnight.

Certain businesses have actual scarcity. The people I acquire rare and first edition books from for my collection, Bauman Rare Books in New York, have actual scarcity and therefore real urgency. If they have a single copy of a first edition of a book I want, signed by its author, I know they are simultaneously notifying multiple clients of its availability and even a minute's hesitation may let someone beat me to the purchase—so I must decide quickly and impulsively; I have no time to consider cost. Most businesses lacking such actual scarcity can, with creative thought, manufacture it, offer by offer by offer.

So how could an ordinary local restaurant and sports bar create an exclusive offer with enormous inherent urgency, publicity appeal to local media, and excitement to its customers? My prescription would be to rent a football celebrity, perhaps a local hero, and craft an afternoon and evening of activities around his presence. One offer, fairly standard: he's there for a meet 'n' greet and photo opportunity during the Sunday afternoon games for any customer, with autographed footballs and jerseys auctioned off during an hour within that time frame, with proceeds to a local charity—a limited number permitted in, pre-registration made possible, with or without ticket fee. Then, the exclusive offer: just 12 patrons can buy a ticket to go into the private dining room or roped-off section, have dinner with, watch the Sunday night game with, and hang out with the star, and get an autographed ball, jersey, and photo—at, say, $2,000.00 per ticket. With that, there's massive urgency because there are only 12. A financial advisor, lawyer, auto dealer, etc. could use the same premise, renting the facility or joint-venturing with a restaurant owner, and still incorporating the local charity. The event itself would be directly profitable, reward good clients, and create new clients. The "halo effect" of the promotion to the business's entire email, social media, and mailing lists is significant, while the opportunity for free—but valuable— publicity is profound. What's most important to understand is that I took a business that is about "come on in" and eat, drink, and be merry, and converted it into a direct-marketing business, with two different, specific offers, both with created and legitimate urgency.

My friend, top direct-response copywriter John Carlton, always advises imagining your prospective customer or client as a gigantic somnambulant sloth, spread out on the couch, loathe to move his sleeping bulk, phone just out of reach. Your offer must force and compel him to move now. Your goal is immediate response. A plain vanilla, dull, mundane offer won't do it.

CHAPTER 3

Make Them
OBEY ORDERS

Originally appearing as Chapter 3
from *No B.S. Direct Marketing*

hy don't we get the results we want from other
people? Husbands and wives routinely complain about
their spouses expecting them to be mind readers.
Managers bemoan employees' failures to perform as expected,
often saying "But I told him once." Most managers' ideas about
training omit a feedback loop to ascertain comprehension and
acceptance, and ignore the need for perpetual reinforcement.
Everywhere you look in human-to-human communication,
there is disappointment. This certainly exists for marketers, too,
although many business owners don't think they should be able
to outright *control* the behavior of their customers to the extent
they should be able to employees, vendors, or family members.
In marketing and sales, control is exactly what we need. Ultimately,

all this is much about simple clarity. Do people really, clearly know what is expected of them? Or are you taking too much for granted, chalking things up as too obvious to bother clarifying?

Rule #3
You Will Give Clear Instructions

Most people do a reasonably good job of following directions. For the most part, they stop on red and go on green, stand in the lines they're told to stand in, fill out the forms they're given to fill out, applaud when the Applause sign comes on. Most people are well-conditioned from infancy, in every environment, to do as they are told.

Most marketers' failures and disappointments result from giving confusing directions or no directions at all. Confused or uncertain consumers do nothing. And people rarely buy anything of consequence without being asked.

When I held one of my mastermind meetings for one of my client groups at Disney, one of the Disney Imagineers we met was in charge of "fixing confusion." At any spot in any of the parks where there was a noticeable slowing of movement (yes, they monitor that) or an inordinate number of guests asking employees for directions, he was tasked with figuring out the reason for the confusion and changing or creating signs, giving buildings more descriptive names, and even rerouting traffic as need be to fix the confusion. "It isn't just about efficient movement," he told us, "it's about a pleasing experience. People do not like not knowing where to go or even what is expected of them."

In-store signage, restaurant menus, icons on websites—everywhere you closely examine physical selling environments and media—you will find plenty of assumptions made about the knowledge people have (and may not have) and plenty of opportunity for confusion. In a split test in nonprofit fundraising by direct mail, four different business-reply envelopes were used. One was a standard prepaid business reply envelope with the standard markings. The second was the same, but with a large hand-scrawl-appearing note, "No postage stamp needed. We've paid the postage. Just drop in the mail." Third was a plain, pre-addressed envelope with an actual stamp affixed. Fourth was the plain, pre-addressed envelope with an actual stamp affixed, plus the hand-scrawl-appearing note, "No postage stamp needed. We've paid the postage. Just drop in the mail." To be fair, the last two add obligation to clarity, and they were the winners by significant margin. But the first envelope was the biggest loser by a very big margin, even against the second, simply because the first presumes knowledge on the consumer's part that is not there. Not long ago, I got a statistically meaningful increase in conversion of visitors to buyers at a website by switching from just a "Buy Now" button to the button, plus the words "Click This Button to Buy Now."

When you put together *any* marketing tool, ad, flier, sales letter, website, phone script, etc., or *any* physical selling environment, it should be carefully examined for presumption of knowledge on the consumer's part, for lack of clarity about what is expected of them, or for wimpiness about asking clearly and directly for the desired action. Stop sending out anything without clear instructions. As illustration, take a look at Figure 3.1 on page 36, excerpted from an actual sales letter (sent to knowledgeable buyers already in a relationship with the marketer). Note that the subhead above the copy is *quite* clear.

It's also worth noting that people's anxiety goes up anytime they are asked to do something but are unsure of what to expect. In my book *No B.S. Guide to Marketing to Leading-Edge Boomers and Seniors*, in Chapter 15 ("The Power of Stress Reduction"), I share an example of a marketing device and copy we routinely use with professional practices, such as chiropractic, dental, medical, financial advisors', or lawyers' offices titled *"What to Expect at Your First Appointment."* Anxiety about anything uncertain grows more acute with age, but is not unique to boomers and seniors. Removing it with very clear instructions, directions, descriptions, or information is a smart strategy.

Last, you should consider the physical device of the order form. The late, great direct-response copywriter Gary Halbert claimed to often spend as much time on the copy and layout of the order form as he did the entire sales letter. In one part of my business life, professional speaking and selling my resources in an in-speech commercial, I've taken great pains to create order forms passed out to the audiences, or at the rear-of-room product tables, that mimic the best mail-order order forms in completeness and clarity, and I credit my order forms with aiding me in consistently achieving exceptional results — including selling over $1 million of my resources from the stage per year, for more than ten years running. A lot of businesses don't even use order forms when they could and should.

The Clearer the Marching Orders, the Happier the Customer

In direct marketing, we have learned a lot about consumer satisfaction, which affects refunds in our world and at least repeat purchasing and positive or negative word-of-mouth in every business. Presented with "difficult" or complex products, many customers are quickly, and profoundly, unhappy. I cannot tell you the number of times I've received a product that disappointed by seeming to be more trouble than it's worth, and returned it or simply trashed it, and I am not alone. A friend of mine, often an early adopter, took her first iPad back to the store to ask for help and was told by a disdainful clerk, "It's intuitive." Not to her. In direct-to-consumer delivery of complex products, we often add written labels to CDs or DVDs *very clearly* stating: Read/Listen/Watch This First. We sometimes even decal *the outside of* a box with "Call This Free Recorded Message, Please, BEFORE You Open & Unpack Your <Insert Product Name>." We include a *simple* flowchart or "map" of how to use the product. Often, we have to "sell" the tolerance for complexity. One of my clients, Guthy-Renker, has the number-one acne treatment brand, Proactiv®, sold and delivered direct to the consumer. Although it's made clear in the advertising, a chief cause of consumer dissatisfaction and noncompliant use has always been that there are three bottles and a three-step process. *Three.* To many, two steps too many. If we don't convince them that this is necessary and worth it, the product comes back for refund. You may not have actual refunds occurring, but more quiet dissatisfaction can be just as damaging.

Consumers like, are reassured by, and respond to clarity. Be sure you provide it.

The Power of Good Directions

Figure 3.1 on page 36 is actual "directions copy" from a sales letter, with the business identity removed. It has reinforced the scarcity/urgency established earlier in the letter. It includes the offer-specific phone number, times to call, and persons with whom they'll be speaking, as well as an alternative route to the website. In previous campaigns, this marketer had used a much simpler instruction—essentially "Call 000-000-0000 to place your order." The copy on page 36 more than tripled the response vs. the previously used instructions.

FIGURE 3.1: Sales Letter

What To Do Next

Only 14 of these xxxxxxxx's are available. This invitation
was sent to 100 of our best customers—like you!—by FedEx,
to ensure everyone has received them at the same time and
has fair opportunity to respond.
Without delay, please . . .

Call 000-000-0000 to secure one of these 14 xxxxxxx's. We
will be accepting calls beginning at 7:00 A.M. on [Insert Date]
and continuing through Noon on [Insert Next Day's Date], or
until all 14 are spoken for—whichever comes first. Helen or
Rob will be available to personally take your call.

Or . . .

If you would like to see the xxxxxxxx, a 9-minute preview
video is accessible online at www.[insert-site].com. You may
also instantly purchase your xxxxxxxx online, at
the conclusion of the video, and receive
confirmation immediately.

As always, your satisfaction is guaranteed with a 15-day
inspection and return privilege. All major credit cards
accepted, and the convenience of three monthly
installments on request.

No Freeloaders

Originally appearing as Chapter 4
from *No B.S. Direct Marketing*

I was taught: Earn your keep. From a very young age, I had chores, I had work to do. When I discovered there was pricey coffee made from cat poop being sold—a demonstration included in my book *No B.S. Price Strategy*—I sat the dog down for a discussion! Having everybody and everything earn their keep is deeply ingrained in me.

Anyway, most of us try to hold people accountable for assigned tasks, but a lot of businesspeople aren't as tough on the dollars they put to work in advertising and marketing. In the boom of 2006–2007, money streamed uphill. If you were once casual or deluded about waste or lack of accountability in advertising and marketing before, it's now the luxury you dare not afford. In fact, in 2017 and 2018, we are in the midst of a collapse of the midrange consumer and witnessing the fast shrinkage or destruction of a number of retailers, department store chains, restaurant chains, and other kinds of businesses dependent on those consumers. Some of the cause is Amazon, but not all of it. One thing is certain, waste of anything—a dollar, a lead, a potential customer, a customer—is no longer affordable.

This is about demanding performance.

As the leader of your business, you must do exactly that.

Rule #4
There Will Be Tracking, Measurement, and Accountability

You are no longer going to permit *any* advertising, marketing, or selling investments to be made without direct and accurate tracking, measurement, and accountability.

You will be given all sorts of arguments against such a harsh position, by media salespeople, by online media champions talking a "new" language of "new metrics," by staff, by peers. You will smile and politely say "Rubbish." Each dollar sent out to forage must come back with more and/or must meet predetermined objectives. There will be no freeloaders; there will be no slackers.

This is now particularly vital with online and social media. Some of it is ad media pretending to be something else. Much of it is wrapped in its own deliberately confusing means of evaluation—likes, views, time of views, viral, etc. In 2017, Facebook was exposed for misreporting and exaggerating views and numbers of minutes viewed for advertisers' videos. Widespread inflation of activity at all sites by "bots" and "fake activity farms" became known. None of this negates use of it, but it should inform your firm insistence on clear, accurate measurements for return on invested money and time in such media, just the same as for all media. You will be told it's different, but always remember you don't get to spend different money or different hours on it.

There are two reasons for holding all media harshly accountable.

First, because management by objectives is the only kind of management that actually works. When an NFL football team takes the field on Sunday, there are team objectives—not just winning, but for ingredients of victory that can be measured. Each player also has individual, measurable objectives that he and his coaches have discussed before the game and will evaluate after the game. So it should be when your team takes the field. Your team includes people you pay as well as marketing you pay for. You can't manage what you can't, don't, or won't measure. Vagueness must be banished.

I can tell you as ironclad fact that of all my clients, past and present, the richest and most successful, the ones who build the best businesses "know their numbers" better than all the also-rans. For a full discussion of the "money math" of business, I'll refer you to Chapter 46 of my book *No B.S. Ruthless Management of People and Profits, 2nd Edition.* That book in its entirety is an excellent companion to this one, and specifically to this chapter.

The second reason for direct measurement is that you need real, hard facts and data to make good, intelligent marketing decisions. Making such decisions on what you and your employees think is happening, feel, have a sense of, etc. is stupid. And you don't want to be stupid, do you?

So let's talk about tracking response. This means collecting as much information as you can, which is useful in determining what advertising, marketing, and promotion is working and what isn't, which offer is pulling and which isn't. Admittedly, this can be a bit tricky. For example, Ad #1 may pull in new customers at $122.80 in cost and Ad #2 at $210.00, so you might decide Ad #1

Resource Alert!

This book is the solid foundation for conversion of any ordinary business to a direct-marketing business. There are specialized next-steps marketing books:

No B.S. Guide to Marketing to Leading-Edge Boomers and Seniors

No B.S. Trust-Based Marketing*

**Ideal for financial, health, and other professionals; for high-transaction sales professionals; and for consultants.

The companion book to this one for management of a direct-marketing business is:

No B.S. Ruthless Management of People & Profits, 2nd Edition

All are available at Entrepreneur, Amazon, BN.com, Barnes & Noble, and other booksellers.

is the winner. But the average first six months' purchase activity of those coming from Ad #2 is $380.00; the average from Ad #1 only $198.00. Now, which is more productive? Further, 30% of those from Ad #2 may refer others, while only 10% of those from Ad #1 refer. Now, which ad is better?

Do not dare shrug this off as too complicated. Think. Set up systems to capture the data you need and set aside time for the analysis. If it's painful and confusing at first, the fog will clear, the difficulty will abate. You will make discoveries that enable you to make better decisions, better allocate resources, create better marketing messages, and grow your business without simply growing the marketing budget proportionately. In a mature business, this is how profits can be grown without growing revenue.

Warning: employees can often be an obstacle to accurate tracking, sometimes out of laziness, sometimes stubbornness, sometimes for more Machiavellian motives, such as concealing their own ineffectiveness. If there's been little or no tracking until now, there will naturally be resistance to the added work and to the revealed facts.

As an interesting example of what can be revealed, consider a company I did some consulting for, with complex advertising and marketing bringing prospects to offices for one-to-one sales presentations. The salespeople were inflating their closing percentages with cooperation of the receptionists, underreporting the number of appointments occurring. When I instituted a gift with appointment into the marketing, the salespeople suddenly had to requisition the needed number of gifts for the appointments they took. Bill could no longer claim he was closing 6 out of 10 when he was really closing 6 out of 20 now that he needed 20 gifts. Of course, the salespeople quickly claimed that giving the gifts was bringing in poorer quality prospects, but a controlled test of another kind firmly disproved that. The really awful thing in all this for the business owner was a lot of prospects he'd paid to get were coming and going invisibly, thus no follow-up on prospects who failed to buy at first attempt was occurring. Installing an effective, multistep follow-up campaign comprised of direct mail, email, and, finally, phone added over $1 million in revenue the first year.

One more example. A chain of stores with advertising that produced a lot of walk-ins had in place a process whereby the clerks were to ask everybody which ad in which media had brought them in, and stick-count it, day by day. Unfortunately, this was subject to an enormous amount of "slop." Employees didn't ask and randomly added to the count in different categories or put a lot of numbers in "Misc." A change was made, giving visitors a little survey card to fill out, pushed by huge in-store signage, entering them in a weekly drawing for good prizes—and suddenly, a lot of accurate data materialized, very contradictory to the data that had been collected or, often, just made up by the staff.

If you loop back and connect this to Rule #1, you'll find an important key to tracking: offers. Different offers can be made in different media, to different mailing lists, at different times. Offer and promotional codes can be assigned to coupons, reply cards, surveys, online opt-in, response, and order forms. Big direct-response advertisers on radio like LifeLock and Boll & Branch tie promotional codes to different talk radio hosts, which the consumer enters at the website to secure a discount or gift, often as simple as entering the host's name: Rush or Glenn or Sean. The internet also offers the local merchant an opportunity to force better tracking. Pre-internet, a local restaurant advertising on several radio shows and in a couple newspapers, giving away a free appetizer with dinner, could only try to find out which ad brought a customer in by having the customer tell the waiter or waitress in order to get the free appetizer, and relying on the waitstaff to accurately stick-count and report that collected information. Now the consumer can be driven to a different, clone website to download a coupon for the free appetizer, the coupons collected and tallied, and a much more accurate result obtained—plus the added benefit of capturing the names and email addresses of those visiting the site, and maybe offering online reservation-making options to the consumer as well.

Tough-minded management of marketing (and of people) requires *knowing* things. Of course, hardly any tracking mechanism is perfect. The job is to get as close to perfect as you can so that you are getting the best information possible.

Rule #5
Only No-Cost Brand-Building

The great GKIC member marketers behind the fast-growing national franchise organization Iron Tribe Fitness Centers, featured in the book *No B.S. Guide to Brand-Building by Direct Response*, gave a presentation to one of my mastermind groups they participated in, of their new "branding campaign"—and as they introduced it as such, a collective groan was emitted by the other coaching group members. They all know better! And they were all confident that I would react badly to a brand-oriented ad campaign and marketing program. But not so in this case, because these smart guys incorporated Rule #4 throughout the entire campaign. Tracking by separate phone numbers, domain names, or promotional codes was built into every item, every media used, every step of this campaign. Also, they obeyed Rule #5, so they weren't actually buying the brand-building. They were letting direct response pay for it. They are exactly right in their approach, they are a stellar example everybody should look at (regardless of the industry you're in), and, because they get this, they are a force to be reckoned with in their industry—where, frankly, really horrible advertising is the norm.

I am *not* opposed to brand-building, nor would I argue against the influence, power, and value of brand. Quite a few of my clients have built powerful mainstream brands, including Proactiv®, HealthSource (400+ chiropractic clinics nationwide), and High Point University; niche brands famous in their respective industries and fields, like the Scheduling Institute (in the dental profession), Advisors' Academy (with financial advisors), American Gunsmithing Institute (with gun hobbyists), and many more. But none of them have bought their brand recognition in the traditional way.

My own business is connected to brands—my own name, me, myself, and I. Dan Kennedy is a brand well-known and well-respected in entrepreneurial and marketing environments. Go Google me and see all you can find. The "No B.S." brand attached to this very successful book series, published by Entrepreneur Books, also extends to five successful newsletters, a full catalog of resources (magneticmarketing.com), and stands as positioning for GKIC. GKIC is fast developing The Renegade Entrepreneur Movement® as an extension of my Renegade Millionaire brand. Again, none of this identity and target market brand recognition has been bought or obtained by patient and hard-to-hold-accountable spending. It has all come as, essentially, a free bonus provided from direct investment only into direct marketing.

By the way, you can create brand power for even the most mundane of commodities. Coca-Cola branded water—Dasani. Victoria's Secret branded undergarments. Omaha Steaks—steaks. Hale Groves Grapefruit—grapefruit. Dasani Water is an off-shelf product. Victoria's Secret, retail. Omaha Steaks and Hale Groves are direct marketers, mail order, and ecommerce.

I am *not* opposed to brand-building.

I *am* opposed to paying for brand-building.

Most small-business owners cannot afford to properly invest in brand-building. Most startups lack the patient capital and luxury of time required by brand-building. I do not believe it is a wise investment for small-business owners and entrepreneurs, nor do I believe it is necessary. Brand power can be acquired as a no-cost byproduct of profitable direct-response advertising and direct marketing. My preferred strategy is simple: buy response, gratefully accept brand-building as a bonus. NEVER buy brand-building and hope for direct response as a bonus. (Unless you are actually trying to spend Daddy's fortune out of spite.)

Paying for traditional brand-building may be fine, even essential, for giant companies with giant budgets in combat for store shelf space and consumers' recognition. If you are the CEO of Heinz or Coors or some company like that, playing with shareholders' money, and fighting it out as a commodity purveyor, by all means buy brand identity. But if you are an entrepreneur playing with your own marbles, beware. Copying the brand-builders can bankrupt you. You should also take note of really big brand-name companies that are advertising brand, but also aggressively and directly asking prospects to go to a website or call a phone number, like GEICO and Progressive in insurance. This direct lead flow is paying for the advertising, with the contribution to brand recognition as a bonus. A relatively small percentage of brand-name advertisers know how to do this well, so you have to be very careful about whom you model.

It's also worth noting that there's no guarantee of success or sustainability with widespread brand recognition and brand equity. Some once very famous and dominant brands are, today, badly tarnished, shadows of their former selves, or dead. In the motel industry, the leading American brands *were* Holiday Inn and Howard Johnson's. Pontiac was once a leading car brand in the GM portfolio, and for a time, Rambler was the brand that stood for reliability, and Rambler dominated the station wagon category. More recently, Borders was one of two top brands in bookselling. Some of the brands you know and perceive to be dominant leaders in their fields and product categories today will be diseased or dead within ten years. The graveyard of once-powerful brands is big, and welcomes new arrivals frequently. Any idea of inevitability of an established brand is foolish and dangerous conceit. Consider Sears, once the Amazon of its era, and the dominant all-goods retailer, and once one of the best-known and trusted brand names. None of that guaranteed its permanence.

Why, When, and How to Do UN-Branded Advertising

There is a case for ignoring branding altogether, entirely or situationally. What I am about to reveal here is a very, very powerful advertising and marketing strategy well-known to Direct Marketers but largely ignored or misunderstood by all others. It is the deliberate use of nakedly un-branded advertising.

What you never want to do is let brand-building get in the way of the most powerful and profitable advertising and marketing opportunities to grow your business. There are many types of direct-response lead-generation ads, designed to motivate qualified prospects for a particular product or service to step forward, identify themselves, and ask for information, which work much better "blind," absent any company name or logo or branding, than they do with identity disclosed. One version is the now classic "Warning" ad:

Warning to Mutual Fund Investors
Expert Predicts Dramatic Change and
Danger in the Next 29 Days.

This Is Information You MUST Have—That
Brokers Don't Want You to Know. For Free
Information and "The Wall Street Secrets Report,"
call the Fund Investor Hotline at 1-800-000-0000 or
go online to www.Xxxxxxx.com

You absolutely kill that ad's pulling power if you attach a big, fat logo, a national brand name, or a financial planning firm's name and slogan to it.

In this category, in financial and investment information publishing, one of the all-time biggest successes was a campaign that dominated print, radio, and cable TV in 2011 and 2012, driving traffic to an online video at EndOfAmerica.com. (You can probably still see it via YouTube.) This ad was aired, seen, and heard so much, the domain name itself nearly had brand identity, but throughout, neither the company nor its brand, the newsletter ultimately being sold, the author, or any other identity, corporate or personal, was disclosed in the advertising. It was completely "blind." I am told it broke all subscriber acquisition records of its company and probably the industry, bringing nearly a million new subscribers into the fold. Incidentally, as a side point, the online video was 90 minutes long, so let that stick a dagger in the persistent and erroneous beliefs about short viewer attention spans and/or need for short copy. The point: zero brand-building was attempted. But if in the hands of most big, dumb companies in publishing, insurance, annuities, gold, or other financial goods and services, they and their nincompoop ad agencies would have insisted on mucking up the ads with their corporate names, logos, slogans, years in business.

You can always brand-build internally with customers once they are acquired. There's no law that says you can't create powerful brand identity and preference with customers, yet never even mention it to new prospects.

There are even instances where a brand suppresses response *because of its virtues*. I have, on more than one occasion, had clients in niche markets who had become very well-known and well-respected, and if you asked 100 people in their market about them, nearly all of the randomly chosen 100 had generally positive things to say about the company, but could also rattle off the five key components of that company's sales story and offerings. No mystique, no curiosity. A been-there-heard-that-done-that-before problem. Success came by trotting out "blind" advertising and marketing with fresh promises and bold positioning, which would have been instantly discredited if voiced by the venerable, old industry leader. Then, once interest in the promises was created, information could be provided that revealed the match of the biggest, most respected brand with the hot, new, daring products.

In short, brand is not necessarily the holy grail. Brand-building is best for very, very patient marketers with very, very deep pockets filled with other people's money. You are likely far better served by focusing on leads, customers, sales, and profits directly driven by your marketing, letting whatever brand equity you get be provided as a free byproduct of direct marketing.

Interview with Rick Cesari: Brand-Building by Direct Marketing

Rick Cesari is the author of a must-read book on direct marketing, *BUY NOW: Creative Marketing That Gets Customers to Respond to You and Your Product*, based on his extraordinary experience bringing products like The Juiceman, the Sonicare Toothbrush, and the George Foreman Grill to market.

KENNEDY: Monster successes like those you've shepherded never begin that way. They begin with proving we have something to sell and proving we can craft a message that people will respond to, starting by playing small ball. I'd like you to talk a little bit about the way you started these businesses, such as The Juiceman.

CESARI: We started The Juiceman business in 1989, and in three and a half years we grew the sales from zero to $75 million. I found Jay Kordich, the inventor and personality of The Juiceman, at a small, local consumer show. 10-by-10-foot booths, people selling products. All the booths had one or two people, but this one booth had a crowd, 50 people gathered. Jay was there, talking about the health benefits of juicing, demonstrating his machine, and he had people captivated. I talked with him and found out he was living on the road, working these kinds of shows, state fairs, that sort of thing all over the country, selling a lot of juice to groups. I'd already been in the direct-marketing field a long time, and I was sure that we could take what he was doing on this small level, move it to media, and build it into something a lot bigger.

Brand-Building by Direct Marketing, cont.

KENNEDY: I think it's important I point out: Jay had a small business, reaching small numbers of customers, by successful direct selling. With direct marketing, you could basically multiply him with media. The reason I push owners of businesses thought of as ordinary to move away from traditional marketing to direct marketing is that they can multiply what they do successfully one to one into one to many with media.

CESARI: That's right. But we didn't run out and make TV infomercials immediately. We made calls to get Jay booked as a guest on local radio and TV shows to talk about health and juicing. Our first breakthrough came on a New York station, on a local morning show hosted by Matt Lauer, who now, of course, is a *Today Show* host. Jay was on for 20 minutes and told people if they would send in an envelope with a dollar, he'd send them recipes. I was told that the station switchboard lit up, but this was before the internet so everything happened through the mail, and it took a week before we saw the result. He was on, on June 30th. On July 6th, the mail truck pulls up, and the mailman brings in three canvas sacks. Twelve thousand envelopes with dollars in them. We sent out a flier selling juicers with those recipes and that's what started this business. We used that strategy, got Jay on show after show after show. We also started using those interviews, then our first infomercial to get people to come to free health seminars, where Jay would sell from the stage to hundreds and hundreds of people at a time.

KENNEDY: Let's be sure everybody gets that there is architecture here that does not go out of date. This doesn't have an expiration date on it.

Brand-Building by Direct Marketing, cont.

CESARI: This model still works, although we get to add the internet, we have more marketing tools—but direct marketing from more than 25 years ago with The Juiceman and the direct marketing we're applying to our latest projects is the same.

KENNEDY: The next question goes to Message. Many businesspeople think that their products, services, or businesses are ordinary, they complain about commoditization and competition, and they just can't see how what you've done and do, how what they see with products sold direct in infomercials, in direct-mail packages, applies to them. When you think about, basically, a blender, a countertop grill, a toothbrush, it's hard to be more ordinary than these products, yet you take them to direct marketing, and turn them into multimillion-dollar brands, and move them successfully to retail where they sell off the shelf. Let's talk a bit about this turning the ordinary into something very salable and very exciting to the public—and let me emphasize the requirement of making whatever you offer, sell, do *exciting* to the public. You just can't afford to accept the idea that your thing is doomed to be ordinary and uninteresting, can you?

CESARI: You have to look at products *in a different way*. In 1989, there *were* a lot of juicers being sold, but they belonged to appliance manufacturers and were being sold *conventionally* as kitchen appliances. The twist we put on it with Jay was to make it a health device, not a kitchen appliance. We never talked much about the blades or motor or size of container. We pushed the information booklets, the immune strengthening diet, the weight loss juice diet, anti-aging. When we brought the Sonicare Toothbrush out, there was one other premium priced electric toothbrush sold through dentists, but there were quite a few sold to consumers for

Brand-Building by Direct Marketing, cont.

a few dollars. Sonicare was $150.00. How to sell a $150 tooth-brush? Nobody understood or cared about sonic technology. So we made our message about reversing gum disease, preventing heart disease, etc. With the George Foreman Grill, there were a lot of little grills, and it was actually originally a taco maker—it's slant-ed the way it is to slide the ground beef into the taco shell. Not surprisingly, it wasn't selling. We determined you could drain the fat and grease that way, and with George Foreman, made it about "Knock Out the Fat." Again, a health device, not just a kitchen appliance. There have been more than 30 million George Foreman Grills sold. We believe there is *always* a unique benefit.

KENNEDY: This is one of the differences between the way most businesspeople and marketers think vs. the way we direct market-ers think. They look to the product and its features for benefits to talk about. We want to be storytellers. We look for the hidden benefit, for the benefit that matches up with consumers' life issues and interests.

Excerpted from and based on an exclusive interview with Rick Cesari for the monthly GKIC Diamond Members' Tele-Seminar & Q&A Conference Call.

CHAPTER 5

How to Find Profit in an Unprofitable World

Originally appearing as Chapter 1 from
*No B.S. Guide to Direct Response
Social Media Marketing*

R egardless of the media, be profit focused.
Some media readily lends itself to direct-response advertising and marketing. Some doesn't. Social media, for the most part, doesn't. It is like trying to use Jell-O as cement.

Marrying social media (which has its own profound culture, cultural norms, and participant expectations) with direct response (which has clear and, by definition, *direct* purpose) is like an arranged or forced marriage between strangers distrustful of each other and from different ethnic, religious, or socio-economic backgrounds. To reach back, it is reminiscent of Lonesome George Gobel's line about feeling like a pair of scuffed brown shoes worn with a formal tuxedo. It is, frankly, a poor match.

Still, it is also now *necessary*.

If I bowed to my own preferences, I'd advise you to ignore all of it. But even if I did, you won't, and I'd be a tree falling in a distant, deserted forest.

If you are going to be drawn into the ever-expanding morass of social media (and it is extremely unlikely you won't be), then you need to insist it repay all the attention, time, and money you invest in it. I doubt you'll stay a stubborn opt-out as I am personally. You obviously bought this book because you're already in and getting deeper.

With two exceptions, all my private clients (as of this writing) are in. Most are managing—with some difficulty—to make it pay. That's the thing. You cannot afford to just let it *play*. It must *pay*.

You can't afford to buy into nonsensical "new metrics" promulgated by the promoters of social media or by users ignorant of—or by virtue of employment by big, dumb companies—divorced from real economics. If you feel you must have presence, if you must participate, you must make it pay. In real dollars, not imaginary, hopeful metrics. *Money*.

We are all in the money business. Not the likes, friends, views, tweets, retweets, and viral videos business. The Money Business.

Most fail miserably at The Money Business. Only 1% get rich, and only another 4% achieve significant financial independence from owning and operating businesses of their own. The other 95% come up way, way short. One reason for all this failure is naïve, fantastical, delusional thinking and false optimism vs. *accurate* thinking. Weak-minded, thus overly influenced by peers, staff, a vocal minority of customers, popular fads, and each new, bright, shiny object vs. *tough-minded* thinking focused on direct profit from every investment. To that end, incidentally, I urge getting and reading my scariest, toughest, bluntest book, *No B.S. Ruthless Management of People and Profits,*

Second Edition (Entrepreneur Books, 2014). You don't want to fail at The Money Business.

Social media as a direct-response marketing tool has another problem: a growing hazard. Its chief owners at Google, Facebook, and others don't like it. They dislike harsh, factual measurement of return on investment. They are openly, busily striving to attract more and more big, dumb corporate advertisers with big buckets of Wall Street money and a love of brand and image and bragging rights through numbers divorced from direct sales. They are in hot pursuit of advertisers who do not insist on direct return on investment. They have outright said as much, and I have been reporting on this evolution in my newsletters, notably *The No B.S. Marketing Letter* (https:// magneticmarketing.com).

The trouble for you is, these big brand advertisers are kings, queens, princes, and princesses moving into the social media castle. They view you as part of a rat infestation, and the castle landlord is very sympathetic to their wishes.

Trying to do marketing that actually works in this environment grows more difficult by the day. In fact, Facebook is regularly throwing advertisers right out the back door of the castle. To get back in, companies are required to redo their sites and behavior in ways that neuter effectiveness. Do not underestimate this problem.

Still, it now seems *necessary* to engage in this struggle—as sanely and smartly as possible. It is for that reason that I agreed to act as "chairman" of this book and that I chose Kim Walsh Phillips to be its "CEO." In a field rife with fools and charlatans, I and my clients have found her to be a rare truth-teller—someone who views this media collection accurately and not through rose-tinted glasses under the influence of Ecstasy, and someone who does understand direct response. She is a trustworthy Sherpa through a dangerous jungle.

My Two Instructions

My message about all social media and about this book is a simple one: Be careful and be demanding. Brook no bullshit.

Consider Twitter's former CFO, Anthony Noto, who infamously erred in sending a private message out into the public arena. As he painfully discovered, once such an error—of mechanics or of impulse—is made, it can be forwarded to the universe—fast—and it can't be stopped.

The news is chock-full of executives, celebrities, and athletes being wounded and, in a few cases, ruined by an ill-advised tweet or Facebook post. Or, for that matter, hacked email. Even the private is no longer reliably private. Sony Pictures execs found this out. These same mistakes made even more commonly by small-business owners and entrepreneurs never make the TV news or get reported in *The Wall Street Journal*, but they foster mayhem just the same. This is also an environment where every complainant and every looney bird has a megaphone. The more you are present and active, the more you expose yourself to their type of social media terrorism: negative reviews, outright attacks, and bothersome complaints to the Facebooks of the world. This must be closely monitored and managed. It's a price of playing in this sandbox. It carries an actual price tag.

Be careful, too, not to treat any or all of this as a replacement for any other media or for a sensible multimedia business strategy. The worst number in business is *one*. Don't count Facebook, Twitter, LinkedIn, etc. as three, five, or 50. Social media is One. If you are overly dependent on any One, you are overly vulnerable—at enormous risk.

My client Chris Cardell in the UK is extremely clever about using Facebook profitably. At the time I wrote this, he was merrily minting money with it. But you couldn't take direct mail away from him at gunpoint. He also uses pay-per-click and email, online video sales letters, radio, TV, and newspapers. He won't be caught being lazy about this. And if Facebook boots him from the castle, he'll survive quite well. More than enough will still be coming for tea 'n' crumpets.

A different client, after months of tussling with Facebook, getting booted and then getting back in, finally walked away. This client has upped advertising in newspapers nationwide and is happy about the results.

I can't tell you what your decisions should be. However, this book can certainly help you make the best possible choice. What I can tell you with ironclad certainty is that overdependence puts you in peril. The *only* secure strategy is a multimedia marketing strategy and a multichannel sales strategy.

If you are a success with social media, fine. This book can be a huge help. But if more than 20% of your leads, customers, or revenue comes from social media or more than 20% of your relationship with customers relies on it, you are a fool who is cruisin' for a bruisin'.

Next, be demanding. In a poll reported in *USA Today*, 61% of small-business owners could not document or prove any direct return on their investments in social media activity, yet 50% said they were increasing time and money commitments—and only 7% said they were cutting back on it. Incredible. The CEO of a social media agency insisted those latter business owners were wrong. He claimed they do get returns from social media activity—*they just don't know what they are when they see them.* If you like being told you are an idiot, you'd love this guy. I sleep pretty soundly, but I know whether I've had sex during the night. Nobody's going to tell me I am having a lot of sex but just not smart enough to know it.

After one of retail's big days, Black Friday, another *USA Today* article reported a 40% increase in social media campaigns by retailers like Walmart, Sears, and Amazon, yet IBM Smarter Commerce (which tracks sales of the top 500 retail sites) reported a decrease in online sales that day. Then an expert said, "While it may be hard to track how all this drives sales, most retailers agree that having people talking about their brand or store is better than not."

Advertising software automation company Nanigans revealed current research in October 2018 detailing retailers' ever-evolving Black Friday strategies. According to their data, "Marketers revealed that a quarter of their annual ad budgets are used to target shoppers during Black Friday/Cyber Monday weekend. With total U.S. digital ad spend by retailers expected to exceed $23 billion in 2018, retailers plan to allocate almost $6 billion in media toward this four-day period.

In terms of where advertisers are putting their dollars, the Facebook-Google duopoly is the clear winner. Retailers indicated that Google Search and Display (35%) and Facebook (18%) dominate their planned channels, but Amazon is a close third (15%). This underscores the appeal of Amazon's evolving online ecosystem to retailers and reinforces the company's growing momentum in digital advertising.

"Nearly half of U.S. consumers now start their product search on Amazon, meaning the retail giant offers an attractive model for brands hoping to capture the attention of active buyers during the 2018 holiday shopping season," said Ric Calvillo, CEO and cofounder of Nanigans. "However, retailers' decision to pump ad spend into Amazon may be shortsighted. The company has built an ecosystem that makes it both an attractive ecommerce ad platform and a retailer's top competitor."

Additional key findings from the study include:

- More than half (51%) of retailers plan to keep 2018 holiday season ad budgets about the same as last year, while 48% plan to increase the amount they spend on holiday ads.
- Retailers don't focus much of their holiday ad spend on last-minute shoppers, which could be a missed opportunity

as it's a pivotal time to generate brand exposure. Almost half (47%) prioritize early-season campaigns, 48% focus on prime-season buyers, and just 5% target late-season shoppers.

- Retail marketers plan to dedicate 14% of their campaign budgets to video ads during the 2018 holiday shopping season.
- 30% of retailers want to see higher ROI from their holiday ad spend, and 87% would reallocate some of this budget to other areas if they could. Specifically, 49% of respondents would reinvest their holiday ad spend in martech and adtech technology, if possible.
- 29% of marketers surveyed agree they can't change holiday ad spend strategy due to organizational leaders holding them back.
- For a majority of retailers, the holidays positively impact acquiring more customers with significant value, but the trade-off is the fact that 25% of marketers report dramatically higher cost of customer acquisition during this time.
- The holiday advertising season starts early for the majority of retailers, with 64% of those surveyed implementing campaigns before Halloween.[1]

If that is consensus thinking, the consensus is made up of morons who've lost a grip on the business they're in. You are not in the business of being talked about. You are in the business of selling things. You are not in the buzz business. You are in The Money Business. Refuse to be dissuaded from that simple, straightforward fact.

The Marketing Success Triangle Has NOT Changed

RIGHT Markets Get RIGHT Message by RIGHT Media.

---

[1] https://www.businesswire.com/news/home/20181016005150/en

Simply broadcasting a message to millions by social media accomplishes little for most businesses. Companies like GoPro (the camera company) and Red Bull are great examples of brand-builders using viral videos and social media to rise from obscurity to fame in the marketplace. But your business is probably not kin to theirs. You have to be very careful—again that advice, be careful—to model and emulate businesses with much in common with your own. Capital and human resources, for example. If you are funding your business's growth from its profits or money borrowed by mortgaging your home and your grandma's wheelchair, you are in an entirely different place than a company into which hundreds of millions of dollars of venture capital and Wall Street money flow.

Further, viral explosions are not all they're cracked up to be, as Greg Levitt, cofounder of www.33Across.com, a social media sharing platform, admits. From his firm's research:

- Consumers are most likely to share articles, news, and content related to science, but only 9% of person-to-person recipients click on the shared links regarding these topics.
- Timely news and political items are less widely shared at 2%, but the click rates are 86% and 77%, respectively.
- Business-related: only a 4% share and a 24% click on the shared links.
- Health: 3% share, 15% click.
- Celebrity and entertainment: 2% share, but 40% click.
- Consumer reviews of products, businesses: 1% share, 4% click.
- Personal finance: 1% share, 11% click.

(The above stats were based on 500 publishers of online content.)

Levitt explains the wide disparity between share and click rates as "ego sharing," that is, senders sharing content they believe boosts their perceived intelligence, informed status, etc., regardless of whether they think recipients will find it interesting or not. The overall average is 3% sharing of content and 24% of recipients clicking on shared links.

To me, this says there are only two useful plays: First, work with a tightly targeted list of thought-leader, market-leader, and influential recipients to deliver content of high interest and value that enhances their status if shared—to hit or beat the 3% bar, but so that the 24% of those recipients who are shared with are ideal for you; or second, you need a massive volume outreach so the 3% matters.

The stats about forwarding/sharing of "reviews" about products and businesses suggest that angst over this—and time and money spent on it—may be overdone.

Ironically, and in the face of what I have pointed out above, you can make a case that it is important to include social media as part of your integrated marketing plan. But approach it strategically, with the same direct-response and sound business principles that you would in any other media channel. Social media is no different than any other media.

The Stuff of Bank Deposits Has NOT Changed

You can't go to the bank and deposit likes, views, retweets, viral explosions, social media conversations, or brand recognition. Bankers are extremely narrow-minded. They won't even accept vegetables grown in your backyard garden or bitcoin. They want real money.

You must insist on exactly the same thing from all media. Contrary to popular belief, no media is different. No media gets a pass because it is different. Don't be fooled. Be open-minded, creative, and opportunistic. But always keep a watchful eye on the bottom line.

Opportunism and skepticism are not mutually exclusive. They can and should work in concert, like partners, like Walt Disney, the visionary, and Roy Disney, the money watcher, worked in tandem. Approach social media this way, and you'll avoid being burnt.

CHAPTER 6

Media Is Not
Marketing

Originally appearing as Chapter 2 from
*No B.S. Guide to Direct Response
Social Media Marketing*

I n the 2012 Olympics, U.S. swimmer Michael Phelps became the most decorated Olympian of all time (beating gymnast Larisa Latynina's prior record of 18 medals). Phelps earned his 19th Olympic medal in the men's 4 × 200-meter freestyle relay. His current medal count of 28 is made up of 23 gold, three silver, and two bronze.

Although he had a great Olympics, it could have easily not gone his way.

In fact, prior to the Olympics Phelps fell short of many people's expectations, including his own. His problems began after the 2008 Olympics when he got lazy. He stopped doing the things that brought him success in the first place, like going to the pool to train every day. Until 2011, when he was bested by his teammate Ryan Lochte in the 200-meter individual medley at the world championships.

That's when Phelps got back to the basics, doing the things he needed to do to win again.

The funny thing with swimmers is that no matter how long they've been swimming, they do the same thing day in, day out to prepare for their races.

Take U.S. swimmer Dara Torres, who at the age of 41 became the oldest Olympic swimming medalist in history when she won two Olympic silver medals in 2008. Despite having swam her whole life, she never forgot the basics. She did the same workouts as every other sprint swimmer on her team, such as kicking and drills. She kept the foundational pieces in place as circumstances around her changed.

Despite his success in the 2012 Olympics, Phelps announced his retirement directly after their conclusion. But like a true champion, he didn't stay poolside for long.

At the 2016 Summer Olympics in Rio de Janeiro, he won five gold medals and one silver. This made him the most successful athlete of the games for the fourth Olympics in a row.

He announced his second retirement on August 12, 2016, having won more medals than anyone else in the Olympics at final count of 28. According to a Fox News story by Chris Chase, if Michael Phelps was a country, he'd be ranked 32nd on the all-time medal count. That's all-time, as in everything a country has won in 120 years and 28 Summer Olympics.

While you may never be an Olympic Record holder, you can follow the success principle of staying true to the same behaviors that got you in there in the first place.

Contrary to Popular Belief . . .

The internet is not as special as most people think, and media is not marketing. The same disciplined business and marketing practices must be kept in place to drive real results. Very few will do this, so very few will ever see results through social media marketing, or any marketing for that matter.

Social media has a lot of the same dangers that email marketing does. It is free and can be distributed quickly with a very low barrier to entry. Not much thought or strategy needs to be put into place in order to launch messaging or paid ads.

WHY SO MANY BUSINESSES ARE FAILING

Just because it is social media doesn't mean it shouldn't use all the same principles as direct-response marketing.

It's been 40 years or more since I replaced old-fashioned prospecting grunt work for a 100% measurable way to attract a predictable, reliable stream of ideal clients.

Success at getting qualified clients, customers, or patients has a lot more to do with understanding the real secrets of direct-response marketing and a lot less to do with chasing prospects through tweets and status updates.

I've been entirely DR (direct response) since 1975 and pioneered a few things of my own. Although the fundamentals and the principles of this do not change, it is still really about applying tested and proven mail order methodology to nonmail order businesses.

The overwhelming majority of commerce of all kinds is driven by direct response.

Everyone from the credit card industry to the apparel industry, from the information business to the local service business is using direct response. The fundamental principle of my approach to marketing is this: Let's make sure we're talking to highly interested, highly motivated, very appropriate prospects for what it is that we have to offer people, who will have a high level of interest the minute we show up.

Do a decent job of selling to them, instead of trying to reduce everything to 140-character tweets, videos no longer than 3.8

minutes, and no sales letters with words more than two syllables so that everybody can pay attention.

WHY YOU ARE THE SAME

Everybody believes their business is different. That this doesn't apply to them. That no one else is doing this in their industry. Just because they aren't using the written word to sell, it must be acceptable because they are making sales. Maybe it's "acceptable." But using better sales copy gives you a competitive edge. Especially when you possess this number-one skill and others *don't*.

Darin Garman was making sales in real estate, but he wasn't happy with the process and was becoming increasingly frustrated doing a lot of work only to lose the sale to a competitor.

No one was using sales letters to sell apartment buildings until Darin decided to do it. Not only did he succeed at selling apartment buildings with sales letters, but he also got the people *he* predetermined were good candidates to respond. Plus, when he did some research, he found he had moved into a position where his office, Heartland Investment Partners, handled 70% of all apartment building transactions. That was *not* the case before he started using sales letters.

It does not matter whether your client is the CEO or the broom pusher or which media channels you use, everybody buys the same way. They all go through the same process. They all go through the same emotional journey.

The Basics of Effective Marketing

There are just a few plain and simple direct-marketing rules to follow, and by committing to them, you'll reap the long-term benefits you desire and develop a long-lasting business foundation.

These basics are skipped by most businesses using Facebook, Twitter, and LinkedIn as their primary sources of communication. Realize you have choices, and you can make your marketing dollars work harder for you by offering people more than one reason and more than one means of responding to you.

However many channels you market in, there are basic rules you need to understand in order to succeed. These foundational concepts must be fully comprehended, practiced, managed, and enforced.

1. There Will Always Be an Offer

There is a popular saying out there that "content is king." I would disagree. The sale is king. Without it, you have no market share and no kingdom to rule over. Your social media marketing needs to have an offer, telling your ideal prospects exactly what to do and why they want to do it right now. It should be irresistible and time sensitive, and give them some type of transformative value if they take action.

Ideally, it's a Godfather's Offer—one that the appropriate prospect or customer can't refuse.

2. There Will Be a Reason to Respond Right Now

The hidden cost and failure in all advertising and marketing is in the almost-persuaded. They were tempted to respond. They nearly responded. They got right up to the edge of response, but then set it aside to do later or to mull over or to check out more the next time they were at their computers. When they get to that edge, we must reach across and pull them past it. There must be a good reason for them not to stop short or delay or ponder. There must be urgency.

3. There Will Be Clear Instructions

Most people do a reasonably good job of following directions. For the most part, they stop on red and go on green, stand in the lines they're told to stand in, fill out the forms they're given to fill out, and applaud when the Applause sign comes on. Most people are well-conditioned from infancy, in every environment, to do as they are told.

Most marketers' failures and disappointments result from giving confusing directions—or no directions at all. Confused or uncertain consumers do nothing. And people rarely buy anything of consequence without being asked. Sharing content alone will not bring measurable results from your social media. You must walk your prospect through the steps you want them to take in order to make the sale.

4. There Will Be Tracking and Measurement

If you want real profits from your marketing, you are no longer going to permit any advertising, marketing, or selling investments to be made without direct and accurate tracking, measurement, and accountability. You will be given all sorts of arguments against such a harsh position by media salespeople, by online media champions talking a "new" language of "new metrics," by staff and peers. You will hear terms like "engagement" and "reach" and "virality," with no data to back up the results. You will smile and politely say "Rubbish." Each dollar sent out to forage must come back with more and/or must meet predetermined objectives. There will be no freeloaders; there will be no slackers.

5. There Will Be Follow-Up

Often, I find business owners with more holes in their bucket than they've got bucket! People read your ad, get your letter, see your sign, find you online, call or visit your place of business, ask your receptionist or staff questions, and that's it. There's no capture of the prospect's name, physical address, email address, and no offer to immediately send an information package, free report, coupons. This is criminal waste.

I've been poor, so I abhor and detest and condemn waste. Just how much waste are you permitting to slop around in your business? Probably a lot. When you invest in advertising and marketing, you don't just pay for the customers you get. You pay a price for every call, every walk-in. Every one. Doing nothing with one is like flushing money down the toilet.

To be simplistic, if you invest $1,000 in an ad campaign and get 50 phone calls, you bought each call for $20. If you're going to waste one, take a nice, crisp $20 bill, go into the bathroom, tear the bill into pieces, let the pieces flutter into the toilet, and flush. Stand there and watch it go away. If you're going to do nothing with 30 of those 50 calls, stand there and do it 30 times. Feel it.

You probably won't like how it feels. Good.

Remember that feeling every time you fail—and it is failure—to thoroughly follow up on a lead or customer.

6. Results Rule

Results Rule. Period. Consider the simple agreement: You want your car hand-washed and waxed outside, vacuumed inside, for which you will pay your neighbor's teen $20. If he does not wash or wax or vacuum the car but wants the $20 anyway, what possible "story" could he offer in place of the result of a clean car that would satisfy you? I would hope none. You didn't offer to pay for a story. You offered to pay for a clean car. The same is true with advertising and marketing investments in social media. Do not let anyone confuse, bamboozle, or convince you otherwise. Further, no opinions count—not even yours.

Only results matter.

CHAPTER 7

The Importance of Creating Your Unique Selling Proposition

Originally appearing as Chapter 3 from
*No B.S. Guide to Direct Response
Social Media Marketing*

I was reading an extensive survey about measuring the impact of advertising slogans. Among the slogans and advertising tag lines for 22 of the biggest U.S. advertisers, only six were recognized by more than 10% of the consumers surveyed.

In other words, not even 1 out of 10 consumers could correctly identify 90% of the slogans. In fact, 16 of the 22 advertisers had slogans no one knew, although each spent more than $100 million a year advertising theirs!

Three of these much-advertised slogans scored 0% recognition. 0%!

Take the test, to see if you can name any of the big, dumb companies that match these slogans:

1. We're With You
2. That Was Easy
3. The Stuff of Life

Only Walmart's "Always Low Prices" was recognized by 64% of the consumers tested. (And by the way, if you can't have the lowest prices, you might as well be the highest. Not much cache in "Almost Always Almost Lowest Prices Most Days.")

Those faring poorly, like #1 above, argued that it had only been advertising its slogan for YEARS!!!! Quote, "It takes time to build brand identity." The spokesman for #3 justified its disaster as "only a transitional slogan," stating the company was moving toward yet another new brand-focused identity, whatever the beejeezus that is. Translation: New slogan being thunk up.

The real laughter is that the copy of this article was from *USA Today*'s website, and at its end, two companies paid to advertise their services, doing, yep, "corporate branding."

Is a Slogan a Brand? Isn't a Slogan Just Like a USP?

No, a slogan is not a brand, and these results are not exactly an indictment of all brand-building approaches.

For example, the kind of "personal branding" I teach encompasses more than a slogan and is usually more targeted to a market.

However, it's easy to have that go awry and wind up with branding that looks good but does nothing. There's a tightrope to walk there, and it's easy to fall off. Most ad agency types do.

A slogan is definitely *not* a USP, although it can represent, telegraph, or at least be congruent with a USP in your small-business marketing.

Actually, Walmart's is the only slogan in all the ones tested via this survey that enunciates a USP. It is, not coincidentally, the only effective slogan. The others not only fail the Dan Kennedy

USP Question #1 (Why should I, your prospect, choose to do business with you vs. any and every other option?), but they are also so generic they could be used by anybody.

For example, "That Was Easy" could certainly work for Boston Market—how easy it is to put a "home cooked" dinner on the family table—or for Ditech—how easy it is to get a home loan.

Warning: If anybody and everybody can use your USP, it ain't one.

If any and every Tom, Dick, and Mary can use your slogan, why on earth would you want it?

In each of these cases, the minute the ad agency charlatans revealed these slogans in the corporate clients' boardrooms, the CEOs should have stood up, pulled out a gun, shot one of them somewhere it would really hurt and bleed a lot but not kill him, and yelled "Next."

This is the kind of chronic stupidity I encountered when working with big, dumb companies like Weight Watchers and MassMutual. (Incidentally, Weight Watchers could use any of the above three loser slogans. Mass could use two of them. And probably would.)

Every company behind these losers had a spokesperson ready with an excuse. Nobody said, truthfully, "We're idiots."

I have the reputation of being anti-brand.

Actually, I'm not "anti-brand" at all and, as you can observe, have diligently turned myself into a personality brand. (Go ahead, Google "Dan Kennedy" and see what turns up. Be sure you've packed a lunch. You'll be there a while.) I also have "NO B.S." as a brand extending over books, newsletters, products, and "RENEGADE MILLIONAIRE" to a lesser extent.

I do counsel *against* investing directly into brand-building, especially with large-company-style "image" advertising that cannot be accurately and ruthlessly held accountable.

A few principles and tips about your brand identity:

1. By all means, work at creating name-brand identity and recognition for yourself and your small business, but do it where it counts, with a carefully selected target, niche, or subculture market small enough that you can have impact with whatever resources you have, defined narrowly enough you can create compelling messages for it. A giant market is only useful to someone with a giant wallet. You do not want to waste your life peeing into the ocean. (For example, I have aimed myself at "entrepreneurs" pretty successfully, but "corporate America" has been sacrificed. Stephen Covey may have 10,000 copies of one of his books bought by American Airlines or Citibank. I most assuredly will not.) Whatever your business, nationally or locally, there is a *prime* market and a *prime* audience. Build brand identity with them.

2. A brand or brand identity is, essentially, a recognized symbol that represents and calls to mind *what* you and your business is about. I maintain it should also be designed to resonate with a very specific *who* your business is for. Many marketers are reasonably clear about their *what* but woefully unclear about their *who*, thus their *what* is often wrong.

3. By all means, work at creating name-brand identity and recognition for yourself and your business, but do it as a byproduct and bonus of solid, accountable, profitable direct-response advertising and marketing. Avoid buying it outright, such as with image advertising. Refer to the "Direct Marketing DIET" on pages 20 and 21 of my *No B.S. Direct Marketing for Non-Direct Marketing Businesses* book.

4. Do not confuse "brand identity" with logos and slogans. Logos, slogans, color schemes, and other imagery are

simply devices used to convey or support brand identity, just as typefaces are a means of conveying words. Brand identity is about ideas first and representations of ideas second.

5. If you do develop brand identity, develop a "customer culture" with it, so your brand is theirs. Think Starbucks or Disney. The customers are part of something, not just people being sold to. But, whatever you do, don't blindly copy big companies' advertising practices. Very, very, very carefully learn from the very few smart ones, like Disney. But remember they are playing in a different league with different rules and different means of keeping score. As an example, you may keep score by profit while they must keep score by stock price (which rarely, formulaically reflects profit). And they have more resources than you do.

6. For most small businesses, personal branding is far superior to corporate/business branding. People prefer dealing with people rather than with nameless, faceless, soulless institutions. Put yourself out there!

7. Most basic, starting-point summary: Begin with *WHO* is your business for? + *WHAT* do you want to be known for, by *WHO?* then *HOW* can you represent, symbolize, and summarize that in a memorable way.

(For more on direct-response branding, pick up my *No B.S. Guide to Brand-Building by Direct Response: The Ultimate No Holds Barred Plan to Creating and Profiting from a Powerful Brand Without Buying It* [Entrepreneur Books, 2014]. I wrote it with two very successful business owners who were building a multimillion-dollar fitness empire, Forrest Walden and Jim Cavale. They use social media for lead generation, but that is only one of many things they do.)

"Don't be in too much of a hurry to promote until you get good. Otherwise, you just speed up the rate at which the world finds out you're no good," said public speaker Cavett Robert.

In reality, the principles behind the USP have been talked about to death. You can call it the Purple Cow, your market position, your winning difference, or just the answer to Why Should Anyone Read Your Blog, connect with you on LinkedIn, "Like" you on Facebook, follow you on Twitter, or click on your ad.

The *reason* the USP has been talked to death is that this core idea is essential to effective marketing. Even though defining your USP is one of the best places to start when you're building a solid marketing plan, it also seems to be one of the easiest places for people to get lost.

USP can be defined this way:

When you set out to attract a new, prospective customer to your business for the first time, there is one paramount question you must answer:

"Why should I choose your business/product/service vs. any/every other competitive option available to me?"

It simply means "justify your reason to exist."

You must know the facts, features, benefits, and promises that your business makes—inside-out, upside-down, backwards, forwards, and sideways. Because if you can't clearly articulate what makes your business unique, how can you expect anyone else to care?

You *will* need to crow about your business if you expect it to expand, but it's pivotal that you trumpet the right things.

The right USP coupled with the right offer, especially at the right time and place, is important for any business. For a business fighting for attention with millions of other blogs all over the world, it's essential.

It is imperative you can answer the following questions:

- What is unique about my product?
- What is unique about my delivery?
- What is unique about my service?
- What industry norms does my company bend or break?
- What is unique about my personality?
- What is my story?
- Who or what are my "enemies"?
- What is unique about my best customers?

Your very first priority as you embark on social media marketing is to get laser focused on what sets you apart. What makes you unique in your industry?

If you cannot come up with very clear answers to these questions, you're going to need to make some changes to your business. Period. This is crucial. This is foundational.

Take a long, hard look at your answers and then ask yourself "How can I incorporate this uniqueness into my marketing? How can I exploit it? How can I use it in every marketing piece I produce?" Then do it. Take action. Implement. Today.

CHAPTER 8

Niche Marketing

Originally appearing as Chapter 5 from
*No B.S. Guide to Direct Response
Social Media Marketing*

T here are riches in niches for your small-business
marketing.

The first official international convention of the
Amalgamated Order of Real Bearded Santas was held in Branson,
Missouri, attended by over 300 professional Santas with real
beards (a niche within the Santa niche!), plus some Mrs. Santas
and a few nebbishy elves horning in on the fun.

I was at a National Speakers Association convention in
the late '70s not much bigger than this. Now NSA has 5,000+
members and is the trade association of that industry. And with
local chapters around the world, and more getting going, GKIC
is an international association of a size to be reckoned with.

Each of these associations and all others (there are thousands)
represents a lucrative niche market for somebody.

After he failed to gain the support of his employer, James Perez Foster, a former partner at Bainbridge Advisors, left his job to focus on the Hispanic market. He saw an underserved market with a lot of potential and wanted to focus on this target market.

He started Solera National Bank, which is dedicated to serving Colorado's growing population of Hispanic and minority-owned businesses.

According to a study done by ShareThis, U.S. Latinos are:

- five times more likely to share content vs. non-Hispanics,
- twice as likely to click on shared content vs. non-Hispanics,
- twice as likely to *purchase the products* they share vs. non-Hispanics, and
- have four times the brand loyalty of non-Hispanics.

The point: In *every* market/business, there are specialty opportunities. Find yours.

When Choosing an Audience: Better to Pick a Small Haystack and More Needles than a Big Haystack with Hardly any Needles

We all know the "needle in the haystack" metaphor. The idea here is it's better to choose a small, well-defined niche and have a ton of followers in that small niche than to pick a large one where your message won't be heard.

How To Use This in Your Own Business

If you already have chosen a niche (whether large or small), you can carve out an even smaller niche for yourself through specialization.

You can do this simply by redefining what it is you do and finding a smaller group of people who are seeking those specialty services. Experts within their space are constantly redefining themselves to serve a smaller, more defined niche—"a smaller haystack."

To define this special space and create that unique niche, you just need to ask yourself a few simple questions:

1. *Who?* Who is the specific buyer or person you are trying to reach? Get to know them, define them, and understand their behaviors.
2. *Why?* Why is this important? Why are you doing this?
3. *Needs/Benefits?* What need are you fulfilling? What does that customer want from you, and what problem will be solved?

And finally, target a very specific niche market to start. Finding and selecting a specialized target market is a safer and better bet than targeting the masses when starting out.

Look at it this way. If you want to sell your product or service to the general public, you need a substantial marketing budget because you'll need to run ads in major publications, do massive direct-mail campaigns, and spend larger amounts on internet advertising.

Why not hitch your wagon to a smaller niche market so you can *really* start to make hay?

CHAPTER 9

What Disney VIP Treatment Can Teach You about Email Marketing

Originally appearing as Chapter 10 from
*No B.S. Guide to Direct Response
Social Media Marketing*

A s a fan of Disney, I think one of the greatest services it offers is a VIP guided tour.

This allows you to do things such as skip to the front of the line, get led in through secret back doors, and basically do more in one day (and in great style) than most may ever imagine.

It's a premium service, so as you can imagine, there are people who say the price is exorbitant. These are the same people who complain about having to wait in long lines at Disney and only having time to go on four attractions during the entire day.

Maybe if they considered that you can, for example, go on 12 attractions in the time it takes others to go on one attraction, they would see the value. Maybe they'd realize in the end, with a guide, you can do in one day what it takes the average person multiple days, even a week, to do.

I see this in business all the time. People look for the easiest, fastest, or cheapest route without considering the whole picture.

Email marketing is a prime example.

Many businesses think, because it's so easy to use, they don't need to put as much thought, time, or planning into it as they do with direct-mail campaigns.

Then these same people complain about their poor open rates, declining clickthroughs, and deflated results.

If you want better results, you have to consider the *whole* picture. And you have to invest in making your emails better.

For instance, one key disadvantage of email is that there are a lot more of them flooding your customers' inboxes every day, many more than there are pieces of mail being delivered to their regular mailbox.

That means a lot more competition for eyeballs.

So you don't want to be sloppy about what you are sending. Rather than firing off an email in ten minutes and blasting it out to your entire list without much thought or consideration, take the time to establish a plan, with response or conversion goals, so you know exactly what you want your audience to do before you ever write your email.

And make sure you've included the core elements needed in each email you send.

Consistency is also a factor. While you can execute a direct-mail campaign at random times, once you start sending emails, you should deliver them consistently week in, week out, without exception.

If you send email in a hit or miss, random fashion, or go missing from their inbox, people will forget about you in a heartbeat—even if you return to a regular, predictable schedule at a later date.

This doesn't mean you can't send emails at other times apart from your schedule. If you take care of the readers on your email list by sending valuable, relevant emails at regular intervals, they will pay attention at other times, too.

There are many strategies you can combine with your email marketing to improve your results and increase your profits—in many cases, well beyond the standard ROI you see quoted in studies.

In fact, rarely do I consult with a client where there aren't untapped opportunities within their email strategy, including ways to combine email with other media to get a higher response.

Strategies to use with opt-ins can separate the looky-loos from hyperactive buyers, increase profits, improve clickthroughs, or even create more loyal customers, clients, or patients.

Split-test your subject lines, layout, email length, time sent, call to action, and so on, and then examine your results to see what is working and what isn't.

There is no free pass to the front of the line. If you want your emails to be the first thing your customers want to open, you have to invest time and resources in making them worthy.

CHAPTER 10

Effective Calls
to Action

Originally appearing as Chapter 14 from
No B.S. Guide to Direct Response
Social Media Marketing

T he most common failure of struggling business owners is not product, place, price, or profitability. Their businesses basically work. They just fall down when it comes to selling. This is something of a lost art and a newly disdained activity. People want to send out proposals by email instead of getting face-to-face to present them. They want an iPad on the wall in their store to do the work of a live, human demonstrator. Sometimes, they hear customers say they prefer such approaches, but it's vital to realize that the customer is *not* always right. We must never surrender to expressed preferences that sabotage the most effective selling. For a lot more on selling, I urge getting a copy of another book in this series, *No B.S. Sales Success* (Entrepreneur Books, 2004).

The worst of all selling failures comes when it is time to ask for specific action. Most advertising peters out and meekly ends, without a clear and direct call to action. People are routinely permitted to wander around in stores, look at merchandise, and leave empty-handed without ever being put through an organized, scripted sales presentation that leads to a "close" or even having their names and contact information captured for follow-up. In social media, there is a cultural idea and a fear about moving people too quickly or definitively to an offer and a call to action—only somewhat justified by the interference of the gods of Facebook, Twitter, LinkedIn, etc. The fact is, there's no money made until somebody sells something, and damn little gets sold without somebody directly asking for the order.

My famous friend and colleague, the great Zig Ziglar, observed that "timid salespeople have skinny kids," and said that what separates the poorly paid professional visitor from the kingly compensated professional salesperson is asking for the order. All advertising, all marketing, all media—social and otherwise—must be engineered to get prospect and seller to a time and place where the order can be requested. Anything else is mere professional visiting.

In advertising, the vital skill is knowing how to ask your prospect to take action. Your experience in effectively closing in-person sales will pay off when you sit down to create effective advertising. The same techniques, words, phrases, and ideas used in personal selling should be used in your marketing.

A "Slam Dunk" Customer

If you're trying to target the entire world, you'd better be prepared to go head-to-head with big, dumb companies with billions of dollars to waste in the effort. Going after every possible person who could ever use your service is a fool's errand.

Instead, you need to figure out who your favorite clients are. Where do they come from? How do they act? What do they read? How much do they earn? What do they like to do for fun? What is it about *you* that they resonate with?

Get a grip on *who* this person is, *where* to find him, and *what* he really wants that only you can provide. And then figure out what *price* you want him to be able to pay. This should be your first step to building a smarter lead-generation system.

An Easy Layup—Your Lead Generation Magnet

Give your leads a clear reason to contact you and get that reason in front of your "slam dunkers." Narrow down your perfect clients from the unwashed masses. This "thing" you're creating is an incentive to respond. It's your Lead Generation Magnet. It can be informational, like a report, guide, book, CD, or webinar, or it might be some other kind of "gift." Obviously, the more desirable your magnet and its offer, the stronger the pull it will have to your perfect prospect.

Here are a few Lead Generation Magnets that work very well:

- My friend Larry Levin, seen often on Fox Business News and heard on radio, offers his options trading technique that made him over $1 million—for free. If you'll just call his 800 number and leave your email address, he'll send it to you.
- My client Ted Oakley, a wealth manager seen on CNBC and other investor-oriented publications, offers his free book, *$20 MILLION AND BROKE* (Keysar Publishing, 2013), for business owners selling or who have recently sold their companies.
- My client ArthroNew offers a free online video about chronic and arthritic pain relief featuring Dr. John Frank,

M.D. and Super Bowl player, and a free month's trial package (to move prospects to tele-reps).

- Doctors with local practices I've worked with offer books like *The Official Consumer Guide to Cosmetic Surgery* and *How to End Back Pain and Golf as If You Were 10 Years Younger—Without Drugs or Surgery.*

- A B2B consultant offers a "Special Research Report" on expense reduction and cost control case histories to hospital CEOs and CFOs.

- A company of which I was part owner taught people how to start homebased information-publishing businesses. It successfully advertised its Lead Generation Magnet in over 50 national magazines for years—its "little yellow book" was titled *How to Make $4,000 a Day, Sitting at Home in Your Underwear, with Your Computer.*

- My longtime client Ben Glass, a personal injury attorney in Virginia, creates and advertises many different free reports and books and is a master at using Lead Generation Magnets. You can take a look at www.BenGlassLaw.com. Ben is so good at this, thousands of lawyers all across the country use his LGM formats and models, and you can see that at www.GreatLegalMarketing.com.

Answer the WHY YOU Question

"Why should I do business with you rather than any other option—including doing nothing?" The answer is what I call your Unique Selling Proposition (USP). Your lead magnet should make dead certain that the factors that make you different are clearly spelled out. This provides fuel to your Call to Action (something else you need in your magnet; do *not* forget that critical piece) that compels them to act without hesitation, knowing that the benefit they want can only be found with your products/services.

Don't rely on hope, networking, or prospecting grunt work to get customers through your door or to your website. Create a lead-generation system that includes these key components to get them to raise their hands and ask for *you*.

The Seamless System Wins

Many big, dumb companies wind up with separate, separately ruled little fiefdoms. Advertising. Marketing. Social Media. Sales. Their princes view each other with suspicion. Often, they compete with each other for budget dollars. They don't respect each other's roles or value. The whole thing winds up a patchwork quilt, with big, ugly seams separating each patch. *You* probably can't afford this all-too-common level of corporate dysfunction.

In its place, you want a seamless system—a customer-centric system.

It's entirely about the customer and totally designed and organized to move someone seamlessly from first point of contact along a single, well-paved and fenced-in path to the point of sale. If that point of first contact is in social media, terrific—but then you must move that person from the avenue through your driveway, onto your garden path, and ultimately to the point of sale.

CHAPTER 11

The Trouble with Trending

Originally appearing as Chapter 17 from
*No B.S. Guide to Direct Response
Social Media Marketing*

I 've said it before and I'll say it again, you should *never* try to be everything to everyone with your marketing.

This is how companies get themselves into trouble when they use social media. It goes something like this: Company sees trending topic, company contributes to trending topic without understanding its context in an effort to appear "relevant" or "hip." Then there's backlash similar to what DiGiorno Pizza encountered in September 2014.

To provide some backstory, the backlash occurred when #WhyIStayed started trending on Twitter to bring to light the issue of domestic violence. This was (and still is) a serious topic of public discussion after the NFL released the video of the Baltimore Ravens player Ray Rice assaulting his then-fiancée in a hotel. DiGiorno Pizza tweeted, "#WhyIStayed You had pizza."

So what was DiGiorno's reasoning behind this tweet? Did it think it was funny? Did it think Ray Rice should have gotten treatment that was more lenient? No. Its answer was so *stupid* it makes me nauseous.

DiGiorno said that it "didn't know what the hashtag was about."

A tenet comes to mind that relates (if you've ever given an excuse when pulled over by a cop, you've heard this one): Ignorance of the law excuses no one.

The alarming revelation here is that this isn't the first and certainly won't be the last example of a company that misstepped in the wild, wild world of social media. As of writing this book, there are over 1.36 billion registered Facebook users, and more than 42 million Facebook pages. There is a lot to learn from companies that are getting social media right and those that, quite frankly, are failing miserably.

So how do we separate the winners from the losers? Dollar-measured results, that's how. Everything else is just a waste of time.

Provided that you are getting a return on your investment, social media can be a valuable asset to add to your marketing plan. That being said, using social media solely is a dangerous (and *not* recommended) path to follow. All of Kim's students have a multilayered approach to their marketing, so if Facebook bit the dust tomorrow, they would still soldier on. The value in social media is how it can complement, *not* replace, your traditional marketing activities like direct mail, email marketing, so on and so forth.

This is especially important considering that new social media networks are developed almost daily. If you are going to chase every social media network down the "Yellow Brick Road," you might as well give your paycheck to the flying monkeys. Seriously. How much sense does it make to deliver a watered-down marketing strategy to multiple audiences, instead of hitting a home run with one social media network? I'll save you the five seconds of contemplation. None.

Multiple social media strategies, case studies, and solutions for the everyday marketer presented are in *No B.S. Guide to Direct Response Social Media Marketing.* Use these examples as a guide for your own journey to social media success. While you may think "My business is different. These steps can't be applied in my situation," I'm here to tell you that you're wrong. You must, however, follow the foundational rules for a high social media ROI.

These many stellar examples demonstrate a high ROI from social media. Don't be fooled. These examples are the exception. And they only occur because of a strict adherence to direct-response marketing with a hawk's eye on measurement.

If you decide to proceed with your social media marketing strategies, keep in mind these foundational rules at all times:

You can (and should) make yourself a celebrity through social media. Utilize social media to create your celebrity status to your target market. This is a platform you can control, and it should be leveraged for celebrity positioning. Think of the Kardashians. They practically built an empire off of what most thought would be Kim Kardashian's 15 seconds of fame. The "video-seen-round-the-world" spawned a reality show that's currently on its 17th season, multiple clothing stores, and an app that earned $43 million in the third quarter of 2014 (Glu Mobile).

However, as a business owner, you might take a less extreme approach than a sex tape. But to each their own.

Niches bring riches. There are niches all over the world— some that you may not even be aware of—that come in the form of associations, groups, interests. You name it, and someone will be willing to pay a pretty penny to work with someone they believe speaks directly to them.

Whether or not you choose to advertise on the platform, Facebook has powerful tools to help you research your list without giving Facebook a dime. At least for now. It's worth checking out before it starts charging. If you do use the platform to advertise, make sure you are not only targeting your ad, but also your audience, too. Too many businesses get a segmented list to market but use the same ad for each audience.

Don't copy someone's social media ad just because it "looks cool." I can't tell you how *dumb* this strategy is, especially on social media, when you have no idea whether or not the ad is even breaking even on the investment.

Kmart had a "viral" video called "Ship My Pants" that was the talk of the web. Did it increase sales of online purchases? Kmart's store sales were down 2.2% again the next year, so my guess? Once again, it forgot who its target market is.

Do not copy what others are doing just because they are doing it.

If someone tries to convince you otherwise, slap yourself in the head. Preferably with this book, so through some act of freakish osmosis, it will remind you of the rules.

Get to know your best customers better, find out their wants and needs, and fill them. Surveying your target audience is a serious exercise that you should use so you can better deliver your product or service. This can be as simple as drafting a survey with only a few questions. It's what comes back in these surveys that is really exciting.

With this data, you can identify potential improvements, referrals, and other business opportunities. These questions can also help you to develop a lead magnet offer (free report, ebook) that will answer a question that is burning in the back of your ideal prospect's mind. Base your marketing strategies on fact, not guessing.

Well, this is where I leave you. If you decide to continue on in your social media marketing efforts or begin them, do so armed.

In *No B.S. Guide to Direct Response Social Media Marketing,* Kim has laid out a thorough, sensible plan for you to establish your presence on social media and, more important to my mind, get measurable return on your investment. This is what works. Personally, I continue to be fed financially through businesses I have interests in, by the social media strategies Kim has described. I'd be the last guy on earth to suggest *not* using it for all it's worth. A lot is done on social media in my name, as if it were me. The work I do for many of my clients incorporates and integrates social media.

But, if you ever find me *personally* tweeting, you'll know the world has ended.

PART II

BRANDING AND LOCAL MARKETING

with selections from

*No B.S. Guide to Brand-Building by
Direct Response*

No B.S. Grassroots Marketing

BRANDING AND LOCAL MARKETING

You want your business to be famous. To be known by name, what it does understood, and some sort of excellence attached to it in the minds of its customers and would-be customers. This ambition is encouraged by what you see giant corporations doing, to create brand identity.

What you *don't* know is:

- Many brand campaigns using all sorts of ad media to hammer home their name and slogan or key promise, like "Save 15% in 15 minutes," are actually failing with a substantial percentage of consumers. Given tests where the brand name is to be matched with its slogan or main product, service, or promise, 25% to 60% of consumers can't make the match! This is not new, by miniaturized attention span. I documented it over a decade ago with the batteries promoted by the rabbit with the drum, my report published in *USA Today*. A big company may be able to afford this advertising inefficiency—can you?

- A lot of the brand advertising done by big companies is about pleasing constituencies you don't have—*not* about attracting customers! It's going on to satisfy Wall Street and shareholders, build the morale of its dealers and sales organizations, even puff up the egos of its CEOs. If you are inspired to follow another company's example as an advertiser and brand builder, you have to ask: Are they pursuing the exact same objectives that I need to pursue?

- Traditional brand advertising, with the money spent to build brand recognition, can take a lot of very patient money, requiring years before getting traction. Just how patient can *your* money be?

What may be good for the Goliath may not be good for the David. What you'll discover here is "the David approach": getting brand identity built without paying to do so. Instead, getting brand-building as a happy byproduct of direct-response advertising that pays for itself in now-time, not someday, you hope. The excerpts here from the book *No B.S. Guide to Brand-Building by Direct Response* explain this.

For the local small business, there is also a nitty-gritty ground game that can build the brand free of direct investment, as a byproduct of community-focused marketing and promotion *activity*. This is more about deploying human capital and relationship capital than money. Excerpts here from the book *No B.S. Grassroots Marketing* tell this story.

This is all as vital and viable today as it was when first written. In some ways, it is even more important, as proliferation of social media tempts random, scattered, and unaccountable spending of money and/or time and labor to build brand familiarity in a way that may achieve it at the expense of profit, even to the point of running out of money just about the time you are well-known. It happens. A lot.

CHAPTER 12

The Golden Opportunity and Harsh Reality of Owning a Brand

Originally appearing as Chapter 1 from
*No B.S. Guide to Brand-Building by
Direct Response*

I am often introduced as "The Millionaire Maker," a nod to the fact that my advice and marketing strategies have lifted hundreds and hundreds, if not thousands and thousands, of people new to business, people with ideas brought to market, owners of established but ordinary businesses, and self-employed professionals to seven-figure incomes and to million and multimillion-dollar wealth. I am also often introduced as "The Professor of Harsh Reality," which is more in keeping with my main brand, which I'll talk about a bit later. This, because I famously rip to shreds illusion, delusion, treasured beliefs, conventional "wisdom," and industry norms and expose charlatans and fakers and theorists. This sometimes makes me unwelcome, and it's possible that will be the case here, if you have treasured beliefs, illusions, or delusions about the magical power of a brand.

On the surface, asking me to write a book on brand-building, as *Entrepreneur* did, seemed odd to me and to many who know me well, with whom I shared the mission. Hiring a heretic to pastor a church. I am a very vocal, near constant critic of big, brand-name companies and their huge expenditures on brand or image advertising. I am incessantly cautioning small-business owners, entrepreneurs, and private practice operators not to emulate the behavior of the big brand advertisers, due to their very different agendas as well as the emperors with no sense in their boardrooms. The potential to brand-build your way to bankruptcy is very real.

I make fun of corporate goofiness, like the pink bunny with the drum that everybody knows but more than half of consumers queried attach it to the wrong band of battery, or the infamous Taco Bell stuffed dog that starred in months of commercials (replacing the food) only to produce a decline in sales, or the fortunes spent tweaking logos and meaningless slogans. When I was writing this book, *USA Today* actually had the unbridled corporate ego to trumpet its new logo—a big blue dot, by the way—as front-page *news*, as if anybody but its designer and his mother cared. Boneheaded corporate CEOs routinely pour millions into brand symbols, logos, and slogans, and issue pompous press releases, even hold press conferences to announce their foolishness. It is routine folly to grossly exaggerate the significance and value of brands.

Of course, there *are* plenty of iconic, powerhouse brands worth fortunes. In entertainment, James Bond, Batman, Superman, The Avengers, Disney. In food, Campbell's Soup and Coca-Cola. Name a category, you can certainly name both corporate and personal brands that have sustained magnetic power. I've never denied that. I've just said that the way many have been built is not by throwing oceans of money into buying recognition, awareness, and familiarity, as most peddlers of brand-building theory and of ad media would have you believe. Also, that there's no warranty of inevitability of brand power or value either.

In autos, Rambler was once a good brand. So was Pontiac. It even owned a craze for a time, the Pontiac Trans Am, made famous by Burt Reynolds in *Smokey and the Bandit*. Oldsmobile, the symbol of having made it, but not wanting to be a show-off. They're all gone. Zeroed out. One of the classic cars I drive around in is a 1972 AMC Javelin SST, then a very hot car (see below). Now, people ask: What is *that?* And often, when I say it was made by American Motors, people ask what that was.

More people know Jeep, of course, and today it is a valuable brand. But it twice flirted with extinction. The Jeep in the photo on page 106 is my restored 1986 Jeep Wagoneer, which I

bought, on impulse, of all places, out of an Orvis catalog. And I felt fine doing so because Orvis is a trusted brand to me. If you're unfamiliar with them, they are a long-established catalog company, selling everything from apparel to hunting and fishing excursions. Orvis shirts, slacks, and a favorite leather jacket hang in my closet. If they say this is a well-restored classic car, I believe them.

Increasingly, a brand is important to consumers—and therefore valuable—in categories of goods or services over-cluttered with competing choices and like or identical pricing, as a shortcut to decision, desperately needed in an overbusy life. Yet, this value and importance can, in some cases, be long-standing, as with, say, Campbell's Soup or Bounty paper towels (you know, the quicker picker upper), but it can also lose its grip, as, say, Holiday Inn, or it can go from firm grip on consumer consciousness to utter oblivion, as, say, Timex or Dr. Spock (once THE name in advice for parents) or Firestone (a brand so weakened its name was even removed from its own PGA tournament held at the country club bearing its name). Brands can be important, until they aren't.

Brand as a holy grail or as a panacea for what ails a business—I buy neither and rail against both. And I strongly caution against pouring capital into a brand, per se.

Yet here I am, adding a book on brand-building to my stable of No B.S. books. When I took it on, I had my doubts it could be done without B.S. But, then again, I have had and have a lot of clients with very valuable brands they grew without having to pour oceans of money into them. That is what this book is about, in terms of strategy and tactics: **getting a great brand—free.** That makes this book radically different from any other books or advice in this category. Everything else about brands is piled high at one end of the library. This little book sits by itself, at the far, opposite end.

A Brand Atheist. A Brand Believer.

I am fundamentally a <u>direct</u> marketing guy. That means I want to be able to accurately, ruthlessly measure a money return on each and every dollar invested, preferably quickly. No ambiguity. No vague idea of gain by awareness. Show me the money. It also means I want <u>direct</u> response. Outreach that brings a customer to the door, credit card in hand. Big, valuable brands can and are created as free byproducts of this kind of direct-marketing activity, including many owned by past or present clients of mine. Weight Watchers, a famous brand built with no brand-building advertising. Guthy-Renker's Proactiv®, an $800-million-a-year business with a brand worth at least five times that much, created, built, and sustained without brand or image advertising—one I'm proud to have made some small contributions to from time to time. Priceline.com, originally raised from scratch by hard-core direct-response radio advertising created and managed by my colleague and friend, Fred Catona at Bulldozer Digital. The fast-growth software Infusionsoft, which you'll read about later in the book. These are all valuable brands that *weren't* bought.

There is one brand I know more about than any other, and we'll start this book's journey with it . . .

This odd photo represents a powerful and valuable brand.

It was first used in 1993, and has since been in perpetual and proliferate use, adorning literature, book covers, catalogs, newsletters, websites, even a bobblehead doll.

It's a (much younger) me, on a rented albino bull—the bull itself a celebrity, having appeared in two Disney films and at countless trade show booths and shopping center grand openings. Its name is Tiny. Mine is Dan Kennedy. And I'm known for being the "No B.S." guy. The actual business logo representing that brand concept is this:

This brand logo has adorned apparel, caps, wall posters, mousepads, jigsaw puzzles, toys, pens, flashlights, as well as books, newsletters, websites, and more.

These brand images mean something to those they mean something to. Maybe you are one of those people, maybe not (yet). But maybe its obvious meaning attracted you to or interested you in this very book. No B.S. is pretty straightforward. It means blunt, unmitigated, unqualified truth. It's said that there is a small market for the truth, and I have found that to be the truth—but it is a small and mighty market: a rabid, appreciative, and loyal audience. Being a truth-teller is not the easiest road to prosperity to travel, but it has proved itself a very reliable and rewarding one.

This Gets to the Question: What, Exactly, Is a Brand?

In the old West, it was an identifying mark burned onto livestock with a fire-heated iron to thwart rustlers and cattle thieves. In similar fashion, businesses and individuals try to mark themselves with a distinct brand and embed that brand in the minds of the public at large or a specific, targeted population, to thwart copycatting and commoditization. It can be said about a very distinctive comedian, like Steven Wright, or Andrew Dice Clay, or my friend Joan Rivers, that they have a particular *brand of* humor. Serious students or even great fans of comedy would likely recognize a Steven Wright or Joan Rivers joke if written out on a 3-by-5 card. For a couple of decades, Cadillac was so branded on the public brain as the symbol of excellence and status that the phrase "The Cadillac of . . ." was used to describe (and nearly co-brand) all sorts of non-auto products. *"This, madam, is the Cadillac of vacuum cleaners," said the door-to-door salesman to the happy homemaker.*

A brand can be a representation of a philosophy or a philosophical position, a reason to do business with a person or entity, an instant message that communicates what a person or product or business is about. It can be aggressive or gentle, bold or subtle. It can represent the values or aspirations of a community of consumers or followers. It can be represented by a name in distinct typeface like Disney's or IBM's or by a distinctive image like Apple's or the Playboy bunny. Many great brands are actually ideas, like *Chicken Soup for the Soul*, or another of my created brands as on page 111.

This is a philosophy and lifestyle brand. It marries two great aspirations. A whole lot of people would like to be rich. If you doubt it, watch the number of people buying Powerball tickets as giant jackpots mount. And a whole lot of people like thinking

of themselves as renegades, and many more would love to be, if they dared or felt they could afford the luxury. A lot of successful brands are aspirational, like Cadillac and Martha Stewart.

A lot of what people believe about brand value, based on academic theory, Madison Avenue ad agencies and their frequent conning of big, dumb companies' leaders out of shareholders' money, and simple assumption that brand automatically equals power, is just B.S., piled high. A lot of money is wasted by small-business owners and entrepreneurs on brand-building strategies that mimic those of big, dumb companies. A brand can be a big drain into which money gets poured. Kind of like a yacht or a California divorce. Or, a brand can be a valuable asset, with much of that value measurable. Very accurate appraisal of brand equity occurs through brand licensing. Personalities like Gene Simmons (KISS) and Martha Stewart have been paid hundreds of millions of dollars to attach their names to all manner of products. There are, for example, KISS condoms and KISS caskets—as Gene puts it, brand licensing money made from the cradle to the grave.

A brand can be important to consumers in different ways. It can, as I said before, help cut through marketplace clutter and chaos and sheer quantity of noise, to make choosing within a category easy and efficient. It can often be a guarantee of consistency, of a certain kind or level of experience, so that the consumer can know in advance what to expect, and what not to expect. It can provide pride of ownership and status; it can enable somebody to be in "the cool kids' club;" it can stroke one's ego: *I am because I own*. It can validate a person's values or aspirations: *I am a good mother because I serve this brand of food*. It can satisfy at an emotional level, as with nostalgia brands.

We will explore everything a brand can and can't be and can and can't do for you or your business in this book. Most important, we will dispel B.S., and we will be clear about *wise* strategies to develop and build brand identity and equity without direct investment.

I have never spent a cent on outright brand advertising of any sort, yet within my chosen target markets my personal brand is strong—meaning, people know me, know what I'm about, and know what to expect when dealing with me. And my business brands are well-recognized by customers, clients, readers, subscribers, and the fields in which I conduct business. The members of the organization built by me and around me, GKIC, which publishes the *No B.S. Marketing Letter*, identify with and have affinity for the No B.S. brand. In fact, many own logo apparel, desk ornaments, and various items linked to that brand. What might surprise some is that I have no interest in *everybody* recognizing these brands. Nor in just anybody recognizing them. I have very deliberately made myself what I call a famous person nobody's ever heard of—except the select audience that is of the highest value to me and best fit with me. One of the great myths of brand-building is that a brand's value is proportionate to the raw numbers of those who know it. That can be true, but it isn't always true.

Business and marketing decisions, especially those about your brands, need to follow a linear path:

Principle > Strategies > Tactics

Great brands stand for something. Sam Walton knew exactly what he wanted Walmart to be when it grew up, and could clearly enunciate a handful of core principles. Ray Kroc had three principles on which to govern the growth of McDonald's. The extremely successful celebrity-entrepreneur Kathy Ireland, who spoke at one of GKIC's annual Marketing and Moneymaking SuperConferences^{SM}, explained there the key principles behind her brand, which now supports thousands of products and drives a multimillion-dollar empire. Walt Disney put his business's number-one principle into its slogan and Unique Selling Proposition, something of a feat: *The* Happiest Place on Earth. The overarching principle of all my work, represented by my brand, is truth-telling. Absolute, unvarnished, bare naked truth-telling. Brands backed by principle tend to outsell, outperform, and outlast brands that aren't. If you stand for nothing, you can be felled by just about anything.

From principle come strategies. Each of the above examples followed that path. If you obtain and read the autobiographies and biographies of these men and women and of other great entrepreneurs who've built powerful personal or business brands, you will find that each of their few chief principles drove a plethora of strategic decisions. I'll use myself as an example here, and rattle off a sampling of strategic decisions mandated by my chief principle, in no particular order:

- I have been selective, discriminating, and deliberate in the clients, customers, members, and fans I've sought and deliberately, overtly repelled others—so that I could be a truth-teller at all times, in every piece of work (book, newsletter, seminar, etc.) without worry over who I might offend or what sale or revenue I might lose by not sugarcoating or walking on tiptoes on the thin ice of political correctness.

- I have focused on entrepreneurial business owners, business builders, and CEOs rather than larger, perhaps more lucrative corporate clients—because I understand and admire the determined entrepreneur but often question the very sanity and competence of corporate executives.
- I've never sold or permitted anyone else to sell anything to my clientele, members, followers without at least a 30-day unconditional guarantee—because if any individual feels they were not told the truth about a product or service, I do not want them feeling stuck with something "false" to them.
- I have been personally transparent with my members and clientele. For example, I have written and publicly spoken about my now long, long ago bankruptcy; my long ago heavy boozing; and I use my marketing misfires and flops as well as my successes as teaching examples. Contrary to the caution that business and politics don't mix, the folks who follow me have no doubt about where I stand on political matters.

Just to give you a couple non-Dan examples:

Farm-to-table restaurants are based on a certain obvious principle. This governs strategic choices about physical location, menu items and food sources and vendors, and tactical decisions about price. Ralph Nader's quixotic presidential campaigns (that made him a bestselling author, popular speaker, media personality—and quite wealthy) centered on being against corporate influence in politics, and this principle governed strategy about who he would and could not take donations or other support from, then tactical decisions about how he could and would raise money and finance campaigns. Bill Cosby determined he never wanted to do anything his young daughter or aging mother would be embarrassed to hear or watch. This principle governed strategic career choices about agents and managers, film and TV projects, down to the tactical choices of jokes, comedy material, and words he would and would not use.

Often, acting in a way that contradicts principle severely damages or ruins a personal or corporate brand. President Bush No. 1 was, in the short term, virtually ruined by his failure to honor his "Read my lips—NO new taxes" pledge. A big-time TV preacher, Jimmy Swaggart, a moralist, never recovered from his public scandal involving underage prostitutes. (For somebody like a rap music star or mogul, the same scandal might be helpful.) Disney has carefully, tentatively negotiated and expanded the serving of alcoholic beverages in select places and at certain times in its parks—something antithetical to Walt's principles for the parks (although Walt personally was a drinker). Strategies that contradict principle are equally perilous. Pierre Cardin and Oleg Cassini were once very elite and exclusive fashion brands, but by extremely aggressive and indiscriminate licensing, including several different price levels and distribution channels for the same category of items—like sunglasses in boutiques at $500.00 but also in department stores at $50.00 and in discount stores for $19.95—their value was destroyed. The minute you can buy a cheaply made handbag with the Birkin brand on it, in unlimited quantity, at Target, the end for Birkin will be near. Disney licensed out the operation of its retail stores in shopping malls and gave up managerial control of the Florida community it created, Celebration, and lived to regret both strategic decisions as damaging to its brand. (It remedied the matter of the stores. It was too late to retake control of Celebration.) With 20/20 hindsight, there is only one strategic decision I've personally made in my own businesses that I consider damaging to my brand, and I'm embarrassed to say I repeated it and made fundamentally the same mistake twice. It was at odds with Principle.

Just as linking Principle to Strategies is powerful, de-linking them is dangerous.

Day by Day, Hour by Hour, Choice by Choice
We Weave Strands of Fabric That Become
the Cape of a Superhero
Or the Shroud of a Disgraced Pariah

Finally, we can get to tactics. This is too often where businesspeople begin or hurry, even race, to implementation. Advertising and marketing content, media, and process decisions are very often made with little or no regard to a principle that governs strategy. Entrepreneurs are often "Ready, Fire, Then Aim" people. Entrepreneurs are often operating under extreme time or financial pressure. The temptations to make tactical moves without full consideration of them against strategies set by principle is difficult to resist. Often, we don't even slow down enough to recognize that is what we're doing!

Martha Stewart risked great brand damage when she took Kmart as her first major retail partner. It was a simple tactical act: They were there with money and no one else was, and they had—at the time—enormous distribution power. She made a similar, apparently money- and immediacy-driven decision when she broke with Macy's and did a huge deal with J.C. Penney, creating a triangle of messy, expensive, and hazardous litigation, ill will, and bad PR. Pharmaceutical companies helped themselves tremendously when they became direct-to-consumer advertisers in print media and on TV, when they copied a favorite tactic of late-night infomercials and hired and showcased celebrity spokespersons, a practice they continue to use. Sleep Number Beds began as a pure direct marketer and built their brand by direct-response advertising, but then made a tactical decision to open and operate their own local, brick-and-mortar retail locations (as opposed to distributing through other retailers or remaining a pure direct marketer), a decision that appears to be working out well for them. It has not worked out well at all for a number of other direct marketers, including brands like The Sharper Image and J. Peterman. Iron Tribe Fitness's owners decided to operate the opposite of most gyms, limiting membership to just 300 rather than selling as many memberships as possible, and selling at a very premium price as opposed to the common, cheap fee. This is working out very well for them. A friend of mine self-published his health book, chooses not to sell it via Amazon or any other bookseller or in any ebook form (where it would probably bring from $4.00 to $9.00), sells it direct to consumers by direct mail only (at a $45.00 price), and has sold nearly 250,000 books at a nice profit. These are all tactical decisions. There are so many tactical options to consider that it's vital to have a fixed basis for evaluating them—such as Strategies based on Principle.

The brands I built and the relationship they and I have with my target market formed the basis for a substantial sale of the company I founded and built, GKIC, to private equity investors, who now own it. It's very rare for an individual author or speaker or thought leader to create a business with real, salable equity. These businesses are mostly income plays, not equity plays. Most are truthfully glorified jobs masquerading as businesses. Not mine. Mine was, in fact, sold twice, first to Bill Glazer, who helmed it with me heavily involved for about ten years, and again to the professional investment group. They valued this company in the tens of millions of dollars. All centered around little ol' me. Why? Because, in my small way, in my niche field, I emulated truly extraordinary builders of brand value like Walt Disney and Hugh Hefner. I made my personal brand and affiliation with me, and my business brands and involvement with them, about high trust (like Disney) and dynamic aspiration (like Hefner). Within the confines and dictates of principle, I was extremely strategic. You will come away with a better, clearer, deeper understanding of why this approach is so important and how you can use it for any business, product, person, or cause.

I pride myself on pragmatism, so I've made this a very practical book. It lays out a productive path, not an ethereal and theoretical jumble of ideas. But this is also an inspirational book. It shows how you can take your business and make it really mean something to its customers. My co-authors from Iron Tribe Fitness demonstrate this clearly. I hope you find this premise exciting and motivational: the making a business into something that really means something to its customers.

Frankly, *just* selling stuff and making money, even a lot of money, is neither mysterious rocket science nor beyond anyone's reach, because of upbringing, education, resources, or any other common excuse for poor life outcomes. I have a happy relationship with money and like making it and like, a lot more, having it, but just making it never really fascinated me. It now seems mundane. I think it's damnably difficult to sustain creativity and enthusiasm for any business if *all* you're doing with it is exchanging goods or services for money. The building of a powerful brand and a positive relationship with a group of customers to whom your work and your business are important and mean something, that is a far more interesting exercise. It is a lie to suggest that, if you do that, plenty of money will automatically follow. Don't believe that for a minute. But it is true that when that is done in concert with the other functions of business, with maximum profits and value as a co-pilot to principle and passion, and sound disciplines of marketing and management applied, it's easier and a great deal more interesting and fulfilling to stack up the pesos.

How Are You to Learn AND IMPLEMENT Brand-Building by Direct Response?

It's possible that the best education is demonstration.

Two of the best practitioners of brand-building by direct response that I've consulted with, coached, and observed closely over the past several years are Forrest Walden and Jim Cavale, developers of a unique franchise concept in the fitness industry. In *No B.S. Guide to Brand-Building by Direct Response*, they provide an in-depth show-n-tell demonstration of exactly how to do it, from startup to local market dominance to national expansion, beginning simply, then becoming incredibly sophisticated. I'll return after these chapters, to talk about different applications of brand-building by direct response.

One quick caution: Please do not sabotage yourself with the small, provincial, and very unimaginative ". . . but MY business is different" thinking. If that's where your mind is at and will stay, you might as well stop right here, return this book for a refund, and move on. NO business is different. ALL businesses require the attraction and fascination and motivation of customers, and ALL successful businesses thrive by converting at least some of those customers to evangelical advocates. In short, to successful tribalism. Few tribes rise and stay together without a powerful brand to which they have allegiance. In this profound way, ALL businesses are the same—so all the lessons of Iron Tribe apply to all businesses.

Attempting success as an entrepreneur with a closed mind is akin to leaping from an airplane and making the rest of the journey with a closed parachute.

Even the Amish aren't this Amish. In GKIC, studying my methods through the *No B.S. Marketing Letter* and the myriad of other resources and at our conferences, right along with the Iron Tribe guys, there are Amish restaurant owners, furniture manufacturers, wealth managers and financial advisors, inventors, publishers, and other kinds of entrepreneurs proactively borrowing "what works" from wildly diverse sources of ideas, information, and inspiration. Everyone with an open mind!

CHAPTER 13

A Demonstration of Brand vs. Brand + Direct Response

Originally appearing as Chapter 15 from
No B.S. Guide to Brand-Building by Direct Response

I read between 30 and 60 different industries' trade journals every month—some because I have clients in those fields, others just because they interest me or often contain information and ideas that might be useful to GKIC Members or because, as a stock market investor, I might gain investing insight. I read *Nation's Restaurant News* even though I don't own a restaurant. I read the Farm Bureau newspaper even though I'm not a farmer. I read *Variety*, the weekly trade journal of the entertainment industry, even though I'm not an actor, singer, or movie producer, although I am a long-term stockholder in Disney and at the time of this writing in the movie company Lionsgate. Anyway, the ad shown in Figure 13.1 (on page 122) runs frequently in *Variety*. It is an ad for a car saleswoman. I do not know her and I have no idea how well the ad performs,

FIGURE 13.1

or if she knows, and since it is a branding ad and not a direct-response ad, it's likely she doesn't. I plucked the ad to critique here, as I sometimes do ads for my five newsletters. It has no copyright, and heck, maybe you'll like it, you live in Hollywood, and you'll buy a car. She looks like a nice lady, and I can help her here, free of charge.

Variety is read by lots of affluent, image-conscious actors, producers, and agents who need to make a good impression with everything they do, including the car they drive. Advertising here could be very good Place Strategy, and she is the only advertiser in her category, so she's practicing my favorite Place Strategy: Show Up Alone. Kudos for all that. She's reaching the kind of customers who want to deal with super-successful people, so her noting at the top of the ad that she is the number-one BMW salesperson since 1999 is a smart proclamation. Visually, the ad is eye-catching and artful. You won't be able to see it as well in this copy on uncoated book paper, as the original is on the slick magazine paper, but there the blue sky looks real, the words "Pleasure in the Job Puts Perfection in the Work" from Aristotle are transparent, so the sky is seen behind them yet they are perfectly legible. The car is sleek and shiny. Neda looks good. She's dressed in a navy blue or black business suit that fits her perfectly, there's just a hint of sexiness, nice smile. The ID in the lower left corner is in white against the steel blue-grey of the road surface. The whole thing looks terrific. It speaks of class and luxury.

This is the kind of personal brand ad you see a lot of real estate agents, financial advisors, cosmetic surgeons, and other professionals often pour money into—which I strongly discourage. They are fine as far as they go, and this one is an excellent example of such a brand ad. But they do not specifically invite you to do anything. This is like meeting her at a cocktail party, being introduced, having her tell you she is the number-one BMW salesperson, then abruptly spinning on her heel and walking away or, if you ask her a question, standing there mute. Or, a better analogy, since we are in sales, is having her knock on your door, introduce herself as the number-one BMW salesperson, spin, and walk away.

The other problem is that this lovely lady is paying this ad to show up in *Variety* for her, but not requiring it to prove it is earning its cost. To her credit, she hasn't loaded it up with Facebook, LinkedIn, and Twitter doorways to make accountability impossible. She's offered only two ways to respond, both direct, and she can obviously ask prospects where they heard of her. Still, there's a lot of room for leakage. And if she's running the same ad in multiple places, it gets murkier.

But the big, big, big flaw is that this ad only gets immediate response from buy-now customers. It does nothing and offers nothing for the many more whom she has intrigued, who are just beginning to think about a new car, who plan to start shopping for a new car when their next residual check comes in. They are left loose, in the hope that imbedding her brand in their minds will be enough 4, 8, 10, 20 weeks later when they are ready to get new wheels. She has paid for those eyeballs to look at this ad, but she has no idea how many or who they are, and can do nothing to build trust and interest with them between now and the time they will actually buy a car.

Don't waste eyeballs you pay for.

Three Ways to Fix this Ad

The least aggressive option does absolutely zero damage to the branding or to the luxury image this ad conveys. We are not going to plunk a big red-and-white cardboard bucket of chicken down on the silver platter on the pure silk tablecloth in the mansion dining room. I'm not going to replace her elegant suit with a red, yellow, and white circus clown outfit and stick a red bulb nose on her. She does not need to commit image suicide. The ad can be shrunk vertically just a tiny bit, just enough to fit a line or two of direct-response copy, black or even grey on white at its bottom. It can be in a discreet and elegant typeface like this:

> To see a BMW test drive with Neda and a fascinating movie stunt man, visit DrivingWithNeda.com. For a Free Report, *How to Own the Perfect Luxury Automobile*, and a DVD including a visit to the BMW factory to see the artisanship and have its incomparable technology demonstrated, complete the quick request form at DrivingWithNeda.com.

By adding these two offers, we create what's called Secondary Reason for Response. We give the person not ready right now to buy a car a reason to respond now anyway. To understand what to do with them when they arrive and how to place them in a good sales funnel, consult Chapter 30 of my *No B.S. Marketing to the Affluent* book, including the funnel diagram. Here, these points: One, Neda still gets the buy-now customers who call her or email her, but she also gets names, at least email addresses, and for the second offer, full addresses of not-ready-now potential buyers that she can continue communicating with directly.

Again, I haven't harmed the beauty of her main presentation in the slightest. Her personal brand is unscathed.

A more aggressive option would be to add a promise/benefit headline to the top or/and place a small testimonial from a famous Hollywood figure in the dead lower right corner AND add the same lead-generation offers I added above.

The most aggressive option would be to replace the entire ad with a black on white, article-look mini advertorial, matching the content typeface of the magazine, actually saying something. That headline might be "The #1 BMW Salesperson in the USA Since 1999 Announces Openings for Seven Hollywood/Beverly Hills Area Clients in Her Exclusive Private Client Group." The article would end with a direct call to action, to call or email her for Private Client details, a test drive, and a gift of fine wine with the test drive, and it would still have the Secondary Reason for Response Offers as well.

I doubt I'd ever convince Neda to buy this third option. I'd be seen as an uncouth beast. But maybe I can persuade you?

How to Accelerate Brand-Building Speed and Buy More Brand-Building Power

Let's assume that one of the above three methods results in the sale of, on average, one more car per month than she presently sells via this ad. Let's assume that equates to a few thousand dollars of commission income. What might Neda do with the money? She could go shopping on Rodeo Drive, but I'll bet her closet's already full. So, she could use it to buy a bigger ad. And if that upped sales yet again, she could go all the way up to a full page, cut in half vertically or horizontally, with a big image ad like hers in half its space and a constantly changing advertorial like I suggested in the other half of the space. With this much bigger presence, she'd be impossible not to notice and remember, and her brand would dominate faster, with more people.

That's how direct response can build a brand, bigger, stronger, faster.

He *or she* who spends the most, the most wisely, does win. But few can spend the most out-of-pocket. By ramping up the proceeds of direct response, someone can spend more and more and more in more places or more often and achieve ultimate brand domination with a market.

Another way to think about this is to envision the paid-for but wasted eyeballs in the eye sockets of not-ready-now prospects who get away and later buy a car from someone else as deadweight your advertising budget has to haul around on its back. The deadweight grows heavier every time the ad runs. Soon it brings the ad budget to its knees. Our ad budget moves slower and more laboriously, bent over and crippled. If we liberate it and lift off the deadweight and convert the deadweight to energy drinks the ad budget consumes as it goes along, it can grow bigger and stronger, stand taller, and move faster. You decide whether to load it down with deadweight or to liberate it and power it up with your decisions about brand/image-only vs. brand/image-with-direct response or direct response with brand/image, Secondary Reason for Response, and a good follow-up sales funnel.

CHAPTER 14

Building a Brand by Building Bonfires

Originally appearing as Chapter 18 from
*No B.S. Guide to Brand-Building by
Direct Response*

M edia publicity, social media buzz, what EST's
Werner Erhard dubbed "sell it by zealot"—now viral
buzz by brand loyalists, deliberately or accidentally
ignited public conversation can be as dangerous as playing with
dynamite and lit matches in a moving pickup truck on a bumpy
dirt road, but it can also be a way to accelerate brand-building
and to activate more brand loyalists as evangelical recruiters.

The old joke about there being no such thing as bad
publicity is no longer universally true. For celebrities, it's a very
unpredictable thing. Celebrity cook Paula Deen's publicized
use of the "N word" seems, as of this writing, to have severely
damaged her brand and business and set endorsers fleeing, but
it did also, immediately, spark a huge surge of purchases of her
cookbooks at Amazon. Tiger Woods similarly saw his sponsors

withdraw en masse, but it appears, at this point, that he may yet be resurrected as a commercial spokesperson. I'll court danger by saying so, but overall, painting with broad brush, it's my observation that the media is more eagerly forgiving of black celebrities' controversial statements and bad behavior than they are of white celebrities who get into similar difficulty. For companies, controversy and/or bad news and bad press can be even more dangerous, yet many brands are surprisingly resilient, and many even benefit from dynamite exploding in their hands.

One thing that the internet has created, that's important to understand, is a remaking of publicity, media exposure, public discussion, and gossip as direct-response marketing, because it's easy for interested people to find you. It's very easy, for example, to find me, if anything seen or read or heard anywhere piques your curiosity. You just type my name into Google. Or Amazon. Or Facebook. Before the internet, this was not the case. Guests on talk shows, for example, had to fight to get an 800 number given out, and were often denied that opportunity. If you were interviewed and included in a magazine article, there was no easy way for readers to locate you or contact you. They might go to a store and ask about your product, but if it wasn't there, that ended that. They might go to a bookstore, but if you weren't the author of a book currently in print, that ended that. Today, you are essentially walking, talking direct-response media. Even a brief mention of your brand in the media can send people on an immediately fruitful search of you. If, for example, there was no contact information of any kind provided in this book for Nick Nanton, but a few sentences I wrote about him interested you, how hard would it be for you to find him and his company online? It takes me longer to microwave my morning cup of coffee.

With this in mind, it's vital to understand direct-response and direct-marketing funnels, so that when people do find you on their own, by whatever provocation, or none but organic search, the trail leads them to and through a door, onto a pathway with high walls on either side, to a series of yes/no actions, ultimately converting them to viable prospects and the highest percentage of them possible to customers. Traffic and visitor counts are, frankly, B.S., flung about by fools and social media promoters and charlatans like monkeys at the zoo fling feces. It's meaningless. Only traffic converted to prospects and customers, converted to sales and profits count. Be very wary of all the "new metrics" gobbledygook. There's no line for it on a bank deposit slip. If the construction of marketing funnels for lead capture and conversion is foreign to you, it will very quickly be made clear when visit https://MagneticMarketing.com.

Also, with this in mind, it's important to understand that there are no longer any protective walls around your brand. It is exposed 24/7/365. And the impact of whatever is said or happens is instant and may spread at the speed of light. There is no news cycle anymore. There's just news now. You can manipulate and use the talk about you more aggressively than ever before. You can also be damaged by it more harshly and more quickly than ever before.

Brand protection includes internal law enforcement. My book *No B.S. Ruthless Management of People and Profits* is the bluntest, toughest instruction manual for brand protection from the inside out ever written by anybody. In it, for example, I recommend full audio and video surveillance of every person who interacts with customers in every place they interact with customers, frequent "mystery shopping" of the answering of your phones, carefully constructed scripts and enforcement of their use, rapid-fire response to mistakes and consumer dissatisfaction, firing fast and hiring slow, and other important measures to protect profit margins and to protect brand. This is the part of business ownership and management people like the least, fear the most, and do the worst. From a brand-equity standpoint, any problem or problem employee not nipped in the bud can bring the entire enterprise to disaster.

The more successful and visible you are, the more important this is. If you focus on brand-building but neglect brand protection, you will likely see, at some point, all your good efforts and investment turn to ruin.

With these cautionary notes made, let's take a look at how we might build your brand with new followers or with loyalists, by taking risks and playing with fire. After all, doesn't fortune favor the bold?

Your Brand and Controversy: Dare You Brand-Build by Being for or Against a Mainstream Issue?

In July 2012, the president of the Chick-fil-A fast-food chain told a Christian publication, *The Biblical Recorder*, that the company and its brand "supports the biblical definition of the family unit." A direct answer to a direct question by a writer for a relatively obscure news outlet made its way into the mainstream, and a major uproar ensued. The mayor of Chicago suggested that the company would not be welcomed if opening restaurants in the city. Liberal TV media like MSNBC attacked the company as bigoted and questioned whether or not its leaders' religious beliefs were creating a hostile workplace or workplace discrimination. A boycott was promoted. But on the flip side, Chick-fil-A brand loyalists and evangelical Christian groups rushed to the company's defense, organized "support days" at the restaurants, and overall, the company saw a year-to-year revenue increase from $4 billion to $4.6 billion. It isn't easy to get that kind of sales boost through regular advertising and growth. Much of it came directly from the heightened visibility and public conversation about the chain, and from the invigorated support of its customer base. If there is any lasting brand damage, it's invisible to me.

For the record, their position was no surprise. This is a company very well-known for closing its stores, even its stores inside malls, on Sunday to celebrate the Sabbath, and for beginning all its business meetings with prayer. Thinking they might be in favor of or even neutral about gay marriage is like thinking the Clint Eastwood movie character "Dirty Harry" might be worried over the difficult childhood of a criminal he cornered in an alley. Still, this rather trivial remark became a Major News Media Event, extended over several weeks, and organized warring groups lined up across from each other in Chick-fil-A parking lots and, more so, all over social media. When all the feathers settled, the net result was a substantial sales increase and a cementing of bond between the brand and its base.

On the other side of this same controversial issue, Howard Schultz, the CEO of Starbucks, received applause at the annual shareholders meeting in 2013 when he stated his and the company's unwavering support for same-sex marriage, reinforcing the company's already announced advocacy for same-sex marriage legislation dating to January 2012. That created a much smaller media firestorm and far less mainstream media criticism than did Chick-fil-A's opposing stand, but it did spark an organized "Dump Starbucks" boycott promoted by the National Organization for Marriage. Regardless, Starbucks experienced nearly a 15% revenue growth in 2012, and continued success in 2013.

These two tales probably indicate that the core customer base owned by Starbucks is a significantly different core customer base than that owned by Chick-fil-A, and both have large armies of brand loyalists likely to agree with the stand taken by the company they already support. Knowing who your customers and who your brand loyalists are, how they line up on issues, who their heroes are, and who their enemies are is important. I'm not suggesting that the CEOs of Chick-fil-A or of Starbucks aren't authentic and sincere in their conflicting viewpoints. I'm not accusing them of simple pandering. Mostly, I personally respect and admire both of them and their companies, and I like one's coffee and the other one's chicken. But they may both have been emboldened by a good understanding of their respective core constituencies. Courage in context is easier than courage in a vacuum.

The bigger and broader point is that a short-term media or social media reaction, pro or con or both, to a company or its owner, CEO, celebrity endorser, or other "face" taking a controversial position or otherwise getting into troubled waters often has little or no lasting negative impact and can, instead, have positive impact, in making a larger population aware of the brand or at least rallying the loyalists. Some entrepreneurs who own valuable personal or corporate brands even intentionally, repeatedly court controversy, like Kenneth Cole and American Apparel. Donald Trump finds somebody to pick a very public fight with anytime he wants media attention and publicity—his targets have included comedian Rosie O'Donnell and President Obama. Hugh Hefner fueled Playboy's rise with controversy. By its nature, the brand was controversial—although it seems quaint now, compared to everything else on the media landscape. But Hef ginned up controversy; he didn't try to tamp it down. In the description of Toby Keith's brand-building (see Chapter 15), a similar strategy is revealed: risking and not worrying about controversy and criticism from media or noncustomers in order to strengthen brand loyalty with the base.

Of course, anytime you personally take a potentially controversial position or attach your company or brand to one, you *do* take risks. Not long ago, you could do it in communications only with your customers, members, or subscribers, or even in targeted media as Chick-fil-A's president did, and never have it see the light of day with the public or the mainstream media. There is still some "spread" between what is said publicly and what is said to supporters and donors by politicians. If you get direct mail for candidates or from the RNC or DNC, you will sometimes see much more pointed and strident position taking and demonizing done there than by the same candidate or organization's spokespersons on the Sunday talk shows. But it is harder and harder to protect that firewall. Governor Romney got caught making derogatory remarks to donors in a closed-door meeting about the 47% of Americans on the dole, taped via a cell phone, and the incident did damage. In the prior campaign, Senator Obama had his disdainful remarks intended only for Left Coast donors about the voters in rural areas clinging to their guns and Bibles captured and made public, but he survived the damage. Cell phone cameras and video cameras, recording devices the size of a shirt button, social media welcoming unfiltered content and spreading it virally and rapidly, and mainstream media increasingly drawing its content from that social media produces an environment where nothing can be "off the record." If you are going to court controversy, you should do it consciously and deliberately, not casually or impulsively.

If You Punch Their Enemy in the Nose, You Are Their Friend

The Trump Technique of picking a fight with a villain or enemy can be an effective way to use controversy with little or no risk if you choose carefully, attack broadly, and know your brand loyalists and target market well. I, for example, have long done well with my audiences of "from scratch" millionaire, multimillionaire, and up-and-coming entrepreneurs and sales professionals by attacking, vilifying, and mocking 1) pinheaded academics, academic theorists, and Ph.D.s (which stands for: Piled Higher and Deeper); 2) Big, Dumb Companies and their corporate suits; 3) Madison Avenue ad agencies; 4) slothful employees; 5) socialist-leaning critics of ambition, initiative, achievement, success, and wealth; and 6) nanny-state meddlers. I can and have attacked Michael Moore, Mayor Bloomberg, Obamacare, named companies doing incredibly dumb advertising, etc., with abandon in my books, newsletters, and speeches, and been cheered. Good places to see this are in my books *No B.S. Ruthless Management of People and Profits*—starting right out in Chapter 1, and *No B.S. Sales Success in the New Economy*—notably in the chapter about sales managers. A lot of people are not consciously completely aware of how much of this I do, and how much I leverage it, but it is actually a major force fueling my own brand.

Life Extension, a major marketer of its own brand of nutritional supplements, uses its own magazine to frequently attack the FDA and the medical establishment. The magazine does have limited newsstand distribution, but it is primarily subscribed to, sent to, and written for its own customers, so its take on medical establishment, big pharma, and government conspiracy to suppress natural health cures is "preaching to the converted," a smart means of reinforcing and strengthening brand loyalty. Life Extension is certainly not alone in this approach in their industry, and when I write direct-response copy for clients in this field, I almost always incorporate the same enemies. They do it as well and aggressively as anybody, though, and can be seen at www.lifeextension.com.

Making Your Brand about a Movement, Not (Just) a Business

I have also worked hard to position myself as a leader of a movement—actually of movements—not just an entrepreneur out to make a buck. I have, in fact, led a movement toward direct-response advertising and direct marketing in hundreds of diverse industries and professions, including those where it was rarely seen or used before I lit the light and ignited the revolution. In more than a hundred fields, there are Dan Kennedy-created, taught, or directly influenced marketing "gurus," each directly guiding the marketing of thousands to tens of thousands of their industry's members to use of my kind of marketing. These include people like Ben Glass at Great Legal Marketing, Richard James at YourBusinessAutomated.com, and Ken Hardison at Personal Injury Lawyers Marketing Association (PILMA), each working with thousands of law firms; Craig Proctor and Kinder & Reese, each working with thousands of Realtors; Jay Geier at the Scheduling Institute, Dr. Tom Orent, and Greg Stanley at Whitehall Management, each working with thousands of dentists; and so on. Combined, we have created a tidal wave of change in these fields. This same change led by Kennedy-linked thought leaders, trainers, and marketing companies has permeated the auto retailing, auto repair, carpet cleaning, landscaping, home remodeling, restaurant, travel, insurance, financial services, chiropractic, cosmetic surgery, retail in just about every category, assisted living and nursing homes, even funeral parlors, as well as B2B environments, like software companies, industrial chemicals and supplies, and industrial equipment. Most of the business owners, company CEOs, private practice professionals, and sales professionals engaged in these groups downstream from me are familiar with my brands and understand they are part of a change movement in marketing, and they're proud of it.

It's like being part of any revolution: It's self-validating, it's cool, it's exciting, it's daring. You can certainly see that the Iron Tribe guys have adopted very comparable positioning for their radical change movement in fitness and health.

I have always taken a position as a champion of "the little guy": the small-business owner, the shopkeeper, the local service provider, the employer of 5 to 50, the true backbone and lifeblood of the economy. Also, the champion of the often-looked-down-upon salesman, who gets knocked down only to get up and knock on the next door, and in doing so, creates all the revenue that ultimately builds every university and hospital and backs every worker's paycheck. I tell them that any other group can take all the vacations they want and we'll still all get along, but if all the small-business owners or all the salespeople went to sleep for 30 consecutive days, the entire nation would grind to a halt. There'd be suffering, starvation, and, soon, rioting in the streets. These people are heroes. They eschew job security, comfort, 9-to-5ing in favor of investment and risk, constant uncertainty, long hours. They don't take jobs—they *make* jobs. They are part of the great entrepreneur movement, the independence and self-reliance movement. Here in the United States, they share legacy with the founders and builders of this nation. When they are demonized as workaholics or evil, greedy capitalists or wild-eyed dreamers or some other stereotype, it is sometimes by the merely ignorant, but often by those of a competing movement toward a dependent, forcibly equalized, socialist state. Together, I and they carry not only the economy but the philosophy that made us a great society squarely on our shoulders. A business made prosperous is a burnishing of the Liberty Bell and a force for real social good, and earned wealth and privilege is admirable and deserved— for all success (and failure) is ultimately behavioral choice. With this sort of message, basically my brand message, I lift the self-esteem and sense of worth of my customers. We are in it together!

All this makes my personal brand and the business brands attached to me more *significant*. To brand loyalists, this is a source of pride, that they are associated and involved with something important, not just a customer of a business.

If you leap to the idea that it's easy for me to do this in my field, but, well, your business is different—it's ordinary, mundane, selling commodities, and you can't follow this path, I suggest looking at the clothing company Bills Khakis. You will see their "mission page" from their Summer 2013 catalog in Figure 14.1 on page 138. I'm sure they won't mind the publicity. Their brand is "cut and sewn in the USA," necessarily clever wording because some of the fabric itself may be imported. They began as a direct-response marketer, essentially a mail-order company, and used radio advertising on the ultra-conservative talker Glenn Beck's programs, in which they emphasized their status as "an authentic American sportswear company," to drive response. Today, they are a strong mail-order catalog company, an ecommerce company (www.BillsKhakis.com), and also have their products sold in hundreds of stores nationwide. They have latched onto the "Made in America Movement," in resurgence after a long sleep begun in the 1960s.

Similar movements that businesses can attach themselves to, which have current and rising influence, are "Support Local Businesses," "Homegrown Produce," and "Farm to Table," and nonprofit causes and the reputable charitable organizations associated with them, like support for veterans and the Wounded Warriors organization, or eradicating child hunger and the nation's or your local Food Bank. Steve Adams, featured in Chapter 12 of *No B.S. Guide to Brand-Building by Direct Response*, does a fine job of linking his pet stores to animal rescue organizations, thus the movement against animal abuse.

FIGURE 14.1: Bills Khakis Ad

SUMMER 2013

Bills Khakis was founded on one simple premise – it's almost impossible to find a great pair of khakis twice. Consistent with this same thought, it's almost impossible to find sportswear from a company that you can truly believe in - a brand that's an extension of you rather than the other way around. In our quality, enduring style, and commitment to American-made craftsmanship, it's our hope that you will wear Bills Khakis with a quiet, confident sense of pride. You wouldn't tell everyone you know about Bills Khakis but you might tell your best friend... simply because they deserve to know. Thank you for buying into our dream of building an authentic American sportswear company. Bills Khakis are also available through the finest independent men's specialty stores in the United States. You will find a listing of retailers who carry a wide selection of our products on the back inside cover of this catalog.

WE MADE BILLS BETTER BY NOT CHANGING A THING.®

Bill Thomas

Bill Thomas, Founder

BILLS KHAKIS®
Reg.

TRADE *Bills* MARK
KHAKIS

Est. 1990

BILLSKHAKIS.COM   1-888-9-KHAKIS (1-888-954-2547)

Finding a Rising Tide

There are big, societal rising tides. Some come and go. Others are perennial. Patriotism is a rising tide. In a local community, its high school football team may be a rising tide, as the focus of the entire town's attention every Friday night for several months. Entrepreneurship has always been my rising tide. Obsession with celebrity is a rising tide, and the GKIC Members in the catering business included in Chapter 11 of *No B.S. Guide to Brand-Building by Direct Response* have risen with it with their local business, just as my longtime client Guthy-Renker Corporation rose with it from their very first TV infomercial as a startup to their multibrand, multidistribution-channel $1.8 billion business now. Home shopping TV was the rising tide for my one-time client Joan Rivers. Reality TV has recently been the rising tide for a number of otherwise rather obscure businesspeople, like the folks seen in *Pawn Stars* or *Duck Dynasty*. Hefner's rising tide was the sexual revolution of the 1960s. Limbaugh's rising tide was the Bill Clinton administration and his role as the number-one Voice of Opposition. In this chapter, we've discussed other rising tides.

Find yours.

CHAPTER 15

Building a
PERSONAL Brand

Originally appearing as Chapter 20 from
*No B.S. Guide to Brand-Building by
Direct Response*

One of the best current examples of brilliant personal branding is the country-western personality Toby Keith, ranked as one of the 100 richest celebrities by *Forbes* on their 2013 list. Many of the facts about him and his business used here come from the July 15, 2013, *"Celebrity 100"* issue of *Forbes.* Keith's career earnings have surpassed $500 million. Over the past five years, he's never earned less than $48 million. He is but one man. And his market is smaller than you might think. Country music accounts for less than 15% of the national radio audience, and it is concentrated in a limited geographic area. Rather than trying to achieve broader appeal, Keith has very deliberately sought maximum leverage within a customer base that can be exceptionally loyal and supportive.

Here are some of the important Keith strategies, in addition to having identified a valuable target market and made himself and his brand a perfect match with it. They're not in any particular priority. They're all important.

Synergy, Synergy, Synergy

Every live Toby Keith concert is not only an exercise in brand reinforcement, it is an epic infomercial for his own sponsors and products, with everything artfully integrated. To his hit song "American Ride," he drives onto the stage in a big Ford pickup truck—part of a multimillion-dollar commercial endorsement deal with Ford. His drink of choice is his own brand of tequila with a worm in every bottle, Wild Shot. When he plays "I Love This Bar," it celebrates his restaurant chain named after it. A beloved, popular, or trusted brand, global or local, always has plentiful opportunities for synergy because its customers have multiple needs and desires. The same homeowner who hires a carpet cleaning company probably needs landscaping and lawn care, gutter cleaning, maid service, and auto detailing. You don't have to necessarily be in all those businesses to put them under your brand via joint ventures and strategic alliances, but what I teach in the No B.S. Business Success book as "the mini-conglomerate theory" certainly applies. Sponsorship money or barter is often neglected but available to all kinds of businesses.

At GKIC, a multiuse, sequential use synergy is often utilized—for example, the featured speaker at one of our major conferences will provide other content in advance of that appearance for newsletters and teleseminars; the presentation itself will be recorded and used afterward as a webcast or DVD to sell an information product built around that speaker. One-time-only seminars beget information products with a long life in catalogs. My book No B.S. Marketing to the Affluent fed a special live training event on the same subject, which birthed an info-product that has been popular for years and a newsletter, *The No B.S. Marketing to the Affluent Letter*, which all GKIC Diamond Members get. I'm big on one thing leading to the next, and it to the next. We could also be more of a mini-conglomerate encompassing more product categories. It's never risen from the back-room "idea board" to priority, but, for example, I've long thought of having my own brand of specially formulated nutritional supplements for brain function and for energy, incorporating the ones I cobble together now. That would be a logical extension of my brand to products people would want. By the way, not only is GKIC Membership useful to you from a training, coaching, networking, and support standpoint, but an added benefit is being able to closely observe and monitor how we market it, and thus borrow our best strategies.

Platform Power

Given a large and loyal audience, Keith has a platform to promote others as well as himself, so why be all about one man? He owns a piece of the quickly made star Taylor Swift. Every time there's a Taylor Swift music CD or download, concert ticket, T-shirt sold, or endorsement deal made, Toby pockets an override. Her recent five years' earnings nearly match his, less, of course, his share. He also owns a piece of the recording company that has Swift, Tim McGraw, and Rascal Flatts. His fast-growing chain of restaurants is organized to provide a 20-to-30-city tour for any rising star he takes on. There, of course, it's his Wild Shot that's the drink of choice. Many business owners, entrepreneurs, authors, and others have platform power that they don't duly appreciate or value, that can be used to aid, promote, and lift others—whether for outright compensation, which I often refer to as "toll position income," or for quid pro quo, reciprocal cross-promotion, or as pay-it-forward investment, or even just because the opportunity to be helpful exists with no harm, foul, or cost. Maybe an investment in karma. I'm frankly very pleased with myself that I've long done this, done it more and more as my own star has risen higher and my influence grown greater, and never worry about creating competition or trading away dollars or any similar miserly concerns.

Ownership and Control

Early on, while still struggling, Keith replaced his band with musicians happy to play for a set salary rather than a share of the take. This and his other ownership moves, like owning the record label, have given him total control over his brand. When his first restaurant opened and he found they had drifted "gourmet" from his prescribed meal items, he stomped his foot and quickly got his way. His preferred fried bologna sandwich, which the suits had removed from the menu, is the chain's number-one bestseller. By owning all or part of everything attached to his brand, he can control the use of the brand and prevent or fix mistakes made by others. It is inevitable that the visionary and personality who builds the brand and its following is judged at some point as having gone as far as he can go with his limited education or sophistication, and newly imported or hired professionals and experts know better. As a company grows, the cries for "professional management" intensify. What happened to his bologna sandwich often happens on a grander scale. No less than Steve Jobs was fired and thrown out of the company he built, only to later be brought back in, with considerable brand damage to repair. Howard Schultz, similar story, with Starbucks. Had he not returned, complete collapse was on the horizon.

You will be challenged about your beliefs about your brand and about your marketing more and more vehemently the more successful you become. You might logically expect the opposite, but you'll be unpleasantly surprised. In my consulting work, I strive to be very careful and thorough in unearthing what makes my client and his relationship with his customers tick, why people have been attracted, what's in the sauce that is invisible to the naked eye and may not be discovered by casual tasting. I am cautious about altering or abandoning what's working, preferring "plus-ing" as Walt Disney called it. Few outside experts or new investors or hired executives are as cautious and considerate. Most are over-eager for change for the sake of change. Many have big but fragile egos and a driving need to demonstrate their cleverness and exert their power as personal validation, not as practical contribution to greater success. Most ask too few questions and are in too much of a hurry to learn about the past or present before making the future. Never, never, never let yourself be intimidated by these people, even though you may need them. Keep my friend Bill Brooks' definition of an expert consultant in mind: a man who knows 365 sexual positions but can't get a date all year. You can't be stupid-stubborn and totally closed-minded, but you don't want to be intimidated or pushed around either. Nobody will be as committed to protecting your brand as you should be.

It's very hard to protect a brand you don't own and own its chief uses. I know this firsthand because I have not owned my brands for a number of years now, and I've had working relationships post-sale with two different owners and companies and three different corporate CEOs, as well as four different book publishers. Such relationships are, I imagine, similar to a man of no means of his own married to a very rich wife. Battles must be chosen judiciously. You can't go to war over every little thing. Compromises, even sacrifices, are required. This is a trade-off you may very well choose to make, just as I did, for my reasons or for other reasons, at some point with your businesses and your brand.

If and when you do, try to get as much as you can while giving up as little control as you can, and know that the devil is in the details. I have managed to coexist with two different owners for nearly 15 years without developing an ulcer, having a heart attack, committing murder, being fired, or being murdered, and with the brands I handed over alive and in reasonably good health. Not all entrepreneurs can do that, nor is it in every entrepreneur's best interests. Just because somebody's standing there with a check doesn't mean you have to take it. One reason not to is the deep emotional connection to your brand as if birthed from your womb and raised by your own breast milk, and feeling it is fragile and vulnerable, so that any and every change made to it or the businesses attached to it feel like personal wounds. I happen to have a knack—a blessing and a curse—for emotional distance and compartmentalization.

My guess, and it is only a guess, is that at some point, probably sooner than later, within years not decades, Toby Keith will wind up selling his entire business, copyrights, and intellectual properties and letting his name, face, personal brand, and brands be used right along with it, while he retires, plays golf even more than now, and does other things unrelated to the entertainment business. If and when he does, the brand will be used in ways he's happy about and ways he's unhappy about, and he'll have forfeited his say-so. But that kind of equity and exit is one of the reasons to build a brand.

Polarization

Toby Keith's hit songs' lyrics have consistently been jingoistic, reflecting right-wing extremes, patriotic themes, and military support. He is the son of a military veteran who never shies from flag-waving. The hit song he put out shortly after the first September 11 Attack Day (NYC, not the more recent Benghazi), titled "Courtesy of the Red, White, and Blue," includes this line: "We'll put a boot in your ass. It's the American Way." He is perfectly happy offending with such material, and responding should someone pick a fight over it. Natalie Maines of the Dixie Chicks called the song "ignorant," and Keith responded by displaying a made-up family photo of her and Saddam Hussein as a giant backdrop at his concerts.

I have plenty of liberals in my fan base, in GKIC Membership, and in various relationships. I do pro bono work for the Cleveland Food Bank and for Happy Trails Farm Animal Sanctuary, both run by liberals. My mystery novel co-author Les Roberts (book title: *Win, Place, or Die*) is a blue-collar liberal who reminds me of Studs Terkel, *and* he's a recently converted vegan. Still, my conservative/libertarian politics are very clear in my written works and speeches and seminars. And I have not held back my ire and disgust for President Obama. The majority of my audience of small-business owners, entrepreneurs, and self-employed professionals skews conservative, at least fiscally if not socially. So I do tread relatively safe ground with most, strongly resonate with many, but undoubtedly offend some who must look past these positions of mine to otherwise benefit—and most important, I repel many.

Deliberately repelling people from a brand is a more common practice than many realize. The CEO of Abercrombie & Fitch made headlines and sparked controversy and criticism by perhaps ill-advisedly detailing who he did not want patronizing their stores or ever seen wearing their apparel, and how he deliberately directed everything from store design to advertising to sizes of clothes stocked to clearly and adamantly tell those people they are not welcome. A & F is a valuable and powerful retail brand, with a lot of its value tied to an aura of exclusivity. There was a lot of expressed shock by pundits over his statements about this, but I was not surprised one bit.

I believe that a price tag attached to power is polarization. Vanilla is only a successful position for ice cream.

Prolific Output

Beginning back in 1993, Toby Keith released at least one new album every year through the year 2000, selling, on average, about 500,000 copies. His 1999 album sold 3.1 million copies. If you want a vibrant brand and brand loyalist population, I do not think you have any choice but to be extremely prolific. You must bring a lot of "new" to the table, frequently. You need constant communication—at GKIC, Diamond Members are "touched" one way or another by me at least 112 times during a calendar year, by GKIC itself above that at least another 100 times, and they see me in person at two national conferences and at least one special event. In total, we're achieving near daily connection. I also strive for omnipresence, meaning every time you turn around in a complete circle in your environment or in your industry, you see, hear, hear about, or somehow bump into me. Just as Toby Keith wants his brand of booze on the bar in your man-cave, his endorsed pickup truck in your garage, his CDs playing in it when you drive it, I want my Dan Kennedy bobblehead, posters, and books in your office, my CDs playing in your car, and No B.S. logo apparel in your closet and on your back. This is a strategy I learned studying Disney.

Even true-blue brand loyalists and longtime fans are increasingly easily distracted. They are under bombardment by seductions every minute in every media. "Brand loyalist" is really an antiquated word still used by all the brand academics, theorists, and agencies selling you on brand, and I've used it in this book as a convenience. But the truth is, loyalty is more of an endangered species by the day, and it is very, very dangerous to presume you have any of it, from anybody. The savvier position is that of the paranoid. You get up each and every morning assuming your fences dissolved during the night and your entire herd has wandered off in 1,000 different directions, and you must ride hard to catch them, re-entice them to follow you, round 'em all up, put up a new fence, grab a nap, and do it all over again. And, by all means, rely more on real, strong, solid fences than simple loyalty. In direct marketing, we build those, for example, out of membership, continuity or forced continuity with automatic recurring payments, and pain of disconnect ideally more complex than an emotional bond. These are strategies and tactics commonly found in businesses of varied kinds owned by GKIC-trained operators and entrepreneurs that you rarely find in the same kind of businesses absent GKIC influence.

Work

There's a dirty word. People who build and sustain valuable personal brands work a lot and work at it a lot. The $1 million or so Toby Keith pulls out of a concert is pale in comparison to the other revenue of his personal empire, but he is nonetheless out there in person, on the plane, then on the bus, then on the stage, doing manual labor, being seen, pressing the flesh. Beyond that, he is writing songs; recording, finding, signing, and promoting other stars; doing deals; visiting restaurants; *working.* The "escape from work" attitude and delusion that has permeated society as a whole and, more troubling, the business and entrepreneur community to a far, far greater extent post-internet than pre-internet, and even more so in very recent years, is a vile, evil cancer destructive to the American and world economies; to individuals' mental, emotional, and physical health; and to society as a whole.

I do not begrudge Tim Ferriss's phenomenal success with his original book titled *The 4-Hour Workweek*, nor with the 4-Hour brand he has built behind it. The content of the original book is better and more honest than its title, picked by popular preference via a Google AdWords test-marketing campaign. Tim has said complimentary things about me, and I certainly respect him. *But*. The very fact that this was the popular and successful title and that people would actually lust after and believe in the idea of grand success and four hours of work per week speaks volumes about the stupid sloth of the public. It's not new. There was, decades ago, a huge seller titled *The Lazy Man's Way to Riches*. But even it didn't dare to say *The Lazy Man's Way to Riches With Just 4 Hours of Work Per Week*. And now it's worse. It's shameful. It makes me embarrassed for my fellow creatures walking upright.

If you closely follow the real schedules, activities, and disciplines of virtually any or every highly successful person, particularly one building or sustaining a valuable personal brand, you won't find a four-hour week; you will find them doing a whole lot of work, out in public, and behind closed doors in private.

I'll quickly mention another entertainer who has built an incredible personal brand, Lady Gaga. If you don't even know who she is, it's perfectly okay. I have very smart and aware clients who only very recently discovered her existence and, predictably, found her bizarre. But you might very well want to study her, and a book worth reading is *Monster Loyalty: How Lady Gaga Turns Followers into Fanatics* by Jackie Huba. A few takeaways: While she has talent and has invested a lot of time and work in developing it, she freely admits she's far from the best singer out there. She is well aware that her openly expressed political and societal opinions are polarizing, but she defines her number-one job as playing to her fan base, and specifically to the top 1% of her fan base, those who buy everything and follow her obsessively, whom she calls her Monsters. She is more interested in keeping her current customers than attracting new ones, and she is not at all concerned with converting people who don't understand her. One of her favorite quotes is, "If you are not pissing someone off, you are not doing your job." That's very close to a principle I've long taught, expressed: If you haven't pissed off somebody by noon, you're under quota. Get busy. Lady Gaga's revenues exceed those of Toby Keith, by the way.

And What If You Have a Tired Brand?

It is relatively common for a good personal brand, and an entertainer, author, other celebrity, expert, or an entire company to outlive its productive, profitable customer base. It is even more common for a good brand to fatigue, to feel "been there, done that," and lose its following to an inferior but newer person, place, or product.

In the 2000s, the famous singer Tony Bennett was a tired brand. If you don't know him for anything else, you might click with his most famous song, *I Left My Heart in San Francisco*. He is of The Rat Pack era, but has outlived all of them and is still performing, recording, and newly popular as I write this. His son Danny reinvigorated Bennett with a marketing strategy known as cobranding. You might be familiar with it thanks to Doritos tacos at Taco Bell, Jim Beam Bourbon enhanced steak burgers at T.G.I.F.'s, or other food cobrands. Ford has a King Ranch truck. Bennett was paired with the just-mentioned Lady Gaga, Carrie Underwood, and other very contemporary singers in a series of *Duets* albums that brought him to the attention of an entire generation of fans who would otherwise have ignored him. The strategy was stolen directly from Frank Sinatra, who did it with two of his own *Duets* albums in the 1990s.

This was a double dose of new life for the tired Tony Bennett brand. First, same brand, same personality, same songs—to an entirely new audience, surprised to find themselves appreciative of their new discovery. Second, same brand attached to other, newer, hotter, trendier brands, making the old one seem and feel reborn as new, too.

Let's Not Forget: Personal Brand-Building by DIRECT RESPONSE

Toby Keith originally built his brand by direct selling of concert tickets and the manual labor of performing. In fact, he built a fan/customer base to make money day to day, while building his brand that could be leveraged far beyond the stage. I built my brand and brand equity predominately with 15 years of intense travel speaking 70 to 80 times a year, accompanied by direct-response advertising in magazines, direct mail, article placement in media, and other direct-response marketing. I built a fan/customer base to make money day to day, while building a brand that could be leveraged far beyond the stage. I have now routinely taken successful business owners in different niches and rapidly made them famous names and known brands in those niches entirely through direct-response advertising.

I have always told my peers in professional speaking, and told authors, that the nifty trick is to avoid going broke while you're busy getting rich and famous. Personal brand-building by direct response makes that trick possible.

CHAPTER 16

Turning a Problematic Environment Upheaval to Your Advantage

Originally appearing as Chapter 2 from
No B.S. Grassroots Marketing

I like to listen to old radio programs on CDs, on the rare occasions I have to drive any significant distance. Many of these CDs have the original commercials intact. In a series of Philip Marlowe detective dramas—based on the character created by the legendary writer Raymond Chandler—there are commercials for the 1950 Ford sedans, and they are really spectacular radio commercials. They feature true Unique Selling Propositions: Ford had the only budget-priced sedan with a powerful V-8 vs. all others in their class with 6-cylinder engines; they had "king-size brakes" typically found only in much more expensive cars, providing maximum safety; and so on. Some of the commercials featured testimonials, like an airline pilot comparing the experience of driving this car to that of flying a plane, soaring above the crowds. They all had a strong call to action, pushing listeners to immediately arrange a test drive. And they all directed listeners where to find their local dealer in their phone directories, plus this line: "... *or perhaps you know him personally*. He'll be happy to arrange ..." The idea that you might know your local Ford dealer personally, whether you do or not, is a powerful piece of persuasion. It suggests that your Ford dealer is a man of your community, a neighbor, a person who is accessible to you, out and about, there to be held accountable. And even if you don't actually know him personally, it reminds you that it feels like you do, because he appears in his own advertisements with his family and pets, and you know things about him as a result of his advertising, marketing, and public relations, maybe, that he was a war hero or a star on the area's college sports team or spearheads a big fundraising effort each year for the volunteer fire department.

This idea of personally knowing the people we do business with may seem to have gone by the wayside given all the broadcast marketing offline and on, all the commerce done at distance, all the automation, and the prevalence of the giant chains. As an example of the dominance of giants, over 60% of consumers involved in home improvement projects in 2010–2011 cited purchasing from Home Depot, Lowe's, and Walmart, while only 3% cited purchasing from independent retailers. So you may think the actual or at least felt personal relationship an unnecessary antique of a bygone era, memorialized only in old black-and-white TV shows about small-town life. To the contrary, one of the few advantages the small, local merchant, service provider, professional, or sales professional can own in the war with the giants and discounters is this kind of personal relationship, or at least sense of personal relationship, to be enhanced with No B.S. Grassroots Marketing.

Please disabuse yourself of the idea that people no longer want this. Ninety percent of college students physically visited their local bank branch at least once a month in 2010, despite being able to do all banking online, from their wizard phones. Some people may not realize how much they want it unless and until they get it, but almost everybody prefers dealing with people rather than faceless institutions, prefers human contact and interaction to distance and isolation, welcomes a warm smile and a kind word from someone who knows them by name and asks how their cat is doing. Further, most people like feeling that they know the people they are doing business with. I have proven beyond any shadow of a doubt that financial advisors', chiropractors', dentists', and in-home service providers' "closing percentages" (conversion of prospects to clients, patients, and customers), average transaction sizes, and referrals go up almost in direct proportion to the extent of personal disclosure done by the seller. In short, the more the prospects know about the person they are contemplating buying from, the more likely they are to buy. For this reason, in most of the advertising I develop as one of the highest-paid direct-response copywriters in the country, for clients in hundreds of different fields, I include personal stories and seemingly unimportant details about the person behind the advertised company or product.

How does all this relate to your advertising and marketing media choices?

First, I am a champion of the idea that there is neither good nor bad media per se, just as neither hammer nor scalpel nor gun is a good or bad tool. It depends on the purpose it is to serve and the capability of the person using it. The merits of any and every advertising and marketing tool, media, strategy, or tactic are totally situational.

Second, the merits of one almost always depend on the context of use and synergy with others. A billboard-wrapped truck in and of itself may have very limited value, largely due to the painfully brief message that can be grasped at 55 miles per hour (and realistically, who drives 55 mph anymore?). But if that billboard-wrapped truck is strategically parked in a neighborhood where work is being done on a happy customer's home, from 5:00 to 6:30 P.M., when all the neighbors are returning home from work AND the people working on the house are in good uniforms and, if approached, are able and eager to answer questions and collect information or immediately whip out a cell phone and connect the prospect with a salesperson back at the office AND the surrounding homes get a multistep mailing campaign immediately after the work on Herb and Betty's house is done, beginning with a testimonial letter from Herb and Betty to their neighbors, well, the billboard-wrapped truck may be very valuable indeed.

Third, and most important—MOST important—when advertising and marketing media are used in a way that makes the connection human, from a person to another person, and reminds that "he is my local Ford dealer I probably know personally"— used in a "grassroots" way—it is all infinitely more effective.

NO B.S. GRASSROOTS MARKETING INCONVENIENT TRUTH #4

There is no substitute for REAL, personal, person-to-person relationships.

My co-author Jeff Slutsky has fairly and accurately assessed the facts of life of advertising and advertising media. The audience is fragmented; the media and the messages are increasingly ineffective; the costs are climbing even as the reach, readership, audience, and attention given is declining; and the need to be present in more media and more places is very challenging to the business owner with limited resources, who already feels stretched too thin. If you want to view all this as adversity, then be reminded of one of the key principles presented in Napoleon Hill's seminal work, *Think and Grow Rich*: In every adversity lies the seed of equal or greater opportunity. There is opportunity here to be had, advantage to be taken: It is being person-to-person and personal in an ever more impersonal marketplace. It is in *the way you use* whatever media you use, not just in choices of media or in hopeful search for the "magic pill" newest media.

The No-B.S. Marketer is and must be ruthless in holding advertising and marketing and sales media, investments, and activities financially accountable, as Jeff emphasizes, and I expound on in my book *No B.S Ruthless Management of People and Profits*. The No-B.S. Marketer must be a militant pragmatist, wary of the kind of creativity for creativity's sake Jeff says ad agencies are often guilty of, and wary of whatever next, new, bright, shiny object is waved in front of him.

But he must also be creative in ways that create that sense of person-to-person, personal relationship. He must use media as an extension of personality and relationship, not as a substitute for it. This is where advantage is to be found, at the grassroots level. The giants have no alternative but to use media as substitute for relationship. The most successful local small-business operators will do exactly the opposite.

CHAPTER 17

Rethinking the Business You Are In

Originally appearing as Chapter 7 from
No B.S. Grassroots Marketing

ip O'Neill famously said, "All politics is local." That was in the Reagan era, when Tip and Ronald Reagan were already old war horses. Surely it can't still be a truism in today's world of social media and online community, a more complex media landscape with so many more options, and a more mobile society, can it? Today, Congress has the lowest favorable ratings in the polls ever, and the "throw the bums out" fervor is high, yet most incumbents get re-elected. How can that be? Because everybody else's congressman is a bum, but my guy answers my mail, got the money to fix a bridge and build a public swimming pool, kept a military base from getting closed during Pentagon budget cuts, and is at every local parade, county fair, rib cook-off, and is just an all-around good guy.

In the very early stage of the 2012 presidential campaign, a candidate on the Republican side, who appeared to have a chance of at least being competitive in the primaries, suffered an amazing campaign collapse when his entire staff quit on the same day. Lots of candidates fire campaign managers and even entire staffs, but nobody can recall an entire staff firing a candidate. Their chief reasons: that he was proving utterly undisciplined and refusing to do any of the real work of political campaigning: calling and speaking to donors personally, getting out to diners and community events, doing living room meetings, pressing the flesh. He believed he could replace all that with new media. His campaign experts, as young as 30-ish, believed otherwise. One of the most famous masterminds of online and social media for politics, who had advised Howard Dean, and then Barack Obama, commented that all the new media is obviously powerful, but none of it can replace a handshake, a look straight in someone's eye, a direct answer to a personal question.

We might add to Tip's admonition that all politics is also *personal*. In the early presidential primary contests, there are caucuses and straw polls, not just elections. Participation is small, made up mostly of party faithful, passionate activists, and donors. In many cases, as incredible as it may seem in this age of technology, social media, and proliferate advertising media, the successful candidate will have met every voter in person, some often enough to actually know them by name. But even in the bigger arena, professional politicians master the making of it all personal. As a speaker, I appeared on about a dozen seminar events with former President George H. W. Bush and wife Barbara Bush. At the first one, I met and very briefly chatted with President Bush backstage. Well over a month later, I encountered him backstage again, and he asked how my books were doing, how my horse-racing was going, and what I thought about an advertising-related news item of the week. There was no reason for him to have bothered to remember me at all, let alone remember details of my business and personal activities. I later asked Barbara Bush about it and she explained that (a) George had trained himself to have an amazing memory for just such information, but (b) that he also cheated, creating notes about everybody he met, that he could use to freshen memory in advance if he knew he was about to encounter that person again, or refer to in correspondence because (c) that was actually what a political career and influence were all about, and—with a twinkle in her eye—(d) you just never knew when it would come in handy, soliciting donations for the next son to run for president or some charitable cause.

This gets us, long-windedly and circuitously, to the core question, the multimillion-dollar question of what business you are really in. Most businesspeople confuse their deliverables with the business they are in. If they own a restaurant, they think they are in the food-service business or food plus entertainment business, but that's like George H. W. Bush thinking he was in the governance business. He knew his deliverable when in office was governance, but his business was list-building, relationship building, influence, and fundraising, all dependent on "local" and "personal." A lot of No-B.S. Marketers advance from confusing the business they're in with its deliverables to thinking of themselves as professional marketers in the marketing business, then a marketer of a restaurant, or veterinary practice, or whatever, and that *is* advancement. But the No-B.S. Grassroots Marketer goes another few steps further. He uses marketing and marketing prowess in ways that create one-on-one relationships at the local level, directly if his business is local, or if his business is regional or national, by making each of its offices, stores, or outposts act as a local business.

For a time, for about two years, I did a lot of consulting with an international conglomerate-owned health products company, with over 1,000 franchised offices across the country. Many were in the hands of multi-unit, territorial franchise owners, who then had hired managers at each location. The franchise owners themselves were distanced from any one office and its community, and, of course, the corporate leaders were even further distanced. Other offices had franchise owner-operators, with the office's owner actually in it, and living in its community. The most successful, most profitable offices achieving top performance in every meaningful statistic, and most important, top performance in client-to-client referrals, were owner-operated in relatively small-sized markets, and on investigation, it became obvious that these owner-operators were not relying on the corporate brand advertising or on their own local media advertising; they were true grassroots marketers, out and about and active in their communities. In fact, as I read the first draft of Jeff's Chapter 5 of *No B.S. Grassroots Marketing*, I saw almost a carbon copy of the marketing plan used by these grassroots marketers who owned these offices.

A big part of my advice to this client was to reverse-engineer what these grassroots operators were doing and push it back upstream. Get the hands-off, multi-unit owners to get better trained, better committed, better paid, and incentivized managers to act as if they were single-office, grassroots marketers. This advice incorporated a lot of what you can read in Jeff's Chapter 4 of *No B.S. Grassroots Marketing*. Sadly, this particular client was unwilling to restructure their marketing in this manner and even more unwilling to impose it on their franchisees, and they have remained a fragile, vulnerable, troubled company very subject to damage by independent, grassroots competitors in many of their markets, skyrocketing costs associated with mass advertising, competitive pressure from discounters, and other evils.

While I did some of the best work of my life for this client, and some of its franchise owners benefited greatly from it, overall I consider the two-year effort a failure, mostly of will on the client's part, the will to do what was and is really necessary to immunize a business of their type to evolutionary destruction by online, cheaper-price marketers, big box discounters entering the product category, excess dependence on costly mass advertising, and vulnerability to little independents in each locality.

This gets us to another subject: *immunity*. Most people understand that they have a personal, physical, physiological, and psychological immune system they need to keep healthy and strong, to ward off disease, delay adverse effects of aging, and protect their ability to perform. Successful athletes pay more attention to this and exert greater effort and discipline regarding it than most ordinary people do, but you are at least aware of the threats to your immune system, and of most common dangers of a weakened or poorly functioning immune system. Many people, for example, consciously eat green, leafy vegetables and "blue" fruits because of their antioxidant and immune system bolstering properties. As cold and flu season approaches, or if you are often surrounded by children, i.e., walking, talking germ factories, you probably take extra vitamin C and zinc. (Note: I'm not dispensing medical advice, just making an observation.) Most businesspeople fail to think of their business as having its own immune system, or of the need and value of keeping their business's immune system healthy and strong, but businesses do have such things, and if they are poorly nourished, inadequately invested in, and permitted to become weak and vulnerable, a lot of very bad things can happen.

The equivalent of a very bad prolonged flu season for a lot of businesses has been the sour economy that fell into recession, affecting just about everybody somewhere around early to mid-2008, and has worsened considerably all the way into the days

I'm working on this particular chapter (mid-2011). Businesses with weak immune systems got sick and have stayed sick, and some have died.

One of the keys to the strongest possible business immune system is positive, direct relationships with customers at the local level, nose to nose, face to face, handshake to handshake, being your customer's neighbor in his neighborhood. The little, local, Main Street bookstore in a small town adjacent to mine has zero immunity against the bigger selection, ease of ordering, and discounts offered me if I simply buy all my books from Amazon, and were I not rich, the recession might very well have added importance to those discounts. Their only immunity is that I like going there, hearing about books they've personally picked and read, being led to the discovery of something I might not have found on my own, and the fact that I identify with this little Main Street and its community, frequently dine at a locally owned eatery a few doors down the street, and buy tailored clothes at a local clothier a few more doors away.

You have to take your immunity against evil forces wherever you can get it.

Jeff has laid out very sensible instruction and examples in Chapters 5 and 6 of No B.S. Grassroots Marketing, whether you are actually a local business owner and operator, or heading up a larger entity with a far-flung network of stores, offices, or sales agents. His suggestions are all about getting local and making it personal. They require you to decide that is the business you are in. I urge making that decision.

Come One, Come All to Your Marketing Event

How to Get or Multiply Large Numbers of Customers at Blinding Speed

Originally appearing as Chapter 13 from
No B.S. Grassroots Marketing

I am a big fan of selling one to many rather than one to one.

I also like getting people physically together, as nothing seems to trump the dynamic results that can be achieved with a good stage presentation and a live audience, but selling one to many via media is fine, too. The boardwalk pitchman who sold kitchen gadgets to small gathering crowds—an early career of Johnny Carson's sidekick Ed McMahon and the place the legendary TV pitchman Ron Popeil started—migrated to TV, first to infomercials, then to home shopping channels like QVC and HSN, and now to YouTube and video presentations at individual websites. In a lot of B2B situations as well as some consumer situations, great use can be made of teleseminars and webinars. All of that is beyond the scope of a single book, let alone a single chapter, so I'm going to stick to the physical-world event typically put on by or for a local business. Most of the principles apply to events held in cyberspace or on broadcast media as well.

Selling Once to Groups in Events

Chiropractors, dentists, and other health-care professionals often advertise and conduct public health seminars or, more often, promote in-office "mini-seminars" to their own patient lists as well as accumulated leads from their websites and email opt-ins or social media. In the chiropractic field, my client Dr. Chris Tomshack, CEO of HealthSource, with over 350 franchised clinics all across the country, has at least two in-office mini-seminars focused on different health topics, to which patients bring family members and friends. The doctor limits the seminar attendance to between a dozen or two dozen people, and frequently gets several new patients each time—patients committed to multi-thousand-dollar treatment programs for chronic pain management or for weight loss. Another client, Dr. Charley Martin, a very successful, candidly very expensive (but worth it!) dentist, conducts in-office mini-seminars for potential cosmetic and implant patients, and routinely creates upward of $50,000.00 in work from one small class.

Restaurant owners who offer membership programs following a model taught to them by Glazer-Kennedy Insider's Circle invite customers to special appetizer or wine-tasting receptions and deliver a presentation to that group about their clubs, often signing up 50% or more of those in attendance.

Well-known companies like Tupperware—brilliantly run by its dynamic CEO Rick Goings—use party-plan selling today very much the same way as in the 1950s, when my mother would attend Tupperware or Stanley Home Products parties. But did you know that Harley-Davidson sells motorcycles to women with "garage parties"? Home-party selling is a grassroots activity by its very nature: The sales agent leverages the hostess's family, friends, and neighbor list, and usually invitations are issued by phone and personal contact and may be extended friend to friend. A lot of local businesses with happy customers could use this business model, but it never occurs to them. A restaurant, winery, bakery, or gourmet foods shop owner could have a customer host an in-home tasting party, and there sell discounted gift cards, gift baskets, or products. A garden center owner could have a customer host a backyard garden party, give lessons in some sort of gardening, and sell gift cards, products, and services.

Financial advisors rely heavily on free public seminars, workshops, and similar events to introduce themselves to prospective clients. I do a lot of work with about 60 such advisors from all over the country, probably bringing more than 150,000 people a year into financial information events. Much of the marketing in the industry for such events is very bland and relies on the lure of a free dinner at a country club, and advisors suffer with very poor response percentages from direct-mail invitations and often, poor-quality prospects. We use a very different approach, with multimedia and an emphasis on referral activity with existing clients, and rarely use free meals as a lure, preferring to bring people to the meetings for the right reasons, notably sincere interest in the subject matter.

At events like these, at some point, there is and needs to be a sales presentation and a call to action, whether to purchase a product or book an appointment. I have been a professional at speaking to sell in such environments, to audiences of 30 to 30,000, for some 35 years, and for many years did so much of it, I earned a seven-figure yearly income just from my speaking and selling from the stage, and I've trained hundreds to do the same. I've written a complete special report on the subject of speaking to sell, which you can request and receive at https://MagneticMarketing.com. Also, my book about the use of humor in speaking and selling, *Make 'Em Laugh and Take Their Money*, is available from booksellers. Jeff also addresses some of these same points in his book, *The Toastmasters International Guide to Successful Speaking*, available on Amazon. com. A caution: there is little point in doing these events if you are squeamish about the selling part, or unskilled and unwilling to get good at it. Just about anybody can get "good enough" to get results at the local level, but you can't take it for granted.

Of a less direct-selling nature, just about any and every business can effectively use and profit from customer appreciation events designed for customers plus family members, friends, and neighbors they invite. Positioned as a genuine thank you, and usually as entertainment, these events can introduce lots of potential customers to your business. One of our Glazer-Kennedy Insider's Circle members who does this brilliantly owns a family dairy farm, dairy store, and home-delivery business in Idaho. Alan and Holly Reed host Farm Days every year, with free hamburgers and hot dogs, a big picnic area, $.50 ice cream cones, music, hay rides, pony rides, cow milking contests, and more. The year I attended as an observer, about 3,000 people came through—two-thirds were present customers, and one-third, prospective customers. Without being heavy-handed about it, they capture guests' contact information for follow-up, and do have a way for guests to sign up on the spot for home delivery if they're on any of the company's routes. The Reeds gain hundreds of new customers each year using this grassroots marketing tactic.

My friend Ben Glass of www.GreatLegalMarketing.com guides many of the lawyers he coaches into grassroots efforts with various kinds of events. Shown in Figure 18.1 is a notice in Mark and Alexis Breyer's client newsletter about their client and community appreciation dinners. As you can see, they are held at four different locations, on different dates, all around Phoenix, Arizona. Another of Ben's member-attorneys, Jason Epstein,

FIGURE 18.1: Mark and Alexis Breyer's Client Newsletter

in Bellevue, Washington, has his own community activism organization, Teens Against Distracted Driving, which arranges school programs to caution teens against dangerous driving habits, such as texting while driving.

Most of these kinds of events—other than pure home parties—tend to be promoted with media, whether internally only, i.e., to current and past customers and accumulated leads, or internally plus externally, i.e., via paid advertising in newspapers, on radio, on TV, etc., and use of online media. But they have a grassroots feel to them, and many are aided by the grassroots activities—the business owner being interviewed on local radio, news releases getting picked up by community newspapers, even broadsheets posted on restaurant and public bulletin boards. Some can be done under the auspices of schools, churches, community colleges, or civic groups.

Dos and Don'ts of Promotional Events

Now that you have an overview of how promotional events can be used to grow interest in your business, here are some tips we have collected from our experience.

- Never assume good attendance just because of goodwill. Events need to be marketed.
- Allow ample time for a good marketing effort. At a local level, this usually requires no less than three weeks to as much as eight weeks.
- Get people to preregister, not just to show up at the door, so you can put them into a "keep 'em excited," reminder sequence of mailings, email, tweets, etc. If your prospects or customers will register online, the confirmation and follow-up emails can be entirely automated.
- If you are holding the event somewhere other than your own place of business, give a lot of consideration to that

location. A convenient, known, or easy-to-find location, safety, and ample free parking are all critical. It shouldn't be too fancy for your crowd, but not bargain-basement either—people want to come to a nice place.

- I'm very big on theme-park thinking, and have used all sorts of themes—including a Desert Cruise (in Arizona), complete with bon voyage party, hotel made over as a cruise ship, captain's cocktail party; an Under-the-Big-Top Three-Ring Circus with all those trappings; Build a Better Business construction-themed events, with rented earth movers and bulldozers parked outside, hard hats for everybody, and sexy "Tool Time Girls," wearing hard hats and tool belts, as greeters; and on and on. For the small, local event, you obviously can't go to the extremes and expense that I and my clients do with an international conference, but I still suggest using a theme and going as far as you can. Make your event sound fun, unusual, and interesting.

- If the emphasis is on delivery of information, that must be made not just interesting but exciting and timely. Again, you can see examples of how we do this in the financial advisory field at www.MattZagula.com. The number-one marketing sin is being boring. You need to generate some tabloid-like sensationalism around what people are going to discover as well as why they need to know about it, now. Emphasize the promise of benefit or gain just from attending. And the speaker(s) need to be made as interesting, authoritative, and given as much celebrity as possible.

Sometimes the value of business to be gained warrants serious investment in a unique and extraordinary event. Jeff Slutsky described his work with a client group of regional pharmaceutical reps working for Bristol-Myers Squibb. To get the undivided, favorable attention of a group of doctors, they organized an evening of fine dining and entertainment. In face-to-face selling in the offices, a rep like these is lucky to get a fast five minutes, but they had four different drugs they wanted to present in some detail. This team of reps was able to get 100 doctors (and their spouses) to an evening featuring the singer LaDonna Gatlin, baby sister of the famed Gatlin Brothers, and comedian Steve Rizzo. The show began with about 30 minutes of LaDonna's regular stage performance followed by Steve's comedy and motivational material. But instead of boring technical explanations of the drugs, the grand finale was presented by LaDonna and Steve in parody songs! Jeff rewrote the lyrics to eight songs from the musical *The Sound of Music*, got them cleared by the company's legal department, and LaDonna and Steve performed them. To *The Sound of Music*: "The halls are alive with the sounds of mucus." To *Climb Every Mountain*: Claim Every Patient. And the crowd favorite about hypertension: You're 216 over 117. No, it won't win a Tony Award, but it did avoid the dreaded, dry technical speech by the corporate executive, and stayed true to the promise of an evening of entertainment.

Obviously, such an event ain't cheap. You need Jeff or somebody like him—and, really, is there anybody like him?—to conceptualize, create, organize, hire talent, secure music use rights, and also speak at the event. He and his creative partner Steve Rizzo are wizards at all this. In evaluating how elaborate and costly to get with your event, you have to consider two things: one, the value of the business as a whole and of each client to be gained; and two, all the costs associated with getting that business and securing those clients by other means. There is probably also a "buzz factor" for you beyond those in the audience and beyond the event itself. You can also consider videotaping it for subsequent use at your websites, on YouTube, and in DVDs used in direct-mail campaigns. Don't "knee-jerk" decide something like this is "too expensive." Think it through carefully.

In B2B environments, Jeff and I are both occasionally used as "drawing cards." A company hires him or me to speak at a seminar or even a teleseminar or webinar, to give them a high-value program as a gift to clients, get clients to bring guests, and to promote to new prospects. Speaking for myself, I'm not a cheap date. I fly by private jet, command a good day fee, and require bulk purchase of my books as attendee gifts and/or book sales. I do have a portfolio of ready-to-use, proven promotional material that can be customized for any client, which is of obvious value. I have been employed this way by various clients selling different services to chiropractors, dentists, small-business owners, and financial advisors. When you hire a speaker for such purposes, it's important that he or she be fully on board with your marketing objectives, not just showing up and delivering off-the-shelf shtick, and not putting your purposes at risk for his own. Furthermore, he or she has to be very promotable—either a famous celebrity who is relevant to your audience or someone of less fame but great authority and relevance—who your clientele can be motivated to be eager to hear.

Whether a high-value, educational program, or a mini off-Broadway production, you need to do some expert planning and very thorough promotion to leverage your investment.

If an event is free, your advertising for it needs to explain how it is being offered free of charge, even if very briefly, to allay skepticism and worry. This can be as simple as "Sponsored by the Elder Law Center as community outreach," but it needs to be said. If nothing will be sold, you usually want to emphasize that. If something is to be sold, I usually prefer disclosing, gently, that there will be a brief commercial on behalf of "x," but also reassuring that beneficial information will be provided and a good time will be had by all.

Skepticism of free events can sometimes be allayed if the event is sponsored or tied to a charity. In B2B environments, my clients using free seminars that sell often get one or more noncompeting vendors to sponsor the events, and sometimes, also, underwrite some or even all of the costs. When I wanted to do free seminars as part of a nationwide book tour, I got the software company Infusionsoft to sponsor and host four events in four cities. Locally, a professional putting on an event could bring another noncompeting professional in to split time and cost and co-promote. Or, a charity tie-in might be created; an elder law attorney might, for example, affiliate his event with the local chapter of the Arthritis Foundation and make a donation based on attendance. Jeff did a similar program with an eight-city tour specifically for comic book retailers, which was sponsored by Marvel Entertainment.

Plan the event itself carefully. People need to be greeted, checked in, and ushered to the event area. If there is a wait time between arrival and the start of a program, they should be given something to look at, literature or an event program, and you may want to have a video showing in the room. At seminars that sell, for financial advisors, doctors, and others, we use five- to seven-minute video compilations of their media appearances, TV commercials, infomercials, and testimonials, and have that running back to back, again and again, during the wait time. The primary speaker should almost always be formally introduced to establish authority—even if you believe much of the audience is familiar with them.

Large Numbers at Blinding Speed

For most businesses, nothing beats an event that gets current customers, clients, or patients to round up and bring family, friends, neighbors, and co-workers to be introduced to you. Multiplying satisfied customers in this way can create exponential growth: If 20 customers each beget 2 via an event, there are 60 customers for the next event, times 2 equals 120, multiplied by 2 at the next event, gives you 240.

Another great way to get numbers and speed is by cooperative list sharing among merchants in an area for one big event. In many areas—including mine, where I saw it firsthand—all the merchants in a shopping village collaborated on a 7 P.M. to midnight Harry Potter night linked to the midnight release of the series' newest book. Every store and restaurant stayed open. Everyone had some Harry Potter-themed gift, trinket, or snack, so kids could go from one merchant to the next to the next, winding up at the bookstore. Kids came in costumes to get the book at a discount. It resembled a giant Halloween party, suggesting that could just as easily be pulled off as a theme. With every merchant at least using its email list to promote, some mailing, and in-store promotion for weeks in advance, everybody got the benefit of everybody else's reach. Customers also brought friends with their kids who may never have been to these shops before. The few shrewd enough to capture visitors' contact info created new prospect lists for follow-up. Many enjoyed a cash-flow surge and gained new customers. Mostly, independent bookstore owners organized these, but any merchant could be the organizer.

Jeff Slutsky is a master of the "blowout promotion"—usually a single day or weekend for a retailer or restaurateur—designed to generate an enormous amount of trial of your product or service in a very short time. It can get a lot of people familiar with a new business or a business in a difficult location in a hurry. It can restart a troubled business. And, as Jeff says, sometimes it is net-cheaper to acquire customers by just giving the product away free than by any other means. I have a client, www.KidsBowlFree.com, who represents a huge number of bowling centers all across the country, and uses their slowest times (days during the summer) as free and nearly-free gifts distributed to its list of over one million family members, bringing first-time customers into those centers.

Jeff describes a fairly typical blowout promotion for a Luby's Cafeteria in Tampa, Florida:

"Their 'Customer Appreciation Day' featured an outrageous 50%-off everything. They brought in a banjo player, a magician, and a balloon artist to entertain guests, decorated the place to reinforce the festive spirit, and, of course, made sure they had enough food ready to support the promotion. Running out of product halfway through this kind of a promotion would be disastrous. Not only do you need enough product, you need enough labor to deliver excellent service. Luby's brought in general managers from other area Luby's to lend a helping hand and expose them to the possibilities of such a promotion. The power of a promotion like this is in getting many first-time customers—in this case, who might never otherwise venture into a cafeteria—to try your business. Since the price is so low, it's clear it's a one-time event, and you don't risk eroding price integrity. Sales tripled for the day and customer counts quadrupled. But the important fact is that store sales were up 13% for the month following the promotion. Approximately half those who came that day were new customers and the boost to sales the following month was testament to many returning. To get those same numbers of new customers over time through traditional advertising or couponing would cost significantly more money."

The way I would try to make this kind of an event even better, looping back to the Harry Potter example, would be to inveigle two noncompeting area merchants of one kind or another who had sizable email or mailing lists and trade them the equal of an exhibit booth with coupon and/or sample distribution inside the Luby's, right smack in the middle of all the activity, for promotion of the event in their name to their list. For a Luby's, it could be a window replacement company, a retail store, or a home services provider like a carpet cleaning company—or even a car dealer displaying their newest car in a velvet-roped area outside, adjacent to the entry. You could also go for a charity tie-in, making a donation for every meal served, in exchange for the charity's promotion of the event to its list. With a charity tie-in, you may find it easier to get free promotion on local radio and TV programs and in community newspapers. In short, I like using events as newly created opportunity for others, thus creating barter currency to exchange for access and endorsement to others' lists.

You can choose to utilize one of your slower days or times of the week, to avoid cannibalizing your peak sales times, although if this event is promoted in a big enough way it will admittedly cut into sales on the days leading up to it as people delay their visits or purchases to take advantage of the sale. In the case of a business like Luby's, though, that trade-off is that they may bring friends who are potential new customers.

One vital point Jeff makes is it's of critical importance to distribute bounce-back certificates. This is the only real way to track how many of the participants in the day's promotion return as customers, and it encourages them to return, within a prescribed time period. The certificate can give a blanket, next-time discount, or a discount on certain items, or offer a gift with the next purchase, and it should bear an expiration date.

It might not occur to you that a good time to run this kind of blowout promotion is immediately before a competitor's grand opening, but Jeff suggests it is. You'll take some of the wind out of their sails and diminish whatever success they may have at purloining your customers.

When the Circus Came to Town, Everybody Went

If you're familiar with the great Ringling Bros. and Barnum & Bailey circus, or have read the outstanding novel *Water for Elephants*, or watched the HBO series *Carnivàle*, you know that once upon a time in America, when the circus came to town, everybody went. This is no longer the case. The box in the living room and the iPad under the arm present a dizzying array of entertainment as well as educational "events" that do not require trudging off to a tent and paying admission. Personally, I never thought of it as "trudging" and I think much has been lost to families and society in general by the disappearance of shared, special experiences into the little electronic boxes, but that's another subject for another time and place. So, today, it takes a lot to motivate people to come to your event. Still, people go. And the putting on or participating in events is the most certain way to gain customers in clumps vs. one at a time, with speed and efficiency. Every No-B.S. Grassroots Marketer should be using event promotions.

The Wizard of Sales

by Jeff Slutsky

With the success of the Bristol-Myers Squibb *Sound of Mucus* show and the National Speakers Association version of *Grease*, it became obvious to Steve Rizzo and me that we were on to something. Steve called me one day and asked me to write him a one-man show that he can do in addition to his standard keynote speech. Steve is a gifted impressionist, so the parodies can involve using his unique talents.

The Wizard of Sales, continued

Both of us speak to a lot of sales organizations, so we agreed that the show should be geared to salespeople. But it should be general enough so that the basic framework of the show could be recycled, and then with a rewrite, adapted to the unique needs and issues of a given client. So it would be a custom show, but many of the most expensive elements of the show would be reusable to help make it cost effective for everyone.

I called Steve back two weeks later with good news and bad news. The good news was I already completed a rough draft of his one-man show. The bad news was that it took a cast and crew of 12 to perform it. That's when I suggested we do a parody of *The Wizard of Oz* for salespeople. First of all, not only does every person know all the music intimately, but everyone knows all the characters and the plot.

For our pilot version, the four main characters would have to overcome four basic selling issues that nearly everyone in a sales audience would identify with (see Figures 18.2 to 18.5 on pages 180–182). Dorothy will have a problem closing the sale. The Scarecrow can't generate good qualified leads. The Tinman will have a problem handling objections. And the Cowardly Lion (played by Steve Rizzo) will have telephone-call reluctance.

The way it's written, the production is both parody and sequel of sorts. Dorothy, after graduating from Kansas State University, gets a job as a sales rep. In her office are three other salespeople: Hunk, Hickory, and Zeke. The sales manager is Mr. Marvel. And her big competitor, who keeps stealing away her best sales, is Elmira Gulch.

The Wizard of Sales, continued

After losing yet another sale to Elmira (this time because of price), she sings, "Somewhere over my sales goals." Throughout the production, each character learns to overcome their particular sales issue.

To ensure that the production was of the highest quality, Broadway director Michael Leeds staged and choreographed the entire production with the help of Broadway musical director Phil Reno. The costumes were designed by Tony Award winner Alvin Colt, who also did the costumes for Forbidden Broadway. His concept was to give each character the "business version" of their movie counterpart. Dorothy wears a blue gingham business dress. Hickory is in a stylish silver gray business suit which later turns into his tin business suit. Huck wears a sport coat and tie but is transformed into the Scarecrow, stuffed with shredded cancellation orders.

Figure 18.2 The sales force before they're transformed.

The Wizard of Sales, continued

The pilot performance was at the Marriott Marquis in New York City for the IDRC, a real estate trade group. Then the first full production was performed at the National Speakers Association annual convention in Washington, DC. In both cases the scripts were rewritten to address the needs and issues of the audience.

Figure 18.3 Dorothy gets advice from Munchkin Corp. with the help of the Good Sales Manager of the East.

The template production is not limited to salespeople. It's designed to be rewritten for basically any audience. Of course, there needs to be enough lead time to research and write a script. Then the cast has to learn a new script each time, even though the blocking and choreography are mostly the same for each show. One interesting point is that the cast has no idea why a certain line is funny to the audience. I tell them where to anticipate a laugh or applause so they can pause accordingly.

The Wizard of Sales, continued

Figure 18.4 The "Great and Powerful Wizard" happens to look strangely like the president of the organization, but just a little greener.

Figure 18.5 Tinman suffers from poor objection handling while Dorothy advises him with wisdom from The Ruby Sales Manual.

The Wizard of Sales, continued

To pursue this kind of production for your event, be sure to look for very talented people who can deliver the final value for you. First find a writer who is not only funny, but understands business. You want someone who can research your business to the point of being an expert. Then he or she is ready to put it on paper for you. Try not to limit this person's creativity. If you want a show but it doesn't matter which music you use, let the writer choose, based on the audience. If you choose the music (unless there's a strategic reason it needs to be something specific), your writer may not be able to give you the best results.

A good director is also important, especially one with "industrial" experience. The staging at most conventions has to be set up specifically for that event, so the production *is not working with the standard stage.* The show has to be adapted to work within the restrictions of the staging, or if possible, when the staging is being designed to allow elements that would make for a smooth production. The same goes for the lighting and the sound.

The sound is very important and seems to be the one area groups scrimp on. The entire show is based on the audience hearing the lyrics. Actors can wear wireless microphones with headsets, like they do on Broadway. But it's super important to make sure that you get a crisp, clear sound from those mikes, or the show is lost. To see a nine-minute promotional video on *The Wizard of Sales*, search on YouTube for Wizard of Sales or log on to YouTube and put this in your browser window: http://www.youtube.com/watch?v=K_I75X9uCg8.

PART III

PERSONALIZED MARKETING

with selections from

No B.S. Trust-Based Marketing

No B.S. Guide to Marketing to Leading-Edge Boomers and Seniors

No B.S. Guide to Maximum Referrals and Customer Retention

PERSONALIZED MARKETING

People like doing business with people—not faceless corporate entities. Proof of this abounds. More importantly, people like doing business with people they like, feel some affinity or connection to, respect, admire, and trust, so their buying decisions are easier and less stressful.

The excerpts in this section, from three different books in the No B.S. series, focus on this available advantage. The great adman Jack Trout of Ries & Trout wrote a book titled *Differentiate or Die!* quite a few years ago, long before the marketplace and media landscape became as cluttered as it is now, and long before one business category after another was being commoditized; price and profit crushed by Amazon and Amazon-esque vendors. His warning is ten times truer now. Everything in this *Best of* book is actually about: differentiation. In the previous two sections we've been creating differentiation by process; by how you attract, acquire, sell to, and keep customers differently from virtually everybody else. The strongest form of differentiation, however, is YOU. No one can swipe and replicate or discount YOU.

Would Warren Buffett Like Your Business?

The legendary investor Warren Buffett talks about preferring businesses that "have a moat around them." He means some sort of advantage or novel "x-factor" that can be protected from copycats, so customers can be protected from poachers. If you watch *Shark Tank* on TV, you'll see that Kevin O'Leary often asks the same question: How can you protect this? Sometimes patents, trademarks, and copyrights enter this discussion. Many protections are only temporary, like first-to-market, a prime location, or a price advantage. In my experience, the ultimate security and ultimate competitive advantage is quality of relationship, which is strongest when a group of customers believes in and trusts the business and its leader.

We live in an untrustworthy world. Every important and once-trusted institution may disappoint us. This fact and this trend is, I'm sorry to say, bad for us as a society, but offers profound advantage to the astute marketer in any field of endeavor, profession, or product or service category. If you can retrain yourself to "sell trust" before and even in place of "stuff," you'll win big.

There are excerpts here from the book *No B.S. Guide to Maximum Referrals and Customer Retention*. Let me leap and present a powerful secret to maximum referrals: Customers *do not* refer much if at all to a business that just satisfies them, just meets their obligations. For a customer to put his ego, reputation, and relationships at risk, he needs more than that. He needs to have maximum trust in that business. He needs the utmost confidence that the business will over deliver and send whomever he refer back to him saying "Thank You," every time, without fail, no excuses—always performance.

These select excerpts are "right on target" for the business peril and business opportunity we confront today.

CHAPTER 19

Trust-Based Marketing
as the Path to Wealth

Originally appearing as Chapter 1 from
No B.S. Trust-Based Marketing

You can get laid with lust. But you get married and stay married with trust.

So a lot depends on your objectives. I've long believed in business that, rather than get customers to make sales, it is smarter to make sales to get customers. The first provides only income. The second provides income *and equity*. If all you're after is a day-to-day income boost for yourself or revenue growth for your company, you'll find plenty of ammunition and firepower in this book to achieve those limited goals. But, even if you don't begin in sync with us, I hope as you proceed you expand your thinking about the impact trust-based marketing can have in building wealth. The majority of businesspeople think only about income every day. The exceptionally smart few who get rich from business, think about both, every day.

You may skip over this chapter if you are *not* interested in getting rich. Chapter 20 begins on page 201.

In my own business, I've very deliberately worked at creating what I call "lifers"—customers who stay engaged with me for decades, continuing to buy whatever I next bring forward, so that the getting of one in the first place is not just consummation of a transaction, but the start of a permanent relationship. Not just the grabbing of some money, but taking title to an oil well. In order to do this in my particular business— essentially the dispensing-of-advice business—I knew I had to earn and keep trust, and I figured out the three key factors in trust-based equity for me: one, being known as a candid, blunt teller of truth, even if unwelcome by many, and never pandering. Thus, the "No B.S." brand I created. Two, establishing certain principles as constants in my writing, speaking—all my works— that were evident and did not change. And three, never abusing my customers for short-term profit. Given these three things, they can trust me not to endorse anyone or anything or sell them anything I don't genuinely believe is honest, beneficial, and the best in its category. For me, this has worked out very nicely. What is now the GKIC business, evolved from my personal business, does in fact have large numbers of members who've been with me for 10, 20, 30, even approaching 40 years. Many who've spent six figures during their tenure—people attending a GKIC SuperConferenceSM now, who first attended a seminar of mine 20 years ago. And this did translate to equity, as the company has been twice sold, and the two sales combined provided a good share of my wealth. This asset can be built upon and leveraged into ever-growing wealth, or it can be destroyed, depending on the thinking and actions of the people who have stewardship of it.

My favorite company of all is Disney. In its present form, it's hard to imagine that, as Walt put it, it all started with a mouse.

And with Walt. In industries that were entirely transactional—amusement parks, films, toys—Walt built trust-based brand equity and relationship equity. Relationship equity is still a major part of Disney's business today, driving premium-priced attractions, time-share real estate (Disney Vacation Club), fraternity (D23), and very frequent repeat purchasing. A series of CEOs that have held stewardship of Walt's legacy have, amazingly, resisted almost all temptations to undermine the trust the company's fans, customers, the public, and even investors have for Disney.

I'm a serious student of Donald Trump. Look carefully behind the Barnum-ism and you'll see that he has done something no other real estate developer and magnate has ever done: built a publicly recognized brand that adds price elasticity to every building and real estate project that bears his name, and, most recently, extends to a successful TV franchise and licensing for a wide range of products, from luxury mattresses to steaks to clothing. Real estate buyers trust Trump to provide "the best." Consumers who aren't about to buy a $3 million penthouse apartment on Park Avenue want to get a small, affordable piece of that, so she buys her husband a Trump necktie at Macy's, he splurges for their stay at a Trump hotel or resort.

These are people who understand the matters of income vs. equity, and of the role of trust in equity.

Income tends to be spent. Equity accumulates and converts to wealth. So everybody needs to be thinking about equity, early, and it is my contention that the only real equity, certainly the best equity, and the source of all equity, is quality relationship with committed, continuing customers. So I would suggest anybody in any business engage in the same thought process I did and ask himself: What are the few, key factors for you, that will make you such a trusted and relied on presence in your customers' lives that they stay with you—and spend with you—for life?

"But MY Business Is Different . . ."

Do NOT reject the question out of hand, because you think your business does not easily, naturally, automatically lend itself to such a relationship. It may seem obvious now that my business lent itself to this, but no one among my peers thought this way. In fact, many in my field joked about making sales and getting out of town before the posse formed. They were all hit-and-runners. Most still are. Today, they're doing it on the internet, sharing massive email lists, driving to one promotion after another, divvying the money like pirates after a raid on defenseless yachts or freighters rather than as traveling salesmen and speakers out on the hustings. But the effect is the same: income, no equity. So don't reject the question out of hand. If you own hardware stores or other retail stores or restaurants, why can't you become a trusted and significant part of your customers' lives? To many, Martha Stewart has made herself just that, and she dispenses much the same sort of ideas, information, and inspiration it would be appropriate for a hardware store owner to dispense. If you are a physician, chiropractor, a dentist, look at Dr. Oz. *Whatever* your business, there is a way to be found and figured out, to elevate your status and cement your importance to your clientele.

What Is Long-Term Marriage About?

It's about always being there, that you will have the other person's back. That they know you care about them. That you find ways to stay interesting and relevant over years of familiarity. Most business owners and sales professionals don't really think about long-term marriage with customers. They either take it for granted or give it no importance. They are focused on income, not equity. They don't think in terms of: *what will this relationship have to be like, for this customer to stay married to me for life?* It's actually not all that difficult to figure it out in any given business. It's more that nobody tries.

I routinely buy things from stores or service providers, visit restaurants, etc., where not even a feeble attempt at creating ongoing, lifetime relationship is made. Some of this is sloth and stupidity: *We did well—he'll be back.* In many of these cases, relationship equal to equity could be very deliberately created. Yet no attempt is made.

Trust, Relationship, Equity, and Wealth

There are profound links between trust and relationship, relationship and equity, equity and wealth.

Brand-name, over-the-counter remedies—the brands we grew up with—continue to substantially outsell generic versions of the exact same formulations and products displayed right next to them on the same shelves, and selling for 20% to 50% less. Why do more people buy Bayer® aspirin than generic aspirin? There's nothing proprietary to it whatsoever. *Because Bayer® is a trusted name.* The 50% price and profit differential, from which much wealth can be derived, has nothing to do with product ingredients, product superiority, distribution, or service, and everything to do with trust.

For most, trust is more complex than just a recognized brand name, and few of us have the resources or patience to wait for generations to harvest our future fortunes from such slowly accumulated trust. We need a more complex approach that can accelerate the achievement of high trust, whether for competitive differentiation or support of premium prices or other motives, and all the components of such an approach are in this book. But, for now, I want to simply demonstrate the bridge from trust to wealth.

A seismic shift begins with a change in the fundamental question of all advertising, marketing, selling, and conduct of business, from: *How can I make a sale today?* or *How can I make some money today?* to: *How can I make sales and money today but also create trust today?*

Let's Go Through a Consulting Session on This

If we were having a consultation, you and I, on this, we would begin very broadly. *What will it take for you to grow wealthy from your business, in a reasonable time frame of your choosing?* This shifts thinking. It switches from the most common *How can I make some (more) money today?* to *How can I conduct my business affairs today and every day to develop the kind of equity that translates to wealth?* We would then examine all the possible kinds of equity in your particular kind of business. That might include unique intellectual property such as patents, trademarks, and copyrights; real estate paid off with business income (as opposed to renting or leasing space); control of distribution; and on and on. But in most cases, it would become evident that all kinds of equity rise or fall based on equity in relationship with continuing customers. Or that the only equity that can be protected is in relationship with continuing customers. And we would ultimately get to the question: *What will this relationship have to be like for this customer to stay married to me for life?*

Inevitably, a big part of that answer will be: trust. And that will loop us all the way back to trust-based marketing. If it is true, and I believe it is, that the value of the equity you have via customers is a reflection of the level of trust they have in you, then it becomes blatantly obvious that developing trust must begin at the beginning, and must never be jeopardized or sacrificed for any other objective. This will color every decision you make.

The questions I've just raised are powerful, if taken seriously. They not only get to equity in customers for life, but to price elasticity, to greater numbers of referrals (thus lowered customer acquisition costs and speed of growth liberated from proportionate capital investment), to stability and sustainability, and more. They translate to more immediate, transactional profit, from which money can

The Question

What will this relationship have to be like for this customer to stay married to me for life?

be siphoned to create permanent wealth, and to greater overall, total, lifetime customer value, which creates equity that can be sold or mined, also to create permanent wealth.

A Wealth Secret from Warren Buffett

If you've read Michael Gerber's work, beginning with the best-selling book *The E-Myth*, you know his core premise: A business (or sales career) should be constructed and systemized as if it would be franchised à la McDonalds, cloned thousands of times, and successfully operated by people with far less talent or skill than you possess. That's a form of operational equity. Of equal or greater importance is customer relationship equity, which can only come from a business deliberately engineered to have it.

I am not a fan of Warren Buffett as a human being. In his meddling in politics, I consider him a charlatan. But he is widely regarded as one of the world's most successful investors, justifiably, and he doesn't just invest in companies: he buys many in entirety based on their equity. As Gerber suggests by engineering a business for cloning, even if you never intend to actually do so, you could benefit by engineering a business to sell to Buffett, even if such an opportunity would never actually occur. You'd think more marketers would dig into Buffett's investment choices to find marketing secrets, but I haven't yet encountered any of my peers or competitors who've had this blinding flash of the obvious. If you did investigate as I have, you'd discover that about 80% of the companies chosen by Buffett have a very high trust component, some by brand identity, others by direct, and in some cases, personality-driven relationship with their customers. In some, a shift to more trust-based marketing has occurred in companies after Buffett's investment in or acquisition of them, so perhaps he is influencing their leaders with such strategic recommendation.

If Buffett were advising you on how to make your business so valuable that he might want to buy it, he'd have to reveal this secret: that he buys trusted companies—companies that have invested in trust.

Buffett knows that the value of equity a business has via its customers is a reflection of those customers' level of trust in that business or even its leaders. Given that, it becomes obvious that the pathway to wealth is in developing high trust with customers from the very beginning, and that this trust must never be jeopardized or sacrificed for any other objective.

Your Navigational System

Most businesspeople are often tactical, rarely strategic. Even this book is loaded with tactical advice. There's nothing wrong with tactics and tactical application, but too often businesspeople are *randomly* tactical. Random is dangerous. Randomly captaining a cruise liner over the ocean can get you and a boatload of passengers killed. Randomly flying a plane hither and yon can stick you nose first into the side of a mountain. Randomly wandering a large forest can get you hopelessly lost, eventually turn you into a meal for bears. Having a sound, reliable navigational system that overlays, governs, and even restricts all decisions is the remedy for the hazards implicit in random activity.

The best such navigational premise for those interested in sustainability, stability, security, equity, and wealth is creating and leveraging high trust.

What Do People REALLY Exchange Money For?

Very few people understand money. Few grasp that money moves from one person or place to another for definitive reasons of its own. This is why all manner of centralized government confiscation and redistribution of money fails miserably. Money itself simply refuses to cooperate with ignorance and stupidity. After the hundreds of billions, if not trillions, of dollars extracted from the private sector and poured into the government's "war on poverty"—declared by President Johnson—we have more people living beneath the poverty line than ever before, and in the very recent Obama administration, more people have been added to the food stamps rolls than in any other four-year period. After coming to foolish consensus that everybody ought to go to college, we permitted government to pour untold sums into subsidizing and financing college educations, resulting in monstrous inflation of tuition and other educational costs, and an entire generation of graduates buried in impossible debt. I could go on. What you want to do is escape all the ignorant and inaccurate thinking about how money functions that lies beneath these epic disasters that, combined, have taken the United States in just 40 years from being the world's biggest lender and creditor, possessing unrivaled economic strength, to being the world's biggest borrower and debtor. You want to align your efforts with the ways that money actually operates, and the only reasons why money ever moves of its free will to somebody and therefore remains with that somebody. I explore all of this in my book *No B.S. Wealth Attraction in the New Economy,* but here is the specific reality most salient to this book:

Something of value to someone must be exchanged for money. Any money moved by coercion or confiscation without this exchange breaks free, runs away, and goes somewhere else for such exchange.

Marketing and selling are about exchange. At the simplest level, Zig Ziglar described his attitude when selling high-priced sets of cookware in homes as: *I've got their pots and pans out in my car, they've got my money in their checkbook in their kitchen drawer, and I'm here to make the exchange.* Fine as far as it goes. It strengthened my spine when I first heard it. But what if we're interested in relationship, not transaction? In equity, not just income? Exchange then becomes more complex and sophisticated.

Most people think very simplistically about their businesses. They have things to sell and they try to figure out how to sell them. To them, business is about sales problems.

Most marketing people are similarly simplistic and narrow in their thinking. They are trained and conditioned to translate products and services into solutions, or desirable experiences, or pride-of-ownership purchases, and to speak about features and benefits. To them, business is about sales message problems.

All this ignores two important facts. One, as I've been beating up here, there's no stability or equity in making sales. Two, everything said by you, your minions, or in media, about products, services, solutions, etc., is grossly devalued and handicapped if not said by somebody whom the prospect or customer trusts.

If I tell you that the Dow will drop or rise by 2,000 points this year, and that you need to re-arrange all your investments accordingly, so what? But if you follow the famous, outspoken economist Harry Dent, Jr., and believe in him because you read his books, get his newsletter, see him interviewed, accept his premise that "demographics are destiny," and know (some of) his past, key predictions are coming true, and he tells you to get your financial house arranged for a 2,000-point swing, you act. Or if you ardently follow Glenn Beck and see him as a truthful, clairvoyant, trustworthy life guide, you may very well have half your garage full of survival food, the other half full of gold bullion, and be guarding it with your own arsenal of guns. And, as advertisers know, if Beck tells you that you can trust one of his advertisers and urges calling them, huge numbers act.

If I tell you that you look pale and sickly, and tell you that heart surgery might be urgently needed, you may start feeling queasy, sweaty, dizzy, or weak if you are highly suggestible, but you are most likely to just go home and take a nap. But if a heart specialist at the Cleveland Clinic is called in by your regular doc, during your yearly physical, and makes the same pronouncement, they can summon the orderlies and you'll climb on the gurney and yell "Go!" Even if I am a sales wizard, I'll find it damnably difficult to make either of these sales, but Dent and the Cleveland Clinic docs can, rather easily. They have the equity I lack: pre-existing trust.

These examples irrefutably demonstrate how powerful and valuable that trust asset is. It sensibly follows that such an asset will produce or make possible production of wealth as no other asset can. You should therefore direct your efforts at the creation and ownership of that asset, more so than any and all others.

CHAPTER 20

Trust Without Trying Is No Longer Enough

Originally appearing as Chapter 2 from
No B.S. Trust-Based Marketing

Trust is a significant part of a great many decisions—including selection of providers of goods and services—without conscious, deliberate, and creative effort on anyone's part to create the trust. It *does* just happen.

Much Undeserved Trust Occurs

We trust casually when we have no practical choices. If you board an airplane to fly across country, you are trusting the factory workers who built it, the mechanics who maintain it, the FAA inspectors, the pilots, and the air traffic controllers. There is abundant evidence none are worthy of trust. The news has revealed sleeping air traffic controllers, inebriated pilots, and improperly maintained planes. If you fly commercial often as I used to, you know the #2 excuse given for departure delays—after #1, weather—is "a mechanical" one. Surely it has occurred to you that if there are that many mechanical malfunctions occurring while the planes are being driven about on the ground, there damn sure must be some you aren't being told about at 30,000 feet up. But, really, what choice do you have? If you want to go from L.A. to Des Moines, you gotta roll the dice.

This breeds a lot of unnecessary casual trust, as a matter of habit. Few people, for example, investigate whether their chiropractors or even their heart surgeons or their investment advisors have complaints against them, settled or unresolved litigation, license suspensions, let alone—with surgeons and hospitals—their comparative track records of success and failure with the kind of surgery about to be performed, even though this kind of information is a matter of public record and can be obtained. Few people personally research a prescribed drug before taking it; they trust their doctor's prescription, even though information about a drug's side effects, history, etc. is readily available. Hardly anybody asks to visit the kitchen of the restaurant they bumble into.

A Lot of Lazy Trust Occurs

In my business book *No B.S. Ruthless Management of People and Profits*, I lay out the strongest possible case for live-accessible and recorded audio and video surveillance of all store, shop, or practice employees' interactions with customers, clients, or patients, and for telephone and in-person "mystery shopping" as enforcement and coaching tools to ensure that sales scripts and policies are adhered to. The business owners who have embraced my advice and reported results to me have, without a single exception, engineered substantial improvements in sales, upsells, customer service, customer satisfaction and retention, and profits (albeit with the inconvenience of having to more frequently fire and replace noncompliant personnel—and outright thieves). Still, most owners will not do this even if it is proven to them to be needed. It's just too much work.

It isn't even accurate to think of this as trust. It's more a knowing, shoulder-shrugging acceptance of mediocrity or worse.

In the same way, people accept a lot rather than take on the responsibility of getting it as it should be.

Still, Most Require Trust to Buy Many Things

All this casual trust occurring should not lull you into a false sense of security. Surprisingly, people who trust irrationally, casually, lazily, still require different levels of trust for different purchases and relationships. Furthermore, is this really what you want to settle for? Hope that you'll be lazily trusted enough to make a sale? You can do a lot better, and see it reflected in many measurable ways, possibly including higher conversion rates, higher transaction sizes, shorter sales cycles, less stressful selling, better retention, increased referrals.

Where Trust Comes From

Throughout this book, we're going to explore many different sources of trust. Not every business can effectively draw on every source, but there's no business in existence that cannot be strengthened by drawing on some of these sources. These sources include:

Authority—doctor, lawyer, accountant, police officer, fireman

Affinity—shared background, experience, philosophy, fraternity

Credibility—factual basis for trust

Longevity—years in business, in the community

Celebrity—being known or being known for something

Familiarity—reassuring omnipresence

Frequency—the more often heard and seen, the more easily trusted

Second-Party Transferal—earned, engineered, borrowed, rented, purchased endorsement

Place—geographic or target market; being for a certain customer

Demonstration—seeing is believing

One of the most important points driven home with relentless repetition throughout this book is that people trust for the wrong reasons. By understanding how people *actually* come to trust, based on the above sources and others, you will be able to deliberately manufacture maximum trust.

Trust as Supreme Marketing Advantage

Consider the backdrop I've painted as a whole. People have an underlying, ever-present, ongoing anxiety and angst about nearly everything—from the news they watch, to the car they drive and the roads they drive on, and the other drivers surrounding them, to the food they eat, to virtually everybody from whom they get advice, services, and products. It's called *"defensive* driving" for good reason. Distrust of elected officials and public institutions has never been higher. As I was writing this, one week's news included: the Penn State sex scandal; the collapse of Herman Cain's campaign to sex scandal; another request by former Presidential contender John Edwards to delay his criminal trial; a recall of 100,000 defective cars by Ford and 50,000 by Mazda; and a news warning about a massive recall of dangerously toxic ground beef. A typical week.

People of my age grew up rarely locking our cars when parked out and about, and never in our own driveways. Many of us left our houses' back doors unlocked. Not now. We feel a level of unease, of threat, outside and even at home. We are an uneasy people, because we know we are trusting people and things unworthy of trust. We are very often disappointed, sometimes harmed, and we expect more of the same. We are not just defensive drivers; we are defensive, period.

The worse this environment gets and the more someone is sensitive to it and affected by it, the bigger an advantage trust is. But few advertisers, marketers, or sales professionals truly focus on this advantage. Instead, they drift to cute or comedic advertising, default to low, lower, or lowest price and discount positioning, or—like someone with a dull knife cutting more furiously—rely on classic product-centric presentations, such as features-to-benefits. This is why this book can be such a powerful tool for you. If you adopt its approach, strategies, and tactics, you'll leave your current cluttered and competitive marketing environment and, via a road less traveled, appear as uniquely attractive to your prospects, customers, and clients. The proof that this is true is that so many people are so desperate to trust, they are bamboozled again and again by obviously untrustworthy people making ridiculous claims, political candidates being at the head of that parade. It is actually quite miraculous that about one-third of the U.S. population votes in presidential and congressional elections, given how consistently disappointed Democrats and Republicans, liberals and conservatives are with their picks when they get power. But people set that aside and hope that this time, it'll be different. That kind of hope is available, and if you find a way to validate it rather than dash it yet again, you will have transformative power for your business.

How Does Trust Affect Buying Decisions?

Even mundane purchases are affected by trust. My wife and I prefer produce and fruit grown in the United States vs. that much more commonly found in most supermarkets, imported from Mexico, Argentina, and other foreign lands. Consequently, we often drive past three supermarkets to go to one 20 miles farther from our home to shop. I eat a lot of blueberries—I'm diabetic, and they are one of the few sweet-tasting fruits I can eat pounds of without damage. I do not want to eat blueberries brought here from Mexico, and if my wife Carla's away at our other home, and I'm hurried and shopping at a close store that has only imported blueberries, I'll do without. We trust U.S.-grown food and we distrust foreign-grown food. But why? I possess no empirical evidence that the U.S.-grown produce is safer. I've done no research, can't recall seeing any news reports, and know of no information to suggest I have reason to distrust blueberries from Argentina or tomatoes from Mexico. Further, I dine out in restaurants frequently and no doubt consume imported produce and fruit, not to mention pasta sauce made from Mexican tomatoes, and think nothing of it. But when choosing the grocery store to shop at, and choosing the foods I purchase in the store, I check labels for country of origin, and I buy or don't buy based on country of origin.

We are obviously in the minority on this particular point about origin of produce, since more supermarkets stock and sell more imported than homegrown product of this nature. But we are not alone. And local farmers markets' success attests to that. The point is, if "Who do you trust?" plays a part in many rather mundane, ordinary, day-to-day buying decisions, imagine how significant it may be for somebody contemplating a more significant purchase or investment.

Certainly the more significant a purchase is to a buyer, the more consciously he seeks a trustworthy seller or provider, but you can't ignore the role of trust in just about every act of commerce.

Trust Is Rarely Rational

As I said, my wife and I eat unknown quantities of foreign-grown produce and foreign-farmed seafood and meat in restaurants, but refuse to buy it at the supermarket to eat it at home. Is that rational? Of course not. A big breakthrough in your own approach to trust-based marketing will be forcing yourself away from rational, logical thought about why your customers would or should trust you. Instead, if you can "decode" how they really process you and the ideas, information, and propositions you present, you'll find yourself holding a new key to the vault. Abandoning rational thought for customers' actual thought is not an easy shift. This is the challenge before you!

The Trust Virus

One of the main sources of trust is "pass along." You trust somebody because somebody you trust trusts him. It's second-party, passed-along trust. We, for example, have a "Mr. Fix-It" handyman who takes care of everything from yearly backyard deck cleaning, to putting up shelves, to fixing squeaky hinges, to dryer vent cleaning, and smoke detector battery changing. He has a garage door opener and keys to the house. He comes and goes as he pleases, and usually does work when we're away. He has the combination to my safe, because he installed it. He hands me an unitemized bill once a year and I pay it without question.

How did I come to place such open-ended, unfettered trust in this fellow? On the surface, he might not engender such trust. He drives an old, beat-up van filled with tools, supplies, and parts. He is scruffy. But the guy who trains my racehorses and with whom I am partner in some of the racehorses has employed the handyman for many years and trusts him implicitly, therefore that trust transferred to me. I do not know much about the handyman. I've never done a background check. I don't even have an address for him. Yet he has the keys to my house. Clearly, this is not rational behavior on my part, yet I'm a pretty rational person most of the time, with most of what I do. I've managed to build up successful businesses, create a modest personal fortune and manage it prudently, and earn the trust of a great many people, including private clients running companies as large as $2 billion in revenue. How can I act so irrationally when it comes to the handyman?

Bernie Madoff sits rotting in prison after a two-decade sustained, epic-sized Ponzi scheme, rivaled only by Roosevelt's concoction, the Social Security system. But Social Security is paid into under coercion and threat. Everybody handed their money over to Bernie voluntarily. And most who did so were college educated, sophisticated, successful, and wealthy individuals, managers of family fortunes and trusts, and paid administrators of universities' investment portfolios and sizable pension funds. All these "victims" had access to competent financial, tax, and legal advisors, undoubtedly routinely relying on those very advisors for guidance on all sorts of decisions. Yet they handed wealth to Madoff. None could explain exactly what Bernie did with their money or how he consistently generated above-par returns. Few wanted money, so Bernie avoided the payout pressure that breaks most Ponzi schemes; he needed only to print fake account statements. Trusting Madoff was inarguably irrational, so why did so many who "should have known better"? Because someone whom they knew and trusted, trusted him. Yes, he had the aid of credibility of having served on the Board of the New York Stock Exchange. He had offices, trappings of wealth, charitable involvements, media recognition, all manufactured with the stolen money.

But at the core, Bernie perpetuated his scam thanks to passed-along trust.

This reveals something very powerful about successfully selling inside the fortress walls of any closed community— and the very wealthy are a closed community. Their fortress walls are their reliance on peer-provided information. They trust each other and distrust all others. This is a strong fortress, difficult to penetrate; yet it is also extraordinarily imperfect and secretly weak, because once it is penetrated at any one point, with just one insider inhabitant, it is erased as a safeguard for all the other inhabitants. One to a few very quickly becomes many, then almost all. There are many such imperfectly fortressed communities; in fact, we all live in one or several. Among all the members of a church it is very common for small Ponzi schemes, mini-Madoffs, to flourish within the congregation. All that is needed is the trust of just one congregant; then all others defenseless. In a small, clannish industry or segment of an industry, the B2B marketer, the consultant, the software developer, the "expert" of any sort needs only the trust of one or a few of the well-known members, and all others' defenses against him disappear.

Further, the harder the trust of any one in such a community is to get in the first place, the more viral it is within that community, and the more valuable its viral nature is.

This is why it is so worthwhile to scheme to gain the trust of key centers of influence within any target group in which you seek to develop a clientele. Why it is so worthwhile to invest in securing that trust.

An Example of a Trust Virus Tactic in Action

This is a true experience of mine, from many years back. One day, in my mail, an envelope arrived, hand-addressed to me, with, in its sender's information corner, the name of a professional peer, another speaker. He and I lived in the same city, both belonged to the National Speakers Association, both engaged in some similar business activity, and he was a well-respected leader in our field. Although I was merely acquainted with the sender, not a friend, I certainly recognized his name, knew his reputation, and I was therefore curious about what he might be writing to me about, so I opened the envelope. That's important. With direct mail, you can't win if your envelope isn't opened, and a great many aren't. In this case, had the business owner being promoted in this surreptitious way been overt and sent me an envelope or other mailer directly from him, I doubt I'd have paid any attention. On opening this envelope, I found a letter from this peer to me that began: "Dear Dan, I suppose you'll quickly wonder why I am writing to you about a plumber." That I did. It was odd. It kept my curiosity alive, so I continued reading the letter. That's also important. With direct mail, readership is required for success, but rarely achieved and usually taken for granted.

The letter went on to tell me a dramatic story of a bit of plumbing trouble my peer had found himself with in his home, immediately before hosting a party (to which I had not been invited). He couldn't reach the last plumber he'd used, and so he found this plumber—Al—in the Yellow Pages. So promptly, brilliantly, and professionally had this fantastic plumber served him that he had decided to send his endorsement letter to everyone he knew in our shared profession in Phoenix. So if I ever needed a top-flight plumber, I'd know to call Al. This doesn't end there, but I'm going to give you the minimum needed to see the tactical play. About a week later, I got a letter from Al, reminding me of my peer's enthusiastic endorsement, offering me a free "plumbing problem prevention audit," and enclosing a couple of refrigerator magnets. Of course, Al the Plumber engineered this entire thing, as means of leveraging a customer's gratitude and satisfaction into a circle of that customer's influence.

The technical term for this tactic is an "Endorsed Mailing #1," followed by a sequence of direct solicitations. Even with the tenuous connection between my peer acquaintance and me, it works because, after all, knowing about a really good, reliable plumber is a good thing, and I said to myself, *Well, if he's good enough for Joel, he's good enough for me.* This is a way to move from random referrals to organized, managed multiplying of satisfied customers.

This particular tactic is transferable to many different kinds of businesses and if you can find opportunities to use it, you'll very likely find doing so very productive, but don't miss the broader point this illustrates, of the power of trust gone viral, passed from one person to many, carrying you over a fortress wall.

CHAPTER 21

The Power of
Prescription

Originally appearing as Chapter 14 from
No B.S. Trust-Based Marketing

This is a very important chapter. In it, I will reveal
a pathway to stress-less selling in a zero resistance zone
of your own making—sort of a zero gravity environment
for making money. If you are more concerned with marketing
than with personal selling, the same breakthrough principles
apply.

Imagine having your advice, ideas, information, recommendations, products, services, and prices or fees easily accepted,
with little question and no resistance! If that's not your experience,
you should know that it *is* the way many "merchants" live.

A person's doctor tells him that his heart trouble is worsening,
he needs to see a specialist, and will likely need surgery to
implant a pacemaker. His doctor refers him to a cardiologist. He
returns home, and the next day calls and makes an appointment

214 ⊛ THE BEST OF NO B.S.

with that cardiologist to whom he was referred. When, two weeks later, he gets in to see the cardiologist, surgery and implant of the device is the now unsurprising prescription, and he agrees to it with only a few questions.

Why Doesn't Your Selling Work Like This?

There are, obviously, many factors in play here. There is the established trust relationship with the primary physician and the established habit of obtaining advice and prescriptions from that doctor. There is the fact that a third party—the insurance company—is paying most of these bills, so there's no thought given to the reasonableness of fees and costs or comparison of them with other vendors. There is the worry about the worsening heart condition. And there is the implicit authority of the cardiologist. It would be smart to transfer as many of those factors to your own selling situation as possible. But the biggest overarching factor is that the proposition isn't being *sold* at all; it is being *prescribed*.

Most business owners, marketers, and sales professionals present and sell propositions. Consequently, they are always selling against resistance—because prospects in selling situations *feel compelled* to resist. Even keenly interested, financially capable prospects who have set out on a mission to purchase something specific for which they must deal with a salesman, like a car, home furnishings, a computer—still tend to put up some resistance when the salesman steps in. They are also, often, selling in a competitive environment, thus having to compare and contrast with others, justify and often negotiate price, win some and lose some. They are also often selling against procrastination and delay. Contrast that with the fact that over 70% of all doctor-issued drug prescriptions are filled, i.e., purchased at the pharmacy immediately, on the way home from

PART III / PERSONALIZED MARKETING

the doctor's office. In short, selling a proposition for a product or service is selling *against*.

In the above scenario, despite presenting something scary and unwanted (like having your chest cut open for dangerous heart surgery), there's virtually no resistance.

How Matt Zagula and I Position to Prescribe

In Matt's financial advisory practice, he replaces the selling of propositions with prescription as best he can. This starts with source, so as many of his prospective new clients as possible are obtained as referrals from existent clients or referrals from other professionals he has cooperative relationships with, such as estate planning attorneys. In his direct marketing, he "wraps himself" in trusted news media, like the newspaper, the local FOX TV affiliate, and popular hosts' radio programs. He uses mailing lists of trust-based marketers' followers—such as financial newsletter author's subscriber lists—and, with his books and other media, establishes authority with the prospects in advance of any meeting or discussion. He attempts to *prepare* the prospective client to accept him as a "financial doctor." Many of these prospects attend Matt's "Evening with the Authors" or workshops, and get to know him as an expert, in a choreographed setting that creates authority. All of this *prefaces* the one-to-one meeting, then structured as diagnosis and prescription. What is being sold here is: first, the person—not the products or proposition, and trust in that person—not in the companies or products he represents; second, the prescriptive plan—not a basket of financial products. The prescriptive plan *is*, of course, a basket of financial products, but they aren't being sold any more than the cardiac surgeon sells the anesthesia, the anesthesiologist, the hospital, or the brand of surgical instruments being used.

Note the above italicized words: *prepare. Preface.* I teach hard-core closing techniques to salespeople and I do know how to close a sale. In fact, I can get a check out of a rock. But it is far better, for a whole host of reasons, to erase the need for brute force to overcome resistance in advance. This requires careful, thorough preparation of prospects in advance of your selling. This requires preface to the act of selling.

In my professional practice, I provide strategic marketing advice coupled with the actual copywriting and development of advertisements, direct-mail campaigns, radio or TV commercials and infomercials, online media, and sales tools. My projects are complex, typically require fees upward from $100,000.00 to $250,000.00 plus royalties tied to results, and the majority of my clients are entrepreneurs building small to midsize businesses—not giant corporations with unlimited funds, and not executives spending other peoples' money. Unlike most freelance copywriters or ad agencies, I neither overtly advertise or directly market myself to a cold market, nor do I ever do free pitch meetings. Instead I've painstakingly created a feeder system, where businesspeople get to know and trust me through subscribing to and reading my newsletters, attending my seminars, listening to my recordings, reading my books, so that by the time they step forward and ask if I can and will personally assist them, they are looking for *my* diagnosis and prescription. Even when a client brings forward a referral, I rarely agree to talk or meet with them unless and until they have prepared themselves by reading, listening, and familiarizing themselves with my work—and when I violate that, I always regret it. Finally, as I said, there is no "free lunch." All possible relationships begin with the client buying an initial consulting day (as of this writing, a fee of $18,800.00), and traveling to one of my home cities to spend that day with me, with it framed in advance as a day of diagnosis and prescription. I do not care if they are inconvenienced or grumpy about trekking to me. If that's a problem, I know there will be other problems, so better we never start.

Keep in mind, Matt is a consumer marketer, dealing with Bob and Harriet Boomer, and their personal life's savings. I am a B2B marketer, dealing with the owners of businesses, entrepreneurs growing midsize companies, and occasionally the CEOs of much larger firms—up to billions in yearly revenue. It doesn't matter if you are B2C or B2B.

If you go back to the heart patient analogy, assume now, instead of merely accepting his family doctor's referral, he is a more discerning patient, and an affluent patient, and he makes calls to trusted friends and peers, he retains a medical investigator, and he determines who *the* best and most trusted cardiologist in America is. He then works his network of contacts to find somebody who can connect him with somebody to get in to see that doctor, a most difficult task. And he travels across country to see that doctor. Or if you wish a more marketing-oriented version, assume he sees a top-rated cardiologist who has written a book interviewed on a news or talk show and is impressed, obtains that doctor's book and reads it, and decides to get in to see that doctor, come hell or high water. When he gets to this difficult-to-get-to-doctor (or seemingly difficult to get to), and he gets his diagnosis done and his prescription delivered, will he then question cost, ask to delay while he comparison shops, resist in any way?

If You Want to Argue That *Your* Business Is Different . . .

All this sounds nifty, you think, but you are quick with some reason it can't work for your business. Yours is more mundane. Or hotly competitive. Or must be mass advertised. Or, for some reason, simply cannot be re-crafted into a process like this. Your conviction is that you must remain in the business of selling, not diagnosing and prescribing, and certainly not having your prescriptions accepted without resistance. That is your choice to make, and given that you have paid less than a foursome's tab at Starbucks for this little book, I'm not going to exert a ton of effort fighting your resistance. I will tell you just a few short stories, though.

The Million-Dollar Dog's Home Away from Home

My wife and I own a Schnoodle dog, which I call "The Million-Dollar Dog," because she is spoiled like a diva heiress. When we needed to board her to travel, there was no way any ordinary kennel would do. We located an upscale doggie hotel near our Ohio home, I believe initially by searching advertisements in this service category. When she called to get information, Carla was politely informed that no new clients were accepted without first having a full informational tour of the facility, and that such tours were conducted only once a day, at 4:00 P.M. Just stop there for a minute. This is, basically, a dog kennel. In a suburb of Cleveland, Ohio, not Beverly Hills or The Hamptons. And they are *dictating* to prospective customers how they may become customers, and the one and only time during the day they may come in. *A dog kennel.* Later, the dog was required to audition and get a psych exam, to determine if participation in group playdates was appropriate. In The Million-Dollar Dog's case, it was not. She is too territorial and aggressive, traits I imagine she picked up from me. Thus, individual playtimes several times per day were part of the prescribed stay plan, at extra fees, naturally. There's more. I won't belabor. Should you wish to see this, visit www.thebarkleypethotel.com.

In Truth, He's Just a Real Estate Salesman, Isn't He?

Story #2. Darin Garman sells heartland-of-America real estate investments, mostly apartment buildings and commercial properties or partnership pieces thereof, mostly in Cedar Rapids, Iowa, to investors, including many first-time real estate investors, from all across the country and even overseas. Over 80% invest without ever meeting him in person, ever visiting Cedar Rapids. They decide and sign documents at a distance, send their tens or hundreds of thousands of dollars by FedEx or wire transfer. Many new investors are now referrals from clients, but still, about half originate from his online and offline advertising, so he starts at zero trust and must get to high trust. He has developed his own media platform and feeder system somewhat modeled after mine. He requires investors to pay membership fees just to be permitted to be his client, somewhat akin to concierge medical practices. He has a well-defined intake process for new clients they must conform to, much like The Barkley Pet Hotel does. For most investors, he is providing these investment opportunities within the context of financial security, retirement, income for life, and tax management planning; thus he is engaged in the diagnostic and prescriptive process, somewhat like Matt is. Place helps him in creating trust and he develops trust by Personality and Process.

The Story of the Now-Famous "Carpet Audit"

Last story. Joe Polish was once, long ago, a dead-broke and struggling carpet cleaner, surviving job to job, selling at the cheapest prices to get those jobs. Joe turned his carpet cleaning business around, then went on to become a "marketing guru" to that industry—and, over years, has installed his advertising, marketing, and sales methods and tools in thousands of carpet cleaning businesses in every city, burg, nook, and cranny in America and more than a dozen foreign countries. Quite a few carpet cleaning business operators pay $10,000.00 to $30,000.00 a year to be in groups coached by Joe and his elite team. Joe has gone far beyond that industry and, in recent years, become a strategic coach and "idea man" for a wide variety of entrepreneurs and celebrities. One of the tactics that began this ascension, back in his original carpet cleaning business, was what we termed a "carpet audit." This is the diagnostic process performed in the home by the expert technician, to determine exactly what is needed in each place, at each spot, to restore the carpet to like-new appearance and condition. The technician even plants little, different-colored flags on the carpet, then walks the homeowner from flag to flag, explaining the varying nature and severity of the soiling or stain at that spot and what must be done to eradicate it. Ultimately, of course, a whole house carpet cleaning, restoration, and ongoing maintenance prescription is issued.

It has been a lot of years now, but I believe I suggested the language—*carpet audit*—to Joe. I can tell you definitively where I got the idea. One of my very first clients ever was a company called Brookside Laboratories. Their customers were family-owned farms throughout the agricultural belt in Ohio and neighboring states. The service they sold was scientific soil analysis. Their tech collected soil samples from many, varied spots all over the client's farm. The lab analyzed these collected samples. After diagnosis, the lab presented the farmer with a color-coded map of his fields, prescribing different mixes of seed, fertilizer, nutrients, and other supplements that would maximize the yield of the crop planted there. Every farmer is a small business owner. The farmer is eminently familiar with taxes, his accountant, and the IRS—he knows the term "audit." For Brookside, I coined the term "soil fertility audit." Years later, when Joe and I were scheming to make the process of selling carpet cleaning in a different and more sophisticated way, to escape the tyranny of competitively advertised, how-low-can-you-go pricing, we landed on diagnosis and prescription, I suggested the audit, and I believe he imagined the colored flags. In any case, with foggy memory, what the heck, I'll claim the credit! And I have been very helpful to Joe and his businesses. At one point, a few years ago, out of the blue, he gifted me a brand-new automobile as a thank-you note. (I'm sorry to say not everybody I've helped get rich or much richer has such undying gratitude.)

Now, consider the heroes of these stories. The operator of *a dog boarding kennel* near Cleveland, Ohio. A *real estate salesman* in Iowa. The operator of a *carpet cleaning business* in Phoenix, Arizona: All found ways to switch from a sales model to a diagnosis and prescription model. If they can, and you insist you can't, the obstacle isn't the nature of your business. It's the nature of your thinking.

What Place Do You Want, in Your Prospect's Mind?

Finally, let's loop back to the matter of trust. That the last thing in the world you want to be identified as is a salesman. I'll broaden that, to somebody engaged in a sales scenario, in the selling of propositions, products, and services. If that's what you are understood to be and to be doing, you automatically, unavoidably place yourself in a low-trust position. You then must fight to overcome that handicap. You can. You can certainly make a good living waging that fight day in, day out, with cleverness and iron-will persistence and dogged effort. But if you will get yourself identified as a "doctor" engaged in diagnosis and prescription, your need for the iron will to wage the endless war against resistance is minimized, because you automatically ascend to a high-trust position.

CHAPTER 22

The Role of Proof

Originally appearing as Chapter 18 from
No B.S. Trust-Based Marketing

Just about everybody reading this book is familiar with customer testimonials. They are ever-present. Many advertisers and marketers use them. As I am writing this, Ford has an excellent series of TV commercials airing, entirely featuring "real customers" talking about their happiness with their Fords, or, in some, just how impressed they are with them as a result of Swap-Your-Ride test drives. I consider customer testimony one of the most powerful trust-based marketing tools of all. Which makes what I'm about to do very unusual—I'm omitting discussion of them from this book. (I refer you to Chapter 8 of the book *No B.S. Sales Success in the New Economy*.)

In a few fields, like Matt's, the use of customer satisfaction testimonials is actually prohibited by law. In others, recent Federal

Trade Commission regulations and expansion of regulatory authority have made the use of testimonials more difficult. (You may want information about this from www.ftc.gov.) Still, in most product and service categories, you will see customer testimonials commonly used—as they should be.

In place of another discussion of the most commonly used sort of proof, the customer testimonial, I want to expand your thinking to a more comprehensive approach to proving your case to your customers or clients. In a legal case, both eyewitnesses and character witnesses are used to the fullest extent possible— the functional equivalent of the customer testimonial—but no prosecutor or defense attorney worth his salt relies only on such "real people" witnesses. Instead, every kind of proof that can be had is used, for much is at stake.

Elsewhere in *No B.S. Trust-Based Marketing*, Matt mentions the use of the expert witness, and I discuss the importance of Demonstration. There is also scientific or faux-scientific evidence available for all sorts of products. As an example of faux-science evidence, there's a legendary marketing premise that has sold freighters full of shark cartilage nutritional supplements: "Sharks Don't Get Cancer!" This is accurate, but it's a very unscientific leap from that fact to the idea that by eating shark cartilage, humans get immunity from cancer. Nevertheless, millions of people made that leap and considered that single fact as "proof of concept." A similar leap used in B2B is: a) *Inc.* magazine is credible and trustworthy and b) our company is on the *Inc.* "500 List," therefore c) our company is credible, trustworthy, and worthy of investment.

There is proof by popularity and sheer numbers, illustrated in Figure 22.1 on page 226. Even celebrity or celebrity endorsement can stand as proof in many consumers' minds. An excellent educational exercise is to become interested in and alert to all the different ways that advertisers and marketers present proof. A good tactical exercise is to apply as many different kinds of proof to your marketing as possible. But here, I'm going to talk about why and how proof is best used, in the context of trust-based marketing . . .

There are four basic kinds of proof that could be important for you to use:

1. Proof of Concept
2. Proof of Personal Relevance
3. Proof of Promised Benefits and Outcomes
4. Proof of Superiority

Proof of Concept

Too often, we erroneously take for granted acceptance of the underlying concepts that drive our businesses. In Matt's business, for example, the concept of having a single, trusted financial advisor coordinating one's financial plans, investments, and funding of retirement is assumed, as advisors compete with each other. But what if the prospect is merely open to but not yet convinced of the wisdom or necessity of that concept? There was a time when travel by seafaring cruise liner or airplane had to be proven safe as a concept or generic, before you could sell competing providers' benefits, fares, or destinations. In one of my businesses, business coaching, many too quickly leap past acceptance of the concept to selling their particular programs, when, first, the concept of having a business coach or being in a coach-led mastermind group needs to be sold. In Figure 22.1 on page 226, you'll find a piece first published in a magazine I controlled, then subsequently used by me and many of my clients as Proof of Concept for coaching. Don't miss the use of borrowed trust via Arnold Palmer.

Another way to think about this is as the formula: a) for you to be trusted, first b) your concept(s) must be trusted.

FIGURE 22.1: Proof of Concept Example

Example of "Proof of Concept" for Business Coaching—Using Borrowed
Trust from Champion Golfer Arnold Palmer, from celebrated success author
Napoleon Hill, and from *Newsweek* magazine.

"I've always made a total
effort, even when the odds
seemed entirely against me.
I never quit trying. I never
felt that I didn't have a
chance to win."

-Arnold Palmer

Origins Of Mastermind Groups

Many coaching programs feature "Mastermind Meetings". Typically with 20 or fewer members, who share experiences and ideas, serve as each others' sounding boards, gentle critics, tough questioners, and in some cases, assist each other with contacts and opportunities. One of the biggest sources of conspiration for the formation of such groups comes from the writings of Napoleon Hill, in his books 'Laws Of Success' and 'Think And Grow Rich', in which he described the powerful mastermind alliance formed by Thomas Edison, Henry Ford and Harvey Firestone. I learned about other aspects of mastermind groups from a number of sources, including Joe Mancuso, expert on family business, and founder of the C.E.O. Clubs, and from a backstage conversation with Henry Kissinger.

"A Master-Mind maybe created through the bringing together and blending, in the spirit of perfect harmony, two or more minds. Out of this blending the chemistry of the mind creates a third mind which may be appropriated and used by one or all"

-Napoleon Hill, 'Laws Of Success'

Early in my career, I saw Arnold Palmer interviewed, and heard about his table, where he mounted as insets the medallions he won in golf tournaments. Each time Palmer won another tournament and brought home another medallion, at the same time he mounted it into the table's surface, he carved out an empty circle for the next medallion. I believe in and teach the use of Visual Psychological Triggers for self-motivation, and that's a terrific example I've emulated one way or another ever since I heard about it. Presently, if you are in my home and see the wall where my win photos are displayed, from my harness racing drives, you'll see all the wins in chronological succession, and one empty frame hung with nothing behind its glass, waiting for the next win picture.

-Dan Kennedy

Reprinted from *Renegade Millionaire* magazine, Spring 2006. All rights reserved.

FIGURE 22.1: Proof of Concept Example, continued

Why Do Top Performers Use Coaches?

- by Dan S. Kennedy

When Arnold Palmer needed to "tune-up" his game, to compensate for his age, he sought out a 26yr old 'swing coach'. Everybody who follows golf knows about the troubles Tiger had with his game after parting with his coach, Butch Harmon. We know most athletes in every sport use coaches, personal trainers and sports psychologists. But do sales professionals and entrepreneurs need coaches too?

Having personally had over 200 high-flying entrepreneurs, small business owners, salespeople and self-employed professionals participate in my coaching groups and telecoaching programs over the past 8 years - some for all 8 years, and been the coach and advisor to nearly 100 business coaches in different fields, I think I have a pretty good understanding of why coaching seems to work so well for entrepreneurs, and why you might want a coach of your own. There are six reasons:

Being Held Accountable
Being Questioned And Challenged
Being Listened To
Being Recognized For Your Achievements
Being Accepted
Being Motivated

Different people have different needs at different times in their lives, but I find most entrepreneurs share all six of these to varying degrees.

Accountability

On many occasions, as a speaker, I was on programs with, and had coach 'green room' time with legendary athletes like Joe Montana, Troy Aikman, Olympian Mary Lou Retton, George Foreman, and coaches like Tom Landry, Lou Holtz, and Jimmy Johnson. The athletes all agreed that high performers personally held themselves to gruelingly high standards, but even so, were it not for feeling accountable to teammates, fans and coaches, and being held accountable by their coach or coaches, who monitored their statistics, replayed film of miss-judgements and mistakes, analyzed and assessed their performance, they would never have reached the levels of success they did. The Jobs of entrepreneurship is good news and bad news. You're your own boss! Having a coach guide you in committing to doing, changing, testing certain things between now and the next call or meeting, then having you report on those things to guarantee to improve your follow-through on your own best ideas! In short, accountability automatically improves performance and results.

Questioned and Challenged

The more successful you are, the less likely the people who work for you or are around all the time are to challenge your ideas. It's easy to end up surrounded by 'yes men', the outside coach with no axe to grind can be both objective and

frank. He can ask the provocative questions that force you to defend your idea. If you can, that's valuable. If you can't, that's valuable too.

Listened To

A Newsweek magazine article about professional business/life coaches described us as "part therapist, part consultant". A lot of entrepreneurs have no one to talk to about business OR personal matters who dare "let their hair down with"... who will listen without any agenda. I often find that a client will talk his way to his own terrific answer, solution or plan of action if I'll just listen. Having a coach with life and business experience relevant to your own, who is personally successful, who can relate to you and who you can relate to is extremely beneficial.

Being Recognized For Your Achievements

Everybody needs recognition and celebration - but to whom can the entrepreneur brag? Certainly not to his employees, his competitors, his vendors. Since most of the people I and the coaches I advise work with are "Renegades", using unorthodox marketing strategies, most of the people around them actually disapprove of a lot of what's working, even if they grudgingly acknowledge the results. And often, if the owner of the business takes the garish black on neon green investiture justified he spent days slaving over; that just pulled a 14-to-1 ROI home to stash his wife and kids', he gets a very disinterested response. A 'that's nice, dear' - not a 'holy crap! 14 - 1! You're a genius! Can I get a copy of that?' Having a 'knowledgeable coach' and associate, being part of a coaching/mastermind group gives everyone of us an appreciative audience who "gets it", who understands our accomplishments, and is able and willing to celebrate our achievements because they are secure in their own success.

Being Accepted

I call no need successful clients (and myself) 'Renegade Millionaires' because we violate just about every norm of our industries and professions... we are actually quite dysfunctional in one way or another... we think and talk differently than almost everyone around us in our day-to-day lives. Because of this, a lot of successful entrepreneurs actually suffer silent frustration and loneliness. In many instances, we can't even explain what we do to our children! Feeling like 'the fish out of water' most of one's

waking hours is not all that pleasant. That's why being part of a coaching/mastermind group with like-minded 'Renegades' is so invigorating. One of the core human needs is to be accepted for who you are, without need of mask or cautious editing of expressed thought.

Being Motivated

Surely a top pro athlete being paid millions of dollars to play a game doesn't need 'motivated' but, actually the fact that they are paid millions, win, lose or draw, means they do need a great deal of other motivation to do all the behind-the-scenes hard work required for peak performance on the field. In almost every locker room after every game, grown men who are paid millions to play their games are awarded game balls. Coaches cry, beg, alta bust', nudge, intimidate, all motivation is self-motivation, but there's definitely contributions made by the people and ideas you associate with, the involvements you're in, the successes of others you're exposed to.

What Exactly Is Business/Life Coaching?

Most of the industry-specific advisors I work with deliver coaching much the same as I do, with different 'levels' appropriate for different people. The most common options begin with simple group tele-seminars or classes often with open question/answer for the participants, sometimes support with website resources or communities. Next, plus some 1-on-1 tele-coaching. Next, all that plus periodic mastermind group meetings. At the highest levels, people travel from all over the country to attend the meetings. New in 2006, I'm also organizing local Dan Kennedy 'Study Groups' combining education, mastermind meetings and coaching facilitated by someone in each city. Information about Kennedy and Glazer-Kennedy programs can be found at www.renegademillionairemarketing.com.

Why Should You 'Plug-In' To One Or More Coaches And Coaching Programs?

If any or all of the six needs I described apply to you, then the best investment you'll ever make is finding and joining one or even several appropriate coaching programs!

Proof of Personal Relevance

Again, to use the above examples, just because I accept financial planning or the use of an advisor or vacationing on a cruise ship as safe, enjoyable, and popular, or business coaching as useful, all as proven concepts, does not mean I accept them as good for *me*. I may accept that thousands love going on cruises, but think that I won't for any number of reasons, including seasickness, claustrophobia, fear of water, eating at designated times with strangers, etc. I may accept that many need and benefit from having a financial advisor, but may feel I won't, for any number of reasons, perhaps that I have too small a nest egg, or am a control freak and will be uncomfortable delegating authority, or that I'm too old and needed that help sooner. Proof of Concept is foundational, but it needs to be connected to Proof of Personal Relevance.

This can loop back to the tactical tool I have chosen not to discuss: Testimonials from people with precisely the same situation and concerns, in sufficient number, with good believability, can serve as Proof of Personal Relevance. But there are many ways to prove this, too, and none should be neglected, all used. If, for example, we are trying to convince a skeptical and recalcitrant senior to begin using Facebook, we can use statistical facts—that the fastest-growing segment of new Facebook users is 60 years of age and up; we can focus on features and uses of Facebook most popular with seniors—like a different way to scrapbook, involvement with grandkids, keeping up with old friends who live great distances away; we can create a story or step-by-step diary of a new Facebook user's experiences, that user matched with the senior we're trying to convince; we could even engineer personal Demonstration. We might use free trial of a few functions set up for the person; in selling, this is called "puppy dogging," and it was once used to popularize odd, new-fangled things like cars, phones, and TV sets; installed or given to people to use for a few days, a weekend, or a week, then removed and taken back if the person didn't come to love them, like putting a puppy dog in someone's home for the weekend then trying to take it back from the kids. If you've never had a puppy dog, and think you wouldn't want one, you might very well find yourself proven wrong in just a few days with a puppy put in your care.

Proof of Promised Benefits and Outcomes

Obviously, to buy, buyers have to feel very confident and reassured, if not rock-solid certain, that the promised and hoped for benefits and outcomes will occur for him.

This is why the GKIC Members and brilliant marketers selling $4,000.00 to $20,000.00 mattresses created The Dream Room in their store (www.gardnersmattressandmore.com), where a customer checks in and enjoys a nap for up to four hours, in a luxury suite, in complete privacy, complete with milk 'n' cookies. You really can't trust a mattress after just stretching out on it for a few minutes, then lying on the next one, and the next. You can only trust it after you've slept on it. Yes, again, a plethora of customer testimonials, especially specific ones about back pain or insomnia resolved, are very helpful. But the only real proof is in the sleeping.

When I was still actively seeking speaking engagements from new clients, I made a point of inviting and working hard-to-get meeting planners who might hire me to sit in on events where I was speaking for a client. If I was going to travel to a distant city to speak for a client's group, I wanted several prospective clients who might book me in that audience, to see living proof of the benefits they would want: my prowess, enthusiastic response of an audience, etc. Sure, client testimonials were a useful tool, as can be "demo" audio CDs and DVDs, credibility and authority tools like books, articles, awards, professional designations. But nothing serves as better proof than actually experiencing the outcomes the prospect desires.

Proof of Superiority

Once somebody has accepted a means of meeting need or desire as a proven, safe concept, and been educated about the existence of a provider, he will quite naturally wonder what other providers and choices may be available. At some point, the issue of choice will always arise. Many tactical tools apply— like Leadership Position and Demonstration. Virtually everything in this book is linked to Proof of Superiority, because the ultimate superior position is: *most trusted.*

Preponderance of Proof

In battle, it's best to have *overwhelming* force. The battle for trust in decidedly un-trusting times, to be secured from understandably anxious, skeptical, suspicious, worried, and mistrustful prospects is best waged with overwhelming proof. That means three things: Quantity, Quality, and *Diversity.* The last may be the pathway to greatest advantage: providing as many different forms of proof in each of the above four categories as you possibly can.

CHAPTER 23

Meet the
LEB/S Market

Originally appearing as Chapter 1 from
No B.S. Guide to Marketing to Leading-Edge
Boomers and Seniors

Americans born between 1946 and 1964 number nearly 80 million and make up about 26% of the U.S. population. Roughly one in four consumers is a boomer. Obviously, these boomers will become seniors, thus "the age wave" will dominate this economy and this marketplace for many years to come. Every day, for the next 18 years, 8,000 to 10,000 boomers will reach age 65. In each of those years, about 3 million.

Younger boomers, age 48 to 57, exhibit significantly different attitudes and behaviors than do older, or leading-edge, boomers, age 58 to 66. This book focuses on the leading-edge boomers, hereinafter referred to as LE-boomers, and on seniors, who have much in common. When no distinction is being made, we'll be referring to them as LEB/S. Mac Brand, partner in Bellwether Food

Group, says, "The lines between seniors and baby boomers are blurring." Jim Gilmartin, founder of Coming of Age, Inc., points out that the combined boomer+senior consumer population tops 117 million, "forming the largest economic group in America, with annual spending power of more than $2 trillion."

What do LEB/S consumers buy? Just about everything, and more of it, at higher average prices than any other consumers. Averaged from research from multiple sources, here are my own numbers, rounded off, in some example categories (percentage of total revenue of the category):

Home Furnishings	55%
Luxury Real Estate	70%
Support of the Arts	60%
Mail-Order Catalogs	75%
Luxury Travel	80%
Charitable Donations	65%
Women's Apparel	50%

Oddly, despite LEB/S accounting for more than half the sales in just about every product and service category, advertising, marketing, and often even product development is still weighted heavily toward other target demographics. This may reflect some strategic thinking; worry about dependency on customers dying off. It more likely reflects companies turning over these decisions to young and even very young people who have little interest in or respect for these consumers.

It is generally true: As restaurants go, so goes the economy. U.S. restaurant industry growth is predicted to fall short of a miserly 1% a year through 2019, not even keeping pace with population growth, according to the "Future of Foodservice Study" reported in *Nation's Restaurant News*. The reason for the near zero growth is the dominance of the LEB/S population. As they grow older, they dine out less, they spend less when they do dine out, and they have different interests in dining. The chief author of the study, Bonnie Riggs, says that "the big competitor is the home. They find it not only cheaper to eat at home, but they believe it tastes better, they can do it more leisurely, and they can eat healthier at home."

My own take on this adds a fourth factor, I think grossly underestimated by the restaurant industry, and a central key to success with LEB/S presented by this book: **Restaurants' delivery of one generic experience for all age groups is unappealing, and is more than enough to tip the scales in favor of "Let's just stay home** *and avoid the aggravation."* LEB/S prefer a relatively quiet, orderly dining experience, so being seated near a family with young children, placed in a noisy environment, hemmed into too-tight quarters, being asked to stand around waiting for a table (holding *a device* that summons them when a table becomes available), feeling hurried at their table, even having a young waitstaff that is impatient or ill-informed all serve up a dissatisfying experience. The answer is in the overarching premise of this book: If you want the LEB/S consumers, you are going to have to create and deliver an experience matched with their preferences, or at minimum, one absent factors they find annoying and off-putting.

It's Complicated

The LEB/S population is far from one homogeneous group. It contains leading-edge boomers in second, third, etc. marriages, many with younger partners, some starting second families, but also empty-nesters and re-nesters with adult children moving back in—sometimes with their young kids in tow—caregivers taking on responsibility for adult parents, retirees, widows and widowers, healthy and active, ill and

infirm, rich and poor. Different kinds of LEB/S have different issues, i.e., buying motives, in their lives. One key point
from this: Few businesses can treat LEB/S as a single market
with one-size-fits-all products and services, advertising and
marketing. Instead, most need to select a segment or segments
within LEB/S to focus on.

With regard to money and spending power, one of the
leading consumer research organizations, Pew, found boomers to be the age group most likely to say they took significant
losses on investments during the recession, beginning in 2008.
Sixty percent of the LE-boomers said they might need to post-
pone planned retirement. Even relatively affluent LE-boomers
have significant concerns about losses suffered during the
recession, from investments or income budgeted to go to
retirement savings. A survey of millionaires for the Centurion
Group of financial advisors found that the number-one worry
of over 60% was overspending, thus running out of money
with too many years left on the clock. Still, over half the
nation's wealth and more of its discretionary spending power
is in the hands of LEB/S.

Convergence of LEB/S and Affluent Consumers

When I wrote the first edition of the book *No B.S. Marketing to the
Affluent* in 2008, I made much of the concentration of both wealth
and discretionary spending power into the hands of the LEB/S population. What was foreseen and documented then is proving true
to the nth degree. Currently, according to the Ipsos Mendelsohn
Affluent Generations Study (www.ipsos.com), four in ten affluents
are boomers—households with median income of $140,000.00, al-
though the income alone is deceiving, as 46% of this group have
net worths exceeding $2 million. This puts the affluent boomers
at about 25 million. Another 9% of U.S. affluence is in the hands of

seniors, putting the combined LEB/S control of the money in the 50% neighborhood. To say it another way, simply, one out of every two dollars available to advertisers, marketers, merchants, and service providers is in the wallets of LEB/S.

LEB/S spending varies widely. The more affluent LEB/S, as the CEO of https:// AgeWave.com, Dr. Ken Dychtwald, puts it, make "the psychological shift from acquiring more material pos-

Resource

Book available at all booksellers.

sessions to *a desire to purchase* enjoyable, satisfying, and memorable experiences." Good news for marketers: They are not *stopping* spending as previous generations of seniors did. Not even spending that reluctantly. Just spending differently for different reasons.

Younger boomers as well as some LE-boomers have been trading down during the recession, when, in the past, this would have been a group almost exclusively making upward mobility purchases, trading up in most categories. A company like McDonald's has been seen attempting to capitalize on this trend with its McCafé specialty coffees and beverages—an open invitation to Starbucks' customers.

The New Senior

For the New Senior, classic or traditional age-defined attitudes and behaviors are pushed further along in years. Jim Gilmartin, founder of Coming of Age, Inc., a marketing agency specializing in the LEB/S market, cautions against using traditional descriptive language. "Be careful what you call them. Euphemisms like 'elder' or 'of a certain age' may not go over well. Many have become upset with being labeled."

This population of seniors is fighting age more than any previous generation, refusing to go quietly into the good night. It has paraded out the "60 is the new 40," now "70 is the new 50" lines, a statement of aspiration if not determined intent. In the skin-care products industry, where I do some consulting and advertising copywriting work, we see the average age of the consumer creeping up. One company selling anti-wrinkle potions has seen its average buyer age move from 57 to 69 in just five years, and further, is finding the older buyer group easier to close on the incoming calls, i.e., delivering a better prospect-to-buyer conversion rate and lower cost per sale, and exhibiting less price resistance. Parallel changes are occurring in cosmetic surgery and cosmetic dentistry.

A big aspiration among LEB/S is quality of life, not just longevity. Seniors are living longer, and are healthy for more years, ill and infirm for fewer years, than in previous generations. The health-care industry's term for this is "compression of morbidity." For a wide spectrum of businesses, this means two things: First, there is greater long-term or lifetime customer value in relationships with LEB/S consumers than there would have been a generation ago, so catering to them makes better business sense than ever before. Second, seniors will remain mobile and actively interested longer in products, services, and experiences that they have historically deserted at age 65.

An Assortment of Facts

How LEB/S *think*—that's the real key to successfully marketing to them. This quick list from the "2010 Del Webb Baby Boomer Survey" conducted by Del Webb, the owner and developer of many retirement communities, offers insight into how they think about themselves . . .

- Boomers set the benchmark of "old age" at—hold your breath—80.
- There is considerable distance between their chronological age and the age they identify with, which is 15 years younger. That has profound bearing on photos and images placed in advertising, the age and appearance of actors or celebrities used in commercials, language used by copywriters. Make a big note of this.
- More than 50% of boomers say they exercise regularly, and feel they are in better shape than they were some years ago.
- Trailing-edge boomers believe they need to accumulate more savings than LE-boomers. Nearly half are skeptical of government benefits being available when they become seniors.
- 72% of boomers intend to keep working past the classic retirement age of 65.
- In their thinking about retirement migration, a warm and sunny climate is not the chief magnet as it has long been for generations of seniors. Instead, cost of living and access to health care are more important.

How Will You Prosper Embracing the Opportunities Presented by the LEB/S Markets?

This book is not an exhaustive and comprehensive examination. I'm not even sure such a thing is possible. Successfully marketing to LEB/S is more a multilayered project than a subject. Our primary purpose here is to be *provocative*: to get you thinking about where you fit in, what opportunities may exist and be best for you, so that you can define your own path forward and then get to work, including gathering the specific information you need, probably from a myriad of sources.

Whether you are left out of the Age/Profit Wave, merely get small benefit by accident, by just being there, or develop a well-organized strategy to mine riches from different segments of this consumer population depends on you and what you do.

After I wrote the first edition of the *No B.S. Marketing to the Affluent* book in 2008, it became clear that couldn't be "done" in a single book either, but it was more an ongoing project. On my end, it begat a series of small group summits, one of which is available in product form now at https://MagneticMarketing.com, and a continuing monthly *No B.S. Marketing to the Affluent Letter*. It led to the book in the No B.S. series immediately preceding this one, *No B.S. Trust-Based Marketing*, which grew out of intimate work with financial advisors, health-care professionals, and others marketing to affluent LEB/S clients. That led to this. It is all an interconnected work in progress. When Einstein was asked how he made his breakthrough scientific discoveries, he replied, "I grope." There is a tendency to want a simple, 1–2–3 recipe and a set of fill-in-the-blanks templates for marketing to a target audience, but I'm afraid real success can't be put into a single, little box. We're hopeful you'll become as fascinated with the opportunities presented by the Age/Profit Wave as we are, and join us in—groping.

A Note About the Rest of the Wave

The explosive growth and impact on markets of LEB/S is not exclusive to America. Asia has 1.2 billion baby boomers. By 2050, the number of people over age 60 in Asia will exceed that number. The combined segment of that population 50+ now controls 55% of all the consumer spending and 80% of the wealth. There is approximately $11 trillion U.S. under their control.

According to the "Investing in Asia Conference's Report," the percentages of spending and wealth will continue to shift to the 50-and-over group in coming years. Europe offers a similar situation. While this book is U.S.-focused with its specific information, the overarching strategies apply anywhere there is spending power and net worth concentrated in the hands of LEB/S.

CHAPTER 24

The Power of Profiling

Originally appearing as Chapter 8 from
*No B.S. Guide to Marketing to Leading-Edge
Boomers and Seniors*

In this book, Chip Kessler and I have been making some sweeping generalizations about LEB/S consumers. These are necessary because this is a book intended for broad diversity of business owners, entrepreneurs, and professionals. But you have an avatar client, an ideal customer, a very particular person within LEB/S who lives in your particular community or operates in your industry. He is an individual, not a human envelope filled with statistics. The more clarity you get about your customer, the better you can serve him, the more successfully and affordably you can attract and acquire him.

There are many different ways to subdivide any market. There are niches and subculture. A niche is occupational or vocational. Auto mechanics are in an occupational niche, as are auto repair shop owners; however, the owners and mechanics think very differently about many things, probably pay different prices for shirts, dine at different kinds of restaurants, and so on, and are likely to carry those differences all the way into retirement. A subculture has to do with interests, shared experiences, and backgrounds. College alumni: subculture. Tea Party: subculture. Harley-Davidson owners: subculture. (Side note: LEB/S are the top Harley-Davidson buyers.) There are demographics: Age. Gender. Marital status. Life cycles, and life-passages positions, such as LE-boomer, trailing-edge boomer, and senior. Income and wealth differential.

Geography can be overrated and underrated. Geo-demographic profiling is based on the idea that you are where you live, from the old tenet that birds of a feather flock together. Companies now spend large sums having their customer files run through geo-demo analytics, dividing them into 50 to 65 different "clusters" and about a dozen "social groups." Different analytics companies use different terminology for the groups, such as Suburban Status Seekers and Affluent Traditionalists. This is pitched as a "simple way to identify, understand, and target consumers." It is simple, but it is also severely flawed, and, by and large, I am not a fan. For certain kinds of fairly large consumer marketers it has a place, and it can provide data that, if used in concert with other data, is helpful. It can at least be used to rule out lowest probability clusters for direct mail. It can be used to tweak copy, broadly. But it is cutting-edge science hooked to a very antiquated idea: that we cluster together by physical neighborhoods. This is just not so. While I am rather reclusive, I know a few things about my own immediate neighbors. Our homes all cost about the same and look about the same, but mine houses a large home office and meeting space in its basement; a neighbor's houses a pool table and poker room. Most here are LE-boomers, a couple are seniors, a couple are younger, one is in a minority group, all others are white. My income is at least five times any of the neighbors' and I know it to be a full ten times at least one of them. I am the only one who owns classic cars. Or racehorses. Only one owns a boat. One is a constant world traveler. I abhor international travel. Need I go on?

Today, the birds flock together on social media more so than by neighborhoods. Sure, parents with young children tend to cluster around schools. That sort of thing is obvious. But again, generalizing about all the parents in a radius around a school is less viable than it was a decade ago. Diversity has invaded a great many neighborhoods in many ways.

There is an excellent, more in-depth discussion of segmentation in the book *Marketing to the Mindset of Boomers and Their Elders* by Carol Morgan. We are in agreement in skepticism about simplified marketing by geo-demo clusters. We also share agreement on another key point: A segmentation strategy should be based on multiple, redundant measures. In other words, more than one source of information overlapped with another is best. I'm not often looking for simple. I'm looking for most effective.

Data mining as well as psychographic mining of your own customers—and of only your best clients you'd most like to clone—is always a good start. Maybe they do cluster geographically. Maybe they are within a tight age range within the LEB/S market. Maybe they all golf. Data may be in your records. The fact that they all golf or attend the theater or vacation in Florida may only be found by asking, by surveying, by gathering information.

Ultimately, you should build a profile of your customer target.

One of the very best examples of this kind of profiling, that shocks many when I show it to them because it strikes them as predatory, is from the famous pastor Rick Warren. You should recognize him as the author of the mega-bestselling book *The Purpose Driven Life*. He is the founder of the huge

Saddleback Church. You should obtain and study his not-so-famous book *The Purpose Driven Church*. It is a marketing manual for pastors. In it he describes in stark and specific detail the profile of "Saddleback Sam," their ideal parishioner, whom they deliberately target—ignoring and excluding a lot of other people. He teaches each pastor to create such a profile.

Carol Morgan advances some lifestyle/life-passages-based profiles for LEB/S. I'll just list them and describe them as briefly as possible, as thought-starters for how you might categorize your customers/target customers:

- *Upbeat Enjoyers.* Optimistic, active, involved. Interested in looking, feeling, and acting younger than their years. Consider retirement a continuation of life, not a destination point marked by a stop sign.
- *Insecures.* Pessimistic, deeply troubled by their lack of financial success and/or by ill health. They view society as obsessed with youth and beauty, and discriminatory and unjust toward them.
- *Threatened Actives.* Concerned with preserving their independence, remaining in their own homes, continuing to drive their own cars. Have a rather traditional attitude toward retirement and a resigned acceptance of aging.
- *Financial Positives.* Responsible, organized planners, conservatively invested, trying not to work in retirement. Most receptive to relocating and possibly moving into a retirement community.

As you can see, these are incomplete profiles. You can also see they might now live in the same zip code or even on the same street, they might even have had similar starting points in life, and other similarities, but it's their profound differences that matter. If you are going to resonate with them, you must speak to each one very differently. Or if you want one as your customer, you must be willing to repel the others and design everything you say and do to match the one desired. In her book, Morgan builds profiles like these, but specific to different product/service segments, such as travel, in which there are Highway Wanderers but also Pampered Relaxers and Global Explorers.

Because I am a price strategy guy, I would think in terms of different consumers' thinking about price. There are, for example, Committed Coupon Clippers, who will always buy by price and will choose brands, pick restaurants, etc. based on

Resource

Highly recommended! My book with Jason Marrs on price, profit, and power.

price or on actually having a coupon in hand. There are Value Buyers, who are concerned with price, but not in a vacuum. There are Complex Buyers, who place many other factors ahead of price, such as expertise, service, and convenience. There are Status Buyers and Elitists. Etc. Most people move about a bit from one of these groups to another, depending on what they are buying.

Again, the more clarity and specificity you can get to with your profile of your desired LEB/S consumer, the better.

There are four chief ways to use your profile:

1. As basis for "attraction copy" in lead-generation advertising
2. In "elevator speech" prospecting, in person-to-person selling
3. In selecting and renting commercially available mailing lists and segments thereof
4. In message matching to segments

246 🌑 THE BEST OF NO B.S.

In lead-generation advertising, we often focus on the person we want to attract rather than the product or service being sold. The simplest template for these is the profile. For example:

TAX AND FINANCIAL ALERT FOR THE 55- TO 65-YEAR-OLD SMALL-BUSINESS OWNER CONCERNED WITH RETIREMENT OR FAMILY SUCCESSION ISSUES. If you own a small business worth at least $500,000.00 to $5 million, are getting serious about retirement, married with children or adult children, and unsure of the best strategic options for structuring safe, guaranteed income for life, the author of the bestselling book *Navigation Guide to Rich Retirement* and Executive Director of the Southwest Asset Preservation Center, William K. Stewart, has new, timely, and important information you need before making any decisions. See his 20-minute video presentation at EndOfIncome.com or call (000) 000-0000 to receive a free DVD sent by mail, no obligation, no salesperson involved. There may be a TAX TIME BOMB HIDING INSIDE YOUR SUCCESSFUL BUSINESS! Find out at www.xxxxxxxxxx.com.

As you can see, virtually nothing about the products or services offered is said. The ad is a construct of profile plus offer, little more. And it could even be further abbreviated to strip out the advertiser's identity:

TAX AND FINANCIAL ALERT FOR THE 55- TO 65-YEAR-OLD SMALL-BUSINESS OWNER CONCERNED WITH RETIREMENT OR FAMILY SUCCESSION ISSUES. If you own a small business worth at least $500,000.00 to $5 million, are getting serious about retirement, married with children or adult children, and unsure of the best strategic options for structuring safe, guar-anteed income for life, you should see the new, timely, and important 20-minute video presentation at EndOfIncome.com, or call (000) 000-0000 to receive a free DVD sent by mail, no obligation, no salesperson involved. There may be a TAX TIME BOMB HIDING INSIDE YOUR SUCCESSFUL BUSINESS! Find out at www.xxxxxxxxxx.com.

With the "elevator speech," the answer to "What do you do?" for cocktail party conversation, a very similar approach is used, placing the emphasis on the profile rather than the product or service, or instantly, easily dismissed description of your business or profession. Stick with this example, the answer would begin:

I work with 55- to 65-year-old small-business owners concerned with retirement or family succession issues, who own a business worth at least $500,000.00 to $5 million, are getting serious about retirement, are married with children or adult children, and unsure of the best strategic options for structuring safe, guaranteed income for life . . .

In renting commercially available mailing lists, the profile is essential to the search. The starting point for this, incidentally, is at www.SRDS.com. You can also learn a great deal from the list search and selection expert I and my clients work with, Craig Simpson, at www.simpson-direct.com.

Finally, the profile allows you to alter and match your basic message to different segments of lists. For example, here are slightly different blocks of copy from the outer envelopes, sent to different age segments of the same business owner and business magazine subscriber lists, for a product and membership offer for GKIC:

1. You worked hard to build your business and your life. Every success, earned. Don't you just wonder about the generation behind you and the world we live in? It seems

upside down: achievement punished, irresponsibility rewarded. Being an entrepreneur can make you feel like the odd man out . . .

2. You are working very hard to build your business—even sacrificing time with your family to do it. You have ideas, ambition, drive, determination . . .

3. Your friends, neighbors, most people your age are totally into their kids, family and entertainment, and recreation. To them, you're strange. You have ideas, ambition, drive. You're willing to invest endless hours in building your business . . .

You should be able to identify which paragraph is aimed at which age group: LEB/S, trailing-edge boomers, and the next age group behind the trailing-edge boomers. They were actually matched paragraph 1 to ages 55 to 65, paragraph 2 to 35 to 55, and paragraph 3 to 25 to 35. You should also be able to see how this demographic customization of the message matters and can lift the response rate.

Most marketers, particularly small-business level marketers, are not nearly this sophisticated. They cast overly broad, generic marketing messages to everybody within their target zip codes, at one website to which all traffic is routed, even to their own customers for whom they should have segmentation data. If you will make yourself more sophisticated, you'll gain competitive advantage and likely boost the profitability of your business as well.

The Power of Reality

There is academic theory, then there is reality.

Michael Lynn, a professor of the Cornell School of Hotel Administration, told *Nation's Restaurant News* that, "The old strategy of segmenting a marketplace and then appealing to different demographics—I don't buy it. Fundamentally, consumers don't differ that much from one another."

Professor Lynn is making a dangerously foolish statement.

First of all, demographic market or list segmentation is not an "old" strategy. In fact, in the direct-marketing world, the old power players were guys like me—the idea people, the copywriters. The new power players are the data mining wizards. My friend, the celebrated economist Harry Dent, Jr., has been more on-target than most with financial and societal predictions precisely because he focuses so heavily on the influence of demographics, and I strongly recommend reading Dent (www.HSDent.com).

Second, I can assure you, from millions of dollars of real-world marketing experience in place of academic theory, that nothing lifts response better than slicing and segmenting markets, lists, or audiences by demographics and by psychographics, and speaking to them differently. Contrary to the prof's assertion, I'll tell you that consumers differ enormously from one another. My friends involved in political campaigns and fundraising would laugh at the professor. They know that the population of northeast Ohio is profoundly different in an important array of attitudes and behaviors from the population of southern Ohio, and that East Clevelanders differ significantly from West Siders, that ethnicity matters, that

The Power of Reality

religious and political affiliations matter. Some media like TV tends to force generic, or "big net" messages, but a great deal of political marketing is about precision, with very different messages directed even to different mailboxes on the same street.

Nothing is more powerful in marketing than *customization*, and I'd say that is treble true with LEB/S (see Chapter 27). Demographics are an essential tool for customization.

CHAPTER 25

Advantages in Marketing to LEB/S

Originally appearing as Chapter 9 from
*No B.S. Guide to Marketing to Leading-Edge
Boomers and Seniors*

There are excellent reasons for preferring LEB/S as your target market, in addition to the fact that roughly half of all the money is in these hands. These are advantages you want to take full advantage of:

1. Classic credibility matters.
2. They accept advice from authority.
3. They prefer mail, open mail, read mail.
4. They will read lengthy material.
5. They value books, articles, and news media.
6. They will listen to/watch lengthy presentations.
7. They act responsibly, so they can be obligated.
8. They are courteous and generally can be trained to be good customers.

9. They are charitable.

10. They can be good centers of influence and sources of referrals.

Classic Credibility at Work

The younger the consumer, the less concern with classic credibility exists. If they're under 30, they have grown up online. Doing business with a bank formed yesterday, with no brick-and-mortar offices, is perfectly normal to them. A bank that was founded in 1913, survived the Great Depression, never defaulted to a single depositor, and has had offices in the community for 40 years has no advantage with them. Longevity is not persuasive, and may even be viewed as a detriment. This is the exact opposite mindset to that of the LEB/S. For those born from 1946 through the 1950s, "Our 25th year of service to the families of Oakbrook" means something. For older seniors, it means everything.

While I was writing this, my wife and I were discussing the ten-year warranty being offered by a particular company. She said, "That's IF they're around to honor it." That would not so quickly occur to our 40-year-old daughter, and it probably wouldn't occur to a 30-year-old at all.

To the LEB/S consumer, longevity can be translated into credibility, which can be translated into security and safety, a chief driver for seniors, and a significant driver for LE-boomers.

The same is true about other security statistics, like numbers of clients served, years clients have stayed, the size of a company. To the LEB/S, the ultimate credibility is what I call "Leadership Position." When you can define your company as THE leader in a category (even if you have to cleverly create the category), you have valuable credibility, thus security and safety to sell. My wife's skepticism about the ten-year warranty can be allayed with facts about that manufacturer's longevity and leadership position in its field—with her. But those same facts would be unpersuasive to much younger consumers. My client, the Guthy-Renker Corporation, owns this oddity with its famous acne treatment product, Proactiv®. It actually has the leadership position, as the #1 bestselling acne treatment, with great longevity, and connection to prominent dermatologists. These facts are meaningful to the parents of the teen and preteen users, although not nearly as useful as they would be if selling to the grandparents. But the same facts are utterly uninteresting to the teens and preteens. They only want to know if it works, how easy it is to use, and how fast it works. Their attention can be gained with endorsements from celebrities like Justin Bieber. But they have no patience for discussions of leadership position credibility.

Since this kind of credibility is persuasive to the LEB/S consumer, you want to make full use of whatever of it you have. If you have longevity, if you have leading citizens or institutions as customers, if yours is a third-generation family business, if you have leadership position, by all means trumpet it, and try not to omit it from any delivery of your advertising or sales message.

Because I Said So

LEB/S consumers were raised under the Because I Said So doctrine, and a good many parented, taught, and coached under the same doctrine. They are conditioned and accustomed to accept authority. Seniors, for example, are still significantly interested by political endorsements from their city's newspaper editors, civic groups, business groups, and their own political party's leaders, while, as you drop in age, these endorsements seem to be of no value to candidates whatsoever. Seniors are also the most supportive of the traditional doctrine of their particular church or religion. Seniors and a good percentage of LE-boomers tend to "do what the doctor tells them."

This conditioned behavior is useful to the advertiser, marketer, or sales professional who can establish authority and gain acceptance as an authority figure with LEB/S prospects and clientele. In my work with clients in various fields selling to LEB/S clients or patients, with a two-appointment selling process (diagnostic, then prescriptive), I have proven without exception that the acceptance of treatment or financial plan at that second appointment can be substantially improved by bestowing the trappings of authority on the advisor or doctor. These professionals' conversion percentages go up, and case sizes go up, and fee resistance goes down when we make them authors of books, guest experts seen on local or, better, national TV programs, and heard interviewed on local or, better, national radio programs, published in newspapers and financial magazines, placed on university or charity advisory boards, properly displaying these things in their offices, and sending prospects such material before and between appointments. In short, when the salesman ceases being the salesman and becomes the exalted authority, just like the doctor, his prescription is accepted without quarrel.

They Have Good Attention Span

Attention span matters, and the LEB/S consumer has more of it than any other consumers, so they will read long letters and articles, read books, watch full-length presentations, and listen to long audio recordings during a sales process. This book does not afford the time and space to make the lengthy, thoroughly documented and decisive case for length in ad copy, in sales letters and other media, and in sales presentations. I make it elsewhere, and I'll ask the skeptics to investigate elsewhere. I will only take a few minutes to appeal to logic, common sense, and what you can see with your own eyes. Common sense tells you that forced abbreviation of a presentation, however it is delivered, can make the task of persuasion more difficult. Logic should tell you that intellectual interest and emotional commitment grow given time, and the more time somebody invests in learning about something or someone, the more likely they are to go forward with a purchase or relationship. These are the reasons for enormously successful staples in direct marketing, like the *30-minute* TV infomercial (even if about a seemingly simple product, like a countertop grill), the *16- to 64-page* "magalogs" used by alternative health and financial newsletter publishers and by nutritional supplement companies—mailed in the tens of millions every year—catalogs that consume *20 to 30 minutes* to page through, the *two- to three-hour* open-to-public seminars and workshops used by financial advisors, implant dentists, and other professionals to interest LEB/S consumers in their services.

In my own experience, for making money nothing trumps a well-written 16- to 64-page sales letter delivered by the postman. Provided it is going to somebody who is prone to open and read it, and that *is* the LEB/S consumer.

In many cases, such letters are accompanied by additional literature, a DVD that may be 30 to 60 minutes in length, and an audio CD that may be equally long or longer. **My objective is usually to get a prospect to spend at least 30 minutes learning about my or my client's proposition, while seated comfortably in his favorite recliner, on the couch, at the kitchen table. My goal is never brevity.** Because this is the most effective approach to marketing and selling, it is a huge benefit to be selling to LEB/S consumers who will cooperate and participate in it. Don't waste that advantage!

The LEB/S also has a healthy respect for media. The senior's home is more likely to have a library filled with books, *hardcover* books, than a media room. Noted elsewhere, the LEB/S still reads and respects the newspaper. The network evening news programs are hanging on, almost entirely viewed by LEB/S. This is an advantage you can capitalize on by authoring a book or books of your own, by getting into print in the newspaper and magazines and utilizing the reprints, by advertising on news programs on TV and radio. To be clear, the new media that is accepted as substitute by younger consumers does not serve the same purpose for you with LEB/S consumers. Your own internet radio show is not the same as your own real radio show or even being interviewed on real radio programs. Your own YouTube video is not the same as real TV. Your blog is not the same as a column in the real newspaper. Jon Stewart, the host of *The Daily Show*, Comedy Central's news-satire program very popular with viewers much younger than LEB/S, revealed something about his own age and mindset when, after being hectored by Arianna Huffington about repeatedly refusing to write a blog on her site, exasperatedly said, "Why would I do *that?* I have *real* media. I have a *real* TV show."

Subject to "Good Guilt"

Seniors are mostly very civilized, responsible, do-the-right-thing folks. They try to be good neighbors. They tend to return favors. In the nonprofit fundraising world, one of the most frequently used direct-mail gimmicks is the enclosure of a gift (in marketing lingo, a freemium), often preprinted return address labels, with a fundraising solicitation. This is done most often and works best with mail aimed at seniors. Why? Because they'll want to keep the labels, they'll even feel guilty throwing them out—*after all, they're useful; waste not, want not; and somebody went to all the trouble to make them for me.* But they'll also feel guilty keeping them but throwing out the sender's letter unread. It's rude. So they'll play fair and read the letter, and they start out a little predisposed to donating if given a convincing argument. I call this "good guilt." It can help get done what I want people to do, and that's a good thing!

The reigning authority on the psychology of this, sometimes called the theory of reciprocity, is Dr. Robert Cialdini, a professor at Arizona State University, corporate consultant, and author of the mega-bestselling book *Influence: The Psychology of Persuasion* (Harper Business, 2021). He and I have been on several programs together as speakers, exchanged information, and I've brought him in to work with one of my coaching/ mastermind groups. I urge getting and reading his book, or to start, visiting his website at www.influenceatwork.com. Everything he describes about the theory of reciprocity applies to the senior market, and will work best there.

LE-boomers are also very subject to motivation by guilt, but in other ways. They tend to be hypersensitive to failing at being "super-parents." Many even start second families with new spouses relatively late in life, in order to "get it right the second time." This can be a leverageable emotion when selling to them if they are still parents with young children, or if you are selling legacy products like life insurance.

On Their Good Behavior

Personally, I'm sorry to say that in my businesses, the best-behaved customers overall are in Canada and the U.K., not here at home in the U.S. Our audiences here, for example, have ants in their pants, are up and down and in and out of the room during a presentation, must be browbeaten to turn off their cell phones, and think little of leaving early, but Canadians and Brits think of all this as rude. I've had doctors compare notes, and the ones practicing in U.S. major cities suffer a much higher rate of no-shows and last-minute cancellations than do the doctors in Canada, the U.K., and some other countries. However, there is profound age bias to this, at least in the U.S., and the LEB/S consumer is far more likely to be well-behaved than are younger consumers. I recognize, in making this observation, I can easily be accused of displaying my own bias of age, of being a grumpy old man. I can only assure you that I work at objectivity on this point. When my wife Carla and I go to a performance at the Cleveland Playhouse, I pay attention to the percentage dressed appropriately or inappropriately, in their seats ahead of time or arriving late, in each age group. I do the same thing at the seminars and conferences where I speak or that I host. In businesses where I have access to data, I investigate refund rates by customer age groups. In various other ways, I try to take an emotionally distanced approach, and I am convinced that the likelihood of customers being on their best behavior rises dramatically with LEB/S. I also believe the differences in good vs. bad behavior between age groups are widening and growing more stark.

When LEB/S customers are given "the rules," and given good reason for them, and benefit by adhering to them, they generally follow them. I happen to be a big advocate of doing business on your own terms, and of having certain well-defined and communicated rules of engagement for how your clients are to interact with you. At seminars, I always begin with what the creator of EST, Werner Erhard, called "The Agreements Process," so that the attendees clearly know what constitutes good behavior and what is expected of them. With my one-to-one client relationships, the same sort of communication occurs in writing and at the meeting in which they are accepted as clients. If you read my book *No B.S. Time Management for*

Entrepreneurs, you'll find a lot more detail about this. I've long taught chiropractors the strategy of communicating desired patient behavior with both an agreements process within their sales presentation (typically called "report of findings") and by promoting competition for Patient of the Month honors, which requires: 1) Keep all your appointments; 2) Show up on time; 3) Be compliant (do the assigned at-home exercises, etc.); 4) Refer new patients who we can help. I teach everybody that clients, customers, or patients are very, very bad things to have, if you have poor control over their behavior! And I do *not* believe that good behavior occurs by happy accident.

Their Charitable Nature, Your Opportunity

LEB/S donors very disproportionately support America's charities, academic and medical institutions, the arts, churches, and causes. For every dollar the rest of the population gives, they give ten. There is some variance by the nature of the nonprofit, but not much. Charities are very vulnerable to the failure of replacement spending/giving of demographic groups following LEB/S.

My client, Nelson Searcy, pastor of the famous ministry The Journey, and a consultant and coach to churches and pastors nationwide, specializes in helping churches grow younger congregations, and one of the things he has to do is guide the pastors in aggressively teaching and training their flocks to be charitable; it's not in their conditioned behavior. To this end, he supplies books like *The Generosity Ladder,* sermons, audio CDs, and DVDs. (You can see his work at www.churchleaderinsights.com.)

LEB/S are different. They were raised to give, are conditioned to give, and they are experienced givers. They've also had sufficient time to become interested in and involved with supporting certain charities and charitable activities. This provides great opportunity to any business that will link itself to a charity popular with a particular audience, especially via direct-mail campaigns.

This is an underutilized strategy, available to both national and local marketers. Shopping for and securing the appropriate donor lists is key, and if you need guidance about that, or about anything involving mailing lists, I recommend connecting with Craig Simpson at www.simpson-direct.com.

Of course, at the local community level, there are often local institutions popular with just about everybody. My long-time student, Dr. Gregg Nielsen, a very successful small-town chiropractor, regularly runs new-patient promotions linked to fundraising for the town's fire department or its food bank.

It is good to be charitable, and to use your business and its marketing to support good charities, causes, and projects. It makes a good impression on LEB/S consumers. It can be used tactically, directly, in advertising, direct mail, and other marketing.

Cloning of Good Customers

Just about every merchant, service provider, or professional knows a referred prospect is more likely to buy, and less price or fee resistant than a prospect created cold from advertising or marketing. I agree, even though I make my living from advertising and marketing. If everybody started getting all the referrals they should and could get, were it their number-one priority, I'd quickly be forcibly retired. I exist largely because of systemic failures in this area.

One of the things most businesspeople don't think about is the comparative quality and value of different customers, by source or demographics or other basis, by which discriminatory marketing could be conducted. Most are very democratic. *Any* customer is just fine. It is incredibly stupid to invest this way. It'd be like a farmer paying the same for certified Black Angus cows, mongrel cows of poor breeding, cows of any age, etc., buying 'em sight unseen by the truckload. You want to exercise some control over the herd you assemble. If, for example, it costs you $200.00 to get a customer from one source but only $50.00 to get one from another source, if you're a dummy, you'll refuse to use the first source and get all your customers from the second, without bothering to calculate their long-term or total customer value, the frequency with which they purchase, whether they buy at full price or only buy discounted promotional offers, whether or not they refer, and without considering how they behave. If the customer acquired for $50.00 is only worth $120.00, but the customer acquired for $200.00 is worth $650.00, then you'd be making a big mistake, in terms of dollars or percentages. Very, very, very few businesspeople track the referral propensity of different customers acquired differently, from different sources, or of different ages, genders, geography. They should, and many would be surprised if they did, but they don't.

I can tell you, broadly, that LEB/S customers have a greater propensity for referring and better ability to refer good customers than customers in other demographic groups. They are more able because they are more likely centers of influence or in leadership roles in groups or communities, they are more listened to and respected by peers, and they have access to and influence with potentially good customers who are their clones. They are more likely because they better appreciate expertise, quality, good service, and good results. In short, the more you focus on doing business with LEB/S consumers, the easier a time you'll have cloning your customers through referrals.

These ten advantages of marketing to the LEB/S market have financial ramifications. They connect to price elasticity and profitability, the amount you can afford to invest in customer acquisition and to retention, and the sustainability and value of your business.

CHAPTER 26

The Power of the Right Media Strategy:

The Online vs. Offline Debate and the LEB/S Market

Originally appearing as Chapter 11 from
*No B.S. Guide to Marketing to Leading-Edge
Boomers and Seniors*

arketers are understandably very, very eager to abandon offline media in favor of online media. Many marketers are also greatly influenced by young advertising and marketing agency leaders and "gurus." Unfortunately, the actual experience of people "on the ground," most successfully selling to LEB/S, as well as the facts obtained from close examination of their results, commands us to stay focused on, and to weight our marketing investments to, offline media.

Here are some very telling facts, drawn from some thorough (and very expensive) research done by an outside, objective team of analysts for a multimillion-dollar producer in the financial services field, marketing to modestly affluent to very affluent LEB/S clients, in 2011, courtesy of my co-author of the

No B.S. Trust-Based Marketing book, Matt Zagula. Clients were interviewed to determine how they were sourced and how the financial firm first came to their attention and garnered their interest. Thirty-four percent cited word-of-mouth—conversations with family, friends, or peers—out of which came a specific recommendation or proactive referral. Nearly the same, 33%, cited the firm's offline media advertising and direct mail for its public, educational seminars and workshops, prompting attendance as response. In specific response, there was overlap: People responding to advertising and attending events also had conversations with peers in which the firm was favorably mentioned. Conversations with peers were also prompted by the events themselves, with attendees not converting to clients still positively influencing others. Another 15% cited the firm's non-event-related media exposure, including advertising on radio and TV and in newspapers, as well as its principals heard or seen interviewed on radio and TV. **Significantly, no one cited any online media as the starting point of their move to relationship with the firm.** *No one. Nada. Zero.*

That should be disturbing to anyone in the financial services field devoting a significant portion of their ad budget, marketing resources, or personal or staff time to online media, notably including social media. Arguably, if it produces 0, it deserves 0%. That would be overly extreme, of course, because *some* presence is essential for credibility if and when potential clients go online at some point, and for the media, and there are things that can be done online to educate prospective clients during and after the sales process, online workshop registration options can be offered, webinars promoted to unconverted leads, and so forth. But to invest in online media as if it was a productive driver of new business is, based on these facts, foolhardy. This cautionary note is not just for those in financial services, but for many kinds of professionals and service providers marketing to LEB/S. I know this flies in the face of a lot of statistics about the rapid growth in numbers of LEB/S using online and social media and is contrary to what you will hear from all the shovel sellers of online media shovels, including Google and Facebook themselves. But statistics are often *not* useful facts. For example, the majority of seniors and many LE-boomers have been driven to social media in order to stay in touch with their adult kids, grandkids, and distant friends, but are resistant to having their data harvested and obviously used to direct advertising messages to them, and do not go to the internet to find services and professional assistance.

As to search marketing, in which marketers invest untold sums of money, time, and energy to stay atop search engines, to build search-engine friendly content and to constantly monitor and respond to changes, it has one very big and severe flaw: It requires search. Most of my clients, in financial services, health, and other fields, make most of their money "knocking on the doors" (via direct media) of people not yet actively seeking what they offer, or even unaware it exists, or at least in circumventing and discouraging search, because search automatically creates comparison.

If we re-examine facts from this financial services firm's productive sources of clients, it tells us where and how to allocate our resources and focus our energies.

Thirty-four percent came from word-of-mouth recommendations and referrals. This suggests that 34% of our resources ought to be invested in encouraging and rewarding that client activity. This is why, in that field—with the advisors I consult with, and that Matt Zagula and I coach—we have led them to the creation and delivery of elaborate new client welcome gift packages, use of one or two monthly client newsletters (you can see the "mini-magazine" we built just for the advisors' LEB/S clients, called *Life, Liberty, & Happiness*, in the *No B.S. Trust-Based Marketing* book), special reports and white papers on different subjects offered to clients via the newsletters, periodic client appreciation events and outings, formal referral reward programs, seasonal gifting, and even more client communication and relationship tools and activities. My rule of thumb is that the client should get an offline "touch" (that is not purely a solicitation) at least 52 times a year. That will certainly include a Thanksgiving or Christmas card or card and gift, a birthday card or card and gift, a spouse's birthday card or card and gift, and at least 12 monthly newsletters. That takes care of 15, leaving 37 to be more creatively concocted.

Incidentally, this same research at this firm found that 43% of clients ranked educational events for clients as important, and 33% said that client appreciation events with a referral component, where they could bring and introduce friends in a casual, fun environment, were important. The research firm reported that as "only" 43% and 33%. I heard that one out of every three clients likes events that are fun, that they can bring friends to. I read this as an invitation to mine these clients for more referrals. As with most research, the way you ask the question matters. Only 14% responded favorably to terming these gatherings as "referral events," while 33% responded favorably to "client appreciation events."

Thirty-three percent came from the advertising for and attendance at public, educational seminars and workshops. This not only suggests at least 33% of the resources be directed there, but an expansion and creative diversification of these events to include different topics, aimed at different LEB/S segments, held in different venues, repositioned as book signings at the local bookstore, and at different times of day. The combined 34% and 33% suggest great emphasis placed on getting present clients to invite and bring guests to these events.

Fifteen percent of the clients came from media advertising and media publicity, on radio, on TV, and in newspapers. This tells us where 15% of our resources should be invested.

The above research work cost a pretty penny, but I've given it to you here, free. Finding these kinds of facts in your own business, as well as observed in the practices of the most successful leaders in your field is important; acting on the facts, even more important!

"You Can't Fix Stupid!"—Ron White

Here is what I find, time and time and time again: direction of resources into media and marketing activity in percentages and proportions in conflict with the facts of where clients come from. In 2011, I met with a major city's food bank's marketing team, which was responsible for recruiting new donors and increasing the contributions from existent donors. Roughly 50% of their donors are LEB/S, and 70% of their contributions come from the 50%, but they have less than 25% of their resources fixated on cloning these LEB/S donors. By far, their number-one means of acquiring donors is direct mail—their least productive, social media—yet they were draining money from direct mail in order to invest hundreds of thousands of dollars into remaking their websites, producing YouTube videos, and adding an employee to manage their social media activity. I might add, there's not a single LEB/S on this team that is making all these decisions and spending all this money to attract LEB/S donors. I also talked with marketing people at one of the largest hospitals in the country, and found them in similar behavior, in conflict with their own facts, and similarly excluding LEB/S marketing professionals and advisors from their inner circle. If that strikes you as stunningly stupid, good! But take a careful look in the mirror.

A hero of many entrepreneurs is Napoleon Hill, author of the book *Think and Grow Rich*. The book, initiated at the behest of Andrew Carnegie, is a summary of 17 "laws of success" built from his in-person interviews and research with hundreds of the greatest businessmen and industrialists, inventors and entrepreneurs, and other peak achievers, in the 1917 to 1937 decades. The laws, not surprisingly, include Burning Desire and Persistence. I often point out that the one Hill cited that is *least* popular is: ACCURATE Thinking. People in advertising and marketing especially love creative thinking. They're not so fond of accurate thinking. People pushing online media as panacea and urging abandonment of offline media love innovative thinking, but they, too, are not as enthusiastic about accurate thinking. These folks love statistics that verify their own predilections but are not as passionate about useful facts that call popular ideas into question.

Google, YouTube, Facebook, et al. are powerful tools as well as fascinating toys, and they have their genuinely useful roles in marketing, and they and the next generation of online media that replace them are inarguably the future. But, contrary to Gen Xs' and Millennials' beliefs, they have not just yet *changed the world.*

If you are to successfully market to LEB/S, you must remain aware of and sensitive to *their* preferences for receiving information, for relationship communication, for advertising outreach. You must collect and consider the *facts* about *their* true behavior as consumers. You must resist the lure of the brightest, shiniest objects, and the seduction of mystics who love and promote them, instead insisting on "what works."

I am *not* claiming that various goods and services can't be marketed or merchandised via online media, online catalogs, webinars, social media, etc. to LEB/S consumers. I do it. My clients do it. I am *not* claiming that utilizing search media in marketing to LEB/S consumers is fruitless. I am *not* denying a shift in these directions. I was integrally involved in the use of online media to drive sales in excess of $1 billion in 2011. While I am, by choice, somewhat famously, *personally*, a conscientious objector to the techno-machine and a near-Luddite, refusing to own a cell phone, never activating my car's GPS, refusing to embrace the iPad, getting books from Amazon by scribbling notes on scraps of paper for my assistant, I study ecommerce and online media, I work closely with the top internet marketing wizards, I write and produce marketing for online media, and I advise companies extensively involved with online media, including those with LEB/S clientele. I am *not* standing as the last horse trader in opposition to the damn horseless carriages. But I am arguing for rational thought and proportionate investment of attention and resources based on useful facts. I am cautioning that the proliferation of online media and its popularity with younger-than-LEB/S marketers is significantly ahead of LEB/S consumers' preferences.

As a general statement, the best approach is media integration, offline/online, online/offline, offline-online-offline, online-offline-online. For example, I have a client selling prepackaged opportunities and coaching programs in real estate investing and finder's fee business operation, at entry prices as low as $149.00, up to $5,000.00. Roughly two-thirds of his buyers are LEB/S. He has made millions in recent years mailing sales letters and postcards of my devising, those driving consumers to websites where full-length sales letters as well as video presentations make the initial sale, followed by both telemarketing and more direct mail to make a series of additional sales. That's offline-online-offline. The brilliant CEO of J.Crew credits their 40 million catalogs mailed during the year as the chief driver of business to their online catalog and websites. That's offline/online. At GKIC, media like this very book push consumers to a website, where they can learn more and, at their option, engage in ongoing dialogue with me via a free trial offer claimed by instant registration online. That's offline/online. My colleague Fred Catona, the wizard of direct-response radio, who built giants like www. Priceline.com with radio, increasingly drives radio listeners to websites rather than to toll-free 800 numbers. Offline/online. I have another client very aggressively using Google AdWords and other Google media, Facebook advertising, and other social media to drive thousands of leads a week to a double-squeeze page, the second obtaining their full, hard addresses, so that an elaborate direct-mail package can be sent that sells his service. Online/offline. Comprehensive integration is the Holy Grail, so that each boat's wake lifts the other boats. However, I have just described a general marketing strategy. As soon as we narrowly target LEB/S and segments within, facts intrude that place other key objectives ahead of media integration and mandate investing resources disproportionately in certain media, and also mandate search circumvention as a chief tactic.

CHAPTER 27

The Power of "FOR ME"
Customization, Exclusivity, and Membership

Originally appearing as Chapter 17 from
*No B.S. Guide to Marketing to Leading-Edge
Boomers and Seniors*

There is a famous story about a major city's streetcars, when doors had to be closed manually by the passengers—and weren't. Signs were posted, reading "As a Courtesy to All Passengers, Please Close the Doors." Ineffectual, they were replaced with "For *Your* Safety and Comfort, Please Close the Doors." I have had similar results with different wording, giving instructions to seminar attendees about returning from break and retaking seats on time, without loitering and requiring herding. FOR ME is very powerful.

When you are a senior, it is even more powerful because you feel you have earned special consideration by your years of toil, your accumulated wisdom, your elder statesman status. You also know you have special needs. You know that the same product,

271

service, place, experience, or person that satisfies a wide swath of ages will likely not satisfy you.

When you are a boomer, FOR ME is also very powerful, for we are the FOR ME GENERATION. It's nearly DNA.

The Power of Customization

Customization is *the* desire. Harry Dent, Jr., wrote, back in 2004, of "the revolt of the affluent"—a rising resistance to off-the-shelf, one-size-fits-all, generic products, services, and experiences. I expanded on the theme in 2008, in the first edition of my book *No B.S. Marketing to the Affluent.* In recent years, I've grown ever more strident in cautioning my clients that "tolerance for ordinary is over."

This is true for all LEB/S consumers, truest for affluent LEB/S, and truer now than it was a handful of years ago. Its edge is sharper. Its influence more powerful. The recession has reminded even the affluent of "value." It has reminded seniors of their parents' Great Depression lessons. For those not required to be frugal, it hasn't really prompted frugality so much as it has encouraged heightened sensitivity to and impatience with poor or even mediocre service, particularly if coupled with perceived disrespect; with less than exceptional experiences. It has made the LEB/S consumer more critical. My friend Pete Lillo, a handful of years older than I, has grown more and more committed to his favorite motto: "You have to give me *a very good* reason to leave my house."

One of the problems in play here has to do with the pleasure of anticipation vs. the pain of disappointment. Studies discussed on CBS's *Sunday Morning* program revealed that taking vacations rarely produces much happiness, and that afterward, people having had a vacation and those who have been home and at work the whole time register no discernible difference in objective psychological measurements of expressed happiness. In fact, most vacation returnees tell their friends and co-workers of the disappointments of the trips, and may also be more irritable and unhappy for days or weeks after their return. Happiness is produced before the trip, from the anticipation of the vacation. People instinctively know this about themselves. The other study mentioned on the TV program had to do with the offer of a kiss from a celebrity of one's choice. You and most people have, at different times, held crushes on celebrities. When offered actual romantic connection with their crush, and given the choice of the little tryst occurring that very day, the next day, two days hence, or three days hence, people chose three days away by a big majority. Immediate fulfillment would rob them of all the anticipation.

Younger consumers have a more resilient response to the disappointment that so often trails great, positive anticipation. Hopes for a great night out fulfilled with only an ordinary night, or even a profoundly disappointing night, are easily shrugged off— after all, it's just one night, life is long. A problem-riddled vacation that falls far short of its anticipation, well, there are a lot of vacations to come. Money spent on a much-anticipated trip, evening out, gift for a family member, or product for the home that proves disappointing, well, there will be a lot more money made and, heck, in 10, 20 years, it will be irrelevant. Not so for us LEB/S. We are, as the saying goes, on or approaching the back 9, and we can see the clubhouse in the distance; we're not teeing off toward the first hole. That *is* a LEB/S saying. We are quite aware of where we are. The number of "next" vacations, next home remodeling projects, next investments, next times we place trust in some advisor, even next nights out is finite. Every night I climb into the racing sulky, take the reins of a racehorse, and head out to the parade to the post, I say to myself, "There will be a last time for this."

Penn, of Penn & Teller, was born in 1955. He is a LE-boomer. His father was a prison guard and, on the side, a numismatic dealer in coins. His parents bought him an Amazing Kreskin magic kit as a birthday present, at a young age, and thereby stamped an ambition that would guide his life. He went through the Ringling Bros. and Barnum & Bailey Clown College. He once performed an act involving riding a unicycle while juggling toilet plungers. (Note: not knives.) Penn developed what he calls "the first rule of show business" early: Never take a restaurant job. A bad day in show business is better than a good day of dishwashing. He worked as an itinerant street performer. He fought his way onto *The Howard Stern Show*. About his (and Teller's) enormously popular, long-running Las Vegas show, I have witnessed him saying and writing, more than once, "There will be a last time for this."

If you are a LEB/S, doing something you like, you know there will be a last time for this.

For this reason, LEB/S consumers grow ever more frustrated by the cycle of hopeful anticipation and sad disappointment. We are conscious of it. We are cautious in our anticipation and keenly interested in avoiding the pain of disappointment. Customization fuels hopeful anticipation, because it promises to prevent disappointment. When you are very clearly positioned and presented as a "specialist" in your category of goods or services, for the LEB/S, you trigger positive anticipation thanks to the "Oh, that's FOR ME" factor. This is what the words "*relaxed fit* jeans" mean to a LEB/S with fluctuating weight or a spare tire around his waist. This is what a "*calm and peaceful* oceanfront resort" means to a LEB/S worried about being surrounded by party animals or families with screaming children. This is what "dedicated to *preserving* clients' *hard-earned life savings* with *personalized* guaranteed-income investment plans" means to the LEB/S considering financial advisors.

But, should you then deliver disappointing experiences, you'll get no second chances. Back in 2004, Dent wrote that "the revolution is about real-time, personalized service at lower costs to meet the needs of a rapidly expanding affluent consumer who expects and demands such service, and creating an ongoing service revenue (relationship) versus a one-time product sale." If you substitute LEB/S consumer in place of the generic affluent consumer in this statement, you have a solid prescription for the best approach to the LEB/S market.

The Power of Exclusivity

Del Webb, the leading developer of retirement communities, has to deal with this issue of age restriction; whether to require residents be of a certain age. This has been a fact of life in the retirement community industry for quite some time, but has oddly not migrated to most other industries. I could definitely see select airline flights to places like Orlando and Las Vegas being designated for LEB/S or seniors only, with planes equipped to more easily accommodate these passengers, and with families traveling with small children precluded. I once suggested Disney setting aside a concierge floor and lounge in its resort hotels exclusively for adults there without children, to create a quieter, less chaotic setting. The Imagineers I had the discussion with thought it antithetical to Disney culture, but didn't summarily reject it—especially given my suggestion that guests might pay as much as a 50% premium for the exclusivity. This hasn't happened, although Disney is a big exclusivity marketer in many ways, notably including extra-priced, variable-priced Fast Pass, VIP Private Guides (Human Fast Passes right to the front of every line), Concierge Floors, and activities only available to those guests, such as the behind-scenes dawn safari at Animal Kingdom, etc.

The question is: How many LEB/S *want* exclusivity by segregation?

The "2010 Del Webb's Boomer Survey" revealed that trailing-edge boomers are ambivalent about age-restricted communities, with about 10% more interest among LE-boomers. Within their own clientele of Del Webb residents planning to make a second move as retirees, the preference for age-restricted communities leaps sky high, to 10–1. This reveals that the exclusivity preference rises with age, but it also reveals it is dramatically affected *by experience.* It is my own pet theory that LEB/S consumers and particularly senior consumers will have greater preference for age-based exclusivity in just about any business category after having experienced it. In that regard, it may be less useful as an attractant of new clients than as a retention/loyalty strategy with continuing customers.

Exclusivity plays a very big role in marketing to the affluent, which I deal with in depth in *No B.S. Marketing to the Affluent.* Exclusivity can also enhance trust, as discussed in *No B.S. Trust-Based Marketing.*

I now travel distances only by private jet. I've been on only one commercial flight—overseas—in the past three years. It is my most outrageous indulgence, although to be fair, the value of my time when invested in my work tops $2,000.00 an hour, and most of my work requires a great deal of focus and mental concentration, so saving a half day, day, or days of time tied to a trip can be worth as much as or more than the cost of the private jet, and arriving at the destination or back home to work in a good frame of mind has monetary value. Still, my best defense aside, it's indulgent. I've paid a lot of attention, the five years or so I've been traveling this way, to my own thoughts about it and to my observations of and conversations with others in the private terminals we embark and arrive at. It's my sense that it is only a minority of these travelers who are glitz-and-glitter celebrities, the famous rich, feeding ego, or even markedly elitist; most of them have more in common with me. Their motives are not so much the luxury of this mode of travel as escape from the profound unpleasantness and inconvenience of the ordinary alternative. Their relationship with the exclusivity of private jets is not so much status as it is segregation.

Most major hospitals now quietly segregate. They have "secret" and not-so-secret suites and even entire floors reserved only for the rich and famous, the rich and powerful, and the quiet rich, including their own chief donors. The area where the "executive physicals" are conducted is set apart from the area that most patients visit staff doctors for routine physicals. Since there is marked convergence with affluence and LEB/S status, most of these privileged patients are LEB/S, and they welcome, even if they didn't at first seek, this exclusivity, as much or more for the segregation as for any special benefits.

In marketing to LEB/S, we're making the point often throughout this book that you need your business, products, services, and messaging to be for LEB/S, and to be clearly for LEB/S. I go further with my advocacy of exclusivity. I believe you also need to be quite clear about who you *aren't* for. Cadillac and Lincoln have, I think wisely, done this in most of their advertising in 2011 and 2012, depicting, at youngest, boomers and more often LEB/S, and using language crafted to call out to LEB/S and exclude younger consumers. It seems to be paying dividends. Were I creating the advertising, I would likely be less subtle.

In its extensive research study of 2010, "Approaching 65: A Survey of Baby Boomers Turning 65 Years Old," AARP noted that "there is a sense among members of the baby boom population that they are special or unique." We LEB/S were raised to believe just that. It is deeply ingrained, and to me, all the more reason to play the age-linked exclusivity card in every way possible.

The Power of Membership

The behemoth of the LEB/S marketplace is AARP.

If you haven't received your first of a very persistent series of mailings complete with your already personalized membership card, I have bad news for you: You most certainly will. You will not be permitted to ignore this pronouncement from on high that YOU ARE OLD!, as you might skip town on your birthday, avoid dinner invites or surprise parties, leave cards unopened. You can't lie or joke about your number either. AARP *knows*.

Few of its 40,000,000 members know of its origins, true purpose, or power, not necessarily wielded in members' best interests. But the majority of LEB/S consumers are influenced by its endorsement for commercial products and services, and their lives are influenced by its lobbying, like it or not.

AARP is the world's second largest nonprofit organization, after the Catholic Church. Both wear the nonprofit mantle yet own and operate a number of richly profitable businesses and investments. While the Catholic Church confines itself more to passive investments than active business invention and operation, AARP is the opposite. It began as a scheme to sell insurance. It is, itself, a boomer. In 1958, a then-72-year-old retired high school principal, Ethel Andrus, was frustrated that she and others like her could not obtain health insurance at fair rates because of age, and had the idea of banding together such individuals to negotiate as a group with the insurance industry. Her noble idea was altered to a moneymaking opportunity by a 32-year-old, ambitious and opportunistic insurance broker, Leonard Davis, who offered to help her in her cause, for a price. He provided $50,000.00 in seed capital and expert advice to launch her organization, initially for retired schoolteachers (not just any old persons). In exchange, he secured the exclusive rights to sell not only health, but also life insurance and other financial products to its members. Permanently. In its infancy, Davis brokered the insurance, but when the organization was morphing into AARP and topping 750,000 members, he formed his own insurance company. You may have heard of it. Colonial Penn. By the early 1970s, Davis was selling insurance to 10 million AARP members. His net profits exceeded $200 million.

That's gumball machine money compared to today's AARP. It is still an insurance sales juggernaut, generating hundreds of millions of dollars of commissions to AARP from a consortium of auto, home, health, disability, life, travel, and burial insurers, plus commissions from approved and endorsed providers of a dizzying array of other LEB/S-oriented products and services, sponsorship fees from giant pharma, bank, credit card, travel, and other corporate partners, and one of the highest per-page ad rates of any print magazine for its publications, the flagship of which is *Modern Maturity*. Exclusivity is often sold, presumably to the highest bidder. Lockout from the captive and controlled audience of LEB/S consumers swayed by AARP recommendation is used as a bloody axe in negotiations. I have witnessed it all firsthand with a client of mine involved with senior health care.

AARP brilliantly melds the power of membership, the patina of an objective advocacy organization, its nonprofit status, and its charitable activities to secure high trust from its members (customers) and create unrivaled value for its advertisers, sponsors, exclusive vendors, and other business partners. It has built a large, powerful "toll booth," virtually uncontested by competitors, and it collects very stiff tolls from any and every marketer seeking to pass through the gates. It may well be *the* ultimate example of what I teach as business and marketing strategy: ownership of the toll position. (A concept I first learned in the 1970s from a brilliant entrepreneur, Harvey Brody, to give credit where credit is due.)

If the AARP were a for-profit corporation, it might very well have run afoul of federal anti-trust laws by now, but its shield of nonprofit status is strong. It is made even stronger by AARP's lobbying arm. It employs dozens of staff lobbyists along with outside PR firms, other Washington lobbyists, and ex-congressmen as "advisors"; essentially a small militia of influencers. It is also able to mobilize its giant army of members in letter-writing, email, and telephone campaigns directed at elected officials and the media. That army, incidentally, dwarfs the membership of the National Rifle Association, the Boy Scouts of America, the National PTA, and the AFL-CIO, combined. When told that both Ronald Reagan and George Bush had "dissed" the AARP by neglecting to involve its representatives in White House-level discussions about health care and other senior issues, President Clinton asked, "Couldn't they count?" Meaning, couldn't the presidents count *votes*? Or *money?*

The AARP also pours millions into "issue advertising" on TV, radio, and in print, to directly influence elections as well as to push or oppose legislation. (There was a view during Hillary's push for universal health care that AARP was opposing it in every way possible, openly and behind closed doors, more because of its own financial interests as an insurance marketer than for any benefit of its members. Its position on so-called "Obamacare" has been more nuanced, but is nonetheless suspected by many.) AARP also funds research on anti-aging, hosts giant conferences in pleasant resorts, and serves as a "source" for the same media that might be critical of it. It is, in effect, a giant octopus, with tentacles reaching to every politician's pocket at every level of government, into every media outlet, and into every area of commercial enterprise touching LEB/S. I have even drawn data from and quoted its research elsewhere in this book—research prepared primarily for use by its commercial partners with purpose common to this book's; guiding them in more effectively selling more goods and services to these consumers.

It can't go without mention that AARP has a major financial advantage over any commercial, capitalist competitors: As a nonprofit institution, it pays no income taxes. However, the strategic principles underpinning its power and success can be co-opted by any business, even at the small local level. They are:

1. Membership
2. Mission Larger Than Itself & Its Own Interests
3. Toll Position
4. Influence

Membership has power because all seniors and many LE-boomers are preconditioned to want it and value it. Seniors have been joiners and belongers their entire lives. All the fraternal organizations, like Kiwanis, Rotary, Elks, etc., have been most actively supported by "The Greatest Generation." Even Fred Flintstone and Barney Rubble belonged to a lodge. Bowling leagues, now in decline, thrived in my parents' day. Joining, belonging to, being identified with and, in many cases, advancing in groups was a path to status for these consumers, in youth and all through adult life.

If you examine the "control" direct-mail pieces of a great many entities marketing themselves to LEB/S, to recruit customers, subscribers, or donors, you will find the already personalized membership card affixed to the sales letter, showing through a window in the envelope, and you will find membership language used throughout. The week I was finishing this chapter, I received a very elaborate mailing of this kind from the Sierra Club. These cards add cost to these mailings, and when hundreds of thousands or even millions of pieces are being mailed, every added cost matters. Most of these major mailers conduct extensive split tests, pitting different offers, mailing formats, colors, and other variables against each other, and it's a very safe wager they've tested membership card vs. no membership card. You can assume the use of the card bumps response more than enough to justify the cost. I'm not necessarily making the micro-suggestion you create membership cards for your coffee shop or beauty parlor (although I wouldn't necessarily rule it out). I call this membership card tactic to your attention as illustration of the broader point: The membership *concept* is powerful with LEB/S.

If you look into GKIC, you will discern that, like AARP, we are a moneymaking operation, in our case publishing newsletters and online training, hosting conferences, providing various exclusive resources and services, and serving as a portal for approved and endorsed vendors, to a "membership association" of marketing-minded entrepreneurs, small-business owners, self-employed and private practice professionals, and sales professionals in the U.S. and in about a dozen other countries. We have local chapters meeting regularly in nearly a hundred cities. We have a ladder of ascension for members to move from one membership level to another. We have achievement awards. We are, in effect, a service organization to our members, and a marketing machine for our own goods as well as for a consortium of vendor-partners, sponsors, and advertisers. Our sister, the Information Marketing Association, is a smaller clone of GKIC, for authors and thought leaders, niche industry consultants and advisors, business and life coaches, publishers, and seminar, workshop, and conference impresarios. The AARP model was not lost on me. I started it all with four subscribers, a newsletter made on a photocopy machine. It now has private equity investment and professional management, a staff exceeding 50, and some 25,000 members, but, beyond that, over 350,000 online, opt-in subscribers and catalog customers, a network of grassroots independent business consultants, a global network of nice industry consultants, and thus a yearly reach of more than one million business owners. Although GKIC members encompass the entire adult age range, the majority of our higher-level members are LEB/S.

Mission larger than self is also influential with LEB/S. After all, seniors sacrificed to save the world and boomers set out from the very start to change the world. Even the small, local business can involve itself in charitable activities of interest to LEB/S residents of its city or community. Organizations like the Arthritis Foundation are nationwide in scope, but have local chapters, local events, and local segments of their national telethon. If you are going to reposition your business as a membership entity, know that LEB/S like belonging, but they are even prouder of belonging to something that is doing good.

Toll position applies at all levels. Often, the best small-ball use of toll position is in cooperative marketing and list and endorsement exchange with another marketer(s) who also owns toll booths to LEB/S customers you desire. The implant dentist and the Lasik® doctor can cooperate and can exchange. The financial advisor and the estate lawyer can co-operate and exchange. But don't neglect opportunities to extract cash tolls for the access you offer or the customers you can deliver. If you can bring 50 affluent LEB/S "members" to a winery on a "member appreciation outing," you shouldn't be paying the winery; they should be paying you. And if one is too obtuse to recognize the opportunity, someone can be made to see it.

Influence. People love those who speak for them. Rush Limbaugh's popularity and wealth is derived from his articulation of philosophies and viewpoints his listeners already have, on their behalf, through his microphone—a microphone they do not have. Any local business owner can make himself into a vocal advocate for groups and causes. At bare minimum, he can "stand for" his LEB/S customers and their values and views via pronouncements in his own media—customer newsletters, blogs, and such. He can write and have published a "viewpoint book" that he gifts to his clients, and through his clients, to his friends. You can go further. You can give national voice to your views, in much the same way I do, by writing articles, by writing books, by promoting yourself to the media. It isn't nearly as difficult as you might think, because the media is now 24 hours a day, seven days a week, huge, with an insatiable appetite for new faces, strong viewpoints, and interesting human interest stories. One tip about relating to the LEB/S consumer that I consistently give to financial advisors, lawyers, doctors, and others I coach is: They want to know who you are and what you think and believe, not just what you sell.

CHAPTER 28

The Power of Aspiration and Ambition

Originally appearing as Chapter 19 from
*No B.S. Guide to Marketing to Leading-Edge
Boomers and Seniors*

L EB/S have been about ambition.
Those coming behind are seriously questioning the
LEB/S concept of ambition, and there is some pandering to
their doubts. In a 2012 commencement speech, media personality,
Kennedy family member, and Schwarzenegger ex-wife Maria
Shriver advised college graduates that it was perfectly okay
to emerge unsure of just about anything including what they
might want to do with their careers or to earn a living (all but
issuing permission slips to move back in with parents and
relax), and promoting what she called "the pause"—the virtue
of pausing *often* in life, in work, to ponder and reflect. The
dearth of jobs for young people, including college graduates,
blamed on the recession, and broad disillusionment with the
American economy coupled with overly tolerant parents are all

contributing to malaise. The youngest newly minted adults are the first generation ever to not even bother getting their driver's licenses at the first available moment, opting for life on Facebook and the couch as an acceptable alternative.

Such ideas are foreign to LEB/S. Seniors and most LE-boomers have been engaged in "racing to the top" their whole lives. In upward mobility. In goal setting. The 1970s were the prime years of the personal growth and human potential movement in America—seminars and workshops on every corner as if convenience stores—and boom years here for the multilevel network marketing industry, led by already old dogs like Amway, and newer emerging titans like Herbalife, enticing millions of people every week into "opportunity meetings" in hotel ballrooms, pancake house back rooms, and living rooms coast to coast. Herbalife even, at one point, aired a multi-hour opportunity meeting and success rally live on cable TV every Sunday night. The concept of "Nothing Down" real estate investing hit its prime, too. At peak, an estimated 25% of the adult U.S. population was involved in a multilevel marketing operation, attending get-rich-in-"nothing down" real estate trainings, or spending weekends at "success seminars," or all three. Leading-edge boomers were right smack in the thick of it all, driving it with their ambition to be smarter, faster, more self-actualized, richer. Seniors lived their own bigger-is-better goal-oriented pursuit of the brass ring in the post-WWII boom. Hardly anybody was content just to be. The phrase "keeping up with the Joneses" was born as their ambitious behavior translated into the purchases of bigger homes with bigger yards, bigger cars, backyard swimming pools, vacation cottages, boats, RVs.

Combined, as a force of nature for the economy, LEB/S pushed the wave of optimism and conspicuous consumption that marked the '80s. After the brief down years with the dour-faced Jimmy Carter telling everybody to turn down their thermostats and wear sweaters, Ronald Reagan re-ignited the Grand Ambition of LEB/S, with his sunny personality, his trickle-down economics, and dramatic tax rate cuts not seen since JFK; tax cuts that said: *Spend!*

All this is important in understanding the LEB/S mind-set. We are, at this point, hard-wired, compulsive achievers. Required to set, pursue, and achieve goals, to crystallize and pursue ambition.

Just as an entire suburbia migration and lifestyle and all its accoutrements and large, luxury cars were sold to the seniors by tying to ambition, and just as racing to the top, second-income entrepreneurship in multilevel marketing, immigration from other fields to Wall Street was sold to LE-boomers by tying to ambition, we can now find exceptionally profitable opportunity in tying to whatever the new ambitions of LEB/S are.

The **"2010 Del Webb Baby Boomer Survey" hands us their *new* ambition list**. The two areas of life that LE-boomers want to improve in are—drumroll, please—physical health, cited as #1 by 35%, and financial security, cited as #1 by 25%. Their improvement goals are to (finally, now that they have time) get their act together with regard to their health or their personal finances. Or both. Further down in the rankings: repairing, improving, and strengthening relationships with family and friends (9%), achieving upward movement in career or business (6%), improving spirituality (12%), more time into and getting better at recreation/leisure activities (10%). Were I you, if interested in tapping the spending power of boomers, I'd be sitting down and trying to figure out how I could link myself, my business, my products and services to these ambitions, preferably #1 and/or #2, or how to reinvent so I could do so.

The AARP research showed that older seniors reveal more "measured perspective." What this means is that their ambition is more tempered. While generally optimistic about the future, they are more cautious in setting clearly defined goals, as their longer span of life experience and knowledge of reoccurring history tells them that things may not work out as planned. In the survey, a large percentage of those 65 and over described their attitudes toward the future as hopeful *and* anxious, confident *and* uncertain. This is not so much addled conflict as it is measured perspective. This gives us guidance in how to talk a little differently to seniors about ambition than to LE-boomers.

This does not preclude them enunciating ambition. Asked, in the same survey, what they want to spend money on and do, travel/more travel ranks highest at 18%, retirement at 12%, improve health at 13%, improve finances at 10%, all others down in single digits. Anyone in the travel field can do a happy dance. But this also suggests the kind of premiums and rewards to focus on: travel. And it suggests not putting as much emphasis on having more free time, more time with family, more time with grandkids as many advertisers do—these do not rank as major ambitions. They do rank high in expectation: 80% said they expected to spend more time with loved ones. Only 9% gave it chief ambition status.

I'll now remind you of the most time-honored formula for getting rich through marketing. It was once stated as "Find a need and fill it," but that required a bit of updating, as greater and greater percentages of our population had their basic needs met. In many product and service categories now, there are arguably no unmet needs. After all, if you need a cup of coffee or a doughnut or cupcake, you need not travel downtown or across town to *the* coffee shop or *the* bakery. Many goods and services once priced beyond reach of the masses are now fully democratized. Seniors will remember commercial air travel as a romantic luxury few could afford. As a young child, I was put on a Trailways bus to go from Cleveland to Pittsburgh, to visit relatives; the idea of going by air was outrageous. Today, Southwest Airlines will fly you across country for bus fare. And so on. So, Zig Ziglar's admonition, taught from the '60s forward, better applies: "If you will help enough other people get what they *want*, you will certainly get whatever you want."

On this premise, dare we make opportunity predictions?

There is the Jewish proverb: If you wish to hear God laugh, tell him of your plans. Still, as business leaders we must attempt reasoned and psychic prediction, and we must attempt to plan and develop strategy, to at least stay apace with the most profitable buyers, if not a step or two ahead. With that in mind, here are a few predictions:

1. **LE-boomers are going to remain in family leadership for some time to come.** John Martin, CEO of The Boomer Project, says that boomers lead more households than any other generation, and now they are at the helm, often reluctantly, of more multigenerational households than ever before. Close to 16% of the American population now inhabit three-generation households, and almost all are headed by boomers. The TV show *Modern Family* portrays a version of this. There are certainly more TV shows of this ilk coming, as TV tends to mirror its viewers. This means, for some years to come, the boomer will be at the epicenter of household, financial, health-care, and other decisions for his own family, his boomerang adult kids moved back in, his senior parents also moved in. This may not be cheery news for some industries, like real estate, but it suggests adaptations by many industries—home remodeling leaps to mind—to capitalize, and a whole new field of multifamily household services and family-leader support services. Family therapists, life coaches, a new wave of personal growth seminars, a spate of self-help books,

a new kind of financial planner, etc., etc.; new designs in refrigerators, garage storage, what else?

2. **Dragged, kicking and screaming, or seeking ways to ease life's burdens, or seeking new social and entertainment options, Martin also predicts that LEB/S will get more and more wired.** I expect this to be pushed forward as physical-world services become less and less available and bear surcharges, compelling and even forcing acceptance of online services. The erasure of service and shift to self-serve was a gradual process that began with the first serve-yourself grocery store chain, Piggly Wiggly®, in 1916, and picked up speed as service stations disappeared and the public was forced to pump its own gas, to the present, where we are asked to check ourselves out at the supermarket, make our own airline reservations online and check ourselves in at the airport, and vacuum out our own cars at the car wash, after depositing coins in a machine for the privilege. LE-boomers dislike some of these conversions from service to do-it-yourself, while the youngest boomers are more accepting, and the next younger people grew up with them and think nothing of them. Seniors dislike them most, naturally. In a very similar way, LEB/S will be guided into acceptance, grudging or not, of conducting their business, doing their banking, interacting with their doctors, and much, much more online. It will happen slower than corporate and government entities would like, but faster than most of these consumers would prefer—and there will be opportunity in being last-men-standing, delivering access to humans and personal service, for a while. The growth in LEB/S use of online social networks topped 80% from 2009 to 2011. The number of LEB/S users of Facebook leapt from about one million in 2009 to over 12 million in 2011, according

to Pew Research and www. iStrategy.com. This, too, has been largely forced, by adult kids and grandkids, and in some cases, business peers refusing to communicate by other means. Once dragged to it, many LEB/S users embrace it for more than the single purpose they were required to use it for; others do not. Still, I predict that the most productive, profitable driving forces in marketing to the LEB/S market for many years to come will continue to be offline media, with increased reliance on direct mail, as other print media is less and less available.

3. **Martin predicts that "health and wellness care will be everywhere."** That is obvious on its face. The real questions have to do with access; and with who will be delivering the care. My own view is that the current trends of consolidation and the absorption of small, independent providers into far fewer, big corporate-owned conglomerates already occurring in health care in the hospital and medical practice arenas will accelerate. I anticipate hospitals taking over a myriad of peripheral health-care businesses, such as dentistry and even chiropractic. Out the back end of it will likely come a fresh wave of fragmentation and new business format invention, but that is a decade away. To his "everywhere" prediction, there's no doubt that "low-end" health care is going retail. CVS, Walmart, and others are already delivering certain kinds of medical care in their pharmacies and stores. The Association of American Medical Colleges has warned of a shortage of as many as 90,000 doctors by 2020, and a growing disinclination toward general medicine or geriatric medicine by students and graduates, due to limits and likely cuts in Medicare reimbursements, other limitations built into "Obamacare," and an overall income disadvantage of at least $100,000.00 a year vs. other categories of medical practice. Given growing doctor shortages and

increasing pressure for cost control, more and more medical care will be pushed downstream, to nurse practitioners,
mini-practices inside retailers' locations, in mobile-van and
in-home practices, and via online, where diagnosis and
issuance of prescriptions is an evolving business very near
the tipping point of a boom.

The Age-Profit Boom will also dramatically change
the health club and gym industry. Already, the fastest-
growing consumer demographic buying memberships is
50 years old—and over. The industry is fast developing
products, services, and classes for LEB/S consumers more
interested in vitality than ripped abs, rock-hard bodies, or
bulging muscles.

4. **I think that health-care centerpiece retirement communities are the coming trend**. If you recall from Chapter 23,
the "2010 Baby Boomer Survey" conducted by Del Webb,
the king of retirement communities, showed that a warm,
sunny climate was not the #1 concern—instead it was cost
of living and access to health care. I live in a community
now that has small townhouse clusters at its perimeter,
large freestanding homes in its main neighborhoods, and
maintenance-free cluster homes, both freestanding and
duplex, in side neighborhoods. Celebration, the Florida
community originally Imagineered by Disney, has apart-
ments and townhouses at its edges, cluster homes, large
freestanding homes, and very upscale mansion-like
homes in segregated but connected neighborhoods, with
a Main Street and small-townish Public Square as its centerpiece. Many upscale retirement communities are built
with golf course and country club as their centerpiece, a
design a client of mine years back, Florida Communities,
copied in miniature scale, with a nine-hole short course,
small lake, small lakeside clubhouse, and modestly

priced premanufactured homes surrounding it all. I think the coming communities built for seniors will mimic these kinds of designs, but with a hospital campus—with hospital, geriatric E.R., every kind of health-care practice, and assisted living facility also likely owned by the hospital— at its center instead of the country club or the mixed-use shopping streets.

5. **Opportunities in the "Independent Living Industry" will grow explosively and expansively.** Fifty-seven percent of Americans older than 65, polled by the Associated Press, said they were "very" or "extremely" likely to stay in their current homes, living independently throughout their retirement. The 57% probably includes some overly optimistic folks, and omits quite a few resigned to other fates but who would profoundly prefer independent living in their own homes, were it possible. We need to find ways to facilitate this aspiration for socio-economic reasons. As the senior population surges and life span extends, the underlying Ponzi scheme not just within Social Security and Medicare, but of our entire economy is exposed. There cannot be enough new money to be taxed, taken, and redistributed to fund the retirement, health care, and nursing home/assisted living costs of the senior population, with those services constituted as they presently are. Some state governors, like Governor Kasich in Ohio, are pushing hard to reformulate state programs like Medicaid to provide more flexibility in paying for home health care, simply because it can be far less costly to assist a person staying in their own home than housing them institutionally for life. Of course, as marketers, we aren't focused on the needy, but on the big number who have financial capability to pay for their own enhanced quality of life. But know that staying at home and living

independently is a huge motivational factor for the majority of seniors as well as the entire LEB/S population. It will be a fortune-making force for a great many entrepreneurs.

One of the fastest growth, opportunity-rich, ill-defined industries ever is and will be what I'm calling "the independent living industry," where products and services devoted to supporting seniors in living on their own their entire lives will converge and synergistically integrate in new ways, and entirely new businesses or modes of conducting business will rise up.

Technologies for "aging in place" is a $2 billion market now, but is projected to exceed $20 billion by 2020, according to Laurie Orlov, head of a Washington think tank studying the field. Jon Pynoos, a professor of gerontology at the University of Southern California, views the $20 billion projection as "optimistic but not unreasonable." He predicts more technology built into houses and more portable technology. The portable products to date are mostly improvements on the classic Life Alert, "I've Fallen and I Can't Get Up" button. But now that we have phones that talk to you, find restaurants that will deliver tomato soup for you, and direct you step by step to the nearest Starbucks, services to remind taking of medications at precise times, direct doctor-to-device monitoring (as with embedded pacemakers), permitting adult children to easily monitor parents' activity in their homes at a distance, etc. are fast emerging and gaining traction in the marketplace.

A company in this field called Rest Assured (www. restassuredsystem.com) marries in-home video safety monitoring (i.e., surveillance) and an array of electronic sensors—to watch over how long a senior has stayed in the bathroom or if they've opened their medicine cabinet at the correct times—with "Tele-Caregivers" who check in with the seniors several times a day. This approach entered test marketing only recently, and is in several hundred homes. I see no reason that both a business of Tele-Caregivers alone, as well as a high-tech/human touch hybrid like Rest Assured won't turn into growth categories. Yes, this does sound a little Orwellian. But sacrifice of privacy to stay out of nursing homes, assisted living centers, or the spare room in the kids' house will prove a price LEBs turning into seniors will be willing to pay.

In the pseudo-tech area, one of the front-runners is a direct-marketing company, FirstStreet, with mail-order and online catalogs devoted to convenience products for seniors, notably the Jitterbug Phone and a proprietary, senior-friendly computer with limited, simplified internet capabilities, the ads for which can be seen online at www.FirstStreetonline.com. Studying this company is very instructive. Manufacturers of virtually any and every kind of product would be well-advised to follow the yellow brick road paved by the Jitterbug Phone, and create senior-friendly versions of their products. The auto industry is doing it, without announcing it or positioning it as such, with cars that slam on their own brakes if backing into an object, park themselves in tight parking places, and give verbal directions to destinations.

Another of my clients, Paul Davey, a veteran owner of construction companies, has converted his firm to Independent Lifestyle Designs, specializing in any and all home makeover installations and modifications to facilitate seniors remaining safely in their own homes. His clients include government agencies, real estate investors, seniors, and the adult children of seniors. He has developed a referral network of hospital and rehab center administrators, doctors, social workers, and real estate agents. In one local area, while most contractors and remodelers have suffered at the hands of the recession, his business has achieved multimillion-dollar year-to-year growth, and he has begun sharing his system with other construction and home remodeling business owners throughout the country. I believe that the consolidation of the products supporting in-home independent living like stair-lifts, walk-in tubs and showers, elevated toilets, security systems, handicapped access home conversions, and full remodeling services in one "expert, trusted advisor" business is going to make fortunes for those participating in this business.

SilverRide, in San Francisco (www.silverride.com), is one of a burgeoning number of on-call transportation services that takes the elderly hither and yon, professionally and safely. With more than 70,000 trips so far, the company's been called on to provide car service for routine trips to the grocery store, late-night runs to 24-hour Walgreens, nights out to the opera, and every other imaginable purpose. The business is complicated by federal and state regulations and insurance requirements having to do with caring for seniors, such as certain first-aid training and certifications required for drivers, handicap accessibility equipped vehicles and the like. But what was once mostly the province of ordinary taxicab companies is fast becoming a specialty business. I recently read of a gerontology dentist closing her brick-and-mortar practice and creating a mobile dental care service for senior patients. Franchisors are invading the home health-care field in increasing numbers. I foresee a growing diversity of to-the-home and taking-seniors-out, individually and in groups, on outings businesses developing.

6. **Financial advice and legal advice will be major growth categories, with clients willing to pay fees for services, for existing and new kinds of services.** A client of mine, Bill Hammond, has pioneered a new subspecialty of elder law, called Alzheimer's law, for the needs of families in which an elder has been diagnosed with or is exhibiting worrying signs of Alzheimer's. He has not only built a hugely successful practice of his own, but has created a nationwide network of thousands of attorneys using his technical work, procedures, marketing, consumer education, and community outreach materials and methods (www.kcelderlaw.com). In Chapter 21 of the *No B.S. Guide to Marketing to Leading-Edge Boomers and Seniors*, you can see the brilliant marketing of one of the top elder law attorneys and business coaches to other elder law attorneys, Julieanne Steinbacher.

7. **The convergence of marketing to the affluent and marketing to LEB/S will escalate.** I am invested in a company, Tuscan Gardens, engaged in the development of small, boutique retirement communities with small but very upscale freestanding homes, nestled together in close quarters, with quasi-assisted living and medical services on-site (www.TuscanGardens.com). I am invested in Kennedy's Barber Club, a classic men's shop with upscale club environment, featuring straight-razor shaves, and operated on a membership rather than fee-for-service model (www.KennedysBarberClub.com). It is squarely aimed at an affluent LEB/S clientele, with monthly membership dues above a hundred dollars. It has grown slowly but steadily during a recession launch to 13 successful locations, and is projected to at least double in number of units by year-end 2012. I made these speculative investments in startup companies with the

conviction that businesses very specifically crafted for the affluent LEB/S offer some of the best growth, margin, and value opportunity for the remainder of this decade and well into the next.

Concierges for the affluent LEB/S will grow in popularity and create new categories. Concierge medicine is already significant, and will only become more appealing should "Obamacare" or some reconstituted version of socialized medicine proceed. I predict the "home concierge" idea will come of age—the handyman, repair, routine maintenance, lawn care, watering of plants when owner's away, etc.—services all in the hands of one concierge. Or the "food concierge," who does the grocery shopping, restocking refrigerator and pantry, and prepares certain meals.

8. **LEB/S will re-assert itself as *the* target market for consumer brands, all sorts of products and services, entertainment, and more.** In 2010, LEB/S consumers spent about $1.3 trillion *more* than Gen X and Millennial consumers combined. Advertisers have been shifting focus, often clumsily. It's now common to see cosmetic and beauty ads in fashion magazines and on TV showcasing "women of a certain age" in place of the young, bold, and hopelessly beautiful. In 2012, Toyota brought forward TV ads presenting a particular car as for the LE-boomers, and not for younger customers. The TV soap opera all but disappeared in the networks' misguided making their main characters younger and younger, leaving their loyal audience behind but failing to attract the coveted young viewers, even as CBS took prime-time dominance with shows chosen for their appeal to LE-boomers, like *NCIS, Hawaii Five-O,* and *Blue Bloods,* and ABC has succeeded with *Dancing with the Stars.* Robert Downey, Jr., the actor best known at the moment as *Iron Man,* has reportedly

acquired movie rights to a decidedly LEB/S character: Perry Mason. Las Vegas wounded itself with its recrafting for the very young. They got visitor counts up, but brought net profitability down. As a sign of their times, a liquor store is opening in the baggage claim area of the airport, so young people can stock up to drink in their rooms before hitting the clubs at night, thus reducing their bar tabs. I believe this will all sort itself out at a now accelerated pace, with advertisers and media aggressively re-engaging with LEB/S.

9. **"Made in America" may make a big comeback.** The global economy isn't going to diminish in importance, but I am tracking—more anecdotally than statistically at this point—a growing aversion to imported goods in many categories, particularly when logic says there should be made-in-America available. I have personal bias here, so, a quick story. A huge box of Harry & David fruit arrived as a gift from a client. My wife and I opened it on the kitchen counter, read the glowing prose about the wondrous Harry & David orchards in Washington state or Oregon, I forget which, and how the seeds for these special pears were first brought there from France, etc., etc., etc. Then, just before unpacking the fruit, we spotted the little label: PRODUCT OF CHILE. I have nothing against Chile *per se*, and I intellectually know that they used very careful wording to skirt past an outright lie, but we still felt deceived, disappointed, and incredulous that pricey Harry & David specialty fruit was being lugged over here from beyond our borders. And we threw it out. And I made a note never to, myself, order anything from Harry & David. It is my opinion that manufacturers and sellers of goods that are homegrown, that are made in America, should promote that fact more boldly and emphatically than seems com-

mon, and I believe it gifts some price elasticity. I think the backlash from a likely long-standing if not permanent unemployment rate at 8% or higher—due to a variety of factors—will be a new isolationism, patriotism, and disapproval of companies exporting jobs and importing goods. There may even be new tariffs and trade wars and taxes tied to this, unwinding the dramatic opening of unfair trade from the Clinton administration.

These are just some of the key areas of opportunity that I'm talking about with my clients, researching and paying attention to for GKIC Members, and considering in my own investment activity.

CHAPTER 29

Across the Rubicon

Originally appearing as Chapter 4 from
*No B.S. Guide to Maximum Referrals
and Customer Retention*

A buyer is not yet a customer. A customer is not yet a committed customer. A committed customer is *not* yet an evangelical ambassador. But only evangelical ambassadors refer in any significant numbers, with any significant frequency.

Somebody can attend your church regularly, yet never really engage with it, with various groups, with other parishioners. Somebody can attend and engage but never or hardly ever invite, let alone successfully invite others to attend. This person can be a satisfied customer or a happy customer or even a committed customer, but never cross the Rubicon to evangelist.

A member of my mastermind/coaching groups I've gotten to know well, Nelson Searcy, is head pastor of The Journey churches as well as the director of Church Leader Insights,

302 ⊕ THE BEST OF NO B.S.

a nationwide support organization for pastors of growing congregations. Nelson freely admits that churches have several advantages over ordinary businesses in the securing of referrals—one of which is that evangelism is baked in. It is part and parcel of being a good Christian and a good church member. No comparable intertwined obligation comes with being the customer of your shoe store, restaurant, financial advisory practice, or software company. Still, he teaches pastors not to take this for granted. If they must convert the person to being an evangelical ambassador, we must do so as well. Presumption or sense of entitlement tied to excellence of goods or services has no place and no power.

The first Rubicon a person gets across is purchasing. He may have hung around as a prospect for some time, reading your online or offline media, seeing your ads, being aware of and interested in you, receiving offers from you. Or he may have seen your sale of the century ad on Friday, and come in and made a purchase on Saturday. Either way, there is absolutely no assurance he will return again and again. All he did was buy something, and all you did is sell something. A transaction happened. A window of opportunity is created that will close quite quickly. Nothing more happened and nothing more should be presumed to have happened.

It's worth noting, hardly any businesses do anything about this. If I wander into a store at the mall and buy something, at best I get my email captured (and I personally don't use email) and get dumped into a generic email marketing and "constant contact" system. Most of the time, even that minimum isn't tried. But I can count on one hand the times I've gotten an actual, personalized thank-you card in the mail with any sort of bounce-back coupon. It occurred with a jewelry store and a rare book dealer last year. Nobody calls, asks if the thing fits or looked good when I got it home or if the dog likes her bed, etc.

In short, follow-up to ensure satisfaction sucks. That pet goods store owner believes: Let sleeping or not-sleeping dogs lie. I guess they assume I'll be back if I liked their shop and if the dog likes her bed.

You want to be assertive and proactive in moving first-time buyer to customer to committed customer. To be a customer, they merely need to return and develop a habituated pattern of patronage. A good example of this was explained to me by a very clever entrepreneur in the dry cleaning business. His grand opening strategy was to aggressively buy habit. The first offer spread through the neighborhood was: Everything you can carry in here in your arms, bag, or box dry cleaned for $1.00. When they came back to pick up that cleaning, they got a ten-day offer to bring in coats, rugs, bedding, or drapes and get a bagful cleaned for just $5.00. These are irresistible offers. By the time the person picks up the second load, she's been to this cleaner four times in under 20 days. He says her car then heads for that cleaner automatically if clothes are piled into its back seat. This turns a buyer into a customer by habit.

The best way to have a committed customer is to have them paid forward or on autocharge, especially if there is pain of disconnect with the autocharge.

In the 1980s, when I was very involved in the "prepay revolution" in chiropractic, I discovered two very important truths. You need to know that then, and now, most chiropractors charged by the visit, and by the treatment modality, as it was consumed. With prepay, the patient was prescribed a treatment plan like "three visits a week for three weeks, then two a week for four weeks, then one a week for five weeks, totaling 22 treatment sessions times $89.00 equals $1,958.00, plus one spinal decompression traction session a week for the 12 weeks times $240.00; $2,880.00; total $4,838.00" then asked to prepay that with a 5% savings or pay it in two monthly installments, right then, bing, bang, bingo.

Here are the two truths that revealed themselves. First, the pay-as-they-went patients were miserably noncompliant. They skipped prescribed sessions, postponed at the last minute, didn't do prescribed exercises at home, and more than half never completed their plans. Second, most did not refer at all or were only milked of one or two referrals early, if the office had a very aggressive approach—like a new patient class requiring "bring a buddy." In contrast, the prepay patients were much more compliant; 80%+ completed their treatment programs on schedule or close to it, 70% referred, and about 25% referred abundantly, and stayed on after their primary treatment programs as lifetime "maintenance" patients. That's the power of prepay.

Autocharge has a similar effect. The person getting his credit card charged $125.00 on the first of every month and getting $200.00 of vouchers for products and services is far more likely to use at least the $200.00 (but probably spend more) than the person paying as he patronizes. He is more likely to be exclusive rather than divide his spending in your category by whim and random convenience. Therefore, you are more likely to succeed at retention and a habituated pattern of patronage.

Sometimes, one of these is helpful while one is harmful. For example, in the GKIC business, the bundled services of membership, subscriptions to newsletters, and other deliverables are autocharged monthly, usually after a free trial period. This is contrary to the newsletter industry norm of one-, two-, and three-year prepaid subscriptions. For GKIC, it works better than term subscriptions and renewals. Significantly, there is "Push," not passive consumption of the goods and services involved. By that I mean, they arrive. GKIC sends Members two packages of newsletters, CDs, and other material each month that arrive at homes or offices, plus email series, calls from Concierges, as well as invitations to online and live events. Many businesses that ask the subscriber/customer to go fetch everything they're being charged for, as digital downloads, content at membership sites, and benefits at physical locations, suffer a much higher loss rate when trying autocharge. Often, businesses built on passive consumption find prepay outperforms continuity.

One way or another, or in multiple ways, the point is to get the customer committed.

Consider visiting Disney World. We went about once a year and sometimes skipped a year and never went more than twice a year until we bought a time-share in the Disney Vacation Club. With that, we own a bank of points applied to lodging at our home-base Disney resort or at all the other Disney resorts, including a few not in Orlando by the parks. These points are added to our account but also expire year to year. We prepaid for them for life. It now feels free to go stay there, but costs out of pocket money to go anywhere else. We now go, on average, three times a year, sometimes four times a year. We are also more habituated: We have favorite restaurants there, favorite shops there, and we know the lay of the land. Every time we go, of course, we spend like maniacs at those restaurants, in those shops. They smartly seed that spending with discounts and promotions exclusive to Disney Vacation Club owners. To not go and let prepaid points expire is unimaginable! We are thoroughly committed customers.

For guests who aren't (yet) DVC owners, Disney is very aggressive in pushing the booking of the next vacation while enjoying the current one, with in-room, in-hotel, and in-literature marketing. They are also aggressive at converting resort guests and park visitors staying elsewhere to DVC. They are also pretty pushy about ascension. One-day to multiday park tickets. From park pass to express line pass. Up to use of private VIP guides.

Very undemocratic. They understand the importance of the committed customer.

My friend and great GKIC Member Alan Reed has hundreds and hundreds of committed customers for his dairy farm in Idaho, hooked up to home delivery—by real "milkmen" in trucks with routes, some customers on autodelivery and autocharge. The customers with regularly scheduled deliveries and autocharge or billing accounts buy more, buy more consistently, and stay as customers much longer than those who "just call when they need something" or "swing by the store."

Many, many, many businesses have opportunities to lock in and automate certain kinds of repeat patronage from at least a segment of their customers, but never bother to figure it out and do it.

The next Rubicon is between (just) committed customers and evangelical ambassadors. This is, by far, the highest level of customer and customer value. I'm a fine ambassador for Disney. Clients who come to my home office encounter a shrine of Disney collectibles, a talking Disney clock, and more, and ask me about Disney, and get enthusiastic testimony. I know of more than 30 people who've become DVC owners because of me. Others who've stepped up to using VIP guides because of me. At one time, when I lived in Phoenix, I was an evangelical ambassador for my trusted car salesman, and brought dozens of family members, friends, and peers to him. Same with my chiropractor of that time. I *liked* telling people my stories about them and, in a sense, spreading their gospel. I *believed in* them—I didn't just buy from them.

You really can judge your efficacy and level of sophistication based on how many evangelical ambassadors you have actively working for you, for free.

It's easiest if this is personal, but companies and brands do achieve it. These are called "passion brands." For a time, Cadillac was such a brand. Apple was and is such a brand. Walt is long gone and the customers don't know Bob Iger, so Disney is such a brand. Good evidence of the strength of a passion brand is customers' cheerful willingness to pay premium prices vs. competitors and alternatives, and shareholders' willingness to overvalue the stock vs. competitors and comparable companies. A Rubicon for a lot of these brands is full integration in their customers' lives and environments, like daily use of products preferably in a ritualistic way, wearing of logo apparel, existence of collectibles, use of its language, and expressed reverence for its philosophy.

CHAPTER 30

The Number-One
Best Retention Strategy

Originally appearing as Chapter 8 from
*No B.S. Guide to Maximum Referrals
and Customer Retention*

he best retention is ascension.
When you figure out how to structure your
business with "membership concept" and then levels,
so customers move from one level upward to the next, and then
to the next, you will have constructed a way to automatically
improve retention. As their level of commitment increases,
their longevity automatically increases. Or, when they have an
ascension aim they are working toward, their retention also
automatically increases. If I'm only two months away from my
next award, "belt," pin, plaque; my next reward or reward level,
rebate, or gift, I'm much more likely to stay for two more months
than if I'm just there, with no target within reach.

At GKIC, there are a number of membership levels, but it
is the step up from the lowest to the next, from what we call

Gold to Diamond, that is most important. The retention rate for Diamond Members is the inverse of the retention rate for Gold. The best way to prevent losses of Gold Members is to upgrade them to Diamond. Diamond Members' dues are about 450% higher than Gold Members' dues, by the way, so don't ever think retention is facilitated with lowest possible prices. Often, as it is for GKIC, the opposite is true. Of course, you'll be tempted to say that the GKIC business naturally lends itself to all this and your business doesn't so easily do so, and you may or may not be right about that. It doesn't matter. You can create it in most businesses. GKIC Members have done it with barber shops, pizza shops, car washes, accounting practices, chiropractic practices, clothing stores, and any number of other businesses. In every case, as soon as a member is ascended to a next level, the length of time they stay is extended, as well as, in many businesses, their frequency of purchase.

Let's take a car wash, and create membership. I'll pick price points out of the air, just to make the example. A VIP Member gets up to three Deluxe Washes and Waxes a month, and is charged $29.00 on the first of each month. A Gold-VIP Member gets unlimited Deluxe Washes every month plus a full winterizing and anti-rust undercoating every October and a full detailing every April, and is charged $59.00 on the first of each month. A Diamond-VIP Member gets unlimited washes, the winterizing, and up to three detail jobs a year and is charged $89.00 a month. The Platinum-VIP has unlimited washes plus up to six times a year, they come, pick up his car, give him a luxury car as a loaner, clean and detail the car, and return it all spit-shined, plus the winterizing—and the car wash operator is proactive, not reactive, and makes sure the Member uses all the service he's entitled to. They also pay for a Triple-A Auto Club Membership for him (which they get at a negotiated discount), and he gets four seats in a luxury skybox sometime during the year for the local team's baseball games. For this, the Member is autocharged $469.00 a month. Which level of Member do you think stays the longest? Further, which level of Member do you think tells the most other people, i.e., brags to the most number of other people, about the amazing Car Care Club that he's a Member of?

I have been teaching "membership concept marketing" to businesses of varied breeds for over 25 years. It seems others are finally catching up, and acting as if they've invented something new! As I write this, there are several new business books about this, much lauded in media, the best of which is *The Membership Economy* by Robbie Baxter. I say: Welcome to the revolution. Too bad you got here so late, but it's nice to have you anyway. Of course, if you did your homework and were transparent, you would not only have given full credit to me and to GKIC for promulgating this throughout the small-business universe before you, but you also would have mentioned originators, like the Book of the Month Club, established in 1926. But that's okay. Go ahead and pretend you're radicals. And, despite all that, I recommend reading this book for the fullest understanding of "membership concept" you can get. But don't miss the main point of leverage for retention: ascension and membership levels.

Why Do Members Ascend?

There are four reasons.

- *First, value propositions.* It simply makes good sense to upgrade and be a higher level member, in financial terms. Usually this means getting more for less per unit. That might be more access, more use of facilities, more quantity of product.
- *Second, exclusive benefits and perks.* Years ago, a very popular restaurant and nightclub in Phoenix converted to a Members First system. Out front, two rope lines: one for

Members, the other for the nonmember public. Members were admitted first, and if there was capacity left over, nonmembers were admitted. VIP Members carrying Gold Cards checked in at the front but were then sent to the back door, where they were always guaranteed immediate admittance. As I recall, it was $100.00 a year for a regular Membership Card, but $500.00 a year for the VIP Card that got you recognized in front, then ushered in the back door, no waiting. They had to stop selling the VIP Cards for months at a time because of capacity issues.

- *Third, peer influence, "being seen," recognition, and status.* You'll see smart charities publishing the names of their donors grouped into levels: Chairman's Circle ($15,000.00 a Year), President's Club ($9,000.00 a Year), Inner Circle ($3,500.00 a Year)—then just Supporters, with no dollar amount. This is both recognition and peer pressure.

- *Fourth, the nature and behavior of the person.* This is the driver of ascension many business operators are clueless about, yet it is very significant. There is a percentage of people in every customer population who typically buy the most expensive option or level offered, or ascend to it as it is repeatedly shown to them, because that's how they see themselves and how they want to be seen by others. By their purchases, they affirm their status to themselves. This is explored in more detail in my book *No B.S. Marketing to the Affluent, Third Edition.*

When you incorporate all four of these drivers into an organized ascension ladder put in front of your customers, many will move right on up! And those moving up are exponentially more likely to stay with you longer, split their business in your category with others less, i.e., be more loyal, spend more overall, be less price sensitive, and refer more and better customers.

CHAPTER 31

Seven Ways to Grow
Each Customer's Value
and Have More Power
in the Marketplace

Originally appearing as Chapter 16 from
*No B.S. Guide to Maximum Referrals
and Customer Retention*

ere is your MONEY MAP.

H You can use this map to uncover more treasure and collect more spoils from every customer you capture!

It is vital to do so. Businesses failing at fully monetizing their customers often fail outright, and many more will in the challenging years ahead. This is so because nothing is more difficult or costly than new customer acquisition. Further, if your customers are middle-income, middle-class consumers, that supply, in the U.S., is shrinking. If you market B2B, many niches, industries, and professions are shrinking in numbers of potential accounts by consolidation, contraction, and attrition. Competition, especially price-driven competition, is fierce and ever more enabled by the internet. Costs related to customer acquisition keep rising, generally outpacing inflation in most product and service categories.

POWER comes from your ability to pay these rising costs and more, and much more than your competitors can, to acquire, retain, and care for your customers. Yes, it *is* that simple. He who can and will spend the most wins. POWER comes from making your customer so much more valuable to you than everyone else's customers are to them that you can outspend everybody else. Obviously, retention—customer value grown by time—and referrals—customer value increased by being a portal to more customers—plays into this in a big way. There are seven specific ways to create the maximum possible customer value so you are the most powerful beast in the jungle.

1. Increase Transaction Size—Initial and/or Repeat
2. Increase Transaction Frequency
3. Decrease Randomness or Division of Spending (In Your Category)
4. Increase Term of Retention and Lifetime Customer Value: STOP LOSSES
5. Increase Profits of Business Conducted with Each Customer
6. Recover Lost Customers
7. Clone or Multiply Customers by Referrals

There is a great deal of work to be done in each of these seven areas of your business. Yes, I said: work.

A little bit of good happens in all seven areas just by being good or great, and having happy customers. I'm right with Keith Lee on this (Chapter 5 of *No B.S. Guide to Maximum Referrals and Customer Retention*). We want *happy* customers. Fine. Well and good. But settling for whatever organic activity that produces will never come close to creating extraordinary income. These are seven areas of opportunity to be aggressive in. Not passive. So work on each is required.

This book is not meant as and lacks room for a comprehensive description of everything to do in these seven areas. Obviously, it has focused on No. 4 and No. 7. But in the interest of giving you at least a complete overview of best opportunities, a few comments about each . . .

#1: Increase Transaction Size

In the Depression, at soda fountains, "soda jerks" were trained to ask, "In your milkshake, would you like one egg or two?" The same basic at-counter upsell is familiar to all fast-food restaurant customers. Unfortunately, what is supposed to be happening often isn't. One major chain recently found eight out of ten not doing the simple upsell, via its mystery shopping.

This is but one method of many to be creatively applied, *then strictly enforced*, for bumping up transaction size. A few dollars more per visit or purchase may not sound like much, until you apply it to the multiyear tenure of a customer and to all customers. That $5.00 more per transaction from a customer engaging in 18 transactions a year equals $90.00, times a five-year retention term equals $450.00. Done with 222 customers: an extra $100,000.00. Done with 2,222 customers, an extra $1 million. You can get rich on the extra money made just from small upsells.

Upselling and cross-selling are the two best ways to bump up transaction size. But every possible method must be considered. All that can be used should be used. You have to know your customer to get this right. My dry cleaner, for example, has a tailor, and he constantly finds little things to fix on the clothes I take there for cleaning. A jacket lining coming loose or bunching up, loose buttons, a frayed pant cuff. These things are fixed and added to the bill without any discussion. He knows I will not squawk, will welcome the service. As I imagine the case with many of his affluent customers. I'm betting he's adding $10.00 to $20.00 to a lot of transactions this way. Many hotels got blowback from automatically adding newspaper delivery and gym use daily fees to their bills, but other chains got little negative feedback, and successfully institutionalized this practice. The in-room minibar is a long-standing way of bumping up hotel stay transaction size. Some now have in-room catalogs, so you can buy the robe, the pillow, the linens, even the bed.

#2: Increase Transaction Frequency

One of our GKIC vendors, NewCustomersNowMarketing.com, and its founder Dean Killingbeck, mastered the obtaining of "cold prospect" birthday lists and birthday-theme promotions and direct-mail campaigns. He administers them for both obvious kinds of businesses, notably restaurants, to less obvious, like auto repair shops, very successfully. Response rates from these mailings to existent customer lists run as high as 25%! But just once in a year for each customer. ⁹ So, the invention of the Half-Birthday. ⚓ From once a year to twice a year, about the same responsiveness both times. This one little tweak doubles sales from this one strategy.

Shaun Buck, my co-author here, has absolutely, empirically proven that transaction frequency (and retention and referrals) improves with the mailing of a well-crafted, monthly frequency customer newsletter. No business owner reading this book should be without one! If you want help or want it done for you, there's no better person to call on than Shaun. Go to his www.TheNewsletterPro.com site without delay. I said: monthly. That's the minimum. You could do more, like a newsletter on the 1st of every month and a magazine on the 15th of every month. Keep this our secret: Their frequency of purchasing has a lot to do with your frequency of friendly, interesting, informative communication.

#3: Decrease Randomness or Division of Spending

Customers are easily seduced sluts. Sorry, but they are. As customers, *we* are. In most categories, they divvy their spending. The same person may go to Walmart and Target and Walgreens all in the same week, even though all three stores sell everything they bought with divided spending. The same thing happens with nonchain, independent businesses of many kinds.

Airlines invented Frequent Flier Programs to curb this, but once they all had virtually identical programs, the power was lost. Very frequent fliers, like I was for about a dozen years, accumulated lots of points in every airline's system, so we still divided our spending, mostly based on convenience of flights for our personal needs. This does not negate the role of a good loyalty rewards program, and a good source to look at is www. RoyaltyRewards.com. But a weak one has nominal impact. Just having one is not enough. It needs constant marketing to customers. Distance to the next reward or reward level promoted. Perks triggered by frequency. It is used often as leverage, not just as a card gotten into a wallet. Barnes & Noble mails its loyalty cardholders monthly discount coupons, with deadlines, and it often triggers an extra trip or two or three for me during the year. The independent Learned Owl bookstore I also occasionally patronize never sends me anything even though I am in their loyalty program, too. I'd wager my spending at Barnes & Noble was 20 times what I spent at Owl last year.

I overheard a guy who walked in and back out of a Sport Clips say, "Line's too long. I'll just go to the place across the street." I asked, "Aren't you in Sport Clips' loyalty reward program?" He said, "Yeah, I've got the card somewhere. But it's not important."

If you're not *important* to your customer, it's not the customer's fault. It's ALL on you. And if you're not important to your customer, that customer will more easily, casually, and randomly divvy up his spending that could be all yours. I feel a little guilty vacationing anywhere but Disney in Orlando, because of how well they manage our relationship. There's not a single restaurant I feel guilty about not patronizing in favor of any other. In fact, when Carla asks where I'd like to go to dinner Friday night with friends, I say: "Let them pick. I don't care." If she raises the prospect of going somewhere other than Disney for a vacation, I'm quick to resist.

Customers divide their spending in various categories for a multiplicity of reasons—convenience of a moment, a heavily advertised big sale, a friend's influence, boredom, and casual shopping, as well as feeling neglected and underappreciated. It's up to you to reduce these temptations and make customers think of you and at least feel guilty about their defection. The amount of divided spending going on in your category, the casualness with which the customer views it, and the loss of rewards it causes all affect both retention and referrals. In other words, the customer with the least divided spending is most likely to stay with you forever and is more likely to refer others to you. Conversely, the customer engaging in the most divided spending is most susceptible to being seduced away and dropping you out of the random rotation altogether, and is less likely to refer. When you reduce divided spending, you automatically boost retention and referral likelihood.

#4: Increase Retention—STOP LOSSES IN THEIR TRACKS!

About half of *No B.S. Guide to Maximum Referrals and Customer Retention* is devoted to this one, so there's only one point I want to make here that isn't dealt with anywhere else in those pages. You need an alarm that goes off, loud and clear, just as a customer is straying. Bill Glazer told me, when he ran his super-successful menswear stores, that for some hyperactive customers it might be four weeks without seeing them; for all the others, a season. Any customer not in for each of the four seasons was straying and shopping elsewhere. If you own a neighborhood diner and Billy Bob comes in every morning for grits 'n gravy, and he's not there on Tuesday, the alarm should go off. Don't wait to see if he shows up. Check on him. Call. If he doesn't answer, drive over to his trailer and peek in. He might be dead. But it's more likely his buddy asked him to meet up for breakfast somewhere else and he did, and if he liked that place, and Bertha smiled at him extra nice, and burnt his toast just like momma used to, he'll be tempted to go over there again tomorrow. If he does that three mornings in a row, he's lost to you. You needed to put an end to that on Tuesday afternoon. Every business has these timing-sensitive issues.

#5: Increase Profits from Each Customer

It's profit that can be reinvested as capital for growth, and it's profit that can be withdrawn for savings and investments, for debt elimination, and for lifestyle. Achieving maximum possible profit *with each customer* can be micromanaged. Somebody should do so, and marketing to each customer varied by use of this information. For example, if Walmart has a customer who very prudently and penuriously buys only staple commodities like toilet paper, paper towels, and a few supplies but never buys its much higher-profit-margin toys, games, apparel, electronics, or seasonal gift merchandise, that customer is a *problem*. There's almost no profit value in that customer. This is, incidentally, the exact kind of customer that Walmart got at the peak of the recession: "trade down" customers who grudgingly came for the dirt-cheap prices on necessities but refused to buy a lipstick or set of bath towels or a giant tub of caramel corn, and went to their usual, more upscale stores to buy high-profit goods. If you were micromanaging that business, you would identify and isolate those customers and concoct a customized sales program just for them, designed to tempt them into buying high-profit goods, hopefully being surprised and satisfied, and then changing their habits.

This is called *account management*.

Most businesses have different products and services with different profit margins. The task is to direct each customer into purchase of high-profit items.

Most business owners are hyper cost conscious, but not nearly as profit conscious as they should be. This is a form of what my friend mega real estate investor and coach Ron LeGrand calls "stepping over dollars to pick up nickels."

Most businesses should have three different kinds of marketing going on with their existent customers. One, generic messages and promotions everybody gets. These are very suitable to mass media, like email and websites. Two, segment-specific messages and promotions crafted differently for different groups of customers. For example, when I'm working on seminar marketing for GKIC or a client, I want to deliver different campaigns to a) customers who attended in prior years but skipped the most recent year, b) customers who've been around long enough to have attended but have not yet done so, c) customers who've attended one kind of event but not another, d) customers located in easy driving or "puddle-jump" flying distance of the event's location, and, sometimes, e) lost customers. Three, customized and personalized messages and offers different for each individual, based on what we know about that person.

#6: Recover Lost Customers

Not all customers are irretrievably lost. Not all broken relationships are irreparably damaged. Lost customer recovery and reactivation campaigns are rarely the highest return on investment things a business can do, but that's no excuse for not doing them. Deciding on what you'll spend is relatively easy; the lost customers have individual and averaged purchase history. Don't write them off without a fight.

The best lost customer campaigns include the following:

1. Acknowledgment, if not apology, that something must have gone awry causing them to wander off
2. Reminding of core reasons they were a customer
3. Introducing "Exciting News" about how you are "New and Improved"
4. Presenting an exclusive, extremely generous, irresistible offer(s) and/or
5. Offer of a VERY appealing FREE gift just for stopping in, calling, etc. to see all the "New and Improved" firsthand
6. Imposing deadlines on the offers

#7: Referrals

Again, about half of *No B.S. Guide to Maximum Referrals and Customer Retention* is devoted to this. Let me just say a word about creating a Referral Culture in your business. Whatever you want from people, they have to know you want it before they can give it to you, they have to know it is expected of them before they can live up to your expectation, and they have to know that they are capable of doing it successfully. So there are actually 11 things that customers need to know for there to be a Referral Culture in play:

1. Our customers refer.
2. Our good customers refer *often.*
3. Our best customers refer *often and a lot.*
4. Referrals are expected. From you.

5. Referrals are genuinely appreciated.

6. Referrals are well taken care of. (You'll only get happy reports and thanks from those you refer.)

7. NOT referring is weird and inappropriate. You should feel bad about it.

8. There are a LOT OF different reasons people do business with us—not just the reason that brought you in. Keep all these reasons in mind . . .

9. Most people don't really know how to find a good, trustworthy provider of what we do, so you are doing others a great service by telling them about us.

10. There are easy ways to introduce people to us and to get our information into the hands of people you think we can be of service to . . .

11. So—here's how to refer. Exactly what to do. 1, 2, 3, A, B, C.

I can train for an entire day just on this list, but you can glean the basic idea just from the list. It's up to you to consistently and effectively communicate these messages.

Years back, I invented an audio program for use by chiropractic physicians titled *Ten Ways to Get Well Faster*. One of the ten was that the patient's level of emotional commitment actually affected his mind-body-linked acceptance of treatment and speed at which his body responded, and the best way to telegraph commitment to the body was by telling the story of chiropractic to others, and referring others to the doctor— which then led into a rundown of this list with some detail. This is just one of dozens of ways we taught the doctors to communicate these 11 points. The most successful ones did it by in-office visuals and handouts, monthly newsletters, recognition for those referring, verbally in conversations with the doctor and the staff; with every media, often and consistently.

Conveyed Expectations

Conveyed expectations matter a lot.

Disney has done a thorough study to determine how far apart trash containers should be and how they should be made visible, to get the most number of people using them, resulting in the least amount of trash on the ground. You might think that's just about convenience for customers, but it's not; it conveys an expectation. Just as the incredible number of sweeper-upper people you see every few minutes keeping the place tidy. They are making sure you know certain things—like: We value the cleanliness of the parks; we work hard to keep them clean; guests do *not* throw trash on the ground *here* (look, there's a trash can within a few steps of you!); we expect YOU to use the trash containers (look, there's a trash can within a few steps of you!). None of this is accidental. I've spoken directly with Disney Imagineers, executives, and former executives about it. In so many ways, they ingeniously manage the behavior of their customers by conveying their expectations.

The person who donates repeatedly to a particular charity is a committed donor but not an evangelical ambassador. The donor feels good about herself because she donates. She must be made to feel bad about herself because she is letting the charity down by not evangelizing for it. She must see all around her, often, gratitude and recognition given for referring others. If this sounds manipulative or harsh, that's because it is. It is a tough position: Being a good and loyal donor is not enough . . . not enough to make you a really good supporter . . . not enough to merit a lot of recognition. Creating a desire on someone else's part to do what you want them to do so that they feel better about themselves is manipulative. Just as Disney's no-trash campaign is.

The person who frequently buys from a business is a committed customer but not an evangelical ambassador. The customer feels good about himself because he is a frequent and loyal patron, because he comes "where everybody knows his name," because he's a part of this business's crowd. But he must be made to feel bad about himself because he is letting the business down by not evangelizing for it. He must see all around him, often, gratitude and recognition given for referring others. If this sounds manipulative or harsh, that's because it is. It is a tough position: Being a good and loyal customer is not enough . . . not enough to make you a really good supporter . . . not enough to merit a lot of recognition. Creating a desire on someone else's part to do what you want them to do so that they feel better about themselves is manipulative.

This specific manipulation is a major driver of most behavior. People do all sorts of things for emotional self-interest, even though they may consciously think and would certainly insist they are doing these things "for" someone else, out of love, appreciation, friendship, religiosity, charity or generosity, or civic duty. If there is one uniting motivation affecting everybody every single day, it is pursuit of feeling good about themselves and better about themselves. We are all defending ourselves and defending our lives day by day, to the critic in the mirror, the embedded, judgmental voices in our head, and to those around us including family, friends, and even foes. If you get past denial of this as an ultimate fact of human behavior and get past any squeamishness or reticence about using it, then getting people to desire doing what you want them to do is suddenly a whole lot easier—including bringing you referrals.

WEALTH BUILDING

with selections from

No B.S. Wealth Attraction in the New Economy

No B.S. Business Success in the New Economy

WEALTH BUILDING

Whatever wealth you want is already in existence, waiting for you to claim it! Although we say it colloquially, nobody actually makes money, except the Fed with its printing presses. You and I dip into the flow of money already in existence and circulation, in motion, moving from one person and one place to another, which it does by ITS rules and operating system. For this reason, the best strategic thinking is about attraction of money in motion, not: How do I make more money?

The select chapters here from the *No B.S. Wealth Attraction* book are based on that important premise. No matter the economy, the other circumstances and conditions of the moment, money is always relocating. Even during the lockdowns and business disruptions made by the China virus, money refused to be locked down, and kept moving around. Some businesses prospered, while others struggled. New businesses were born, others died. In EVERY category, even in restaurants, some creatively adapted and altered their businesses so as to attract money, and did so. There are "magnetic PRINCIPLES" that override conditions and circumstances, and it is good to know them and to use them, in "good" or in "bad" times.

There are psychological aspects of this and there are practical aspects. In other words, ways to think and things to do. None of it is far-out, meditate about your navel, metaphysical manifestation voodoo. Money is likely the most rational actor you will ever deal with.

You Can Magnetize Yourself and Your Business to Money, Right Now

I wrote the original *No B.S. Wealth* book and adjusted subsequent editions from deep study of the transference of wealth, of money in motion, and from hands-on experience with clients who used understanding of these principles to "magnetize" their businesses and themselves to more money, and from my own personal experiences in going from "zero," bankrupt and broke to quite wealthy—and staying that way. The book is a synthesis of several multiday Trainings that I've conducted for different groups, each commanding per person fees upward from $2,000, and of literally billions of dollars attracted and assembled by hundreds and hundreds of entrepreneurs with whom I've worked personally on implementing these principles. You are getting a look at some very valuable stuff!

There are also excerpts here from the very first book in the entire No B.S. series, *No B.S. Business Success*, including a critical chapter on using your business to achieve personal financial independence. It's surprisingly easy to "get lost" and lose grip on your reasons for starting, investing in, owning, and growing a business. Wealth Attraction requires clarity. Clarity of purpose. Here, you will be emphatically reminded of that, and challenged to be purposed.

Building wealth requires a fundamentally sound, reliable foundation. The *No B.S. Business Success* information is foundational.

Does Money Grow on Trees?

I have in my office, received as a gift, an actual Money Tree. Its leaves are made of $20 bills. It first reminds of what we heard from our parents, often in an irritated voice: Money doesn't grow on trees. Yet there are money trees. The pine tree sold at the corner Christmas tree lot. The trees converted to lumber. To paper, then converted to this book, for which money left you and moved to the bookseller, from him to the publisher, and ultimately, a portion—called a "royalty"—to the author, me. Our Dad or Mom meant to impress that money is hard to come by, and that can be true, but it doesn't have to be. I keep my Money Tree to remind myself to attract it, not do hard labor for it. And to utilize opportunities for conversion, upvaluing, leverage, synergy as multiplication, and other strategic methods for transforming dollars (seeds) into $20 leaves, like felled trees are transformed into more value, again and again. And, finally, to remind myself to think well of money and wealth—to be welcoming, respectful and appreciative, unintimidated, and guilt-free.

Maybe these select chapters will plant a Money Tree, or two, or three in your business.

CHAPTER 32

Wealth Magnet 1
No Guilt

Originally appearing as Chapter 1 from
*No B.S. Wealth Attraction in the
New Economy*

Most people's worldview of wealth is as a zero-sum game. A big impediment to attraction of wealth is the idea that the amount of wealth floating around to be attracted is limited. If you believe it's limited, then you believe that each dollar you have came to you at someone else's expense, your gain another's loss. That makes your subconscious mind queasy. So it keeps your wealth attraction power turned down. Never to full power. To let it operate at full power would be unfair and harmful to others. If you are a decent human being, and you have this viewpoint, then you will always modulate your wealth attraction power. If too much starts pouring in too easily, guilt is produced as if it were insulin being produced by the pancreas after pigging out on a whole pizza. You can't help it. Your wealth magnetism will be turned down *for you.*

Think about the words *"fair share."*

They are powerful, dangerous words.

As an ethical, moral person, you probably think—*"hey, I don't want more than my fair share."* But that reveals belief that wealth is limited. If you believe wealth is unlimited, there's no such thing as a share of it. Everybody's share is unlimited. There's nothing to have a share of. There's only unlimited. Your fair share is all you can possibly attract. As is anybody and everybody else's.

In business, there's a similar idea: market share. But again that presumes a finite, limited market, instead of an infinitely expandable market.

In the New Economy, market share is one of the most antiquated of concepts. Boundaries are broken—even the smallest of businesses can be global in reach, thanks largely to the internet. Consumers have access to a multiplied and multiplying range of choices, so classic brand loyalty has been replaced by search for and expectation of the thing that is precisely, perfectly appropriate. The market for all manner of goods and services is greater than ever before yet the fragmentation of the market itself is greater and more complex than ever before. The attraction of wealth in this environment has little to do with somehow "locking up" a limited portion of a limited market and everything to do with directly connecting with individuals and meeting their needs and interests. When you think in terms of being in the business of creatively meeting the needs and interests of individuals, it's obvious that the size of the market available to you is limited only by your own creativity and initiative. Further, that whatever connection you create and accomplish has no relationship to what anyone else does, whether a lot or a little. Clinging to old ideas of limitation blocks access to new opportunity!

A Tale of Two Teenagers

Imagine being a teenager in a family in severe financial trouble. Money is very scarce. There's you, two brothers, father and mother. When everybody sits down to dinner and Mom puts the food on the table, you know that's all the food there is. The bowl of mashed potatoes is all the mashed potatoes there are. You are hungry. You really want a big second helping of mashed potatoes. The bowl is right in front of you, within easy reach. But instead of just reaching out, dragging it over, and scooping out a pile of potatoes, you stop to look around and see who has potatoes on their plate. You look to see if your father's had plenty of potatoes. You hold back from fulfilling your desire out of concern that others may not yet have had their fair share, may be hungrier than you. You do not want someone else going hungry as a result of your appetite.

I don't have to imagine that. I lived it.

Now imagine being a teenager in a family living an abundant life, with great prosperity. When Mom puts dinner on the table, you know there's plenty more where it came from. The refrigerator's full of food. So are the cupboards. There are always leftovers after dinner. You are hungry. You really want a big second helping of mashed potatoes. The bowl is right in front of you, within easy reach. Without a second thought, you reach out, drag the bowl over, and scoop out all the potatoes you want.

In these examples, of course, you're acting consciously. In the first case, in the financially troubled family, you consciously hold back, sacrifice, do not take what is right in front of you for the taking.

Similarly but subconsciously, if you believe, at all, on any level, that wealth is limited, that there's not plenty to go around, you will hold back, you won't take everything that's right in front of you. Your emotions about wealth will be cautious, measured, restricted, suppressed, timid.

If you can make every last smidgen of belief that wealth is limited go away, your attraction of wealth will suddenly, automatically, go from modulated, limited, and suppressed to full power, and opportunity, money, and wealth will quickly flow to you in greater quantities and at greater speed than you've ever before experienced.

People get ingrained in their heads that money taken from Person A and moved to Person B enriches Person B at the expense of Person A. Certainly, the liberal politicians either believe it or pander to it, one or the other. Some religious doctrines and religious leaders posit this idea. There are lots of ways this belief might be firmly planted in your head; maybe even in elementary school math class. If Johnny has 4 pieces of candy and gives 2 of them to Jim, how many does Johnny have left? The answer needed to ace the quiz is 2. But the "problem" ignores the fact that Johnny can simply open his hand and have as many pieces of candy appear in it as he'd like. After all, there's no global shortage of candy. When you actually understand wealth, you know that Johnny can have 4 pieces, give Jim 2 pieces, but then have 42 pieces.

What's even weirder and tougher for math teachers is that Johnny is much more likely to have 42 if he does give away 2 of the 4 than if he hoards the 4. But that's another topic for a different place. For now, let's keep it simple:

> The opposite of wealth attraction is wealth inhibition.

Most people are so wealth-inhibited they never even think in terms of getting wealthy. Their thoughts on this subject are limited to buying a lottery ticket or fantasizing about some unknown, long-lost uncle leaving them a fortune in his will. But there are a lot of people who do, at some point, start seriously trying to figure out how they might convert their knowledge, ability, time, energy, and effort into real wealth. You may be in that group—it may be the reason you were attracted to and purchased this book. So, a warning: the majority of people in this group never get traction, never get going, never get wealthy because they suffer from wealth inhibition.

If you believe wealth is limited, if you view it as a zero-sum game, you are inhibited. This inhibition affects all sorts of things you do or don't do, such as what you'll charge, for example, or who you'll ask for money.

I've spent a lot of time working with people in sales. Those who identify themselves as salespeople, like folks selling insurance, cars, fire alarms, as well as those who don't identify themselves as salespeople but are, like dentists and psychologists. Two things are true for all of them that reflect wealth inhibition.

One has to do with price. Most fear discussion of price, fear raising prices, are paranoid about pricing higher than their competitors. I have had to work long and hard to get some people to raise their prices or fees far beyond present levels, industry norms, or competitors' prices, in order to charge what their service and expertise is really worth to their clientele. In numerous cases, I've forced fee or price increases of 200% to 2,000% with absolutely no adverse impact—that's how far underpriced a lot of people are! In these situations, we are not dealing with practical issues. We are dealing with the businessperson's own inhibitions and fears.

335 @ THE BEST OF NO B.S.

Second is pulling the punch when closing the sale. I some-times joke about one of my own businesses—freelance advertis-ing copywriting—where I routinely charge fees of $100,000.00 to $150,000.00 or more for a complete project, no less than $25,000.00 for a single ad or sales letter. Plus royalties. I say that the primary requirement for getting such fees has little to do with my prowess as a copywriter and everything to do with my ability to keep a straight face and voice free of stammer when quoting the fee! This may be the reason a lot of art and antique dealers write the price down on a piece of stationery and slide it across the desk to you. There's truth in the joke. When the dentist quotes his $70,000.00 case to the patient, when the private residence club quotes the $215,000.00 membership fee, when anyone speaks any price or fee, there is the tendency for tremors, the temptation to discount without ever even being asked, out of fear, inhibition, and presumption. In short, to pull the punch.

Consider the salesman who goes into a person's home to sell fire alarms. (I have a corporate client in this industry.) The fire alarm salesman with the stuffed Dalmatian under his arm and the burning house DVD marches in and discovers that he is in a place of relative poverty—at least by his standards. The two kids are on a threadbare carpet in the living room. They prob-ably have a good television, but pretty much everything else in the house is obviously hand-me-down, beat-up, falling apart, springs sticking up out of the couch seat. He can clearly see that these people aren't doing well. Conversationally, he discovers Papa hasn't worked in four months and one of the kid's got some kind of problem that causes big medical bills, and on and on and on. The salesperson becomes increasingly queasy about clos-ing these people on the $2,000.00 fire alarm sale. And, in many cases, he will not close the sale. He will subconsciously pull his punches, accept the first objection easily. Or he'll consciously, deliberately throw the game at the end, toss that one aside, and get out of there.

This is an analogy to the way everybody behaves in all sorts of situations, if operating from a belief of limited wealth.

My friend Glenn Turner tells the story from his earliest selling days of actually being chased by somebody who was mad that he wouldn't sell him a sewing machine. Glenn thought the person couldn't afford it, shouldn't go into debt to buy it, and obviously cut his presentation short and abruptly got up and left—only to be literally chased down the street and caught by the husband, who called him on not trying to make the sale. "How dare you think for me? I've got a right to buy that thing for my wife if I want to."

My speaking colleague Zig Ziglar has a similar story from his earliest days selling cookware, about the customer that was saving up the money to put in indoor plumbing. Discovering that they didn't even have indoor plumbing, Zig backed off and didn't try to close the sale on the cookware. And the people were annoyed, they really wanted the pots and pans. The husband said: We can put the plumbing in later. Mamma wants those pots now.

The queasiness about price, about whom somebody is selling to, about their ability to pay, their ability to afford it is all deadly. And the truth is, anytime you start to make those decisions for other people, it really reflects more about what's going on internally with you than it does with anything else.

Oh, and by the way, if you were that fire alarm salesman who deliberately threw the sale, how would you feel about not exerting your best efforts if you turned on the TV news the next night and saw that family's house burned to the ground and they had died in the fire? Oops.

There's something else to get clear about the people who are without money, that you perceive to be disadvantaged for one reason or another and you question whether you should sell something—regardless of whether you get any of their money or not—they're going to be without money next week, too.

The reason they're without money has absolutely nothing whatsoever to do with your existence, what you sell or fail to sell, nor does it have to do with the way money works in the real world. It has to do with them. And whether you take it, somebody else takes it, the liquor store takes it, the church takes it, whoever takes it, I promise you somebody's getting it. Because if they're without money now, they're going to be without money again. And most of them are going to be without money permanently, because they never gain or act on an understanding of how money works.

I know that sounds harsh. And you may not be a face-to-face salesperson and never need to sit across a desk or table from someone you think "can't afford it" and sell to them anyway. But the truth about this particular situation is the bigger truth about the entire world of money and wealth. That truth is, whatever amount you get has nothing to do with how much or how little anyone else has. Ever.

If you want your wealth attraction glowing and functioning at full power, you can't have *any* queasiness. You can't have *any* reluctance. You can't have *any* inhibition. You can't *ever* pull a punch. In the bigger sense, you have to understand that whatever financial position anyone you know is in, anyone you do business with is in, anyone, period, is in, has nothing to do with you. In the biggest sense, you have to understand that whatever the state of economic affairs in the world, it has nothing to do with how much wealth you accumulate. **Your wealth is addition for you but subtraction for no one.**

Unless and until you buy this premise hook, line, and sinker, you will always suffer from wealth inhibition.

One of the many great masters of wealth attraction worthy of your study is Gene Simmons, creator of the rock band KISS. In recent years, you may have seen Gene in the reality-TV show about his life on A&E, *Gene Simmons Family Jewels*. We had Gene as a guest speaker at one of the conferences we hold each year for our Glazer-Kennedy Insider's Circle.™ Members got to hear his life story and entrepreneurial strategies firsthand, and I spent a fair amount of private time offstage, kibitzing with him. I routinely recommend his book *Sex, Money, Kiss* as a good, candid look into the way a made-from-scratch, multimillionaire entrepreneur adept at wealth attraction thinks about money. You may be offended or shocked, but you'll learn a lot from Gene.

"Be clear, be truthful.

Stand there proudly,

unapologetically,

unabashedly, and say,

'I love cash.

It will get me

everything

I want in life.' "

—Gene Simmons

Newman's Own

No one mentioned this when reporting on the death, life, and work of Paul Newman. Much was made of his extraordinary acting career, including, I think, accurate observation that there was much more depth in some of his later roles than in his early, more popular performances. If you never saw *The Verdict*, rent it. A little bit was said about his auto racing investments and activities, including his own somewhat improbable, late in life driving—a clue to his competitiveness. More was said about his liberal politics and protest; he was proud of being on President Nixon's enemies list. And he was a liberal even we conservatives could admire and respect, because he was knowledgeable and informed, principled, consistent, and walked his talk. Most was said about his development of his famous food company, which donates its profits to charity. But no one said anything about this, in Newman's own words:

> *"Now that I'm heavily into peddling food, I begin to understand the romance of business, the allure of being the biggest fish in the pond and the juice you get from* **beating out your competitors.**"

He also said that he could not "lay claim to some terribly philanthropic instinct—it was a combination of circumstances." Had the business stayed small, as the lark it was to start, he says it would never have gone charitable. Of course, it quickly grew big, and hundreds of millions of dollars of the Newman's Own brand products have been sold, and the charitable support provided will now continue long after his death, a fine legacy. Somewhat accidentally, the business Paul Newman created and lent his celebrity to has

Newman's Own, cont.

become a new model for many for-profit companies with the purpose of funding social causes or supporting charitable activities.

But my main point here is that behind the legendary blue eyes lived a ferocious competitor. In his acting career, in his racing, in his business, Newman derived immense pleasure from beating out his competitors. A truth not often included in highly successful entrepreneurs' press kits and autobiographies, but that is revealed in interviews and others' profiles of them, is that they are not nice. They are tough. In specific competitive situations, they are even ruthless. They play to win and are not usually "good losers." I listen to people and watch people closely, to try to determine the extent and depth and constancy of their competitive drive—or lack thereof. Personally, every single day that I choose to work, I compete. I compete with the clock; I compete against the odds, to develop successful marketing campaigns; I compete in the cluttered, crowded marketplace for attention. When I was a speaker at events with a number of other speakers who also sold from the platform, I always wanted to hit my targets but also beat all others' dollars per head, and connived to get that information so I could tell whether I won or lost. It's my observation that winners have an emotional need to win, find a way to score themselves in everything they do, and rarely shrug off losing, however that may be defined. If you intently, thoroughly study any famously successful entrepreneur present or past about whom a wealth of information is available, you'll make that same observation.

CHAPTER 33

Wealth Magnet 2
Unequivocal Belief in
Abundance

Originally appearing as Chapter 2 from
*No B.S. Wealth Attraction in the
New Economy*

Water, water everywhere but not a drop to drink.
Our world is no desert island. There's money, money
everywhere. Drink all you want.

If you do not hang out with people who own private planes
or shares in private jets, or at least fly first class everywhere
they go . . . if you do not hang out with people who have their
shirts and suits custom-tailored . . . if you do not hang out with
people who own racehorses or boats or vacation homes . . . if
you do not hang out with people who are extremely prosperous
and adept at wealth attraction, you might be fooled into thinking that money is "tight" or in limited supply or hard to come
by. And based on those thoughts, you might inhibit your own
wealth attraction. Or you might think such people are rare, in
small number. They are not.

While it is true that the recession, stock market collapse, real estate value reversals, and related economic trauma of past, recent years did take its toll on the super-rich, the merely rich, and the mass affluent or nearly rich, it's also true that it left plenty of people in these populations, with plenty more moving up as we speak. After all, if you are worth $100 million or $10 million and temporarily see 10%, 20%, or even 30% of your net worth disappear, you are still worth $70 million, $80 million, or $90 million, or if starting with $10 million, still worth $7 million, $8 million, or $9 million. The loss is annoying, possibly scary, briefly. But it doesn't change the fact that you are wealthy. Further, one thing about everybody who has amassed most or all of their wealth through their own ingenuity, effort, investment, and attraction (as opposed to inheritance, hitting the lottery, or having been president of the United States and then cashing in afterward) is that they know how to replace wealth lost; they know how to attract it, and are quite confident of their ability to do so.

It happens that I travel by private jet myself, and I can tell you there was, recently, a downturn in all aspects of the private aviation business. But I can also tell you that there are still waiting lines to land at and take off from private terminals at many airports, multimillion-dollar jets being purchased every day, and companies like NetJets ferrying about more self-made affluents you've never heard of than celebrities you have heard of, to and from their second and third homes, weekend golf games, vacations, and, of course, business meetings.

The rising tide of affluence is so great we even added a newsletter to our stable, which I edit, devoted entirely to marketing to the affluent, and wrote an entire book on the subject, *No B.S. Marketing to the Affluent.*

Anyway, if these are not the circles you hang out in, then poking your nose in there will be very good for you. Exposure to the reality of a world you may only think of as fodder for

Be Where the Money Is!

I edit a special newsletter entirely devoted to the subject of marketing to the affluent and mass affluent, the *No B.S. Marketing to the Affluent Letter*. Information at www.DanKennedy.com. There is also a book on the subject in this series, *No B.S. Marketing to the Affluent.*

TV and movies and a few glossy magazines can alter your entire attitude about attracting wealth for yourself. The very idea of personal wealth attraction is easier to accept the more you personally see, experience, and understand just how much free-flowing wealth there is to attract. It's a bit like never actually seeing the ocean from a penthouse balcony and only reading about it in a book or seeing pictures in a magazine—the enormity of it, the vastness of it just doesn't hit you until you experience it in person.

I suggest the following experiences: visit The Forum Shops in Las Vegas, Rodeo Drive in Beverly Hills, or Bergdorf Goodman in New York City. Vacation in Boca Raton, Florida, Scottsdale, Arizona, or Aspen, Colorado. Immediately go to your nearest bookstore and pick up copies of *The Robb Report, Millionaire, Worth,* and *Town & Country* magazines. Go on a field trip to a classic car auction or a racehorse auction. In short, in person and at a distance through media, immerse yourself in the lifestyles of the affluent. Not only will you be surprised at the prices cheerfully paid for goods and services, you'll be more amazed at the vast array of very high-priced goods and services designed for affluent consumers—you'll be even more amazed at just how many affluent consumers there are.

The more aware you make your own mind—conscious and subconscious—of just how much affluence there is, just how much money is moving around, the more easily you will attract wealth. So this is no idle exercise I suggest. It is an important step in conditioning your mind to attract wealth. And, just as your body must be conditioned for health and fitness and longevity, your mind must be conditioned for wealth. This observing of money flowing around the affluent is such an important and beneficial exercise, I have taken one of my Wealth Attraction Coaching Groups to Disney's Animal Kingdom Lodge on a "field trip," all staying on the concierge floor, taking the Sunrise Safari, lunching with a staff Imagineer, eating in the five-star restaurants. I took my Coaching Groups on a field trip to The Forum Shops. I give subscriptions to *The Robb Report* as client gifts. Even if you are not yet living an affluent lifestyle, you must immerse yourself in expanded awareness of what it is like and how many people are.

To believe the streets are awash with money, you need to see streets awash with money. If there aren't any in your own neighborhood, you just need to get out more!

Neiman Marcus invented the idea of offering extraordinarily expensive, unique items in their annual holiday catalogs years ago—initially, more as a means of getting publicity than making spectacularly profitable sales. However, over years the practice has led to Neiman Marcus and many other catalog merchants inventing unusual gift offers. Several years ago, Victoria's Secret offered a diamond-encrusted bra for a million dollars. One of my favorites was presented in a catalog called *Gentleman's Domain*: a product from the Eli Bridge Company, a manufacturer that builds amusement park rides, has been building them for the industry for 100 years. With the offer in *Gentleman's Domain*, for a mere $300,000.00 you could have the real thing in your backyard, a 67-foot-high, 16-seat Ferris wheel. The catalog copy warned that you'd need a 220-volt power outlet. And since it weighed almost 20 tons, you may have wanted to have the patio checked out before getting started.

There are two lessons here. One, another illustration of the amount of money flowing, and two, the opportunity to dip into the flowing stream as you wish, given enough ingenuity to create something captivating to people. While these kind of outrageous gift examples date back to 1955, when Neiman Marcus began the creative exercise in response to the blossoming of the new oil-rich in Texas, it is a terrific success clue for the New Economy in which everybody expects something unique, of particular and precise relevance to them, and is willing to pay premium prices or fees for it. (In Neiman Marcus's Christmas catalogs: a jewel-encrusted tiger, a $588,000.00 stocked and staffed Noah's Ark, and his-and-her jets.)

Of course, most people's reaction to an outrageous example like this is to cry "irrelevant!" After all, your customers don't have this kind of money to blow, your customers are tight-fisted cheapskates, you have a hard time selling to your customers, yada yada. Pfui. A few years back, I produced an infomercial-style video brochure for a client who builds top-of-the-line, expensive backyard sheds. Not the tin jobs you think of. These are more like miniature houses, with peaked roofs, doors, windows, flower boxes, and complete interiors, with workbenches, bookshelves, and cabinetry. The priciest of them could even be sold in the Neiman Marcus catalog! To shoot the video, I took a crew to a number of the customers' backyards, to see their sheds and tape their testimonial comments.

One happy couple with not one but two sheds in their backyard, his-and-hers sheds, are both retired and on Social Security, and he's got one small pension. They're totally on a fixed income. Two sheds.

Another guy with the biggest shed and a big pond in his back-yard started out telling me something of a sob story. If you heard it, you'd assume he didn't have two nickels to rub together. But somehow, miraculously, he dug up about $20,000.00 for land-scaping and a koi pond, and another $10,000.00 for the shed.

The truth known to all smart marketers is: Everybody some-how finds plenty of money to buy whatever they decide they want to buy. There's always a lot of "hidden money" in the mar-ket as a whole and in the vast majority of households and busi-nesses. It hides from everyone failing to offer sufficiently moti-vating and interesting offers. It is invisible to entrepreneurs with vision blocked by their own ideas about the absence of available spending power.

Lots of people complain about how tough they have it, rais-ing a family, three kids, both parents having to work. Both par-ents and all three kids have cell phones; about $90.00 a month in charges. Both of the older kids are in not one but several activi-ties: dance, karate, Little League. Both parents drive new autos. There's a satellite dish on the side of the house, a big flat-screen TV in the den, a TV in every bedroom. They wouldn't know "tough" if it bit 'em in the butt, and they freely buy whatever they decide to buy.

It is a huge, huge, huge mistake for you to accept any part of the suggestion that money's tight, hard to get, that your custom-ers don't have money or won't spend it. And if by some freak, rare, incredible chance you actually have managed to put your-self into a position where the people you are doing business with are short of money or are tight about spending it, bubba, you choose your customers. Switch to some who freely spend. There are plenty of them out there. One of the keys to turning your wealth attraction power on to max is acceptance of all the respon-sibility for your outcomes in life. The nature of your customers, the responsiveness of your customers, the buying behavior of your customers in their relationship with you is your responsibility—not theirs and not anybody else's.

Don't Buy What the Bad Newsmongers Are Selling

Beware the news media. For some perverse reasons of their own, about which I have my suspicions, the mainstream media constantly under-reports good economic news and over-hypes bad economic news. During the recent recession, the media loved to compare it to the Great Depression, to such an egregious extent that my friends at the prestigious Business and Media Institute at Media Research Center issued an entire, detailed report for the media, the public, and groups like my clients, debunking the comparison. It is a huge, huge, huge mistake for you to accept the mainstream media's biased, liberal agenda-driven misrepresentation of the state of the economy or of the amount and level of opportunity in this country—at any time. And whatever you do, do NOT listen to any of the even more outrageously inaccurate assertions from Michael Moore and his ilk. There is a contingent of Moore-types who insist on promoting the idea that there is a teeny, tiny group of evil rich vs. a gigantic population of viciously oppressed masses for whom there is no opportunity. The spew of Moore, and others who echo it, is toxic. I have written a lengthy article about this, originally intended for the *No B.S. Business Success* book, omitted through editorial decisions, and subsequently published in my autobiography, *My Unfinished Business*, which you can find information about at https://MagneticMarketing.com.

The truth is that the biggest, fastest-growing, most expansive and expanding segment of the American population is mass affluent, not poor. Admittedly, this trend was temporarily slowed by recession, but demographics guarantee that it will pick up steam and hit a faster stride than ever before, post-recession, in the New Economy.

> $\bigvee$ isit www.BusinessAndMedia.org for research-
> based analysis of media reporting on business,
> financial, and political issues. BMI publishes my politi-
> cal column and numerous other leading columnists and
> thought-leaders, and posts new information and com-
> mentary daily.

Here's something interesting about affluence. I was born in 1954. Owning the color TV in the neighborhood was a sign of affluence. When I was a kid, we were the only people in our entire neighborhood near Cleveland, Ohio, to have a swimming pool. That was a big deal. Getting a new car, a big deal. In the '70s, the two-car household was affluent. Now it's a two-home household. A few years back, when I was still flying commercial, on a flight from Cleveland to Orlando, I realized through conversation that every single person in the first-class seats owned a home in Cleveland and another home in Florida. There is, right now, this minute, more disposable income by any measurement—dollars, percentages, ratios, you pick the statistics you like—than ever before. There are more people invested in real estate in addition to their homes and in the stock market than ever, and despite stalls and reverse in values and value growth of these assets, there are more millionaires than ever before. The biggest wealth transfer in American history from my parents' generation to mine is in progress, with another to follow, from my generation to the next.

On top of that, new categories of products and services, new entertainments and recreations, new industries, new opportunities abound. Stop and think about all the businesses that didn't even exist when you were a kid. I marvel at it all.

It seems that every day, somebody invents another new means of attracting wealth. Consider the simple but fast-growing homebased business of mommy-blogging. If you've never heard of it, it's nearly nine years old, and expanding exponentially. A growing list of major corporations have moved from merely giving free product samples to paying sponsorship fees, per-posting fees, and ad dollars to stay-at-home mommies who use and write about their products on their blogs, giving mom-to-mom recommendations. Most of these bloggers are small-time operators, picking up free products, a few hundred dollars a month, maybe an all-expense paid junket now and again, like a family trip to Sea World. But an increasing number are moving up to thousands of dollars in monthly income, some even more. There are even aggregators, organizing these fragmented solo operators into groups, under single umbrellas, so bigger dollars can be secured from advertisers. The activity has become so significant that, in mid-2009, the Federal Trade Commission began discussions about regulating it as advertising media and imposing requirements for disclosures about payments received by the bloggers. This grass-roots, made-by-moms activity is likely to morph into an organized, substantial industry generating hundreds of millions of dollars a year and, yes, creating wealth for many involved—as well as for up-and-coming businesses that find ways to use this unusual advertising and marketing media. This is but one of literally thousands of examples of new wealth-creation devices and opportunities springing to life all around you.

I am absolutely convinced that if you don't do well financially in America today, it is either due to utter ignorance of opportunity or choice. It definitely is NOT due to lack of opportunity. You need to be convinced of this, too.

These fact-based beliefs are essential to turning off wealth inhibition and turning up wealth attraction. If you do not share these beliefs, if you doubt and question the fact of unlimited, readily available abundance of both opportunity and money, then you need to invest time and energy on your own fact-finding research mission and make this sale to yourself. Otherwise, to borrow from a past friend, the late Jim Newman, author of the fine book *Release Your Brakes,* you are driving down the highway to wealth, one foot on the gas but the other foot riding the brake.

The Day That Changed a Doctor's Money Awareness Forever

Let me tell you about a Critical Day in My Life.

I was making small talk with a female patient, Sally R., who constantly fought me on receiving care, complained about what her insurance covered and didn't cover, and told me she just couldn't afford "all these adjustments"—even though she felt better with them, felt worse without them. This fateful Monday, Sally casually mentioned, "Could you be a little careful today? Saturday I had a deep tissue massage and I'm a bit sore still, mostly in my neck."

I was stunned. As if a bucket of ice water had been thrown in my face.

But I stayed calm and in the same casual tone as hers, asked where she'd received the massage. And she told me—in glowing terms—of going to the new, fancy spa on Columbus Avenue. "My husband's partner's wife told me to go there to get a great facial. By the way, I don't think you've ever met my husband. He and his partner own the big law firm across from the courthouse downtown, the one with the clock on the building's tower. Anyway, when I went to the spa for my first appointment, they asked me if I had any other issues . . . I told them I come here to have my back cracked . . . and they suggested I sign up for a package of deep tissue massages that would complement the adjustments and help me feel better longer."

The Day That Changed a Doctor's Money Awareness Forever, cont.

I was angry. Felt betrayed. Sally'd been poor-mouthing me to the point I'd reduced her per visit charges, and agreed to send her a bill at the end of each month rather than having her pay per visit. Now I knew she was paying big prices—CASH—at a fancy spa. And was married to a prominent attorney. (I later got over being angry at her and rightfully got good and mad AT ME.)

When Sally left, she even put off making her next appointments because "it's just so expensive and I don't want to run up too big a bill. I'll call you if I start feeling badly. Thanks, Dr. Johnson."

Thanks Dr. Johnson, indeed.

This was a Critical Day in My Life. I sat down and thought about what had just happened—and how it was certainly a "dirty little secret" among many of my other patients, and other chiropractors' patients from coast to coast. Maybe you've heard the author and speaker Jim Rohn talk about "the day that turned his life around." This was such a day for me. It *liberated* me, from being slave to what I thought others could or would pay, and *emboldened* me to charge what I was worth—and work for no less.

—Dr. Michael Johnson, D.C.

Dr. Johnson operates a thriving, successful, multi-therapy clinic with emphasis on treating patients with chronic pain conditions in Appleton, Wisconsin. He also provides consulting and business coaching on "The Johnson Methods" for innovative treatment, practice development, and practice management to thousands of chiropractic physicians nationwide.

CHAPTER 34

Wealth Magnet 7
Speak Money

Originally appearing as Chapter 7 from
No B.S. Wealth Attraction in the
New Economy

Most people speak lack, poverty, inadequacy, doubt, and fear.

You have to be careful about the vocabulary you use because every word thought, spoken, or written, if inner-directed, constitutes programming, instructions to your subconscious mind. It is overly simplistic to believe that what you say in your head (think) and speak out loud manifests. The title of Napoleon Hill's most famous book *Think and Grow Rich* is slightly misleading; more accurately it should be *How to Think to Grow Rich*. Thought alone will not override behavior or certain physical realities and circumstances. However, it is accurate to say that the way you think about money and the language you use about money matters a great deal. How you speak about money reveals the programming your subconscious is actually being directed by; and your subconscious is accumulating programming to which it is trying to respond. Further, your spoken words convey to others your relative comfort and confidence or discomfort and fear about money. Any sales professional can tell you that prospects "smell fear" like animals. This is not superstition on their part. Experienced sales pros know it is infinitely harder to make the sale you desperately feel you must make than the sale that doesn't matter much one way or the other. Professional negotiators all know that the person who wants it least has the power. Money is naturally attracted to the person most confident and comfortable about it.

People tend to transfer their money to these same people. When you are talking to others, there's text and subtext, heard by others' conscious and subconscious minds. When you say that you just don't "feel good" about somebody or that your "intuition" tells you not to trust or do business with somebody, it's your subconscious processing impressions from sight, sound, the other senses, searching its files for past information and experiences. You can't actually enunciate why you feel as you do. You just do. So you might not consciously realize that when you're around Joe he often talks in terms of lack, poverty, failure, and fear, so you do not want to buy from him, invest with him, or otherwise be involved with him. But that may very well be what has occurred within your subconscious.

For all these reasons, what you speak about money matters.

As an example, consider the term: "Hard-earned dollars." You all recognize the term, don't you? Hard-earned dollars. You probably heard your parents say it. Your friends may say it. You may say it, or some variation of it, without ever considering its true meaning. If you translate it to programming, it is: money is very hard to get. You get money only through difficult and unpleasant work. If money somehow arrives without being connected to hard work, there's something wrong with it. It's tainted or toxic. It's incorrect and dishonorable to get it easily.

Now consider the phrase "easy money." For most people, this is "bad." The perception is that "easy money" is somehow tainted, dirty, undeserved. The perception is that the person seeking "easy money" is a lazy bum or a fool.

What a barrier! This is a tall, wide, thick wall that prevents entrepreneurs from looking for or seeing many great opportunities in their own businesses, lying there within easy reach. I think this explains why a pair of fresh, expert eyes like mine can so easily and frequently see unexploited opportunities in others' businesses. It's not just that the owner of the business is too close to the trees to see the forest. There's a wall he can't see through at all.

What a barrier! If things start to get easy, if money starts flowing in faster, in bigger sums than ever before, the entrepreneur will subconsciously reject it and engage in all manner of self-sabotage to slow the unjust flow.

The fact is, there's no reason money has to be hard to earn or earned in hard ways. I've taught thousands of entrepreneurs how to earn much larger incomes more easily. There are so many ways this can occur, a hundred books couldn't chronicle them all. I'll try, though, to give you a sense of the range.

For example, there's Dr. Chris Tomshack, who had developed an extraordinarily effective marketing system for attracting patients to his chiropractic practice; on the back of this system, he went from owning and operating one clinic to two to three to four. But there he hit the wall. He found himself spread too thin trying to manage four clinics as well as one. He became frustrated by declining quality, burdened by more and more time going to managing staff and being taken away from his expert attention to advertising and marketing, and ended up actually working harder and harder for less and less. Expansion from four to six to ten was unimaginable. At my suggestion, he switched to franchising and, as of this writing, his company, HealthSource, has over 240 franchised chiropractic and weight-loss clinics throughout America, his income leapt from a very hard-earned six figures to a much more easily and pleasantly earned seven figures, and he is positively affecting the health of hundreds of thousands instead of thousands. Make no mistake, his life is not absent of work. He is now CEO of a fast-growing company, recognized by national magazines for its meteoric growth. But his work is not the "hard work" most think of, and his financial rewards have no proportionate connection whatsoever to hours worked or numbers of patients treated with his hands. His wealth is not limited by his own work, or by his ability and tolerance for hands-on management, or even by geographic boundaries.

My client Dennis Tubbergen has changed the way thousands of upper-tier financial advisors secure clients and earn millions in fees and commissions, with the switch from arduous one-on-one prospecting and presentations to small-group "focus groups" for qualified prospective clients, effectively leveraging the same work to a power of 8 to 12.

Diana and Pierre Coutu, in a field dominated by low prices—pizza—focused on upscale, gourmet products, with their average large pizza priced from $22.00 to $38.00. The work of delivering 100 pizzas is virtually the same at their pizzeria as it is at, say, Pizza Hut or Domino's, but the profit is substantially greater. Their business doubled, by the way, in a peak year of the recent recession.

Another client, Owen Garratt, a pencil artist, decided not to sell his art in traditional ways, like exhibiting weekend after weekend after weekend from morning to night at community art shows or endlessly soliciting and "working" gallery owners for a few spaces on their walls or a show now and then. Instead, Owen focused on the corporate market, where companies buy his works in series, collections, and in quantity, on a continuous basis, as client gifts and awards. He also used the internet, a newsletter, and other direct-marketing media to build his own passionate, loyal following of fans who eagerly await his next new life-adventure and the artworks it inspires. As I write this, he has his own reality-TV show in the works. By controlling his own distribution, from pencil stroke to customer, he shares revenue with no one and builds equity not just in his creative product but also in his customer list and relationship with it. Also, because of the large customer base and the willingness of some to buy quantities of a drawing, he is never selling one drawing like an artist might at an art show, but he is able to turn that same drawing into several series of different-sized prints, selling hundreds of copies often within a matter of days of their release. I imagine the work of finding the ideal location, subject, and story and actually doing the drawing is about the same for one artist or the next, but one may only convert all that work into a single $100.00 or $1,000.00 sale, while Owen converts it to tens of thousands to hundreds of thousands of dollars.

My longtime clients Greg Renker and Bill Guthy, with whom I worked beginning with their very first TV infomercial (for an audio product based on the book *Think and Grow Rich*), led a veritable revolution in the way skin care and cosmetic products are sold—in the process building a billion-dollar business. Traditionally, specialty skin care and cosmetic products have been sold by direct sales forces such as Avon and Mary Kay, or at department store counters and in-store boutiques also staffed by trained sales forces. Beginning with a line linked to actress Victoria Principal, Guthy-Renker brought over a dozen different celebrity-brand cosmetic and skin care product lines to TV infomercials and thus direct to consumers, erasing layers upon layers of distribution, and all the work of recruiting, training, and managing salespeople, distributors, or retail operations. By far their biggest success

358 @ THE BEST OF NO B.S.

has been with skin care products for acne sufferers, Proactiv, a business I helped push them toward. Their billion-dollar success brought about by replacing traditional work with direct media follows a principle or strategy long used to create business break-throughs; marry a fundamentally successful product with a different means of distribution. Every time you see a product demonstrated and sold on a TV commercial by a frenetic, high-energy pitchman—from the grand old master Ron Popeil to the recently famous Billy Mays (who died suddenly at a young age in 2009)—think about the origin of the pitch and, very likely, the product itself: the booth at the state or county fair, the pitchman there working hard all day to sell to small groups of people rather than tens of thousands of TV viewers. If you get your shoes shined at a stand at the airport or get a therapeutic massage in a chair at the same airport, remember such services were transplanted there by somebody with imagination and vision. If you pop into the convenience store and fill your car's gas tank at its pumps, get yourself a Subway® sandwich or Krispy Kreme® doughnut inside the store, remember there was a time when there were gas stations and there were convenience stores but never together, and brand-name fast-food concessions weren't found at either. Even more germane to this topic is the switch from service stations to self-serve gas stations—the company pays fewer workers, the customer does the work, and the wealth still flows to the oil companies.

I could go on forever, with examples of hard-work elements replaced by easy-work elements, or work leveraged through multiplication, in varied businesses small and large, and small made large as a result. The entrepreneurs connected with these examples had to be open to and alert for different substitutions for hard work and for traditional work.

Even consider me. In 1996, I earned over a million dollars from speaking, requiring nearly constant travel, delivering more than 60 presentations during the year, as well as writing, publishing, and selling information products at every speech, and requiring a staff person to process all the orders and a vendor to ship products. In 2004, I earned a million dollars from coaching just five small groups of entrepreneurs who came and met with me, requiring only 26 days of meetings in my home cities plus 16 days talking on the phone while sitting in the sun on my backyard deck or in my big leather recliner in my library. Counting travel days and speaking days, in 1996, it required more than 200 days to earn what only 42 days provided in 2004. Considerably easier, less strenuous, less stressful days. This shift involved procedural changes in my business, changes in strategy, but also, of equal importance, continuous improvement of my thinking, understanding, even imaginings about money.

Breaking free of the Work-Money Link has not been easy for me. I was raised to have enormous respect for work ethic. My youth experiences taught me that money is hard earned and earned hard. Shaking that, replacing that thinking is no simple trick. But that link is an illusion, not a reality.

This is not to suggest that I don't work or that you shouldn't. In fact, I think work of some kind is necessary for sound mental and physical health. But there is work and then there is work. My Platinum Member Ron LeGrand's motto is "The Less I Do, the More I Make." It is subject to misinterpretation. It is meant as a variation on the "work smarter, not harder" theme. Personally, I work at working on my terms, on things that I enjoy, on high-yield opportunities and tasks, and I coach others to do the same. I am all about finding ways to make things easier, not harder. To do more with less. To gain leverage. But if you think and speak the belief of "hard-earned dollars," you reinforce a barrier to doing any of these things.

This is just one example of hundreds of negative, limiting statements routinely thought and said about money. They are all bricks strengthening and reinforcing the wall between you and attraction of maximum wealth.

What You Speak Reveals What You Are

Do you have kids? And how many times, in the past month, did you explain to the kids that money doesn't grow on trees? Where's that come from? Maybe you've become your father. Maybe you are simply repeating what you've always heard. It's been programmed in. And now, at a particular point in your life, you are regurgitating it and spitting it back out with no thought about what it's doing to you or what it's doing to the person that you're saying it to. When you say this, what belief system is it communicating and reinforcing?

I am not for spoiling kids; that's another discussion for another time and place. For now, let's keep the harsh spotlight focused on you. When something like that spews out of your mouth, it came from somewhere. It came from your own mind, your subconscious, your belief system, the recordings that play inside your head. Whatever you say about money is simultaneously revealing and reinforcing.

There is a unique language used by wealth-attracting entrepreneurs. I hear it all the time, because I hang out and work with them most of the time. I've been surrounded by them for years. They speak one language; the outside world speaks another. I'm not going to hand you a vocabulary list here and suggest you try memorizing it, or suggest you read positive affirmations 20 times a day from 3-by-5-inch cards. That can be useful, but it is a tiny piece of this puzzle, and overly simplistic. Trying to use a vocabulary list won't cut it. The language has to be an honest, natural reflection of your beliefs about money and wealth; everything in this book has to come together and support the changes you choose to make in your own belief system.

But make no mistake: What you speak matters. And you can attract more wealth more easily by speaking the language of wealth.

Trump-Speak

Not since Muhammad Ali went around yelling "I AM THE GREATEST" has anybody become so famous for hyperbolic, super-lative statements about himself and everything he does, as has The Donald. With almost every breath, he declares something made-by-Trump as the biggest, the grandest, the greatest, the most amazing, the most successful. Listen to him speak about his TV shows *The Apprentice* and *Celebrity Apprentice* and you'd think there were no others. When we had Trump's daughter Ivanka come and speak at one of the Glazer-Kennedy Insider's Circle™ SuperConferences (the name, a bit of hyperbole of our own) and I sat in the backstage "green room" with her, I imme-diately noticed the exact same Trump-Speak as she described the real estate projects she was working on and her jewelry line. So I asked her about it. She said she'd grown up with it, it was ingrained and natural, and was a way not just of promotion, but of reaffirming commitment to an ideal and a position in the world. "After all, if we can't make what we're doing the best," she said, "why would we choose to do it?" I believe "Trump-Speak" reflects a deeply felt ideal, the more often and consistently spo-ken, the more deeply felt. A closed loop of extreme confidence construction for self and assertive, pre-eminent positioning to the marketplace.

Donald Trump has been asked about this himself many times. In his own words . . .

Trump-Speak, cont.

". . . key to the way I promote is BRAVADO. People may not always think big themselves but they get very excited by those who do. People want to believe something is THE biggest and THE greatest and THE most spectacular.

"Some people have written that I'm boastful, but they are missing the point. If you're devoting your life to creating a body of work and you believe in what you do, and what you do is excellent, you'd damn well better tell people you think so. Subtlety and modesty are appropriate for nuns, but if you're in business, you'd better learn to speak up and announce your significant accomplishments to the world."

Wealth Magnet 26
Energy From People

Originally appearing as Chapter 26 from
No B.S. Wealth Attraction in the
New Economy

here are very practical obstacles to wealth attraction that short-circuit your wealth attraction.

The first big obstacle is incompetent people. Sometimes these are people incapable of handling the responsibilities or doing the jobs entrusted to them. More frequently these are people able but unwilling to do the jobs. They are lazy and uncreative. They have no sense of urgency or initiative, so they will do only the minimum, they will not figure out solutions, they will let their progress be stalled by the slightest challenge, and return everything to your lap. Dealing with such people is a miserable, sadly common experience. Every entrepreneur wrestles with these people. They may be employees, vendors, advisors, others.

Another, related obstacle: people who waste or abuse your time, what I call "time vampires." This bunch can just as easily include certain clients or customers as employees and vendors.

Another, related obstacle: people who drain or divert your mental energy, who disrupt the flow of your wealth attraction. Negative people, gloom 'n' doom people, whiners and complainers. Mike Vance, former Dean of Disney University, calls them pissers and moaners. This bunch can just as easily include friends and relatives as employees, vendors, customers, or clients.

They must all go. The minute you detect their toxic odor, take action to get them out of your business, out of your life, to distance yourself from them. You need to develop a Zero Tolerance Policy about all these people and be decisive, even ruthless in enforcing it. Hesitancy and timidity in doing so will always cost you more than whatever temporary trauma and disruption results from making changes in your staff, vendors, or others around you. Always.

I'll give you a very common example. A client with five staff members in his office brought me in, to observe, interview, analyze, look at his business from top to bottom with my "fresh eyes." I told him that his majorette domo, his key office manager, the employee who had been with him the longest had to go. I told him she was sabotaging his new initiatives behind his back, ignoring procedures he wanted followed, damaging morale, and driving away good clients. I told him she was the equal of an open vat of toxic chemicals. He insisted he needed her, relied on her, couldn't function without her; at bare minimum, the disruption caused by firing her would be disastrous. It took me over a year to convince him to give the old battle-ax the ax. Immediately after doing so, sales increased; he made no other changes; no increased advertising; she exited, enter more income. Within the year, the business was 30% more profitable, the remaining employees measurably more productive, my client happier, more relaxed, and more productive. By the following year, his net worth had increased by nearly $500,000.00, and he had enough liberated time to finally launch a second business he'd been back-burnering for years. A "wealth block" had been surgically removed, vibrant health created by its removal.

Think of your wealth attraction power as electric current. Years ago, strings of Christmas lights could be short-circuited by any loose bulb, any burnt-out bulb, or any bad fuse. If there was one of these anywhere in the entire string of lights, it disrupted the flow of power, and the entire string shut off. I remember helping my father unscrew and test bulb after bulb, fuse after fuse, to find the one bad one. The power cord that runs between you and the world supply of wealth and the world supply of wealth and you has a very similar flaw. One disruptive person laying a finger on it anywhere along the line shuts down the entire flow of power.

I try my level best to operate a Zero Tolerance Policy toward people who disrupt the flow of my wealth attraction power. Be they employee, vendor, associate, or client, I will not tolerate their interference with the flow of wealth to me. I rid myself of them, even if at considerable, temporary cost. I have, on several occasions, stopped projects for clients after I've done a lot of work on them, refunded as much as $70,000.00, just to get rid of the client who was a "problem child," seriously interfering with my flow of power.

One of my rules:

> If I wake up three
> mornings thinking about you,
> and I'm not having sex with
> you, you've got to go.

Most people tolerate others causing them undue stress and aggravation, without realizing how costly such tolerance is. I want you to understand: it is very, very costly.

The opposite of all this is the assembly and organization of your own small cadre of exceptionally competent, highly creative, extraordinarily reliable and trustworthy individuals who are in sync and harmony with you and your objectives, who facilitate and even multiply your wealth attraction power. If you read Lee Iacocca's autobiography, you saw his description of this as his "horses," the few key people he relied on. If you carefully observed Donald Trump during his *Apprentice* television programs, read his books, and read his biography, you realized that George Ross and several other key people make Trump possible. Without them Trump wouldn't be and couldn't be Trump. You will find this "theme" true of all incredibly accomplished, successful, and wealthy entrepreneurs.

In short, the people around you, the people who populate your world, the people you rely on either enhance or sap your wealth attraction power. No person with whom you interact is a neutral factor. Each and every person either drains power from you or contributes power to you. One or the other. Power source or power drain. Ally or enemy. Black or white.

Refusing to face the black-and-white nature of this, with clarity and accuracy and honesty, is a major obstacle to wealth attraction. Refusing to act appropriately and decisively about what you deduce about a person, about a power drainer, is a major obstacle to wealth attraction.

How to Build a "Power Team" Around You

I have been very, very fortunate in my life to have had a number of people around me who have added to my power. They have changed over time, some left, some came. Change is inevitable. But I have certainly had an enormous amount of support.

Mine is in tiers.

In the first tier have been spouses, close associates, close friends, people I've relied on heavily, at different times, in different ways. My second wife, Carla, for example, was an important, chief source of support and power for many of the 22 years of our marriage. After a brief divorce, we are remarried and, in different ways than before, she is a greater source of support than ever before. At present, Bill Glazer, who publishes my *No B.S. Marketing Letter*, is president of Glazer-Kennedy Insider's Circle™, and his crackerjack staff, and Pete Lillo, who publishes another of my newsletters, are enormously valuable business associates I can rely on without equivocation. Vicky Tolleson, my lone employee, office manager, personal assistant, time-and-access sentry, problem solver, and client services director, is valuable beyond description. These people and a very short list of others, past or present, work with me pretty much on my terms, with the prime purpose of supporting and facilitating my productivity. They view their responsibility and best interests as making it possible for me to function at peak performance. I also have a very short list of people I can rely on for advice, counsel, information. It features Lee Milteer, a close friend and associate, who is a reliable sounding board, encourager but also questioner. The total number of people in this tier, at any given time, is less than a dozen.

In the second tier are both suppliers and clients. For example, for 11 years, I've run a formal "mastermind group" exclusively for information marketers in business akin to my own, all highly successful and innovative, all wealthy. While they pay me well to organize, host, facilitate, and direct the group and its meetings, I also participate as a member and benefit from the exchange of ideas and information. This tier also includes my CPA firm, the person I am most involved with in real estate investments, Darin Garman, and other paid advisors.

In the third tier are all the other clients I work with, the other vendors I rely on, the other sources of information I access, trade associations I belong to. Included here, for example, is the publisher of this book, its editor, its marketing people, my other publishers, my literary agents, my publicist. Also included are my consulting and copywriting clients who I work for and who support me, but toward whom I must still act discriminately. Also included, editors, graphic artists, web masters, other professionals and vendors I use intermittently, project by project.

This is "Planet Dan," a world I create and own and control, populated only by people I permit to be there, governed by laws I legislate and enforce. It's a small planet, so I have some level of personal relationship with every inhabitant of the planet. Every one of these relationships is a two-way street. They all influence me as I influence them. That's unavoidable. They all either enhance or drain my energy. They all either support and facilitate or interfere with my productivity. They all either enhance or disrupt my wealth attraction.

This is true of every single person you permit existence in your world, too. Rule your world accordingly.

Additional, Essential Reading

FOR RULERS OF THEIR OWN WORLDS: My books *No B.S. Time Management for Entrepreneurs* and *No B.S. Ruthless Management of People and Profits*, available from bookstores or online booksellers.

CHAPTER 36

Positioning Yourself and Your Business for MAXIMUM SUCCESS

Originally appearing as Chapter 4 from
*No B.S. Business Success in the
New Economy*

P ositioning is admittedly an advertising buzzword, but it's legitimately one of the most important marketing concepts you'll ever consider in your entrepreneurial career. One of the definitions of positioning is controlling how your customers and prospective customers think and feel about your business in comparison to other, similar businesses competing for their attention.

I have several specific suggestions about this process. Maybe they'll seem obvious to you, but I can tell you that I have seen many business people overlook the obvious, and cost themselves a lot of money as a result.

Positioning Strategy #1:
How to Describe What You Do to Attract the Customers You Want

Let's start with the name of your business. I insist the best business names telegraph what the business does. This may sound elementary, but start looking at the businesses in your town and notice how many of their names, boldly displayed on their signs, do not instantly tell you what the business offers and does. I, for example, prefer Dunkin' Donuts® to Starbucks®; although to be fair, their real name is Starbucks Coffee—the public has abbreviated it themselves with familiarity. Obviously, we can point to many hugely successful, brand name companies with mystery names: Apple and Amazon.com, for example, consumers know now, but didn't know at the start. The question you have to ask is whether or not you want to invest an enormous amount of money and patience in creating awareness and understanding of what your name represents or to start with a name that clearly represents what your business is and does.

For every successful name that doesn't telegraph what the business is about, you can find hundreds that do. Outback Steakhouse®, for example, tells us what we get there—steak, but also conveys its theme. *Entrepreneur* magazine, *The Wall Street Journal*, and *Investor's Business Daily* all bear names leaving no doubt about who they are for or what they are about. Our own *No B.S. Marketing Letter*, *No B.S. Marketing to the Affluent Letter*, and *No B.S. Info-Marketing Letter* all identify their different subject matter, and all convey the theme. Men's Wearhouse, a successful chain of many years, tells us who they are for, and, with a play on words, tells men they can get what they need to wear in an environment men (who generally don't like to shop) are comfortable in—a warehouse—and can get direct warehouse prices, implying good savings. With the same play-on-words technique, the Planters brand at Kraft Foods has a line of *NUT-rition* nut mixes; one for a healthy heart, another to improve digestion, another to boost immunity.

An old favorite of mine, a product I named for a company I had an interest in, was "Kills Weeds Dead." It was poisonous goop in an aerosol can that, when sprayed on pesky weeds, penetrated their root structure and killed them dead.

You have to consider very specific language choices in naming businesses, or in describing them. Consider these three: 9-11 Emergency Chiropractic Clinic . . . Family Chiropractic Clinic . . . Health & Longevity Chiropractic Clinic. In all three, fundamentally the same services are provided. But they would clearly attract different types of patients with different priorities. Do these three suggest different things to you: Hamilton & Wesley Wealth Management Advisors . . . Hamilton & Wesley Investment Management Advisors . . . Hamilton & Wesley, Financial Planning?

Titles matter. A lot. I have fought with all my publishers over my own book titles, except this publisher, which cheerfully accepted the long, awkward title and "No B.S." positioning of many of the books: *The No B.S., No Holds Barred, Kick Butt and Take No Prisoners Guide to* . . . (which we finally abbreviated with this one, in favor of *in the New Economy* added). That is my position; I have cultivated a reputation as a blunt, direct "no b.s." individual. Tim Ferriss, author of the monster bestseller *The 4-Hour Workweek*, revealed to Glazer-Kennedy Insider's Circle™ Diamond Members on one of their monthly teleseminars that he had arrived at that title by testing a number of options via Google Ads.

Titles matter beyond the book business. Titles or names are important for products, for offers. Our Member, Dr. Nielsen, a famously successful small-town chiropractor, comes up with a new name for a package of services every month, in connection with the feature story in his newsletter. One month might feature the Fast Injury Recovery, Back to Work Program; another the Golfers' Flexibility and Long-Ball Hitting Strength Program. All involve chiropractic treatment.

I have a Member in the photography business who split-tested via direct mail a particular offer and in the test altered only the name of the offer—version #1 was "Family Portrait Mother's Day Gift"; version #2: "The Ultimate Mother's Day Gift: The Family Portrait." Version #2 out-pulled version #1 in response by better than a 3-to-1 margin, a 300% difference.

Someone once told me about seeing a sign for an upcoming free seminar titled "12 Roadblocks to Financial Success" and concluding he had no need to attend—because he already knew more than 12! Maybe he was joking. Maybe not. But it certainly would have been improved by adding "How to Overcome" to its title.

There is the naming or titling of your "process." You can more clearly communicate and you can add value to what you do solely by its name. For example, THE 10-MINUTE OIL CHANGE is perceived differently if it's THE 9-MINUTE OIL CHANGE or if it is the GUARANTEED 10-MINUTE OIL CHANGE or the INDY 500-STYLE 10-MINUTE OIL CHANGE. Little words can make a big difference. For my client HealthSource's weight loss programs' marketing I coined the term Weight Loss Resistance Syndrome®, to describe the collection of weight problems and both physical and psychological barriers to weight loss that their program counters. In my book *No B.S. Marketing to the Affluent*, I also show how you can illustrate your process, to make it appear valuable and unique.

Positioning Strategy #2: How to Price

You'll hear a lot of different opinions about pricing strategy. Personally, I don't think I'd ever want to be in a business that procured its customers with the lure of "lowest prices." You cannot build long-term customer retention via the cheapest price. The way you get a customer has great impact on how you will sell to that customer again. There will always be someone willing to offer a cheaper price. If the only thing binding your customers to your company is the lowest price, your business will be as fragile in its tenth year as in its tenth week.

Dan Kennedy's Eternal Truth #6

Live by price, die by price.

In every business I'm involved in, we sell quality, value, service, and unique benefits. We do not sell price. I'm very pleased that I've become very well-known for guiding countless business owners among Glazer-Kennedy Insider's Circle™ Membership to creating premium versions of their goods and services and to selling at substantially higher prices or fees than they or their competitors ever imagined possible. At my urging, business owners and professionals discover what I call Price Elasticity. Usually, businesspeople underestimate the elasticity available to them and afforded by their customers.

I have vivid and permanent memory of such a lesson delivered to one client. He was one of 15 business owners in a group I coached. I and every other member of the group insisted he was underpricing a particular service he sold for $1,000.00, with the number of customers accommodated each time limited to 100. Finally, exasperated with the debate, I left my conference room where the group was meeting, returned with my checkbook, and offered to buy all 100 positions in the next group for $1,000.00 each with the intent of reselling them at $3,000.00 each and keeping the profit, letting them deliver their service as usual. They went home and—with fear and trepidation—doubled their price, with no ill effects. My best calculation is that they've pocketed over $2 million a year extra every year since, having discovered their price a lot more elastic than they believed.

The worst thing for any business, for any provider is "commoditization," being perceived as interchangeable commodity. When you sell emphasizing cheap price, you invite that perception.

Another interesting thing about price is how fearful most business owners are of raising prices or offering premium priced options. **Here's a scary thought**: you are selling everything you sell for less than you need to. **Scarier thought**: you're selling less of it at lower prices than you would at higher prices.

One of the most interesting things about price is not its impact on profit and income, but its impact on positioning. Often, underpricing sends the wrong message. The business owner thinks he's optimizing sales by offering the lowest price possible when he's actually creating skepticism and causing discerning customers to look elsewhere. One ad I have in my files even includes the line "Reassuringly Expensive." For years, I have cheerfully told everybody I can that I am the highest paid direct-response copywriter on the planet, and that most have chest pains when they first hear my fees. Taking this position has gotten me a lot more interest and, as a result, clients than it has cost me, and it has definitely saved me from a lot of time wasted with clients I wouldn't have wanted under any circumstances.

In most categories, as few as 10% to no more than 20% of consumers make their choices based on lowest price or fee. The other 80% to 90% look for more information and strive to make their decisions based on more complex criteria, factoring in quality, value, reliability, service, reputation, pride of ownership, and overall confidence they feel for the seller. The New Economy Customer is even more thoughtful about complex value vs. simple price. You'll find a more detailed discussion of the New Economy Customer in my book *No B.S. Sales Success in the New Economy*. The final piece of advice on price I'll give you here is that successful businesses based on factors other than low or aggressively competitive pricing outnumber successful businesses that feature low or lowest price promises by at least 500 to 1. Play the odds.

Price, Profit, and Power

Price strategy, price confidence, and presentation of price are so important that I developed and conducted an entire day-long workshop about it, now converted to an online learning program you can go through at home, at your convenience. You can find more information about this at https://MagneticMarketing.com.

Positioning Strategy #3:
How to Make Your Image Work for You

As long as I live, I will never forget a bank manager looking me straight in the eye, and in a genuinely sincere, shocked voice saying, "You can't be president of a company—you're not wearing a tie." To be perceived, without risk of exception, as a successful entrepreneur, you must match the image of a successful entrepreneur. To be perceived, without risk of exception, as successful and trustworthy in your field, you must match the image of a successful person in your field.

Places of business, product packaging, literature, and advertising, all are subject to the same image concerns as are individuals' appearances. Whether I walk on stage in a suit or in jeans has nothing to do with the quality or value of the speech I'll deliver, but it will have everything to do with how that speech is received. If I come on in the jeans, I instantly create psychological obstacles to acceptance. I've proven to myself that the most authoritative look makes a difference. At most of my speaking engagements, I sell my books and audio learning programs. I've tested, with identical types of audiences, tie, sport coat, and slacks vs. light-colored suit vs. dark, navy, or black pinstriped suit, and I always enjoyed greater sales with the last "look."

Is this fair? Of course not. It, unfortunately, allows racist, sexist, and other prejudices to live on. And you can certainly have a lot of moral outrage over it if you want to. But I'm going to ask

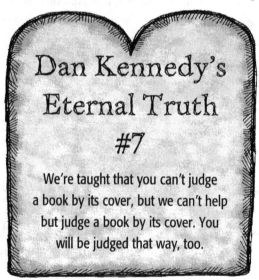

Dan Kennedy's Eternal Truth #7

We're taught that you can't judge a book by its cover, but we can't help but judge a book by its cover. You will be judged that way, too.

you a **defining question: would you rather be right or rich?** I call this a defining question for entrepreneurs because it challenges you to be totally realistic and pragmatic, give up your excuses, and succeed. A lot of people would rather live mediocre lives under the protection of the "it's not fair" excuse umbrella than to face the world as it really is and do what is necessary to win. A lot of people will cling to certain beliefs and behaviors even at the expense of desirable results. The most successful entrepreneurs I know are willing to change their beliefs and behaviors whenever that change can facilitate the most desirable results.

Now, don't misunderstand; I'm not suggesting the politicians' chameleon game, changing minute by minute, audience by audience, dressing up for one group, down for the next, telling anybody and everybody what they want to hear with no regard for truth or contradiction, having no core philosophy other than desired results. There has to be a "you" in there somewhere. There has to be a collection of core values not subject to easy change. But there are many things not nearly as important as core values that can be easily modified to permit success.

I once counseled a struggling attorney who couldn't understand why he wasn't attracting or keeping solid business clients. The day he drove me from his office to a lunch meeting in his canary-yellow, four-year-old pickup truck, I told him why. Of course, he protested mightily; he loved his truck, it was paid for, it shouldn't matter, etc. but his practice started picking up when he started driving a Cadillac. Individuals and businesses have images and are judged by them, usually long before the customer has an opportunity to fairly judge the actual competence or expertise of the individual or the quality of the products and services.

On the other hand, with regard to advertising or literature or direct mail, I must strongly caution you against image over substance. All too often, marketing material is pretty (and expensive) but fails to deliver a compelling direct-response message. Most businesses are better served by thinking about their marketing tools as "salesmanship in media" rather than as "advertising." In simple terms, copy is king. Message matters most. Yes, the wrong presentation for a given market can sabotage even the best message. But the more common error is a beautiful presentation of—nothing.

Ultimately, there must be an appropriate marriage of substance and style. Customers' expectations must be met and exceeded, anxiety avoided, reassurance given by the image presented by you, your staff, your physical location, your marketing material.

Positioning Strategy #4: Self-Appointment

When we are kids, our parents "appoint us" old enough to stay home alone, old enough to babysit our younger brothers or sisters, old enough to date, and so on. At work, employers or supervisors "promote us." In all these experiences, there is someone else, some authority figure determining that you are qualified to do a certain thing or handle a certain responsibility. This conditioning is not particularly useful when you step into the entrepreneurial world.

People often ask me: "How do you become a professional speaker?" They're looking for some kind of organized path such as going to a school, passing tests, and, finally, getting appointed as a professional by some kind of group. They're disappointed when I say, "Be one." I give the same answer regarding "business coach" or "consultant." Of course, there are alphabet soup designations you can go and get from groups that have set themselves up to sell them—themselves masters at manipulating perception, but clients care nothing about these things. Only peers do and peers do not make deposits to your bank account.

Early in my career, I read Robert Ringer's book *Winning Through Intimidation*, which made me understand that the biggest problem with getting to the top is getting through the crowd at the bottom. Ringer suggested simply "leap-frogging" over them. I've done that all my life. But I notice most people waiting around for someone else to recognize them, to give them permission to be successful.

Please understand, you do not need anybody's permission to be successful. And, if you wait for "the establishment" in any given field to grant you that permission, you'll wait a long, long time. And remember, success is never an accident, no matter how it appears to outsiders.

Jay Leno got Johnny Carson's job, arguably the best job in show business. At one time, comedian Gary Shandling was considered the front-runner for that job, and David Letterman was after it, too. But only Leno quietly went out and appointed himself to the job. In his travels, he went to the local NBC affiliates in different cities and towns, befriended the station managers, did promotional spots for them for free, and operated as the self-appointed ambassador of goodwill for the network and the show. By the time Carson retired, Leno was the only candidate with the solid support of all the NBC affiliates. Who told him he could do this? Nobody. He just did it. How dare he? That's the point.

Business success just isn't conferred upon you.

Power and influence is not granted—it's taken.

"Expert positioning" is all about self-appointment, self-promotion, and self-aggrandizement. Years ago, a client of mine, Dr. Robert Kotler, a Beverly Hills cosmetic surgeon, wrote and self-published a book titled *The Consumer's Guide to Cosmetic Surgery*. He was then able to promote himself as the

> "There are no wishy-washy rock stars, no wishy-washy astronauts, no wishy-washy CEOs . . ."
>
> —Karen Salmansohn, author of *Ballsy: 99 Ways to Grow a Bigger Pair*

doctor who wrote the book. You may have seen him on the TV program *Dr. 90210*. Easy for a doctor, you might think, but not so easy for me—I own a shoe repair shop or my company installs windows or I own a landscaping company. Actually, every business, every business can benefit from its owner or its "face" being promoted and then recognized as an expert. Examples abound if you'll look for them.

Make this note: you become a promotable expert by decision, acquisition, and organization of information, pronouncement, and promotion. Not by anointment by some authority on high.

A Story of Positioning Success

A longtime Member as well as a private client of mine, Darin Garman, was once a commercial real estate broker in Cedar Rapids, Iowa, handling apartment building, shopping center, and office building transactions in that area, by soliciting and securing listings, then hunting for investor-buyers. His business was local. It was helped enormously with my kind of marketing, so that he became the dominant leader in his field there, with over 80% of all such transactions going through his office. But his transformation from having a very good local business to a truly exceptional international business came by positioning himself as the expert in "heartland-of-America commercial real estate investing," and reaching out to investors outside the area. Today, 90% of his investors buying all these properties are from states other than Iowa and even overseas, most invest in or buy the Iowa properties sight unseen, all pay membership fees to be clients just for the privilege of having access to Darin's expertise, property owners listing properties with him pay client fees above and in advance of customary commissions, and he's never pressured to discount commissions. His business held up just fine during the recent recession years, too. In fact, there was flight of investment funds to

An Example of Darin's Marketing

An example of Darin's marketing can be found in my book *The Ultimate Sales Letter*. You can also see Darin's business at https://MagneticMarketing.com.

him from clients taking their money away from the stock market and other places.

In just a few short years, Darin has gone from a "salesman" with a nice six-figure income to a nationally respected expert and sought after advisor with a very nice seven-figure income and a multimillionaire investor partnering in many projects with clients.

There's a lot to this business story. Darin transcended traditional geographic boundaries of his business. He created unique concepts. He wrote books, gave teleseminars, built a list of interested investors-in-waiting for good opportunities, through advertising in national publications like *Forbes* and *The Wall Street Journal*. But all that hinged on a positioning decision.

What does this have to do with your shoe store, restaurant, insurance agency, or widget distribution business? Everything! Darin's "trick" shows the income-multiplying power of positioning.

Who Do You Think You Are?

There's an old story that many speakers have appropriated and told as their own: the featured guest speaker seated at the head table says to the waiter, "Bring me some more butter."

The waiter says, "Can't. One pat of butter per person."

"Do you know who I am?" asks the frustrated speaker.

"Nope," says the waiter. "Who are you?"

"I am a famous author, here tonight as the featured guest speaker. After dinner, I'm going to share my wisdom with all these people. This group has brought me in at great expense. That's who I am. And I want another pat of butter."

"Well," says the waiter, "do you know who I am?"

"No," admits the speaker.

The waiter smiles triumphantly. "I am the man in charge of the butter."

The point of the story is that we all need to maintain some modesty and some appreciation for everybody else's right to be important. But in positioning yourself and your business for success, you have to clearly determine who you are, then drive that message home to your marketplace. And it's important to make the right decision. The marketplace will usually accept the positioning you choose for yourself and present to others. You really are in control.

CHAPTER 37

Why and How to Build Your Own Mini Conglomerate

Originally appearing as Chapter 14 from
*No B.S. Business Success in the
New Economy*

Over the years I've often been asked how I managed to keep up with all my different businesses. It puzzled many people. But one of the things they didn't see is how my businesses and activities fit together, so that I viewed it as managing one synergistic conglomerate rather than wrestling with an assortment of different ventures.

Early on, some of my companies shared office and warehouse space, computer services, a telephone system, and some personnel. By sharing this way, each business entity got better things than it could afford on its own, and no entity spent more than it had to for its needs. There was synergy. For example, one company produced videos and serviced a number of my consulting clients with infomercial and promotional video production. It also produced videos that my publishing company sold.

My publishing company's catalogs also advertised my consulting, copywriting, and speaking services. My speaking activities provided new customers for my publishing company's mailing lists. The books I wrote for other publishers, which were sold in bookstores, provided new customers for my company's mailing lists and provided consulting clients, so I counted my writing as a form of advertising.

I carefully and strategically started, acquired, and developed businesses and business interests that were profitable and valuable in and of themselves, but that also assisted each other, so that the whole was greater than the parts. Many savvy entrepreneurs follow this same pattern.

The current Glazer-Kennedy Insider's Circle™ business, while much larger, is much the same, in having a number of business "units" under one umbrella. Further, I still strive to make my outside business interests and activities feed and support Insider's Circle, just as I rely on it to feed and support my other interests.

On a bigger scale, consider the Disney empire. Its cable-TV Disney Channel, its Radio Disney network, and its magazines are good businesses in and of themselves, but also a huge promotional system for its parks, movies, videos, and products. Its character-licensing business is immensely profitable, and everywhere those famous characters appear, they silently, subtly advertise Disney. Their substantial mail-order catalog and online catalog businesses advertise their movies and parks and cross-promote their retail stores. Their retail stores promote their movies, parks, and time-share real estate, Disney Vacation Club. And on and on it goes.

This kind of "cross-fertilization," done carefully and intelligently, on a big or small scale, can make your business more profitable and a lot more fun. This is the way to create a big income out of a small business.

In media, the term "platform" is used. Disney has a very substantial platform—its magazines, its television and radio network, its websites, and its parks—nearly guaranteeing the success of many new products or services. These days, book publishers prefer authors with their own platforms for promotion, virtually guaranteeing a significant number of sales. That might be the number of Facebook friends, the size of an email list, or influence in a given industry. For me, the entire Glazer-Kennedy Insider's Circle™ business provides a substantial platform: there is an online networking community, heavily trafficked websites, an opt-in email list of hundreds of thousands of entrepreneurs, four newsletters reaching all the Members, monthly teleseminars and audio programs, over 150 local Chapters meeting regularly, and two major international events a year. With this in place, we can roll out a book and confidently predict a sales number larger than 90% of all nonfiction business books ever achieve—not counting new people who find it on bookstore shelves, while meandering around Amazon, or by recommendation from a friend. In the other direction, the book will introduce many people to me and to Glazer-Kennedy for the first time. I'll get speaking engagements and consulting engagements directly.

Of course you're not an author nor do you have an international membership organization, so what does this have to do with you?

Three Strategies for Big Income Even if Starting as a Small Business Owner

There are three important strategies every entrepreneur should strain his brain over, to find a way to put them to use for his business.

386 THE BEST OF NO B.S.

Strategy #1: You want to develop and control an effective promotional platform, and think in terms of owning that, not just owning a business.

It can be local or global, niched or broad, facilitated predominately online or offline. But it should be multimedia, reaching an organized audience of customers as well as new, potential customers, ready for your use to roll out a new product or service or promotion. You want to be a mini-media mogul with your own media conglomerate.

Let's assume you own a local fine restaurant or wine store. You decide to organize a food and wine cruise, which you will host. If you can put 250 people on the cruise, you'll net $125,000.00 and, of course, go free. If all you have to work with is the traffic through your store or restaurant, it could take months to forever to make that happen. But if you have thousands of people getting your twice weekly email gourmet cooking, healthy eating, and wine education tips; if you have hundreds actively using your searchable database for cool recipes; if you have a mail-order business shipping wines and food-gift baskets all over the country as well as delivering client gifts for local businesses; if you have a monthly newsletter featuring famous celebrities' favorite recipes; and if you have made yourself into something of a celebrity . . . selling out that cruise in 30 days is not only possible, it could be a snap.

So think about using your business to build your multimedia platform, then using your platform to not only promote and support your business but to make all sorts of other income opportunities possible.

Strategy #2: Think synergistically.

When you layer one business on another, and another on top of that, or create horizontal product or service extensions, it should all work together in closed loops, feeding on and feeding back

PART IV / WEALTH BUILDING

to the main business. Be very wary of unrelated, nonsynergis-
tic involvements' distractions, diffusion of resources and energy,
and trade-offs, producing dollars in one place but costing them
in another.

For example, so far, several financial advisors have chosen
to acquire Kennedy's All-American Barber Club™ franchises in
their local areas. The Barber Club clientele tends to be affluent,
many are business owners and entrepreneurs, and the Club is
much more than just a barber shop, so it is a perfect vehicle for
the financial advisor to become known to and get to know potential clients for his practice. Conversely, most of his financial advisory clients are affluent men, so gifting them with rewards at the
Club works, and they can more easily refer their friends there—
and all roads lead to Rome. There are other local businesses with
whom the Barber Club has similarly good synergy, but there are
some with which it has none. In a similar way, most of the 150+
Glazer-Kennedy Independent Business Advisors operating our
local Chapters and Kennedy Study/Mastermind Groups in their
areas have other, full-time businesses that work synergistically
with their Business Advisor status.

I always like businesses with vertical synergy opportunity,
meaning you can build one business on the back of the first.
For example, one of our Members, John Du Cane owns Dragon
Door Publications, marketing a variety of books, manuals, DVDs,
and courses having to do with health and fitness disciplines, including the very popular "kettlebell" training. His is basically a
mail-order company selling products. It has spawned two other
businesses: one, a training and certification program for personal
trainers and coaches who want to teach John's disciplines in their
local areas; two, a distributor and affiliate organization, selling
his products. In a related field, in the martial arts industry, a Platinum Member of mine, Stephen Oliver, owns Mile High Karate,
with academies in his own, local area and franchised academies

throughout the country. Stephen chose to acquire the major trade and professional association in that industry, NAPMA, the National Association of Professional Martial Artists, which publishes the *Martial Arts Professional* magazine reaching every martial arts school in the country.

In horizontal extensions, one of our Members, Dr. Barry Lycka, started with a private cosmetic procedures practice, then opened a retail day spa next door. Many chiropractors opt to own massage therapy offices. Restaurants add bakeries, party centers, catering. My client Dr. Tomshack has a nationwide network of franchised HealthSource® chiropractic clinics that, once established, he added a weight loss franchise to. Sometimes this can even involve multiple business owners in a joint venture. In our Membership, for example, there is an M.D., a dentist, and a nutritionist who jointly own a "stop snoring" sleep disorders clinic, primarily treating sleep apnea.

Think about how to reposition your present business within a synergistic spiderweb, with other opportunities created vertically and horizontally.

Strategy #3: Give yourself something other than your business to promote.

When you set out to directly promote a business, media wants you to buy advertising—they're not eager to give it to you for free in the form of publicity. Much of the public is immediately resistant to your outreach and messages, viewing you as just another salesman arriving at their doorstep.

I'll first use myself as example. I have written and had published 13 books. As the author of a book, a great many doorways to customers and clients have welcome mats in front of them. Radio program hosts, industry advisors and associations conducting teleseminars, trade journals, and mainstream magazines are all happy to interview me or get content from me they can use.

If I simply want to directly promote Glazer-Kennedy Insider's Circle™ Membership, many of these doorways slam shut.

If you own several dollar stores in your area, you may find getting invited on all your local radio and television stations to be interviewed and promote your stores difficult. But if you have a new, free access website to help consumers in a tough economy, featuring 101 ways to save money at home, on clothes, when buying a car, dining out, etc., with contributions and ideas from many experts that you've gathered, and a forum for people to submit their best money-saving ideas—with a $500.00 shopping spree awarded each month for the best one . . . that you can promote much, much more easily than your four stores. As you can see, an idea like this links back to Strategy #1.

What else can you promote but your business? A website providing useful information and services like the one in my example, a book, a special report, results of a survey, an event, a cause.

Dan Kennedy's
Eternal Truth
#17

A "normal" small business can only yield a "normal" small business income. To earn an extraordinary income, you must develop an extraordinary business!

This entire discussion has taken us back to differences between ordinary business owners and entrepreneurs. Remember, ordinary business owners think inward and provincially. Entrepreneurs think much more expansively and creatively.

How to Get Rich by Accident

The way to wealth as an entrepreneur is continually, creatively redefining and reinventing a business. Entrepreneurs need to be open to and alert for completely unexpected opportunities for alliances and ways to expand businesses on top of the business. When you can do this, you can *just about* get rich by accident.

The large mail-order marketer of office supplies, Quill Corporation, provides a good example. They got in the mail-order business completely by accident. They originally had a tiny, struggling retail business; to try and attract business, the owners experimented with sending out new product announcements and special offers on postcards. The response to their simple direct-mail campaigns was so good, they started selling directly rather than through the retail system.

The Miller Brothers started Quill in 1957 in a remodeled coal bin in Chicago with $2,000.00 they managed to scrape together. Today, they mail millions of catalogs a year, have a thriving ecommerce business, serve over a million customers, and generate hundreds of millions of dollars in annual sales. "Being in the mail-order business was never our intention," Jack Miller says. "It just sort of happened."

I had a client in the industrial chemicals business who discovered his employees sneaking bottles of one of their products out the back door and selling it to friends and neighbors. To their eternal credit, instead of putting an armed guard at the back door, they instead seized opportunity. They reasoned: if it's good enough to steal and sell to consumers, we ought to be selling it to consumers. Today, the sales of that one product bottled for consumer use and sold on TV, in catalogs, and in retail chains including Home Depot and Walmart far exceed the entire sales volume of the original business.

Careful expansion and diversification, linking businesses within a business, building businesses on businesses, forming strategic alliances, and keeping the doors wide open to accidental, additional opportunity all added together can give the small-business entrepreneur a big income—a huge fortune.

The New Mandate of the New Economy

New Economy Customers increasingly reward the businesses of greater and greater and greater service to them. Amazon has become strong and successful by going far beyond bookselling, into countless other product categories, even into making its platform available to authors and small, self-publishers. My clients who are enjoying the greatest success are constantly finding ways to provide a better range of products and services to their customers. Convenience is key. The mini-conglomerate approach is a path to greater influence with your customers, value to your customers, and profitability for you by increasing Total Customer Value.

The New Economy punishes waste of resources. "Waste not, want not" applies to the nth degree. And the last thing you want to waste is customer value. The second most important thing not to waste is the full value in every advertising or marketing dollar invested.

The Antidote to Advertising

Yes, I'm an "adman," but I recognize that for most business owners, advertising remains an expensive and frustrating mystery.

I'm a marketing guy, but I understand that most business owners prefer other aspects of business, and are least comfortable with marketing. If this is you, and you find the entire responsibility of advertising and marketing to obtain new customers painful and problematic, there is a simple solution: do a lot more business with the customers you do get—so you need less of them. That begs a "mini-conglomerate" approach.

One of the greatest drains on a business's profitability is the high cost of acquiring each new customer, to replace those lost, and to grow. It can also be a challenge to capital. The antidote is doing more business with each customer you have. This puts the less-is-more principle to work for you. Personally, I've always preferred small numbers/big income businesses.

Recently, the automatic garage door at one of our homes turned Linda Blair from *The Exorcist*, opening and closing by whim, refusing to stay closed when asked, and emitting frightening noises at random. No spewing of green glop, but still. I picked a garage door service company out of the Yellow Pages, a service tech arrived, did a fine job, and that was that. Sad, I thought. They spent quite a bit of money to get me. Then they did so little with me. At barest minimum, some attempt should have been made to sell me an extended warranty and a routine service arrangement, so a tech periodically came, oiled, greased, tightened, and "whatevered" the door, the springs, the motor. But the opportunity for them was so much bigger than that. They had a capable person in my home who had gained my trust for himself and for his company by arriving on time, performing capably. If they owned or had strategic alliances with a garage cleaning, junk removal business . . . a garage organizer company . . . a house painting or gutter cleaning or door and window company or handyman service or car detailing or carpet cleaning, etc., etc., etc. business, they could have secured me as a customer for that at zero cost; the cost already paid for by the garage door company's advertising.

Two weeks have passed as of this writing, and no follow-up has occurred. No courtesy call from someone at the office to verify satisfaction—and offer or recommend additional services. No letter endorsing another kind of home services company with which they have a reciprocal relationship. Nothing. Nada. Zip. Safe bet, this company's owner is pretty clueless about TCV, Total Customer Value, and completely clueless about the mini-conglomerate approach. Fortunately, you are now well-informed.

CHAPTER 38

Using Your Business as a Path to Financial Independence

Originally appearing as Chapter 15 from
No B.S. Business Success in the
New Economy

W hy are you in business or getting into business? You might be surprised at some of the answers I get when I ask this question of clients or at seminars. You see, getting into business is actually pretty easy, even too easy for some people's own good. Getting in is often a lot easier than getting out. And getting in is definitely a lot easier than getting what you really want from being in business. For most, that's the tough assignment.

For starters, viewing your business as "the end" is a mistake. It's not an achieved goal; it is a means for achieving many other goals. For too many people, the desire to own their own business is so powerful and exciting that little thought is given to "what's next?"

You don't want to marry the business. Marry the goals.

Years ago, in connection with a writing assignment, I interviewed a woman in the muffin business in Atlanta. Her name has long since been forgotten, so I'll call her Margie.

Margie's experience provides a great example. Margie determined that she wanted to open her own muffin and cookie store. She researched the field, found a location she believed was viable, and developed some of her own creative recipes. She was very excited about her business plan. At night, she lay awake, staring at the ceiling, visualizing her sign—Margie's Famous Muffins and Munchies—over the door of her store.

After some struggle to get the money together, Margie opened her shop just as she had visualized it. Just one month later, she was in financial trouble. The location wasn't as "hot" as she'd believed, and there were other problems. But, by happy accident, the manager of a nearby supermarket chain stopped in and was so impressed with Margie's muffins that he asked her to supply products for resale in his stores. That was a big success, quickly requiring a full night-shift operation to meet the demand.

The retail store was losing money, but the wholesale baking operation was a success. Finally, Margie did the obvious and closed down the high-rent, unsuccessful retail location and put the wholesale baking operation in a cheap rental space. But she cried for a week over the death of her dream. By the end of that year, she was supplying more supermarkets plus numerous restaurants and made a huge net profit. By not having to be at her retail business every day, she had the opportunity to expand by selling new accounts. She's got the makings of an enormously successful business, but not the business she originally married, and that caused her quite a bit of emotional distress. Her emotional difficulties come from being too focused on *modus operandi* rather than being focused on life goals.

Don't Let Your Business Own You

It's ironic that in order to get what you really want from owning your own business—wealth, security, freedom, for example—you must do the most unnatural, difficult thing for an entrepreneur; you must systematically reduce the dependency of the business on you. Don't overlook this. This is the secret to becoming financially independent through entrepreneurship.

Most entrepreneurs have no understanding of this and give it very little thought until it's too late. They wind up being owned by their businesses. To their surprise, they find that they've traded one old boss for a plethora of new ones: stockholders, investors, and lenders, employees and associates, customers and clients, vendors and government agencies.

There's an old joke about the government bureaucrat descending on the small-business owner. He says: "We've received a report that you have some poor fellow working here 18 hours a day, seven days a week, for nothing but a room, board, meals, all the tobacco he can smoke, and all the liquor he can drink. Is that true?" "Yes, I'm afraid it is," admits the owner. "And I'm sad to say, you're looking at him."

You're probably wondering about the security of your business. If the typical entrepreneur leaves the business alone for a week, it does a Jekyll-Hyde transformation. You have got to be there! I know many business owners who go years without a vacation. And those who do go on vacation don't enjoy it. One half hopes everything's okay back at the ranch, which he checks every few hours by phone, and the other half is disappointed if it is OK; after all, how could it be without his indispensable presence?

I'm embarrassed for business owners connected to their businesses every waking minute, constantly, compulsively, truthfully fearfully jumping as if electroshocked every time their cell phone sounds its little ringtone, checking text messages and emails every other minute, their devices always at hand if not in hand. I tell men they have traded their testicles for an iPhone. Pathetic. What is the point of being the Boss and the Owner if your every minute is dominated by things buzzing, beeping, pinging, and prodding you?

Too many people get into business only to discover they've acquired a new, tougher, more demanding, more stressful job, and they cannot see any way to change it. They tell me they see their stress climbing on the exact same ascendant line and pace as their success. Was that the goal?

The trick is to let the business mature—and the faster, the better. An immature business is entrepreneur driven. In its early days, that's OK and usually necessary. You are the business. From Day One, though, if your business is to provide security, freedom, and wealth, you should be working at weaning the business from dependence on you and creating dependence on systems. My friend Ken Varga, who has built huge companies, says any business still dependent on your day-to-day presence after three years is not a business at all. It's a job.

I've appeared as a speaker on several programs with Michael Gerber, author of the bestselling book *The E-Myth*. His advice is to systemize your business as if you would franchise it and replicate it in a hundred distant sites, even if you have no intention of doing so. Good, liberating strategy.

Getting Out of Your Own Way

Some people tie their egos up in their minute-by-minute, indispensable importance to their businesses. I have made this mistake myself: carrying data around in my head, making every decision myself whether for a dime or a dollar, being the first one at the office in the morning, the last one there at the end of the day, the guy able to do every job in the place—and meddling in every one of them.

I was probably indispensable and irreplaceable. I was also stressed out—a nervous breakdown looking for a place to happen. I started getting in the habit of stopping off "for a couple of drinks" after leaving the office and going home hours later, half-drunk. This is not the way to get your sense of importance satisfied.

Instead, you can be important and make the most meaningful contributions to your business—without sacrificing your health, family, and sanity—by freeing yourself from in-depth involvement in day-to-day operations, so you have more time for the few business-building things you do best. In my case, in my publishing company, what I did best was create new products or improve the ones we already had, create advertising and marketing materials, and deal with key clients and contacts. But if I gave equal time to purchasing raw materials and supplies, bookkeeping, organizing records and mailing lists, product quality control, and so on, I cheated the business out of my best and I cheated myself out of the business's best.

Be sure you're not cheating yourself and your business out of your best.

How to Help Your Business Mature

A mature business is some or all of these things:

- MARKET driven
- PRODUCT driven
- SERVICE driven
- SYSTEMS driven

For example, a retail store in a busy mall is driven by its market. Very little, if any, outside advertising or marketing is done; the business is designed to feed off the mall traffic.

A manufacturer of a little widget that goes inside a bigger widget that makes the windshield wiper switch work is product driven. The bigger widget maker has to have the little widget; the little widget is only made by a couple of companies. A quick-print shop is service driven; its customers are usually concerned with and wooed by speed, convenience, and reliability.

In the beginning, these businesses will also be *owner driven.* The retail-store owner makes all the product, pricing, window-display, and other decisions for the store. The manufacturer watches over the widget making, hiring, firing, buying raw materials, keeping the customers happy, and so on. The copy-shop owner solicits accounts, deals with customers, and keeps the copy shop hopping.

Over time, these businesses can mature to a great degree. Each owner can isolate the one or two things he or she does best and delegate the rest. But the way to get to that stage is to develop your systems, and the development of effective *marketing systems* is the most vital job overlooked by most entrepreneurs.

For example, consider John G., a roofing contractor. He told me that he wanted to diminish his day-to-day work in the business, but as he is the one who brings in most of the business, he doesn't know how to go about it. He's been able to hire good crews and good managers and delegate all the labor, but, he asked, how do you delegate the prospecting and selling that gets the jobs?

The answer is to develop a marketing system that delivers predictable results from repetitive use. In John's case, we worked together to create a direct-mail campaign aimed at qualified leads (provided by a list broker), then a telephone procedure to convert a predictable number of those inquiries to appointments. Then, the big step, we worked on a standardized sales presentation using a flip chart, a video, and a cost-quoting computer program. This made it possible to hire sales representatives, train them quickly and easily, and put them in the field to secure just about the same number of jobs per appointments as when John dealt personally with all the customers. Bingo! This fellow was able to replace himself with a marketing system.

Over the next two years, not only did John achieve his objective of cutting by half his time devoted to the business, but the business was able to increase by nearly 30%!

The time to start thinking about all this is not 6 or 12 months before you'd like to change your role in your business. In fact, you should start planning for flexibility and change from Day One. You must accept that the unbridled passions you feel for your business at the beginning, that have you happily there from dawn to midnight up to your armpits in work, will change as time passes. The activity you can't wait to get at today may bore the blazes out of you three years from now. It's smart to build your business in a way that allows you to satisfy your changing interests.

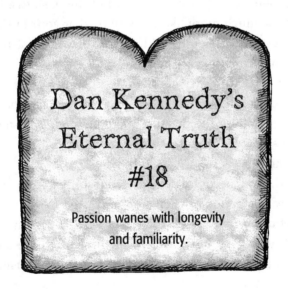

Dan Kennedy's Eternal Truth #18

Passion wanes with longevity and familiarity.

> # To Build Marketing Systems for Your Business
>
> Consult the book *No B.S. DIRECT Marketing for NON-Direct Marketing Businesses*, for a detailed direct marketing blueprint and actual examples from a diverse variety of businesses . . . and Chapter 36 of *No B.S. Marketing to the Affluent*, which provides a diagram and a complete explanation of a fully automated customer attraction, capture, and conversion system.

You can also think of this as a form of insurance. You could be injured or become ill. The statistics I've seen indicate that one of every three business owners experience some period of disability during their careers. For many, even with an insurance policy in their desk drawer, this can kill the business. Imagine, though, how much more likely it will be that your business can survive a period of months without you if you've structured it with systems from the very beginning.

The first thing you must do is ensure that the routine processes of your business are really routine. That means they happen by procedure so that just about anybody can step in and follow those procedures. You shouldn't have to have your nose in everything.

Second, you need to develop your business to the point where new customers or clients are attracted to your company by marketing systems, not through your direct personal efforts.

Third, you must have a plan for directing more and more of your time and energy to the few aspects of the business you enjoy and do best and for reducing the commitment of your time and energy to the many aspects of the business you do not enjoy or do best.

How Does a System Work?

First and foremost, a system works without you being married to it 24 hours a day. Let's say that there have been a number of burglaries in your neighborhood, and you are suddenly more concerned than usual with making your home look occupied all the time. One way to do that is to stay home. Another would be to hire a house-sitter for the times you aren't there—in other words, delegating the responsibility. Or, you could get some simple, inexpensive electronic devices that can be set to turn different lights and appliances on and off at different times. That would be a system. Once in place, it works with little or no attention from you.

Systems deliver predictable and consistent results.

A marketing system is arguably the most important kind of system that an entrepreneur can ever give the business. One restaurant owner I know, Bill H., exemplifies the success of initiating such a system. He sends two letters and a postcard to residents of the neighborhoods surrounding his restaurant and to people in businesses around his restaurant. He has this system streamlined to the point that he has a formula for determining what percentage of response he will get from each mailing, and how many of those responses turned into reservations and revenue for his restaurant. This means he can guarantee his restaurant a certain predictable base of business each and every week. If, say, a seasonal slump is coming up, he can increase the number of letters mailed in order to increase revenue. He can go to sleep at night knowing that a certain number of new clients will call the next day, and, because this is an entirely mechanical process, he could go on vacation for three weeks and still guarantee a certain amount of business to his restaurant. His system gives him immense power, leverage of time, less stress and frustration, and better positioning with new clients.

Always strive to put systems in place; the right systems can totally transform a business.

PART V

PRODUCTIVITY AND MANAGEMENT

with selections from

No B.S. Time Management for Entrepreneurs

*No B.S. Ruthless Management of
People and Profits*

PRODUCTIVITY AND MANAGEMENT

How you define PRODUCTIVITY, for yourself and for your business, determines outcomes. I define it as things getting done, effectively and efficiently, that move me measurably closer to my meaningful goals. Thoreau noted that the ants are very, very busy—but busy at what? It is easy, it is seductive, it is deceptive to be very, very busy. It's tough-minded to be constantly asking: But busy at what?

I originally wrote the *No B.S. Time Management for Entrepreneurs* book for two chief reasons:

One, all the time-management books, articles, seminars, and "systems" seemed made for people with relatively few real problems with time management, mostly executives and cubicle dwellers. I couldn't find anything for the *extreme* challenges confronted by entrepreneurs.

Two, people taking note of my own, personal *modus operandi*, and my unusual rules of engagement I imposed on others, my control of access to me and inbound communication, my refusal to take random phone calls without pre-appointment, and who took note of my impressive productivity and prolificacy asked, more and more, for me to explain it all to them. In consulting days with individual clients paying upward from $18,000 for a day purposed to discuss their advertising and marketing, I found myself being questioned about how I got so much done. How I exerted so much control. How I "got away with it" and still earned a seven-figure income? I decided to write it all down for everybody.

Over the years, literally thousands of entrepreneurs in hundreds of different kinds of businesses have adapted and adopted much of the philosophy and methodology in this book for themselves, and often to their surprise, successfully re-educated the world around them about how to work with them, under *their* system—odd or unreasonable as it might seem.

In a Time of Endless, Competing Distractions, Applied Discipline Is More Important Than Ever

The book has aged well. I still refuse to own a cell phone or use text, email, or social media, and I still use and advise clients to use carefully determined, clearly articulated, and rigidly adhered to "laws of productivity success." Too many people have given up all their sovereignty to constant connectivity. President Trump was 100% accurate in constantly saying: No borders, no country. Same thing with your personal autonomy and productivity. No borders, game over, you lose.

One of my favorite quotes for entrepreneurs about all this comes from Pastor Mike Murdock, author of *Secrets of the Richest Man Who Ever Lived: From the Life of King Solomon*. Pastor Murdock says: "Always keep in mind that few people around you have any *SERIOUS* plans they are pursuing on a daily basis." If you do, then you cannot accept and conform to their ideas about time and self-management, you cannot worry much about them approving of your methods, and you must organize a personal operating system that suits your purposes. Not theirs. Yours. In a seminar I presented a number of times called the *7-Figures Academy*, I made the point that you do not raise yourself from a five-figure or six-figure income to a seven-figure income by doing more of the same things and running harder and faster doing them. You get there by doing different things, differently.

The other book excerpted from here is *No B.S. Ruthless Management of People and Profits*. Interestingly, it's the book I've received the greatest number of thank-you and praise letters about and the book I've received the most horrified and disapproving letters about. Many of the latter are from folks who obviously did not read the book. They were just outraged by the word "ruthless." I might have said "unambiguous," but it's awkward. Its premise is zero tolerance for deviation from maximum productivity, period. It has to be *zero*, because whatever you accept, you get more of.

The #1 Ruthless Question that I like to challenge clients (and myself) with often is: *Where's the profit in that?* That person, that job as it is constructed, that client or account, that product, that procedure, that dispute, that decision you are about to make. After all, the first mandate of business management *is* profit. There is a lot going on in most businesses that can't stand up to this question.

In the new introduction to this book, I mentioned my issuing of permission slips. Combined, the excerpts here equal a big, fat permission slip to make demands of your choosing on your business. And a challenge to you to do so.

CHAPTER 39

How to Turn Time into Money

Originally appearing as Chapter 1 from
No B.S. Time Management for Entrepreneurs

W
hat is "entrepreneurship" if not the conversion
of your knowledge, talent, guts, etc. — *through investment
of your time* — into money?

In other chapters of *No B.S. Time Management for Entrepreneurs*,
we dive into very specific how-to strategies, but first, I think you'll
find it useful to understand how I arrived at my philosophy of
valuing time and how I value time.

In time-management books and in time-management
seminars, authors and speakers love to show off charts and graphs
depicting the dollar value of each workday hour, depending on
your income or the income you want to achieve. Maybe you've
sat through one of these painful PowerPoint sessions before. You
know, Mr. Lecturer up there, laptop computer wired into the
overhead projector, lights dimmed, even a laser-beam pointer in

hand, so he can show off his beautiful five-color bar graph. If you use his numbers, for example, based on eight-hour workdays, presuming 220 workdays, earning $200,000.00 a year requires that each hour be worth $113.64.

Unfortunately, it's all a pile of seminar-room B.S.

Here's why: it's all based on eight-hour workdays. Eight hours a day. But there's not a soul on the planet who gets in eight *productive* hours a day. Not even close. You see, the workday hour is one thing, *the productive hour*—or what I call the billable hour—is another. In Chapter 4 of *No B.S. Time Management for Entrepreneurs*, there's a definition of productivity you may want to use to determine which of your hours are productive. (If you can't or won't define it, you can't own it. If you don't own it, you won't achieve it.)

Now, if you happen to be an attorney, none of this matters. It seems lawyers bill out hours whether productive or not. Here's a joke: 35-year-old lawyer in perfect health suddenly drops dead. He gets to Saint Peter at The Gate and argues: "You guys screwed up. You pulled me up here early." Saint Peter checks his clipboard and says, "No sir. Judging by your total billable hours, you're 113 years old and we're late." *Lawyers.*

But the rest of us can only collect on genuinely productive hours.

Can One "Number" Change Your Life?

Let's go back to the math game and assume that $200,000.00 is your base earnings target. (We'll talk more about what that term means later.) How many of your hours will be productive, directly generating revenue? How many will be otherwise consumed: commuting, filling out government paperwork, dealing with vendors, emptying the trash cans (I hope not), whatever? Let's say it is one-third productive, two-thirds other. That's pretty generous. One study of Fortune 500 CEOs revealed they averaged 28 productive minutes a day. The business legend Lee Iacocca, who made the Mustang happen at Ford and who rescued Chrysler from the brink of bankruptcy in the 1980s with mini-vans, cup holders, and bold warranties, personally told me he figured top CEOs might squeeze in 45 productive minutes per day—the rest of the day fighting off time-wasting B.S. like a frantic fellow futilely waving his arms at a swarm of angry bees on attack. And that was then; this is now, with all the intrusive communication: email, texts, expected participation in social media. All those distractions in the device in your hand. I have a lot more to say about this in Chapter 14 of *No B.S. Time Management for Entrepreneurs*. But let's generously label 33% of your time productive. With that, only one of three hours counts as "billable." So you've got to multiply the $113.64 times three, $340.92. This becomes your governing number for $200,000.00 a year. For $600,000.00, three times that: $1,022.76.

When I wrote the first edition of this book in 1996, I was charging about $3,500.00 to write an advertising campaign for a client. By the time I updated this book in 2013, that fee had multiplied five times. Today, a full campaign bills at $75,000.00 to $150,000.00 plus royalties. Since the time required is about the same—possibly less as my memory bank of material and proficiency have grown—this puts more and more weight on any time wasted. I also now target a yearly income upward from $1.5 million, so the ideas and methods I describe in this book are a lot more important to me financially today than they were in 1996 or in 2013. Of course, it's arguably true that I can more easily afford to repel some clients and annoy some people with these methods now than then, but I contend I got here, in part, by thinking about time in this fashion and doing these things long before I could ostensibly afford them.

Anyway, let's roll back the calendar and assume that my base earnings target number required an hourly average of only $340.92. If you travel in business, you have to think about this a lot. I once lived in Arizona, and then traveled for business constantly. I currently have homes in Ohio and in Virginia, grew to loathe travel, and now do it as little as possible, insisting that the clients, coaching groups, and even events I speak at occur in my home cities. But when I was traveling, if there were two days of travel bracketing a day of work, that put three days' cost to that work. Using the $340.92 hourly number, that's $8,182.08 of cost.

Few people ever factor cost of their time (or their staff's time) into product, service, or deliverable cost, or the maintenance of each client of variable value or much of anything else. But you should. At just $340.92 an hour, a client who comes to you costs only for the hours he is there. A client you must drive an hour to visit and an hour to return from costs $681.84 more. If that's four times a year, one costs $2,727.36 more than the other. Consider two customers, each worth $3,000.00 a year, but one is needier and more demanding than the other. One consumes eight hours—the other three. The first may not even be worth having, particularly if there are enough of the second to be had. This, by the way, is why I book 20-minute, not 30-minute, calls with my coaching clients. I can do three per hour at 20 minutes each but only three per one-and-a-half hours at 30 minutes each. In a year, ten minutes saved per month per client = two hours! Times 20 clients, a full week!

So again, let's say my number is $340.92, calendar rolled back. Here's how I have to use it.

First, it has to be on my mind constantly. Is what I'm doing worth $340.92 an hour to do? I believe you need to be *hyper-conscious* of the disappearance of time by the minute or the hour—not in retrospect at the end of a week, month, or year—and *hyper-conscious* of the dollar value of what that time is disappearing into.

Second, it puts a meter on others' consumption of my time—that unnecessary 12-minute phone conversation just cost $68.18, and the same goes with 12 minutes on Facebook or Twitter. This exercise forces you to think of time and activity in terms of investment and expense. It enables you to quantify what is going on in your life. About this, something of a discovery I've made in just the past ten years: the more you think like an investor-entrepreneur than just an entrepreneur, the better you do financially. It is "investor-think" that makes you wealthy. If some activity, project, person, series of meetings, etc. is going to consume 40 hours in total, using the $340.92 number, you have to ask yourself: would I invest $13,636.80 in this as a venture? You also have to consider lost opportunity cost, meaning: if I wasn't investing $340.92 . . . or $13,636.80 . . . of time in this, is there something else I could invest that time in more profitably?

Third, for me it sets the base cost for hours given to a speaking engagement, consulting assignment, copywriting assignment, and other things I do that are directly billable. And if you do anything but earn a fixed salary, you have to weigh this base cost against every activity to set your fee or to decide whether or not to bother.

I've learned to think about time cost and time cost of travel a lot. When I first started shifting from going to clients to getting clients to travel to me, I used differential pricing. At that time, a consulting day billed at $8,300.00 if I came to you but only $7,800.00 if you came to me. Why? Because it's worth money to me to stay home, be able to write for an hour in the morning before the consulting day, finish and be at home at 4:30, be able to drive in harness races and not miss any, sleep in my own bed, and be at work in my home office promptly at 7:00 A.M. the next morning vs. losing that hour the day of, losing a half day or so to travel on either side. Gradually, I eliminated the differential pricing and simply mandated that clients travel to me. I finally converted to flying only by private jet, and that exorbitant expense to be absorbed by a client has pretty much ended any discussion of me coming to them. In a way, that expense added to fees has recreated differential pricing; the cost of even the client plus a couple staff people traveling commercial to me is a lot lower than my fee plus my private jet bill. Looked at side by side on a sheet of paper, it's dramatic if the client fails to factor in the dollar value of his and his staff's travel time, which most clients do not calculate. Differential pricing is useful for a variety of purposes—within GKIC membership, there are a lot of lawyers, accountants, dentists, and others who charge a higher fee if they do a client's work than they do if they only supervise the work done by subordinates.

You don't have to be flying the unfriendly skies to do travel-time cost math. Many years ago, when I was in the field, selling, I quickly figured out that you could fit in two, three, four, or five appointments per day, depending on how you routed yourself. A salesman half as good at selling as a competitor but twice as good at efficiently routing himself and clustering prospects makes the same amount of money. With this in mind, I've long "clustered" as much productive activity as possible, if traveling, or even when leaving the house. By not "clustering," most people allow a great deal of inefficiency to sneak into their lives.

By working at home, as a writer, consultant, and tele-coach, as opposed to going to an office, I make a lot of money each day just by *not* commuting. I have conditioned myself to go directly from bed to shower to work in 15 minutes. If I were leaving the house to go to an office, I'd have those 15 minutes plus another half-hour, maybe an hour commute, then another 15 minutes getting settled in at the office—not to mention the commute at end of day. And the stops at Starbucks.

I have nothing against Starbucks. At different times, I've owned the company's stock. If I'm at the mall, I might stop in for a cup. But the person who stops there every morning easily surrenders at least a half-hour every day, 110 hours per work year; about two full workweeks to parking and standing in line. At the $340.92 per hour number, $37,501.20 has been spent plus the price of the coffee! Get a Keurig and buy Starbucks K-cups, and do something more valuable with those two weeks! Heck, even take a two-week vacation. Almost anything beats this very expensive Starbucks habit.

Seek Leverage

In whatever ways you can, in your business, you need to seek leverage. In terms of work productivity, leverage is, in essence, the difference between the base cost for your hour and the amount of money you get for it or from it. One good way to evaluate your personal effectiveness is measuring and monitoring this differential, hour by hour, for a week.

Now, let's set up your **base earnings target**. Since you are your own boss, you write your own paycheck and you decide how much that paycheck is going to be. For most entrepreneurs, that number is whatever's left! This is a huge mistake for two reasons: it indicates zero planning, and it means you pay yourself last—the number-one reason entrepreneurs wind up broke. So, let's reverse all that and start with the planning. You've got to decide how much money you're going to take out of your business or businesses this year in salary, perks, contributions to retirement plans, and so on. What is that number?

*I'll tell you this: eight out of ten entrepreneurs I ask **cannot** come up with this number.*

If you do not have a base income target, then you cannot calculate what your time must be worth, which means you cannot make good decisions about the investment of your time, which means you are not exercising any real control over your business or life at all. You are a wandering generality. Is that what you want to do—*just wander around and settle for whatever you get?*

Now, you may not have a situation that lends itself to clear-cut billable hours as I do, so how can this strategy work for you? *It has to.* It's even more important to you than to me. Let's say you own six stores. Each store has a manager. Hey, this is complicated. Well, you'll have to decide how much of the business's bottom-line profit goal will be provided by the managers whether you sleep or work and how much is still inextricably linked to you. If you want $500,000.00 at the bottom line, and you figure half is dependent on you, you've got a $250,000.00 target.

For me, it's reasonably precise. For you, it may not be such an exact science. But that's OK. I promise you that coming up with a number, even if it is arrived at through some pretty questionable calculations, is still a whole lot better than not having a number at all. Having a number is going to make such a dramatic change in so many of the decisions you make, habits you cultivate, and people you associate with, that the benefits will be so extraordinary, it won't matter

> *E*ntrepreneurs should think about the purpose of business. A lot of business owners lose sight of that altogether. The purpose of a business is to make its owner rich. Time must be invested accordingly.

if the original method of getting to a number had a technical flaw or two buried in it. At least for the sake of our conversation, in this book, get a number—YOUR base earnings target for the next full calendar year. (See Figure 39.1.) Divide it by the number of workday hours. Multiply it to allow for unproductive vs. productive hours. If you haven't a better estimate of that, use the three times multiple I've used here. Now you have what your time is supposed to be worth per hour and divided by 60 to see per minute.

That little number may just change your life.

It's sort of like a heart attack being required to really get somebody to change their eating and exercise habits.

A lot of your decision making gets easy with this number staring you in the face. It's hard to con yourself with this number

FIGURE 39.1: Calculating Your Base Earnings Target

Base Earnings Target:	$_____
Divided by (220 days x 8 = 1,760) work hours in a year	÷_____
= Base hourly number	$_____
Times productivity vs. nonproductivity multiple	X_____
= What your time must be worth per hour:	$_____

confronting you. In fact, I suggest having it stare you in the face a lot until you internalize it. Write your number "$___ per Hour" on a bunch of colorful 4-by-6-inch cards, in bold black letters, and stick these cards up in places where you work and will see them often. (See Chapter 41: The Inner Game of Peak Personal Productivity.)

Generally speaking, two business life changes probably come to mind immediately, with this number confronting you.

First, you realize that you've got to surround yourself with people who understand and respect the value of your time and behave accordingly. This is not easy, and they will forget often. Familiarity breeds contempt. Periodically, you will have to reorient them. You also must get people who do not respect the value of your time out of your business life. If you let people who do not understand and respect the value of your time hang around, you won't even have a fighting chance.

Second, you have to eliminate the need for doing or delegate those tasks and activities that just cannot and do not match up with the mandated value of your time.

Dan Kennedy's #1 No B.S. Time Truth

If you don't know what your time is worth, you can't expect the world to know it either.

When I started in real estate, despite high ambition, I was constrained by the same 24 hours as everyone else. My early success came from a grueling schedule, long hours, and the high price of near burnout. In self-defense, I devised a system that featured direct marketing in place of traditional prospecting plus a highly effective team, with all the non-rainmaker tasks delegated to them. This took me to the top of the profession, twice #1 in RE/MAX worldwide in commissions earned, and 15 years as one of the top agents—working less hours than most. While an active agent, I consistently sold over 500 homes a year, even while starting and developing a second business, training and coaching more millionaire agents than any other coach. Without the inspiration of Dan Kennedy's direct-marketing methods and his extraordinary, extreme time-management philosophy, these achievements simply would not have been possible. **LEVERAGING yourself**, by media in place of manual labor, and with other people is very intimidating to most real estate agents and to most small businesspeople. It frankly is not easy to get right, but it is the quantum leap that uniquely and simultaneously lifts income and supports a great lifestyle.

—CRAIG PROCTOR, HTTPS:// CRAIGPROCTOR.COM

The Amazing Power of Time Valuing

My longtime private client and friend Craig Proctor mentioned my time-management *philosophy*. It can be boiled down to this: time valuing. Every one of my working hours has to be worth a certain amount of money; I do everything I can to create and protect that value and anybody screwing that up had better watch out.

Another, related issue is "project valuing" or "opportunity valuing" or "account valuing" for salespeople. In short, a "thing" has to be worth X-dollars, whatever you decide X must be, for you to even touch it, think about it, or be involved with it. Many of my best clients have adopted this idea and now have their own litmus test, helpful in quickly and decisively saying yea or nay to whatever comes along.

Most sales professionals hang on to clients and accounts that consume far, far more time than they can ever be worth. Better to send them to a competitor. Most entrepreneurs perpetuate projects that consume far, far more time—theirs or employees'—than they're worth. I've done it more times than I care to confess. But I'm getting much better at NOT doing it with each passing year. As a good reminder, my friend Lee Milteer, a top business performance coach (https:// Milteer.com) and the host interviewer on my Renegade Millionaire System audio program (https://MagneticMarketing.com) gave me a wall plaque that reads:

Dan's Other Business

It Seemed Like a Good Idea
at the Time, Inc.

There's an old joke of Bob Newhart's: an executive is engaged in mad, passionate sex with his secretary, clothes strewn about the office, she on her back on the desk, legs wrapped around him; he thrusting; she, overcome by the moment, screams "Kiss me! Kiss me!"—and he says: "Geez, I shouldn't even be doing *this!*"

Deciding what you *shouldn't* be doing—this moment, or at all—is at least as important as deciding what to invest your time in.

Disciplining yourself to say NO is vital, yet very difficult for the true-blue entrepreneur. Our conditioned response is summarized in reality-TV entrepreneur Mark Burnett's book titled *Jump In!* Often, jumping in without every answer, without every needed resource, at inconvenient times is what differentiates the entrepreneur from corporate drone or civilian and what yields outsize success. This cannot be denied or discounted. Still, operating in an ALWAYS-YES mode absent any restraint or discretion moves past entrepreneurial to reckless.

The week that I wrote this part of this book, I said NO, candidly after some weeks of procrastination, to two different promising opportunities brought to me by two people I like, respect, and would enjoy working with on the projects. Saying NO was painful—not just because of the money that might have been made, but because emotionally, by conditioning, and philosophically, I prefer always jumping in. Admitting limitations makes me feel weak. Turning my back on opportunity makes me feel guilty. Disappointing good allies makes me anxious. Yet I knew that I did not have the bandwidth for these projects, having only recently entered into other time-demanding commitments. I knew that adding these would place me under considerable pressure and stress, and even though I am a stress camel, I am also cognizant of each year's toll on that capacity. I do not want to be running as fast as I can and juggling as frantically as I can every waking minute. I've worked hard not to financially need to do so, so why still say YES as if I did? It's easy to be ruled by habituated reactions and behaviors that once served you well in the past but no longer match your circumstances, needs, or desires.

I have superpowers. You probably feel that you do, too. Good. But making more time isn't one of them. Time, capacity, and bandwidth are *facts*.

ONE **chapter** of Dan's *No B.S. Time Management for Entrepreneurs* literally changed my life—and it did it almost overnight. The simple exercise in this chapter made me realize the REAL value of my time when I'm performing productive work. This was a huge "Aha Moment" for me. Of course, we all know our time has to be valuable. That wasn't a new idea for me, and I'm sure it won't be for you either. But **the *clarity* this exercise created for me was new. Many things changed for me right then**, not only in how I managed my time and work, but also the time and work of my employees in our busy, successful, but often stressed insurance agency. We had good people and good processes, but we had a lot of bad management of time. Pushed by this book, I focused on devoting the right shares of time to the most profitable processes and activities with the right people performing the right tasks and everything held financially accountable.

I already had a very *successful* career and business. Guided by this book, I created a better career and a stronger business.

—Bɪʟʟ Gᴏᴜɢʜ, Pʀᴇsɪᴅᴇɴᴛ, BGI Mᴀʀᴋᴇᴛɪɴɢ (www.ʙɢɪsʏsᴛᴇᴍs.ᴄᴏᴍ),
Nᴜᴍʙᴇʀ-ᴏɴᴇ Tʀᴀɪɴɪɴɢ/Cᴏᴀᴄʜɪɴɢ Oʀɢᴀɴɪᴢᴀᴛɪᴏɴ ꜰᴏʀ Aʟʟsᴛᴀᴛᴇ Iɴsᴜʀᴀɴᴄᴇ
Aɢᴇɴᴛs

NOT Being Your Own Worst Enemy

Success and productivity are not the same things nor does maximum productivity necessarily translate to success. You might, for example, achieve a very high level of productivity at cold-call prospecting and pushing through CEOs' doors in order to sell your services but come to understand that you do not feel at all successful as a result. Instead, perpetually stressed and anxious, demeaned by the "numbers game," the rejection, and the burnout, you might then come to realize you would have been better served devoting productive energy to building a marketing system that brought interested prospects to you.

As you set out to get a far stronger grip on your time, to enhance your performance, it's important to be constantly assessing your reasons for doing so and the validity of the objectives you are pursuing and achieving.

Entrepreneurs tend to be under more constant assault than executives or others, so it is easier to lose grip on the thread that leads through the muddle to the prize. Prizes you don't really want get set up in front of you by others, and you race to get to them while losing the critical thinking that questions the appropriateness of the prize. This takes your time and invests it where it can't get a desirable return. Entrepreneurs are, by conditioned habit, often by ingrained compulsion, and perhaps even by nature, Problem Solvers and Mountain Climbers. It's what we do. But not every problem is one you need to solve or should care about solving. Not every mountain you are led to needs conquering by you.

My racehorses are incapable of critical thinking. They are bred, trained, and conditioned nearly from birth to race. They are noble and fierce and *automatic* competitors. When I climb into the sulky and drive the horse to the track, get him moving behind the starting gate among the other horses, never, never, never does he stop and think—*gee, maybe this is a race I don't need to run*. But you and I are capable of such critical thinking. We can rein ourselves in. As entrepreneurs, we are automatic competitors, automatic problem-solvers, automatic mountain climbers—but we are capable of overriding our automatic inclinations.

If you put a business problem or opportunity in front of a true entrepreneur, he automatically leaps on it and begins solving it or capitalizing on it. He reacts as if a lion thrown a hunk of raw, red meat. The lion will respond even if he has just had a big meal and is not hungry. The entrepreneur will respond even if he has more on his plate than he can handle, no need to respond, or no time to respond. In this way, entrepreneurs are dangerous to themselves.

You can reduce that danger with more disciplined time management. With entire weeks scheduled and scripted in advance, the new and unexpected must take a lower place in line, patiently wait, and instead of reacting impulsively, you can attend to it more calmly and thoughtfully. One of my principles is that nothing is ever as bad or as good as it initially appears. Before acting hastily based on first impressions, each new thing—problem or opportunity—must be carefully inspected.

CHAPTER 40

The Ten Time Management Techniques Really Worth Using

Originally appearing as Chapter 7 from
No B.S. Time Management for Entrepreneurs

My business, the information business—as well as businesses such as weight loss, diet, and financial advisory services—revolves around the public's stubborn belief that there must be a "secret" to success concealed from them, possibly by conspiracy, that, if uncovered, would change everything. This concept can be useful to remember if you work in advertising, marketing, and selling, but it is a useless, or even harmful, delusion otherwise. With regard to time, I promise you, there's no secret magic pill you don't know about, and no new, color-coded appointment book, smartphone app, or super-duper gadget is going to change that.

In business, there are good strategies poorly executed and poor strategies executed well, but rarely is there a truly new, revolutionary strategy. In this chapter are ten good strategies. Nothing earth shaking, nothing revolutionary, and probably nothing you don't already know. The issue is execution—not innovation.

The "joke" in the weight-loss industry, where I find myself doing marketing consulting from time to time, is this: if there was a diet that worked, there'd only be one diet. Similarly, you could reasonably argue that if there was one time management system that worked perfectly for everybody, there'd be only one system. The good news is that, in a way, there IS just one time management "system," and it's all here in this chapter.

If you read every time management book ever written, go to every time management seminar offered and, more importantly, observe and analyze lots of people who get an exceptional quantity of important things accomplished, you will be able to boil ALL the technique "stuff" down to only ten things worth doing. So let me save you all that time and just hand them to you here. I'll note, too, that all ten might not apply to you and your situations. When it's all said and done, you sort of have to find your own way. Ultimately, there is only one system that will work best for you, and it is up to you to try different methods and tools until you figure it out. Then, lock it down and stick with it, as I have done with mine over decades.

Technique #1: Tame ALL the Interruptions

You've got to free yourself from the tyranny of phone calls, text messages, tweets, emails, faxes, and similar stuff. If you refuse to limit and control access to you, the war is lost even if you win a few battles here or there.

Technique #2: Minimize Meetings

Find every way possible to minimize your time spent in formal meetings. Most meetings end where they begin anyway.

I deal with one company that has six conference rooms—a very bad sign. If Noah had convened a meeting of architects, interior decorators, goat and sheep herders, lion tamers, navigators, we would all have fins. Nothing ever got done in a meeting. I hate 'em.

For a lot of people, meetings are a place to hide out—or preen and be important—but not a place to actually do work or get anything done. You need a strategy to avoid them. If you lead meetings, you need a strategy to abbreviate and focus them. If you must attend meetings, you need a strategy to escape from them at will.

> Oh, and here's a "little tip" that saves me quite a bit of time: stop meeting people at restaurants for lunch or drinks, or whatever. Four out of five times, they'll keep you waiting. For years, when I spent time at an office, if I was going to lunch with somebody, I had them first come to my office, then we would go from there. Then, when they were 20 minutes late, I got to do 20 minutes of real work. If you must go to such an "off-site" meeting place, have something to read or some work to do with you.

After reading your book when it was first published, I imposed a new rule: I only accept lunch invitations if they come and meet me at the restaurant across the street from my office! This *has* cut down on *some* lunch invitations, which is just fine. Having lunch with someone, especially if driving across town to do it, will literally eat up two hours of time that, often, could be put to better use—a better time *investment*.

But most acquiesce to my restaurant choice even when they are doing the inviting. Life lesson learned.

—LEE MILTEER, MILLIONAIRE SMARTS® COACH, BESTSELLING AUTHOR,
SPEAKER, HTTPS://MILTEER.COM

Technique #3: Practice Absolute Punctuality

See Chapter 5 of *No B.S. Time Management for Entrepreneurs.*

Technique #4: Make and Use Lists

There is not a single time management discipline or system on earth that doesn't revolve around making and using lists. You CANNOT carry it all in your head. For years, I've operated with four basic lists:

1. *My Schedule.* This is for the entire year, day by day. It gets updated as there is reason to, on average about twice a month. While this is principally for use by me, my assistant, and my wife, a tweaked version is sent to key associates and clients so they can know when I'm utterly incommunicado or potentially accessible.

2. *Things to Do List.* My basic "Things to Do" list is organized by the month, the week, and each day prioritized as As, Bs, and Cs. Management consultant (and "hustler") Ivy Lee reportedly sold this idea to billionaire industrialist Andrew Carnegie's right-hand man, Charles Schwab, for $25,000.00. It worked for Schwab. It works for just about everybody who uses it now.

3. *People to Call List.* My third list is a "People to Call" list, also prioritized alphabetically.

4. *Conference Planner.* And finally, I have the "Conference Planner"—just a page for each person I interact with a lot, where I jot down things I need to talk to them about as they occur to me in between meetings or conversations.

To be perfectly honest, I do this with a yellow legal pad and pages I most often carry folded up in my pocket. Maybe this is not exactly a shining example for a time management "leader" to set, but I've found that this works just as well for me as a number of different, more organized, and formal systems I've tried. Over the years, I've experimented with the Day-Timer and several other systems—even one I designed myself. Anyway, the "magic" is more in the making and using the lists than in the particular tool, medium, or format you use. My current incarnation of this, which I've used for several years, is a page from a legal pad, divided in half vertically and into five horizontal sections, giving me ten boxes covering ten days at a time. In each box, for that day, my To-Dos and my To-Calls.

I also have a project list with deadlines up on the wall. Can't miss it. I also sometimes use a "storyboard" for planning, somewhat like the storyboard used to plan a TV program or movie. I got this from the late Mike Vance, and he got it from his years working with Walt Disney.

Incidentally, if you are a "free spirit," you might think something like these lists to be intolerably confining, like a pair of jockey shorts mistakenly bought one size too small. (What?—like I'm the only one to ever make that mistake?) Actually, once you get used to using these lists, you'll find them mentally, creatively liberating. Why? Because the more details you get on paper, the fewer you must remember and worry about remembering. This frees your mind up for more important tasks.

I'm usually amused by people dependent on their devices and laptops for their schedules, plans, and lists. On more than one occasion, I've heard them wailing about the machine gleefully erasing everything and leaving them with a blank screen or watched their batteries go dead. So far, the trifolded pages in my jacket pocket and pen have not failed me.

Ultimately, though, whether with crayon and pad or computer, you have got to get some sort of regimented, regularly used list-making system working for you. **If you aren't making lists, you probably aren't making a lot of money either.**

Technique #5: Fight to Link Everything to Your Goals

(The secret reason why there aren't more millionaires.)

The late, great success philosopher Jim Rohn, a friend and speaking colleague, often said that the only real reason more people do not become millionaires is that they don't have enough reasons to. It's certainly not lack of opportunity! Look around. You can't pick up a magazine without reading of people who've taken very ordinary ideas, even weird ideas, and used them to become rich. You can't pick up a magazine and not read of someone who has scrambled up out of poor circumstances and gotten rich. So why don't more people become millionaires? They just don't have enough reasons to.

Similarly, I insist that the only real reason more people aren't much, much more productive is that they don't have enough reasons to be. A secret to greater personal productivity is more good reasons to be more productive. That's why you have to fight to link everything you do (and choose not to do) to your goals.

Frankly, this is very difficult. You've undoubtedly heard the adage: when you're up to your neck in alligators, it's difficult to remember that your original objective was to drain the swamp. And, having been up to my neck in alligator-filled swamp water more often than I like to remember, I know just how tough it is to keep at least one eye fixed firmly on your list of goals. But that's EVERYTHING. That is what gets goals achieved, and that is what creates peak productivity, as I'll explain.

In the 1980s, "productivity" was a big, big buzzword. There were all sorts of folks running around teaching businesses and businesspeople every conceivable gimmick for improving productivity—without ever defining or (I contend) knowing what the heck productivity was. For corporations, there was regurgitated Demingism, Japanese management styles, MBO, MBV, and on and on all in search of an invisible, ill-defined intangible.

If you're going to achieve peak personal productivity, you've got to *define* peak personal productivity.

So, here's my definition:

> *Productivity* is the deliberate, strategic investment of your time, talent, intelligence, energy, resources, and opportunities in a manner calculated to move you measurably closer to meaningful goals.

Note that this definition presupposes the existence of meaningful goals. I don't know of a single successful individual, in any field, who isn't goal directed and who is not involved in measuring, preferably daily, movement toward those goals. Paul Meyer, founder of Success Motivation Institute, once stated that if you are not achieving what you feel you should in life, it is because your goals are not defined well enough. But my definition of productivity goes beyond that. It says not only that you cannot be productive without goals, in fact, without linkage with goals, it says you cannot be productive without *measurement.*

This gives you a very simple standard for determining, minute by minute, task by task, choice by choice, whether you are being productive or unproductive:

> *Is what I am doing, this minute, moving me measurably closer to my goals?*

Now, to be reasonable, and to be human, let's cheerfully acknowledge that nobody can—or should—be able to say "yes" to that question all of the time. We need, want, and deserve time for casual conversation, for baseball scores, for political arguments, for reading the comics, and for just plain goofing off. But you want to do those things knowingly, consciously, and by choice, not by random accident or others' direction.

I'd say that anything beyond a 50% "yes rate" qualifies as peak personal productivity. Incidentally, measurement alone will enhance your productivity. Just asking the question will enhance your productivity. Any athlete will tell you that measurement alone improves performance.

One strategy in your book that I live by is linking time to goals. I am a *recovering* pleaser, enabler, and rescuer of others, so forcing myself to put myself and my goals first, and to set and enforce boundaries is critical for my success. Linking my time to my goals now influences how I plan my days, who I say Yes to, and who I say No to. The question in your book is on a sign where I see it often: Is What I Am Doing, This Minute, Moving Me Measurably Closer to My Goals?

—LEE MILTEER, HTTPS://MILTEER.COM

Technique #6: Tickle the Memory with Tickler Files

I've got a memory like a steel trap. A rusted steel trap. Seems a lot seeps out through those rust holes. For example, I seem to have mental blocks about how old people are (the ONLY person's age I know is mine), birthdays, anniversaries, holidays, and people's names. With this in mind, I wrote a country-western song: *"I Love My Wife but I Can't Remember Where I Live."* Perversely, I can perfectly recall the lyrics from 20-year-old songs, obscure actors' names, and a collection of other useless trivia. If I could remember to phrase it as a question, I'd go on *Jeopardy!* and get rich. Seriously, I need tools and systems to substitute for memory. The Tickler File is one of my favorites.

The more I use this technique, the better I like it. The idea is simple: you have 90 file folders—red, numbered 1 through 30; blue, numbered 1 through 30; and white, numbered 1 through 30 representing the current month, next month, and the month after that. This has been most commonly used by accountant-type folks, to keep track of bills to be paid. But it can be used for anything. Let's assume you agree to follow up with a client on a particular matter on the tenth of next month. Take either that client's whole file or just that piece of correspondence or just a handwritten note and plop it into the blue file folder numbered 10. And forget it. On the tenth of next month, it'll pop up all by itself and remind you to do it. Used right, these Tickler Files reduce clutter, serve as automatic memory, and help organize daily activities.

Yes, I am well aware that there are all sorts of "contact management programs" for computers, tablets, and phones that can substitute for the file folders in a drawer, and if you prefer that, by all means, be my guest. (I have more to say about technology later in this chapter.) Personally, I'd be scanning in stuff, which requires time, and I'd have a hard time accommodating the lumpy, bulky material that is part and parcel of my work. But manual, automated, physical, virtual, or hybrid, a Tickler File System can be a very good friend.

Technique #7: Block Your Time

Here is one of the real, hidden secrets of people who consistently achieve peak productivity: make inviolate appointments with yourself. You know, we all do a pretty good job at keeping the appointments we make with others. We have this skill down. So, why not use it to get things done?

Most people's schedules only have their locked-in-stone appointments with others. Mine also has my pre-allocated, locked-in-stone appointments with myself and with my work, including start and end times. For each year, a lot of time gets locked down months to a full year ahead. For example, I clump most of my necessary phone appointments during a month into one day, along with the group coaching calls I conduct and the random teleseminars, radio interviews, and discussions with clients that pop up. While many of these things can't be known specifically six months ahead, I can and do book my Phone Day in each month a year ahead; then all needed calls are put on those days. Speaking engagements and coaching meetings are also booked way ahead. Then month to month, the various work appointments and time blocks for writing my monthly newsletters or for work on a book. My goal

Some years back, I was counseling a chiropractor new to practice and advised her to close her office for one day a week, call that "Marketing Day," and devote that entire day to calling patients, visiting health food stores, calling on businesses, giving speeches, and so on. Left to be "fit in" as time allowed, most of these very productive things would never have happened.

is to have as little unassigned time as possible. The less open and flexible time, the less wandering and meandering, the less waste, and the more discriminating you have to be in saying yes to things.

I treat the work appointments (or play appointments) that I have with myself just as inviolate as I do a speaking engagement or a consulting day.

I've been busy starting businesses over the last 14 years. Currently, I'm managing four businesses, while most struggle just to manage one— therefore never really getting to be true entrepreneurs. It became very clear to me that there was often a competition between my purposes and agenda and others' agendas, particularly those Dan calls Time Vampires. **This is why planning and Time Blocking is so important. Having appointments with yourself so that others must wait, having start and stop times for everything, and, in the business, differentiating between low and high value and low and high time-consuming customers is critical.** If anybody knows that time IS money, it's me—I'm a chartered accountant often analyzing the hidden reasons for struggle, losses, and missed opportunities in diverse businesses. I have conducted over 3,000 business growth consultations with companies in the U.K. and found or created over $100 million in documented gains for my clients.

—SHAZ NAWAZ, CHARTERED ACCOUNTANT, ENTREPRENEUR, AUTHOR,

SPEAKER, AA-ACCOUNTANTS.CO.UK, SHAZNAWAZ.CO.UK

In short, if you lay your calendar out before you and pre-assign or block as much of your time as possible, as much in advance as possible—carved in rock and not written lightly in pencil—you will then leave yourself only a small amount of loose, unassigned time. Further, by blocking time for important, high-value functions you perform, you prevent demands of others from moving your highest and best-value activities from number one to number ten on your list over and over again.

When to Work, Workout, or Whatever

As men age, their testosterone declines and their peak testosterone is early in the morning—a fact that many wives are unenthused about.

It may well be that your body has its own clock for everything—not just sex. There's a growing body of research supporting the idea that your body and your mind are best equipped to most effectively perform different tasks at different times of day. For example, exercising first thing in the morning may waste the time when you are mentally fresh and best able to do your most important work. Late in the afternoon, when the mind is fatigued and waning in cognitive function, could be the better time to hit the gym.

For more on this, see Sue Shellenbarger's *The Wall Street Journal* article "The Peak Time for Everything."

On the other hand, I believe you can train and condition your mind to your schedule. I, for example, have trained my subconscious mind to solve assigned problems and to write advertising copy or content copy for me while I sleep. Scoff, but virtually every morning, at 6:00 or 7:00 a.m., I go directly from bed to computer, put fingers on keyboard, and race, race, race to input all the copy pouring from my subconscious, which it has accumulated during the night and has been impatiently waiting to get it committed to the printed word. It feels somewhat like having waited way too long to pee, rushing to the bathroom and barely getting your clothing out of harm's way before explosively powered urine floods the bowl—not that I'm comparing my writing to pee. Others make that comparison, and I'll leave them to it. But now, when I have to write, I have to write!

I am an Amazon shareholder and my books are sold by Amazon, but I have never once gone to Amazon and bought a book there. I can more quickly jot a book I hear or read about and want on a list or scrap of paper for my assistant to fetch. On the other hand, I will still go to a bookstore and meander about, looking at new titles and types of books I would not ordinarily be exposed to like the newsstand. Doing this is an inefficient but effective method of discovery and a relaxing entertainment, so, for me, a two-fer: the same hour is productive in two ways.

This is an example of: know thyself. The more you know about yourself and what works best for you, to liberate your creativity and to power your performance, the better you can arrange things to your satisfaction.

As another example, for the past 20 years, I've rarely had an assistant in my own work environment, and when I've tried it, I've found it disruptive and unproductive. That person actually takes over my time—the exact opposite of my reasons for employing her. There must be work organized for her to do when she arrives. Her questions must be answered. She requires supervision. Instead, my assistant has been in her own office at the opposite end of the country, and we speak briefly no more than once a day—for which we both accumulate, organize, and prioritize what must be covered. I put together her work at my pace and convenience and send it by FedEx once or twice a week; she organizes all my inbound mail, faxes, phone messages, periodicals, and her work and sends it each Wednesday. We do not email or text because I never use either one. We are both safeguarded from interruptions by the other. Neither of us wastes the other's time. Clients, vendors, and others learn that we are not in the same space and that she does not have immediate access, so she is able to ward off pressure to "just get him for me for a quick conversation now." I recognize full well most people would not want this sort of arrangement even if proven to be the most productive of all approaches to having a personal assistant. Many bosses get psychic satisfaction from buzzing a buzzer, literally or figuratively, and having their assistant drop whatever he or she is doing and appear in front of him, panting and eager. This is food for their ego. Many like the social interaction of staff. I doubt many really need it, but many want it. It's far beyond the scope of this book to deal with psychosis. I am simply explaining to you that I have figured out how I am most productive and completely ignored convention in order to create the best work conditions for myself. It is those two things that are important:

One, to figure out how *you* are most productive.

Two, to throw out all norms, "rules," preconceived ideas, others' opinions, others' schedules, etc. and create the best work conditions for yourself that facilitate your best productivity.

This is very important. Being thought of as odd or strange, as unreasonable, as a luddite, etc. is a cheap price to pay for the best possible personal productivity. Understand this is the polar opposite of the trap most fall into. Most try to improve their productivity and manage their time inside boxes already built by others and approved of by others. You have a key decision to make about all of this: whether you want maximum personal productivity or the approval of others.

Technique #8: Minimize Unplanned Activity

By reducing unscheduled time and unplanned activity, you automatically reduce waste.

If you look around carefully, you'll see that most people just sort of show up. They arrive at the office and react. If you press them for their day's plan, you'll find they may have only one or two scheduled activities—one of which is usually lunch. (That attitude reminds me of the *Peanuts* cartoon: what class do you like best? Recess.) They may also have a few things on a "loose" things-to-do list. All the unscheduled time somehow gets used up, but if you again press them at the end of the day—or better yet, at the end of the week—they cannot tell you where it went.

Just as the person who cannot tell you where his money goes is forever destined to be poor, the person who cannot tell you where his time goes is forever destined to be unproductive—and, often, poor.

Ideally, you should schedule your day by the half-hour from beginning to end. I now use the term "script" in place of "schedule." Many days, *every minute* is accounted for in advance and outcomes are preordained.

If you do project work as I do, it's important to estimate the minutes or hours required and work against the clock and against deadlines. Every task gets completed faster and more efficiently when you have determined in advance how long it should take and set a time for its completion. This, too, minimizes unplanned activity.

Doesn't All This Create a Pressure Cooker Environment?

Yes. When you play "beat the clock" on a daily basis, with virtually every activity, from a phone conversation to writing a sales letter or answering inbounds booked as appointments with start and end times, you *do* create pressure for yourself. But once you grow accustomed to it, you'll discover an important difference between pressure and stress. Chaos, juggling priorities, randomly responding to interruptions, letting work expand its consumption of time as it sees fit, and constant compromise of your intentions to accommodate others, leaving many intentions unmet and carrying over endlessly, creates a lot of pressure and stress. Being organized as described in Techniques #7 and #8 creates pressure but actually reduces stress.

Pressure to Perform Can Make Performance Better

This may be contrary to what you've been told by others, but I know it to be true. Focus is everything and nothing forces focus better than intense time pressure. One of the things I do is drive professionally in harness races about 150 times a year. A race is two minutes or less, the difference between first and fifth place often just a fifth of a second. There are eight or nine other horses and sulkies in tight quarters, the width of a piece of paper separating the wheels. There is zero time to think about any of the three or four critical decisions and myriad of small ones that must be made during the course of the race, and being distracted can get you and others killed. The pressure is intense, so the focus is nearly perfect. The mind does not wander.

The cohost of Discovery Channel's show *MythBusters*, Adam Savage, is a movie special effects fabricator. He told this story in *Wired* magazine (2013):

> I'm working on an alien costume. I've got the suit. It was built for me, and it's gorgeous. But I'm making the head myself, and it's kicking my butt. The problem: I have too much time.
>
> I've learned over decades of building that a deadline is a potent tool for problem solving. This is counterintuitive because complaining about deadlines is a near universal pastime . . . When I'm stumped without a deadline, I tend to let things go. So the head has pretty much sat on my bench for seven months. Any cursory perusal of a fan/

maker forum on the web reveals two distinct kinds of projects: the long, meandering, inconsistently updated but impressively detailed effort and the hell bent for leather, tearing toward a deadline build. Solutions to problems of the first type are often methodical and obvious. Solutions for the second type are much more likely to be innovative, elegant, and shockingly simple. Invariably, the second type of project is propelled by an upcoming event. *Deadlines refine the mind.* They remove variables like exotic materials and processes that take too long.

His experience with his work is much the same as mine is with mine—writing advertising and sales copy for complex, multimedia campaigns and writing content for books, info-products, newsletters, and seminars.

Walt Disney and Steve Jobs were both notorious for placing "impossible" deadlines on projects and the people who worried over them and worked on them—and look how their ventures turned out. Watch the movie about Walt and the making of the original *Mary Poppins* movie *Saving Mr. Banks,* and take note of the incredible time pressure he put the music composers, the Sherman brothers, and others under. My wife and I saw Richard Sherman at a D23 event, and he spoke fondly of his times working for and with Walt, including times when an entire new song that would be a key part of a movie was needed overnight. There is a false idea that "creative people" work liberated from deadlines and time pressure and need the freedom to wait for inspiration. Not the successful ones. Not the productive ones.

Everyone needs pressure to perform at their best. Everyone needs deadlines—even the beavers. They loaf around all summer, but when they are faced with the winter deadline, they work like fury. If we didn't have deadlines here, for everything, for everyone, we'd stagnate. I've found that the best way to get started is to quit talking and begin doing, and the best way to get something done is to have to. The best way to get a lot of things done is to be under a lot of pressure to pull them off.

—WALT DISNEY

There is a popular idea that one should escape and avoid pressure. I believe the opposite. I believe the more pressure you put yourself under to perform, the better you perform—and the less time each performed task or accomplishment requires, giving you time to tackle another and another and another. Both your conscious and subconscious minds are capable of much more than you now ask of them, and they and you can be conditioned to thrive under intense deadline pressure.

It Can't Take More Time Than This: The Power of a Time Budget

Certain pieces of business have certain relatively or perfectly predictable value for me. Not all entrepreneurs have as clear-cut a basis for making these determinations as I do, but everybody can develop some basis. In my case, for example, I know what a book like this can be worth to me in total income, from the royalties from the publisher and from promotional considerations. There is a dollar number. I take that number and divide it by $3,000.00, and that dictates the maximum number of hours I can invest in writing this book, getting it through editing, correspondence with the publisher and others about it, and promoting it. It will get not a minute more. I know how much I will earn from a particular seminar. The hours required to travel to it and present it times $3,000.00 equal an amount deducted from the total. The remainder divided by $3,000.00 dictates how many hours can be invested in its promotion and preparation. It cannot have more. It does not deserve more. I could take you through virtually every piece of business within my entire realm of business activity and conduct the same math exercise.

This creates a time budget for each piece of business, project, client relationship, etc. that has to be binding. If I can see that something will require, or even risks requiring, more time than it is worth, I pass on it. If I am running out of time, compromises must be made in order to finish within the time budget. In most of what I do, you can tinker and tweak and try to improve endlessly. In my book *No B.S. Ruthless Management of People and Profits,* I talk at some length about the GE Spot: the Good Enough Spot. Different businesses, different customers, and different products all have GE Spots. In most cases, there is insufficient value in exceeding the GE Spot, but many entrepreneurs get caught up in far exceeding the worth of a piece of business by striving for perfection beyond the GE Spot. I work against the clock, within the time budget, and to, but never beyond, the GE Spot. I can frankly tolerate some compromise of desired quality, but I *cannot* tolerate winding up underpaid.

Very few people think this way. They make open-ended commitments and work at things for as long as it takes to complete them. This guarantees you will invest too much time in relationship to the financial worth because work expands to fit the time available to it.

Very few people develop time budgets, and even fewer engineer their work backward based on those budgets. If I know the maximum number of hours that can be invested in this book's writing, I know the maximum number of minutes that can be invested in each page. I know page by page if I'm on pace, falling behind, or getting ahead. It's cool to get ahead. That banks time that, later, I can invest in more polishing than I'd planned on, or transfer to a different aspect of the piece of business like promotion, or pocket as bonus profit. It's bad to fall behind. Falling behind sets up the worst-case scenario: being underpaid for this piece of business and having to steal time from another piece of business. That's why falling behind has to be watched out for and fixed.

As an owner of more than 90 companies, and a world traveler for speaking engagements, effective time management is an absolute must. Yet I've learned **you can't** *actually* **manage time; you can only manage yourself and those around you.** I learned keys of self-management that I implement with my team from Dan Kennedy. He has been a personal mentor of mine for years, and I continue to invest in private coaching from him because of his unique ability to get straight to the core of a problem or opportunity. Many things taken from Dan and the summary of his **methods in this book have become my NON-NEGOTIABLES. For example, I use the Time Budget and "It Can't Take More Time Than This."** The amount of quality work my team and I complete exceeds most of what my peers get done and into the marketplace with teams three and four times the size of mine. This is because of structured, definite time pressure.

—LORAL LANGEMEIER, INTERNATIONAL WEALTH EXPERT, AUTHOR/PUBLISHER,

COACH, FOUNDER AND CEO OF LIVE OUT LOUD, INC.,

HTTPS://WWW.LORALLANGEMEIER.COM

Technique #9: Profit from "Odd-Lot" Time

Everything is now portable. A seminar by a great speaker, just about any and every book ever published, how-to information of every variety, on audio CDs and DVDs, accessible through online media, on YouTube, inside your Kindle or iPad. Or you *could* still make sure you have an actual book with you at all times. You can use YouTube for something other than watching kittens water ski. There is no excuse to simply waste time while waiting in an airport, stuck in traffic, or parked in a reception room. In Washington, DC, they say a billion here, ten billion there, and before you know it, you've spent real money. Well, five minutes here, 15 minutes there, pretty soon, you're spending months *and* real money.

The audio program is the greatest educational invention since the Gutenberg press—and has the superiority of not requiring exclusive attention to be beneficial. I've been producing and educating others for 40 years* as well as educating myself with audio programs for 55 years, starting with records, then audiocassette tapes, and now CDs. You can turn your car into a classroom. You can listen, think, and absorb while doing mundane, relatively mindless tasks you either can't escape or don't want to (some people *like* mowing their lawns). You can condition your subconscious with spaced repetition learning most easily with audio; 7 to 21 repetitions of the same messages automatically embeds. Few will read the same book seven times.

Some people, instead, give their odd-lot time to returning calls, texts, or emails, or to talking on the phone. This is usually a mistake for three reasons: one, you'll be doing it hurriedly and without proper preparation or organization, and if any of it is important, it's too important to do poorly. If it's not important enough to do properly, why are you doing it at all? Two, it's a bad precedent to set with those who have access to you and with whom you communicate. If you inject randomness, you lose the ability to impose organization. Three, it steals time you need to

---

*A current catalog of all my audio programs can be accessed via https://magneticmarketing.com.

think, to read, to listen, and to get and process input. Constant connectivity makes Jack a dull boy, dull meant as a synonym for: stupid.

Disciplined use of the time everybody else wastes can give you an edge. The now rich and famous writer of legal thrillers, Scott Turow, wrote his first novel using only his morning commutes into New York City on the train. All around him, others just killed the same time. If I have big gaps between races I'm driving in, I take a stack of trade journals to skim or accumulated "B-pile" mail to go through, sit in the car outside the barn, and make an hour serve a productive purpose.

For most people, these minutes don't matter. But they can. In a sense, this is the penny argument. It's *only* a penny. A lot of people won't even pick one up if they drop it. But if you ask Warren Buffett if he pays attention to pennies, you'll get a different answer. When you say to yourself "It's only ten minutes," you miss the entire point of time. You either take it seriously or you don't.

Technique #10: Live off Peak

Why make life more difficult than it already is?

There are obvious ways to use this technique. For example, avoid going to the bank on Fridays, especially after 11:00 A.M., and especially if it is the 1st or 15th of the month. Avoid going to the supermarket the day before a holiday weekend. Avoid going to the post office the day before a rate increase (an unfortunately increasingly common occurrence).

I suppose everybody knows these things. But there are many similar patterns and instances of "herd behavior" that you can avoid. In Phoenix, where I lived for 24 years, I could drive from my home to my office in ten minutes if I did it after 9:00 A.M., but it took a half-hour or more if I tried it between 7:30 and 8:30 A.M.

Thanks to the idiotic refusal by the Phoenix authorities to install left turn arrows, it was often easier, faster, and safer to make three right turns and go around a block than to wait in line and make one left turn. If traveling, I try to avoid having to check out and leave a hotel between 8:00 and 9:00 A.M. or check in between 4:00 and 6:00 P.M. because that's when everybody else checks in and out.

What Is the Average Length of Time People Spend Waiting in Line?

Sweden	2.2 minutes
U.K.	3.3 minutes
Italy	14.4 minutes
Russia	27.1 minutes
United States	16 minutes
@ Disney World	48 minutes
To be first to get newest iPhone	5.3 hours
U.S. emergency room	4.7 hours

Data from: *The Book of Times* by Lesley Alderman; Disney Guidebook: *Little-Known Facts about Well-Known Places: Walt Disney World* by Laurie Flannery; *The Unofficial Guide to Walt Disney World 2013* by Sehlinger/Testa; *Time Use Survey*, Grey Research Group.

Time Waiting in Lines, continued

There are three possible attitudes to have about waiting in lines, and they are revealing of a person's overall attitude about their time and waste of their time:

1. **Waiting in lines is for other people but not for me.** I am smarter than most and can arrange my activities to reduce waiting, I can delegate it and have others do whatever requires standing in line for me, I can buy privilege and by-pass lines. (At Disney, you can hire a private guide by the hour and be escorted to the front of every line. You can travel by private jet and never stand in a TSA security line. You can sign a power of attorney and send someone to the DMV line in your place. You can avoid going to restaurants that do not accept and honor reservations.)

2. **Waiting in lines is just a necessary part of life, and there's nothing to be done about it.** Patience is a virtue. Life is made up of random chance. *Note*: Acceptance of ordinary realities that are counter to deriving maximum benefit from your time equates to surrender of control.

3. **Somehow scheming to skip waiting in lines or paying to bypass lines is unfair** and unjust to everyone else and something I *shouldn't* do. Having the idea that my time is more important than other people's is arrogant, egotistical, and shameful. *Note*: Guilt about creating benefit for yourself blocks any benefit coming to you.

Each of us chooses one of these three philosophical positions. Whichever you've chosen has been established in your subconscious mind as a governing, navigational principle lording authority over all your other decisions, largely without you being consciously aware of its influence.

When you take note of these things and organize your life to work around them, you can save a lot of time and avoid a lot of frustration.

Bonus Technique #11: Use Technology Profitably

I first wrote this book in 1996. It was updated once in 2013. Now, here we are again. In these elapsed years, the quantity and diversity of business and personal technology has mushroomed wildly.

There are so many tech tools to choose from, it's hard to make good choices. People are wearing special jackets with multiple, variously sized pockets to carry three, four, or even five different devices. The devices connect you to a nearly infinite number of apps that do things for you, count things for you, communicate for you, but—truth told—mostly are part of a mobile toy chest and not a mobile cache of productivity-boosting weaponry. When there are too many, they all lose value and become more time-consuming than they are worth.

Few reading this book will share my personal view. Most of the tech gadgetry is an anathema to me. That does not prohibit me having it used for me or having it deployed for me or my clients as advertising, marketing, and sales media. It hasn't even barred me from investing in technology companies. I also own tobacco stock but have never smoked. Nor should my personal preferences be the advice I dispense. Instead, I have three cautions:

One, ask the tough question: where's the profit in this? If it does, in fact, honestly, conserve and improve the value of your time, aid you in faster or surer implementation, or otherwise boost your or your business's performance, then, of course, use it. But be very careful to consider its direct cost, that is, the time required to use it as well as the indirect cost, i.e., what relying on it is doing to your brain.

Two, beware using something just because it exists. The piling on of things to use and do because somebody invents and markets them puts you on the wrong side of the cash register. Kohler is selling a very pricey toilet/bidet with a touch screen pad attached to "manage it." But, really, is there any practical benefit to a computer-operated toilet?

Three, beware peer pressure. You are an adult entrepreneur. Don't act like a kid in junior high. Just because "everybody" around you has rushed to get the latest tech thing or stuff does not mean it is productive and profitable for you to have it—and the fact that "everybody" has embraced it should even give you pause. What's popular, what's normal, and what's productive often do not match up.

Automate or Stagnate

Automation can certainly facilitate implementation that would not be possible or would be considerably less profitable otherwise. My friends who invented Infusionsoft brought something forward that is a terrific example of this. If you read my book *No B.S. Direct Marketing for NON-Direct Marketing Businesses*, you'll be introduced to lead generation in place of one-step selling, multimedia, multistep marketing campaigns, and multistep follow-up campaigns for unconverted leads, new buyers' retention and ascension, and cross-selling. If all that was gibberish to you, please, please, please, do yourself the very profitable favors of getting and reading the book and accepting the free offer in it. Anyway, all this comes from big direct-marketing companies with big computer systems filled with custom software they had built for them and teams of employees buzzing about managing it all, and the small-business owner or entrepreneur has none of that and can't afford it. For years, we all did the best we could, doing all this manually and, as computers came to every office and kitchen table, with various types of programs that didn't communicate well with each other. Most could, candidly, only implement everything I taught—and they understood represented great opportunity—to a very limited extent and with a relatively high quotient of struggle and pain. Infusionsoft is the only small-business marketing management software built from the ground up to properly, easily run complicated, multistep campaigns. It combines database and list segmentation functions, CRM functions, tracking, automated email, and many other capabilities. I encourage looking into it, at www. infusionsoft.com. Most of my clients and many GKIC Members power their marketing with Infusionsoft, including many sophisticated campaigns that they can set up and forget and know they'll occur perfectly.

As an example, for one group of entrepreneurs who sell by bringing prospective clients into introductory seminars and there scheduling personal, follow-up appointments with as many as they can but always a minority of those in attendance, I devised a 16-step, 4-week follow-up system for those not scheduling that produces from a 2-to-1 to 8-to-1 return on investment. Hardly any of these busy entrepreneurs would ever consistently implement it without Infusionsoft. Now, they only need enter or database-migrate the people from the seminars not booking appointments, and those prospects automatically get 12 email and 4 direct-mail follow-up communications, all customized and personalized, with precise timing (i.e., Follow-Up #1, 3rd Day, Follow-Up #2, 5th Day, etc.). Most businesses can be revolutionized with this kind of automated, no-fail follow-up.

Other companies in my world that brilliantly assist entrepreneurs and their companies in sophisticated, automated marketing, selling, and customer service processes are www. eLaunchers.com and https://magneticmarketing.com. Their services in this area are all about being able to do a lot more with prospect and customer engagement, with less time from you or your team and with greater consistency and certainty. This is also for the good. So, make no mistake, I am for automation where it provides clear advantage. Where it too often turns sour is when the technology requires constant oversight, change, maintenance, and involvement of you or top-tier team members and *consumes* time rather than liberating time.

All of it, though, needs to be added to your business life carefully. It's best if what gets added replaces more time-consuming or cumbersome things that can be subtracted. Trying to give attention to more and more and more added with no subtraction gets problematic in a hurry.

Turning Time Management into Achievement and Achieved Goals

What is the point of these techniques? They are achieving goals you choose and develop for yourself. This is treacherous territory!

According to a 2015 University of Scranton poll, 62% of Americans make New Year's resolutions. Only 8% keep them. Sounds about right to me. Although this is the most unserious goal-setting that ever occurs, the ugly truth is that most goal-setting has similarly poor results.

The most common New Year's resolutions have to do with losing weight and getting back in shape. This sparks sign-ups in gyms and diet groups, enrollment in home-delivered preportioned diet

Goals, continued

food plans, buying diet and health books, and purchasing of all sorts of home exercise equipment. The joke in that industry is that the handles on all exercise machines and treadmills put into homes must point *up*—so the laundry doesn't fall off. I've done a fair amount of work in that industry as a marketing strategist, and I can tell you, joke aside, that the most important product feature is that it folds up, to stow away under the bed or in a closet. Years back, I did a big consulting and ad copywriting project for a major brand-name, national weight-loss company and discovered that 70% of its customers were its own dropouts, back for a second, third, fifth, or even seventh bite at the apple, and virtually all of the other first-timers cited having tried and been disappointed by at least four other competing programs. Most dieters are on an endless merry-go-round, getting off the gray horse to get on the red one and then getting off it to get on the black one. Children acting childishly. There are goals in all of this failure.

The second most common New Year's resolution—more in sync with this book—is to finally get organized. This sparks spending sprees as well—all kinds of containers, shelves, filing systems, planning calendars, devices, apps. Most left by the wayside within months if not weeks. There are goals in all of this failure.

Of course, I live by goals and advocate doing the same—but not as most do or as most teach. The goal or target has to be taken very seriously, has to be created in a context of practical application, and has to be supported in every possible way—most beneficially, via commitments you can't not keep. Just writing down a goal and hastily buying a few things related to it means nothing.

Goals, continued

It's good for the economy, but it's not good for you. In fact, it's a very unhealthy behavioral pattern.

Making New Year's resolutions or their equivalent any time during the year is literally a waste of time. To quote W. H. Auden: "The only way to spend New Year's Eve is either quietly celebrating with friends or in a brothel"—*not* making resolutions.

If you are to take a goal, objective, or target seriously and have hope of its achievement, you need to link it to time. Time must be made for it, allocated to it, budgeted for it, and booked into your schedule as firm, inviolate appointments with yourself and/or with others. I need and want (best if both need and want are in play) to get a certain, set amount of writing for my projects (like this book) done, and it's best to get it done in daily doses because if I fall behind by a week, I'll never catch up. Therefore, I have no less than one hour booked first thing every morning to do this—before I start writing for clients or do anything else. Every day. This makes successful, rein-forcing accomplishment a daily thing and not some distant event like the completion of an entire manuscript. In a way, the activity itself becomes the goal that can be achieved on a regular, recurring basis. You can engineer the same thing for just about any purpose. If I replaced the first hour writing with a first hour of walking on the treadmill, I would lose weight and build stamina.

You also need, importantly, to safeguard the goal and everything you're doing to achieve it from NIOP: *Negative Interference from Other People*. A strong fortress must be constructed around the goal and the linked activities and responsibilities—with snipers in the tow-ers atop the wall, an alligator-filled moat around it, and land mines in the ground for miles around it. People who negatively interfere

Goals, continued

with no negative intent or malice aforethought are just as dangerous to you as those deliberately trying to stop your forward progress or upward mobility. The person who constantly says "Oh, John, you've been burning the midnight oil on that thing for two weeks—you can certainly take the weekend off from it, and you deserve it" is just as much The Enemy as is the burglar who breaks in and steals what you've been working on. You have to view them as such.

Their motives, conscious or unconscious, authentically kind or secretly evil, do *not* matter. If they are encouraging you to break and dishonor the commitments you've made to yourself and your goal, they are the Enemy.

If you can't identify your enemies, you damn sure won't ward them off and defeat them. Chapter 3 of *No B.S. Time Management for Entrepreneurs*, "How to Drive a Stake Through the Hearts of the Time Vampires Out to Suck You Dry," tackles this in detail.

The Ten Techniques just presented in this chapter are the arrows in your quiver—the weapons in your arsenal. To achieve goals, you'll need them all.

CHAPTER 41

The Inner Game of
Peak Personal Productivity

Originally appearing as Chapter 12 from
No B.S. Time Management for Entrepreneurs

Y ou can load yourself up with big, hunky day-
planner devices, computer software, notepads, different
colored pens, stickers, strings tied around your
thumbs, and a million little "techniques" and still be pitifully
unproductive if you don't have your "inner game" under
control. Productivity is an inside-out game.

Psycho-Cybernetics and Getting More
Value from Your Time

You probably recognize the term "Psycho-Cybernetics." The
book of that title has sold more than 30 million copies worldwide,
and several different audiocassette adaptations have been sold
via the famous Nightingale-Conant catalog, the SkyMall catalog,

and a television program as well as published and distributed through bookstores. The mental training techniques created by Dr. Maxwell Maltz that make up Psycho-Cybernetics have been endorsed and used by famous pro athletes and coaches, leading corporate executives, star salespeople, entertainment personalities, and me. Salvador Dali gave Dr. Maltz an original painting as thanks for Psycho-Cybernetics's influence on his career.

When Dr. Maltz first began putting his techniques down on paper in the 1960s, he was far ahead of his time—so far ahead that people first discovering his material right now are amazed by and profit enormously from them.

What does all that have to do with you and peak productivity?

There is a certain state of mind that best facilitates achieving peak productivity. You can best create that state of mind as needed, when needed, and at will by mastering certain Psycho-Cybernetics techniques.

For example, Dr. Maltz talked about "clearing the calculator." If you have a simple calculator lying around, get it and take a look at it. You'll find that you have to hit the "clear" button and either store in memory or completely clear away one problem before you employ the calculator to solve another. In his studies of human behavior, Dr. Maltz observed that all too often, we're trying to use our minds to work on several problems at once without ever stopping to hit the "clear" button.

Achieving maximum personal productivity requires that you become extraordinarily facile at stopping, storing, and clearing so as to direct 100% of your mental powers to one matter at a time—to the matter at hand. One client of mine, the CEO of a $20 million-a-year corporation, is a compulsive, obsessive worrier. He admittedly lets a dozen worries loose to run around in his mind at the same time he is trying to do something else and says he is constantly interrupted by his own thoughts. He marvels at me and tells others that "it is amazing how Kennedy can just box up a problem, put it away on a shelf in his mind, focus totally on some task, and only go back to work on the problem when he wants to." This is because I have practiced and practiced and practiced the technique of "clearing the calculator" until it is second nature to me.

A big reason for my prolific output as a writer is that I never have to "get in the mood" to write. Many people go through great physical and mental gyrations just getting ready to get ready to write. I don't. I can sit down, put my fingers on the keys, clear my calculator in 60 seconds or less, and write.

This is just one of a number of simple but very powerful Psycho-Cybernetic techniques, but it illustrates a very important point: *If you can't control your thoughts and manage your mind, you can't control or manage your time.*

Creating a Peak Productivity Environment

You can do a number of things to make certain that your environment works *for* you instead of against you. The following are some key ideas to consider and experiment with:

- Psychological triggers
- Organization vs. clutter

I am a big believer in populating my work environment with "psychological triggers"—objects that remind me to think a certain way. I work at mentally attracting wealth, for example, so my primary work environment is full of things that represent wealth: at last count, 27 such pictures, objects, and artifacts were within view.

I have visual motivators all through my workplaces.

One coffee mug, a gift from a client, is emblazoned with the word HUSTLE. Another mug has a happy little monster who says, "The sale begins when the customer says no." Another, a

Disney mug with a character from *Cars* reads, "I eat losers for breakfast." A painting on my wall of a black tiger devouring a man in the jungle reminds me of the quote, "Tigers starve last in the jungle," and reminds me to be tough and aggressive.

I am also surrounded by clocks. The conference room has clocks on three of its four walls, one of which is the famous Kit-Cat Clock® of 1950 kitchens—its tail and big eyes move back and forth every minute accompanied by a slight ticking sound. In the kitchenette, there is a giant Disney clock that goes off every hour with Mickey and Goofy announcing the time. It can be heard anywhere in the six rooms. On a wall next to it, another Disney clock: a giant Mickey Mouse watch. In the bathroom, yet another Disney clock: a Mickey that works just like the Kit-Cat Clock. In my writing area, there are five clocks every which way I turn. Above my computer, a miniature wood hangman platform with a rope noose, a chair, a hole that pops out beneath one's feet— subtle its message to me is not.

There are nine additional clocks scattered about on bookshelves, on the fireplace mantle, and on tables.

This is done to keep me hypersensitive to the disappearance of each minute.

My huge library of over 3,000 visible books is also a visual motivator for me. It is a writer's environment. Walter Gibson, one of the most prolific writers ever—including the thousand or so *Shadow* novels, novelettes, comic books, and radio broadcasts of the 1940s—had a workspace similarly surrounded by towering bookshelves. Harry Houdini did as well. In my case, there are custom built, floor to ceiling, deep shelves on one wall, a double-sided unit across from it, another such unit next to my desk, and in another room, a built-in wall of floor-to-ceiling shelves. There are still piles in corners. The unit next to my desk houses books I frequently use, like collections of quotes and jokes. The shelf above me has dictionaries, thesauruses, and reference books.

From a time standpoint, I prefer not having to get up out of my chair to get any of these. *Stay put. Keep working. The clocks are ticking.*

Book titles themselves are psychological triggers and sources of ideas. I can take a few minutes to scan a set of shelves and let a title leap out and prompt a thought. Often, that thought is: *Get back to work!*

There are other psychological triggers all through my workplace. There is, in one chair, a huge stuffed Yogi Bear who has been with me since childhood. Yogi, you may recall, has his own tag line. He is "smarter than the average bear," as am I. The walls feature the winner's circle photos from my years of driving professionally in harness races with one frame always empty ready for the *next* win photo—an idea from the late, great golfer Arnie Palmer. The message of the walls is: win. I won't name the other 50+ objects, knickknacks, little signs, etc., each there to trigger a productivity- and performance-bolstering thought.

I have designed my entire workplace to be practically and psychologically supportive.

Most people try to be productive in very opposite conditions . . . I think you can "surround yourself" in three possible ways:

1. By accident and happenstance, with no purpose in mind and no purpose served.
2. Consciously or unconsciously, with things that trigger negative responses, frustration, anger, resentment, or depression.
3. Deliberately with things selected to reinforce positive—productive—responses.

"A Clean Desk Is a Sign of a Sick Mind"

Let's not be dogmatic about this. I suspect that a person with a constantly, pristinely clean and neat desk and work environment—a "Felix"—may very well be neurotic. Certainly

I *prefer* to believe that. On the other hand, the person immersed in clutter and a chaotic environment—an "Oscar"—MUST waste time by hunting and searching and must be distracted. There is a broad band of acceptable style between the two extremes.

Personally, fortunately, largely by "clearing the calculator," I can sit down and work effectively surrounded by clutter or in chaos. However, I will tell you that I am most productive in what I have come to call a "semi-organized environment." As a writer, for example, I think it's unavoidable to have stacks of papers, reference materials, and other documents around, but I find it very helpful to have those piles organized by topic or project.

Really creative, innovative thinking seems to come out of chaos more often than out of neatnik organization. But the successful implementation of innovative ideas seems to come about in a most organized, disciplined way.

It's worth noting, to paraphrase management guru Peter Drucker, that what we are after is *effectiveness* and not necessarily *efficiency*. Put a time-and-motion analyst on the typical entrepreneur, and he will come up empty; how do you analyze the guy who sits on the floor of his office watching daytime TV talk shows and thumbing through magazines for hours on end, then suddenly hits upon the right "pitch" for his company's new fitness product?

The most important thing here is to be honest with yourself. Is the level of clutter and disorganization around you helping or hindering? Is it out of control or just about right?

> One big time-saving tip I can give you is:
> When in doubt, throw it out.

Many people are compulsive keepers. I find a bit of ruthlessness toward paper is beneficial. If you seriously doubt you will need or use it again, go ahead and throw it out immediately. If it becomes really important, it will be provided to you again. At least once a year, usually in December, I conduct a violent purge of my correspondence files, client records, desk drawers, etc. and throw out as much of it as I dare. In all these years, I've had that come back to haunt me only a couple of times.

It's also important for your "work space" to make it easy for you to work. My own, in my home office, is not unlike a pilot's cockpit; without getting out of my swivel chair, I can operate my computers, my TV, and my CD player. I can reach my most important reference books, and I have two "surfaces" for paperwork. Once you get to work, you ought to be able to stay at work without having to jump up and down every minute or two to fetch something or put something else away.

Finally—The Militant Attitude

I have come to really, deeply, vehemently, and violently *resent* having my time wasted. I place a very, very high value on my time, and I believe that the value you really, honestly place on your time will control the way others value it and you.

I have talked about this elsewhere in this book and do not want to redundantly beat on any one single point, yet this self-determination is so important. You set your own price. And you determine whether or not people "get it" and respect it.

When I was in direct sales, managing, motivating, and trying to help others build their businesses, I was constantly amazed and often depressed at how little value people placed on their time and how pitifully unwilling they were to protect it and wisely invest it. I heard, "I didn't because . . . my mother-in-law

459 THE BEST OF NO B.S.

decided to surprise us with a visit . . . my buddy Bob dropped by and took up the whole evening . . . the roof started to leak and I had to work on that . . ." Etc. Etc. But if you already had something very important to do, that you were committed to doing, mother-in-law would have to sit home alone and watch TV, buddy Bob would be bounced out, a bucket would be put under the leak, and you'd stay focused.

How tough are you on those who would undervalue your time? How tough are you on yourself?

Your Rules

According to the actor Michael Caine, stated in his autobiography *The Elephant to Hollywood,* Frank Sinatra had a 20-minute rule. If he was invited to a dinner, party, or meeting and he was in his car for more than 20 minutes, he would tell his driver to turn around and take him home.

You need preset rules.

Discipline doesn't get made up as you go along.

Like Sinatra, I, too, have a 20-minute rule. Mine is about the phone. Ninety percent of my phone appointments with clients, would-be clients, and people doing work for me are booked in 20-minute increments. In my experience, 20 minutes is enough if both parties are properly prepared for the call. If not, no call should occur. This allows me to fit three calls per hour. With a few breaks—because I'm a camel—in a 7:00 A.M. to 7:00 P.M. "Phone Day," I can dispense with 30 phone appointments in only one day a month and keep nearly all the other days phone free. Stop and think for a minute how the productivity of your days might change if many or most were free of any phone conversations and you locked your phone away in a desk drawer.

Also like Sinatra, I'm not big on the inconvenience and time-suck of distance. When clients come to me, they are required to stay at a very modest hotel that is less than 15 minutes from my house. Most of my everyday life is arranged within 8-minute and 15-minute to 30-minute radiuses around my house—the racetrack where I drive professionally and where most of my horses are, a favorite restaurant, two additional satisfactory restaurants, the copy shop, the package shipping and receiving store I use, a movie theater, the supermarket, and the aforementioned hotel are all in the 8- to 15-minute radius. The shopping area with a large Barnes & Noble store in one direction, the upscale mall in the other, Imperial Auto Castle, where the classic cars I drive are housed, the airport I fly in and out of, etc. are in the 15- to 30-minute radius. The distance between home and racetrack was the chief controlling element in selecting our home, but all things were considered. Ninety percent of the time, I do not want to drive more than 15 minutes in each direction for anything or anybody. This is achieved by living in a semi-rural small town not an elbow-to-elbow dense, traffic gridlocked city.

My specifics need not be your specifics—that's not my point. But you should want to and can consciously, deliberately, and strategically choose and control where you live and work, what you will and will not do, and how others are permitted to consume your time. **You really have to get that it is all** *your* **time.** *All* **of it.** *Every* **minute of it.** *Yours.* If I let a client stay at a hotel 30 minutes away instead of 8, I have let him take 22 minutes times 2 equals 44 minutes of *my* time that I could have kept for myself. Didn't I have something to do with it? When you permit people to take 30 minutes for a business phone conversation that could have been accomplished in 20, you let them take—and waste—10 minutes of *your* time. Let that happen twice a day 250 workdays a year and it's 5,000 minutes. In 5 years, 25,000 minutes. 416 hours. 52 eight-hour days. In a 40-year career, 200,000 minutes. 3,334 hours. 416 days. Now, what is it you said you don't have the time to do? Read and study? Write a good newsletter for your customers every month? Exercise? Take a decent vacation?

My rules—or Sinatra's—need not be your rules. The point is you should have rules. Without rules, you have anarchy. That anarchy equals freedom is an epic lie. It destroys it. The absence of curfews of any kind does not constitute the absolute freedom to stroll about the streets at any time as you please if those streets are unsafe and you risk mugging or violent assault at any time. The absence of winter street parking bans so that everyone has absolute freedom to park as they please on both sides of the street gives no one true freedom if the snow plows can't clear the street and no one can go anywhere for weeks. These sorts of rules imposed by others chafe but are pretty much necessary to prevent a "Lord of the Flies" scenario. But the rules you make and impose on yourself and others need not chafe you. You craft them to your benefit. You use them to organize your life and the world around you to safeguard your time, energy, productivity, and peace of mind. This is even a constitutional right in the United States—"pursuit of happiness."

There's an old, little book I've had for decades in my library with a beautiful title: *The Kingship of Self-Control*. Its title alone is a course. Kingship: yes, you can be king of all you survey. You get kingship by controlling yourself and by you exercising control over others. Conversely, you get peonage and enslavement by failing to exercise control over yourself and others. Do you want to live as king or peon? A king is a ruler. By definition, a ruler makes and enforces rules. Only by adopting the behavior of a king do you get to be a king.

The Inner Game of Kingship

You need not impose control in a mean-spirited or diva-like manner.

There's no need to be mean. You can be polite yet firm. You can present your rules of engagement as beneficial to those you work with as well as to yourself. You can good-humoredly acknowledge eccentricity on your part. You can *sell* your way of doing things. (I didn't say: *negotiate*; I said: *sell*.)

There's no need to be a diva about it. This isn't about demanding only blue M&Ms and Hawaiian water in your dressing room. This isn't about egotism at all. Your decisions about how and when the world interacts with you are pragmatic, albeit personal. They should be reasoned—not arbitrary.

For these reasons, you must not let yourself be made to feel guilty. There's nothing in this to be guilty about. The bus driver never feels guilty about not pulling up to any bus stop in the city the instant you arrive there—he makes his appointed rounds on a set schedule. If that inconveniences you, there are other transportation choices available. I think of the way I work in much the same way. There are other choices. If someone is or feels unbearably inconvenienced by the way I make my appointed rounds on a schedule set by me, they are free to get the services I provide from another source; they are free to reject me as customer and sell to someone else. I hold no monopoly.

In my Renegade Millionaire Training, I make the point that there is never any need to be or behave like a prick in order to be successful, but you must be okay with some, possibly many, people thinking of you as an insufferable prick. If you're too thin-skinned for that, extraordinary success and autonomy as an entrepreneur is well beyond your reach.

Guilt is a very powerful emotion. Most people are routinely and easily manipulated with it. Criticism, another. Most people cannot hold up to others making fun of them, being critical of them, or thinking them odd. Outright dislike, another. Most people try to be liked by all and likeable to all. Most are very needy of others' approval. The entrepreneur must raise himself above these ordinary concerns. An entrepreneur seeks income and financial rewards, independence and autonomy, and other outcomes that are profoundly different, apart from, and superior to those ever achieved or experienced by 95% of the people around you. That requires you to think in profoundly different and superior ways. You can't have one without the other. Success is a conceit. If you are to have it, it will be at an intellectual, emotional, and behavioral distance from most others.

The very idea of "time management" is itself a grand conceit. It says that you—*and just who do you think you are, anyway?*—are going to manage, i.e., impose control over, dictate to, and govern, God's minutes and their movement, clock and calendar, and people of all sorts around you. It announces that you will have your way with time. This is not a humble idea.

In the great film starring Michael Caine and Sean Connery, *The Man Who Would Be King,* directed by John Huston, Caine's character, in reacting to a grandiose challenge, says, "We are not *little* people." This is what has to be decided by the entrepreneur who sets out to control his time.

Most time management training, books, courses, and lecturers focus almost entirely on mechanical methods and on tools: a better appointment book, a better software program, colored stickers, and one kind of list or another. But these are no better than guns: useless without *the will* to use them.

CHAPTER 42

How to Turn Time into Wealth

Originally appearing as Chapter 15 from
No B.S. Time Management for Entrepreneurs

Tere is an old joke that says: "I've been rich, and I've been poor. Rich is definitely better." Well, I concur. I make absolutely no apology for striving to be rich and for teaching and inspiring others to do the same. Furthermore, I believe you have every right to figure out ways to make maximum money from minimum time. When you can honestly apply the axiomatic advice of "work smarter—not harder," more power to you! I do not think any special heroism comes from earning your money through backbreaking work or long hours.

I suspect I am unique in working up close, personal, and hands-on with more than 500 first-generation millionaire and multimillionaire entrepreneurs, most of whom built their wealth by creating and building new businesses from scratch and many of whom hit the million-dollar mark in a hurry. I have been in their offices and they in mine, had hundreds of hours of telephone conversations with them, worked with them individually and in groups, and had countless opportunities over years to observe their behavior and probe their psyches. One of the key factors in their success is the way they link time to money and think in terms of investing time. Most are always looking for ways to get more for less, invest fewer minutes of work, and extract more dollars.

One way they do this is by making themselves into bona fide experts in some field—one thing from which wealth can come. There is the old story about the customer angrily demanding an itemized bill from the plumber, who submitted a $250.00 bill for two minutes' work—smacking the clogged pipe with a hammer. The plumber wrote out the itemized bill as follows: For hitting pipe with hammer: $5.00. For knowing where to hit pipe with hammer: $245.00. Getting into that position—when you can be paid not (just) for what you do (physical labor) but for what you know (intellectual equity)—is a very worthy objective and a good investment of time.

So, let there be no mistake: I think you deserve to be rich if you earn it. I think you have a right to be rich. I think you provide enormous service to society by getting and being rich. I think the government should be forbidden from penalizing or attacking you for being rich.

"On the Other Hand . . ."

With all that said, though, I have to suggest that money isn't everything.

It is a lot easier to give the "money isn't everything" and "money doesn't buy happiness" lecture after you have a considerable amount of money than before. Personally, I always resented hearing it when I was broke, and believe me, I understand that a person NEEDS a certain level of financial success before he can give a great deal of quality thought to the bigger philosophical issues of life. And I think in our land of great opportunity, it is disgraceful not to do well. I don't see any honor in being poor. I see no shame in it as a temporary condition but there should be shame if being poor is accepted as a permanent way of life. But, to be certain, money is only part, and maybe a small part, of "wealth."

On a surprisingly cool summer morning in Cleveland, Ohio, I sit in a dirty jog cart (the work-a-day version of a sulky), reins in hands, and bouncing along behind an aging but still game Standardbred horse on the Northfield Park backstretch. Damp dirt, gravel, and bits of manure are kicked up past the mud screen onto my boots and pants, occasionally hitting my face. I am in seventh heaven. Of course, I'm just fooling around. But most of the folks there doing the same thing and taking care of these horses as work are in seventh heaven, too. They couldn't imagine doing anything else.

On this particular day and night, a 70-year-old man, Earl Bowman, and his wife, Joanna, were celebrating their 50th wedding anniversary. Earl, a retired driver and still a very good trainer, took his horse to the paddock, took care of it, and worked just as he would any other night. After the race, Joanna joined him as he led the horse into the winners' circle for the photo. Then he took the horse back to the barns where he had another hour's work ahead of him, stripping off the harness, bathing the horse, walking the horse to cool him out, bandaging the horse's legs, and so on. And if you asked Earl if he could have gone anywhere else or done anything else on that night, what would he wish for, he'd have no answer. *This* is wealth.

I am often asked what, of the varied but intertwined things I do, I like doing best. I like speaking to audiences as small as 250 or as large as 25,000 for 60 minutes or 60 hours in a multiday seminar. At some of those engagements, I am sharing the day with celebrities including ones I enjoy meeting or with top CEOs I find fascinating; at others, I'm solo. There is the private consulting—a day or two in a room isolated from the world working with a client or client and his team. There is the development of advertising, marketing, and sales strategy and the copywriting for advertisements, webinars, radio commercials, TV infomercials, and direct-mail campaigns. There is the content writing for books like this, five monthly newsletters, weekly client group memos, and home study courses. So, the oft-asked question: of all the things I do, which do I like best?

My first answer is: receiving and depositing the checks. Of all the writing I do, writing out bank deposit slips is my favorite. I'm with Mark Twain on this: nobody but a blockhead writes but for the money. And more is better. You will hear people say that they love what they do so much they would do it for free. I have yet to meet any wealthy person or top achiever who means it. Being very well compensated is what I enjoy most. Taking time plus other ingredients, mixing it, and turning it into very respectable sums of money is, to me, richly satisfying—pardon the pun. Then, you get to turn that money into other things, too. But the starting point of each dollar of wealth and all it can, in turn, buy is in the remaking of time into productivity and profit.

I manage assets, mine and clients', for a living. Most people naturally think of financial assets: home and property, business, stocks, bonds, pension, money. But what Dan Kennedy correctly emphasizes is that **time itself is an asset class all its own**, and you can contend that it is more valuable than all other assets yet managed less than all others. My sense of this has been heightened greatly by being Dan Kennedy's client, observing him, and listening to his thoughts on this subject. To the degree that you or I do not control our time, our time controls us, just as is true with our money.

—TED OAKLEY, CEO, HTTPS:// OXBOWADVISORS.COM, AUTHOR,
$20 MILLION AND BROKE AND *CRAZY TIME*

My second answer to the "what do you like doing most?" question is possibly more instructive; I do not *dislike* any of the things I do. On the few occasions that has occurred and I have found myself engaged in work or activity or relationships that I did not like, I changed the situation—often abruptly—when I could afford doing so and when I couldn't. I have a high work ethic, I work a lot, and I convert a lot of work into a whale of a lot of money. This is only possible because I generally like the work I am doing, and the conditions in which I'm doing it, and the people I'm doing it for and with. It's very, very difficult to sustain performance and productivity for very long if any of those three things are reversed.

Wealth of this kind—liking your work, the conditions in which you work, and the people you work for and with—almost automatically begets financial wealth.

This does not mean it all has to be *fun*. Not disliking some of what is required is good enough. I do not subscribe to the theory that all your work should be fun, fun, fun, as if a day at Disney World with short lines and mild weather. As Larry Winget says, in the title of one of his blunt-force books, *It's Called WORK for a Reason*, and it's called a workplace for a reason. I am not a believer in the playground, happy place, come 'n' go as you please approach that you find at Google. The Happiest Place on Earth, Disney, does not run their workplace that way, and I'm siding with Disney. The insistence that your work has to be just as much fun as an evening at the circus is ridiculous, and if you are going to be successful, you are going to be engaged in a myriad of un-fun and even uninteresting things that are necessary to facilitate the important, interesting, productive, and profitable things. There's nothing fun or interesting to me about travel, but if I am to stand in front of an audience that can't be brought to me and collect a lot of money for it and I make that choice, I am going to have to suffer an airplane flight, a limo driver who wants to tell me his life story or argue politics, and a hotel bed that makes my back ache. You avoid, change, replace, automate, and delegate what you can, but so far, for me to be there, I have to go there. Yes, I know I can Skype, and we do broadcast live and prerecorded webinars, but to date, nobody's willing to pay me $50,000.00 to $100,000.00 to Skype it in. Every business has the same kind of elements that the operator considers no fun but still must do. Everything one likes doing has a price tag attached.

The idea of succeeding by pursuing your number-one passion is also a pile of B.S. Success for entrepreneurs is, first and foremost, market driven, and there are marketplace realities that must be dealt with. Not all passions offer productivity or profit. There is usually some way to integrate what passionately interests you with a business, but it can't necessarily be the business or the way a business decision is made. An entrepreneur's time and other resources must be invested where there is excellent profit—if not the best possible profit. That is the prime consideration.

Ultimately, it's pointless to invest your time in pursuing success doing something you fundamentally dislike. Success is not just about how much money you can make, but also, maybe more so, how you make the money. That is what this book is really about. There is no shortage of opportunities, or of clients, customers, and patients. Some, maybe many, may prove unwilling to cooperate with the way you want to make money. But others will. I am often told about this book's recommendations and my other rules of engagement about the way I make my money that are impractical for others. They disqualify themselves for all sorts of silly reasons, not the least of which is the delusion that I am special. For the record, I'm a high school graduate who never attended college. With zero formal training or apprenticeship in anything, everything I've grown to do so well and now have long lines of people willing to pay princely sums for and willing to do business with me on my terms, I was bad at when I started. The processes of going from dumb to smart, inept to exceptionally capable, barely knowledgeable to expert, or unknown to respected and/or to celebrity as well as the processes for autonomy are all well-known, well-documented, and repeated constantly by large numbers of people. You can invest your time in those processes or invest the same time in making the list of all the ways your business is different, your opportunities are fewer, and your handicaps greater.

You can also invest time just in getting rich but at expense of your autonomy. Or you can invest time in getting *wealthy.*

Many people manage to get rich, but comparatively few get wealthy. As long as you're going to put in your time on the planet, why not invest it in a way that makes you *wealthy?*

Napoleon Hill, most famous for his classic bestselling book *Think and Grow Rich,* spent his entire life encouraging people to pursue great goals, including financial riches. Hill was originally sent out on his mission by America's first billionaire, Andrew Carnegie, who believed there were "universal principles of success" that could be taught and learned just as any other collection of mechanical skills could be learned. Carnegie helped get Hill in-depth interviews and relationships with hundreds of the greatest achievers of that era. Hill identified 13 commonalities and wrote about them, first in *The Laws of Success* and then in *Think and Grow Rich*. Following publication of that book in 1937, Napoleon Hill lectured, trained large sales organizations, recorded inspirational messages, and in various ways, distributed his "science of success" based on those 13 principles.

Late in his life, Napoleon Hill wrote a lesser-known book I highly recommend: *Grow Rich with Peace of Mind*. In this book, after acquiring great riches, losing great riches, and a long career, Napoleon Hill did his best to reconcile the issues of pursuing great financial success and achieving total wealth in the bigger, broader sense.

How Much Is Enough?

So, how do you turn time into wealth? Reverse engineering. Decide what "wealth" means to you. This includes what I call your "enough-is-enough number"—the total of investable assets you need to feel secure and spin off sufficient income to support you and your family as you wish to live. I don't mean wild-fantasy, win-the-lottery, own-a-castle-in-Spain levels, at least not for most people, but a reasonable yet desirable level. Develop a clear, detailed picture of what your life would look like and how you would live if you had that "number" in place. Does this picture include a second home, a big vacation twice a year, or owning a bed-and-breakfast? In this picture, how do you use, spend, and invest your time?

Once you have this entire picture built, with detailed clarity, you can begin looking backward to where you are now. You identify the obstacles in the path and begin looking for and thinking about all the possible ways they might be removed. You can construct a plan. Establish yearly, monthly, and weekly targets and benchmarks. Then, most important of all, you can judge whether your present moment's choices made with your time are linked to creating the wealth you desire.

I am occasionally derided as *just* having built a "lifestyle business"—what I would call an enough-is-enough business, and not having gone further, to make it bigger, more independent of me, more valuable if sold. The most recent person voicing this critique is, I happen to know, deeply in debt with big mortgages on two homes as well as business debt, has a staff of more than 30 people—all useful but also all needy—and is under incessant pressure to hit high revenue goals every week. I have no debt, employ only one person, use a handful of outsourced support people, and am under zero pressure to produce thanks to accumulated wealth. I also happen to know that this critic's net income last year was about the same as mine. I have all the respect in the world for what I call empire builders. Our nation needs them and their boundless ambition and so does the world. They make great clients. But I want you to keep in mind that your time is your life, no one else's, and you should ignore criticism and needling, guilt mongering, emotional manipulation, or obligation about the conscious, thoughtful choices you make about what you do—and don't do—with it. My hope is this book makes a positive contribution to you getting what *you* want from your time.

To be always intending to make a new and better life but never to find time to set about it is as to put off eating and drinking and sleeping from one day to the next until you are dead.

—Og Mandino, author, *The Greatest Salesman in the World*
AND OTHER CLASSIC SUCCESS LITERATURE

CHAPTER 43

The Willy Loman Syndrome Moves to Management

Originally appearing as Chapter 4 from
No B.S. Ruthless Management of
People and Profits

illy Loman is the lead character in Arthur Miller's play *Death of a Salesman*. The death of a salesman is a desperate desire to be liked, above all else—including making sales. This is so common a disease among failing sales professionals it's called the Willy Loman Syndrome. However, it is contagious beyond salespeople. Managers get infected, too. A manager is severely handicapped, dangerously vulnerable, and certain to be ineffective if he is an approval seeker, a person who needs to be *liked* by his subordinates.

Why the word *ruthless* in this book's title? Isn't that a bit harsh? Most business owners are anything but. They give chance after chance after chance, tolerate incompetence and insubordination, twist themselves into a pretzel trying not to fire even the worst employee ever to walk the earth. Most business owners try too hard to be "a good boss," meaning a boss liked by the employees, rather than an effective boss, or one who sets and enforces standards and procedures in order to create maximum possible profits. I find even ex-Marine tough guys who are pretty ruthless in other aspects of their business soft as mashed potatoes when it comes to managing the people they pay. Many enunciate fear statements like "If I demand she does that, she'll quit" or wimp statements like "My people just won't do that." Even though in my consulting and coaching relationships I'm supposed to be dealing with marketing, I find myself fixing these travesties, helping business owners grow a pair. So I think *ruthless* is the direction most need to move in.

One of my favorite stories from the trenches involves the owner of a company with 22 offices scattered over three states, and a corporate office really running three businesses in one. After about three years of working with me, his longtime executive assistant came out and told him: "You were a much nicer guy before you started listening to that Kennedy guy," and "I don't like working here anymore." Notably, his company's profits had increased nearly 35% over those three years. He correctly suggested to her it would be most appropriate for her to find a different place of employment where she could be happier. As an accountant, he was able to grasp the fact that there's no bonus added by the bank to his deposits nor extra contribution made to his retirement fund because Bertha is *happy*. Of course I'm not advocating intentionally making everybody unhappy. But somehow, employees and opinion makers have gotten it into their heads that it's your job to make your employees happy. They forget you are paying them to work and generate profits. There are businesses that make people happy, ranging from Disneyland® to Nevada brothels. They all charge fees *for* doing so.

So, yes, I very deliberately used the word *ruthless* to grab attention. One person's *ruthless* is another person's *sane* approach to business. After you read this book, you can draw your own conclusions.

I expect some very harsh, critical reviews. I expect about 33% of the business owners to recoil from what I've put between these pages as they might if finding a bevy of large snakes busily consuming rats under the bed sheets. If that's you, I offer no apologies. Only sympathy. I will probably hear from some of you. It won't be fan mail. You might want to know before writing that I practice as policy "immunity to criticism."

I expect about 33% to rejoice that—*finally*—somebody is speaking the truth and providing both permission to behave in a sane manner as a business owner toward employees and honestly practical advice for doing so. I expect to hear from a lot of you. Of your relief. Of being emboldened. Of your success.

I expect the middle 33% to just be perplexed. But then, the middle 33% is pretty much perplexed 100% of the time about 100% of everything. You know who they are, in your company and out on the street. Easy to spot. They have that perplexed look on their faces.

If you're in the 33% who are rejoicing, congratulations and welcome.

What you need to know most is that Willy Loman would be even more of a failure as a manager than he was as a salesman. There is absolutely no evidence whatsoever that a manager liked by the employees creates more productivity or more profitability for the company. In fact, in sports it's rather common to see underperforming players rallying around the unsuccessful coach they like, trying to keep him from being fired. Not only is the boss who's liked by everybody not any more successful than the boss who's not liked at all, he may even be less successful. It's OK and probably advisable to take "being liked" off the table altogether. There are a number of other more important priorities.

The new-style "fun palace" workplaces can't go without comment. This is a popular fad, born of Google® and its workplace environment, and academic theorists' love for it, and media infatuation—including creation of a plethora of awards for "best place to work" in a given city or industry. There are even "most fun place to work" awards. So companies are busily putting in playrooms, nap rooms, having recess and nap times, and employees are zipping around on electric roller skates and *playing*. I am a founding stockholder in a fast-growth software company that has a "Cereal Bar" for its employees, with a range of flavors of cereal and milk, free, and this firm has won some "best place to work" awards. It makes me nervous over my investment. I actually cashed out a lot of my equity during a round of expansion financing with Goldman Sachs because of this.

I *guess* you can't argue with Google's success, but everywhere else I've seen the "care and feeding of" approach taken, it has ruined productivity and profits. As I was writing this, Facebook was publicly discussing plans to build its own town for its employees to live in, where they can be cared for 24/7, have their laundry done, their refrigerators stocked, and have little buses ferrying them to and from work. This is something of a throwback to the company towns of the early steel, coal, and other Industrial Revolution companies. It suggests these people dare not be left to care for themselves, and that the best productivity might be obtained by waking them up, getting them up, getting them dressed, feeding them, and bringing them to a job as if the mother who must get her small, utterly unreliable child to school. Amazon took and takes a very different approach.

The workplace as kindergarten and the coddling of employees as little children may be uniquely necessary with tech-tots in Silicon Valley. I suspect it also reflects some egotism of certain companies' founders and leaders, a new form of bragging right—look how progressive we are!

With 40-plus years' long backward view, I count it as just another management fad, in a long line of such fads, most that have come and gone. I am with Jeff Bezos. When you come to work, you should be in a workplace, and you should work hard, fast, and intensely. You should be laser-beam focused. You should be under pressure of urgency. In the book *The Everything Store: Jeff Bezos and the Age of Amazon*, its author, Brad Stone, who has reported on Amazon for 15 years, says that a great many past and present Amazon employees bemoan the fact that Bezos is *extremely* difficult to work for. Stone reports that despite Bezos' cheerful public persona, he is capable of the same kind of acerbic outbursts as Steve Jobs—who could terrify any employee who stepped into an elevator with him. Bezos is a micromanager who reacts harshly to efforts that don't meet his rigorous standards. About working for him, one former executive referred to the company motto, "Get Big Fast," and said, "There were deadlines and death marches." I can tell you that my most successful clients surround themselves with very self-reliant people, not babies who need to be brought their blankies and warm milk, cooed at, sung calming songs. I am also right there with Marissa Mayer who took the very unpopular position that Yahoo! employees should actually come to work at Yahoo! rather than at Starbucks, the park, or at home. Her move on this is somewhat akin to Bezos' unpopular banning of prepared PowerPoint presentations at all meetings, instead dictating that employees be able to enunciate and argue for their ideas, be interrupted and challenged, and think on their feet.

A big entity like Google, with extraordinary profit margins, with no manufactured goods costs, and unlimited access to other people's money, can conceal a lot of dysfunction. It can afford four people to do the work of one. Growth can mask a lot of sins. It's when growth levels off, and profitability becomes the governing mandate, that a lot of chicanery and foolishness gets exposed. This, a version of Buffett's line: You can't really tell who's naked until the tide goes *out*.

Your company is probably not anything like Google. It's unlikely that you have access to an unlimited ocean of investors' money. You probably have to make things, inventory things, deliver things. You probably don't have anything close to monopolistic power. You probably need to make real profits, consistently, day in and day out, and for you to wind up taking home enough to grow and stay rich—your reason for being in business—those profits need to be substantial. They must cover reinvestment needs and growth financing, a dizzying array of taxes, the occasional trauma or crisis. You probably do not have the luxury of throwing money about carelessly. Therefore, being "inspired" by Google or some similar "magic enterprise" in managing your work force, your workplace, or your money is a bad idea.

There will be a day, mark my words, when some turnaround guy with a steel spine and a bloody hatchet has to be brought into Google, as well as to companies copying its culture, to ruthlessly slash away at all the accumulated, out-of-control fat and waste and sloth. Harsh accountability for costs will occur. Demands will be made for proof that happy-making expenditures are producing profits.

So let's be clear. You can't have *as goals* being beloved by your troops, being the provider of the coolest place to work, being recognized as a cool place to work by media, or being envied by your peers for your progressiveness. The last item's even juvenile, like Chevy Chase's character trying to best his neighbor with the biggest and most elaborate Christmas light display. If these things occur naturally as byproducts of you creating and managing (and policing) the most productive workplace and the most profit-producing work force, fine, take the plaque and hang it proudly. But you can't afford to pursue that award plaque.

CHAPTER 44

The Two Most Crucial Management Decisions of All

Originally appearing as Chapter 10 from
*No B.S. Ruthless Management of
People and Profits*

A crucial management decision is: What kind of employee do you want? When I ask that question of individual clients or groups of people, I usually get a litany of vague and nice-sounding responses. *I want productive employees. Employees that care. Loyal. Ambitious. Intelligent. With good communication skills. With good attitudes.*

This is akin to, when asked to define goals, answering with "I want to be happy." Not a target. Just an idea.

The only rational answer to this critically important question is: "I want a PROFITABLE employee."

Contrary to a lot of silly ideas, the only sane reason to have an employee is profit. Somehow you get more profit by having the employee than by not having the employee. The only reason to have an employee is that you make a multiple of what he costs by having him. Unfortunately, a lot of people pile up employees around them for remarkably irrational reasons!

In addition to all the management stuff to be discussed in this book, this goal requires four other things: 1) buying into the premise; 2) calculating true and total cost; 3) creating a means of measurement for return on investment (ROI); and 4) vicious intolerance for unsatisfactory ROI.

The Premise

Liberals, most Democrats, some Republicans, and most employees think you, the business owner, exist to provide people with jobs. This is bullshit. If you can make more money by employing fewer people, that is exactly what you ought to do. In fact, it is your responsibility to do so because your first and foremost responsibility as CEO is to maximize company income and shareholder value. If you own the thing, then you are CEO *and* shareholder. You have a responsibility to yourself to maximize profit. Only you are invested, only you are at risk, only you truly care. If you go belly up, they'll go get jobs someplace else. It is not your responsibility to provide Mary with a job, nor your responsibility to pay her enough to support herself, her uneducated and refusing-to-get-educated husband, three kids, dog, two cars, five cell phones, and cable TV with premium channels. It is Mary's responsibility to make herself so valuable your business can't live without her. It is Mary's responsibility to continue making herself more and more valuable so you keep paying her more and more. If she doesn't, if she's an interchangeable commodity, so be it.

It's really important for you to get clear about who owns which responsibilities. Mary might never get clear about this. Mary's family may never get clear about this. Liberals and media pundits will never face this. But at least you can get clear about it. A lot of business owners get bullied into having and keeping unprofitable employees because those employees need their jobs. It seems incredible but it's true. This sense of obligation or this guilt over doing so well yourself must be resisted with all your might.

The *only* reason to have or keep Mary around is profit.

The Other Reasons to NOT Have Employees

Other unforgivable reasons business owners have employees, more employees than they need, and unprofitable employees are ego, poor self-esteem, and a need for reassurance, social activity, and friends. Some equate success with having a bigger staff than the next guy. When the brother-in-law who's the doctor visits, the business owner doesn't feel good about showing him a 600-square-foot hole in the wall with one employee at a desk counting money—no matter how much money he's counting. The business owner wants to show

More than half of McDonald's franchise owners and 40% of its corporate executives started out as crew in entry-level jobs, working in the restaurants. Chipotle, operator of 1,400 fast-food restaurants, has an aggressive promote-from-within program, allowing employees to rise to manager and qualify for educational assistance, paid vacations, stock options, even company cars. They have 300 managers who've risen from their ranks; their average salary is $90,000.00 a year. Do not let anybody convince you that people are imprisoned in entry-level, minimum-wage jobs or that we must make all such jobs pay a "living wage." Opportunity beckons!

SOURCE: WWW. *NATION'S RESTAURANT NEWS*/NRN.COM. 5-13

his brother-in-law, the doctor, a big beehive of activity with worker bees buzzing about, flying hither and thon. Other business owners lack confidence in their decision making and need a bunch of people around who are paid to agree with them. Other owners can't stand working alone and need to populate a place with people. Instead, I recommend getting a dog. The only reason to have or keep an employee is profit. (There are lots of good reasons to have a dog. If you are unfamiliar with them, read *Marley & Me*, quite possibly the best book ever written by anybody about anything, period.)

It is your role to keep wage costs to the lowest possible number. That said, I do believe in Chapter 27's title in *No B.S. Ruthless Management of People and Profits*, "Exceptions to All the Rules." I also believe in suppressing wages for ordinary people who deliver only ordinary performance or people in mundane jobs with inherently low value by any and all legal means necessary so that you, the owner, take home as much money as possible from your business. As I was writing this, by the way, much noise was being made about the U.S. wages for bottom-rung jobs in service sectors like hotels and restaurants actually declining in recent years. So there was a lot of noise about again raising the minimum wage. About it having to be a "living wage" that allows an employee to own a home, raise a family, and retire. This idea ignores two facts. First, getting certain jobs done is only worth a certain amount of money. Doesn't matter who does the job, how long he's been doing the job, or what his needs are. Getting those red things packed in that brown box is only worth $4.18, no more. Second, minimum wage jobs are not supposed to be *careers*. They should be called entry-level jobs or first-rung-on-the-ladder jobs. A place to start, not to stay. Many people do understand or learn that. To be very clear about where the responsibility for a good living wage lies, it is the responsibility of the person doing a job that pays an unsatisfactory wage to somehow move himself up the ladders of skill, value, and income. It is not the responsibility of any employer to pay more than a job is worth because of other people's needs.

When employers are forced to do so, they do other things instead. They automate. In *The Future of Employment: How Susceptible Are Jobs to Computerization?* Carl Frey and Michael Osborne of Oxford University forecast that 47% of all U.S. jobs are at risk of being automated. How fast probably depends on how much government, unions, and other sources raise the cost of labor. Amazon paid $750 million to buy a robotics company, making mobile robots to replace human workers in its warehouses. The fast-food industry is racing to replace counter clerks with self-order computer screens, just as supermarkets did and are doing with checkouts, airlines did and are doing with check-in, banks did and are doing with ATMs and online banking. Faced with Obamacare, countless companies, universities—even staunchly liberal ones, hospitals, and even unions began replacing full-time jobs with part-time jobs. The idea that employers/owners are just going to roll over, lie down, and have their profit structure forcibly changed without a reaction is ridiculous. The big companies can't and won't. They'll shutter their least profitable outlets, they'll

> Bad, bad, bad news for humans who need to work for food: A recent survey indicates that 61% of consumers would be willing to shop in a fully automated store absent any humans, and 42% claim they would prefer it. 58% of shoppers are happy to have stores or online retailers keep track of their purchase history (now advertised as a benefit in Lowe's TV spots), so that a machine can serve as their memory, tell them what they bought, and tell them what to buy.
>
> SOURCE: CISCO CUSTOMER EXPERIENCE RESEARCH/RETAIL SHOPPING RESULTS. WWW.CISCO.COM

shift investments overseas, they'll automate, they'll outsource, and they will even shrink in size if need be to protect net profits. After being held up by President Obama as a shining example of progressiveness in health care and used as the site for a speech and photo op, when actually faced with the costs, the Cleveland Clinic announced $300 million in budget cuts and erasure of as many as 9,000 jobs. Nobody can compel business to hire or to pay a set wage above value of job or to absorb newly invented costs. Business reacts, by raising prices, eliminating jobs, freezing pay, and reducing employee benefits.

You must react in a similar way. You can't be bullied. The last person at your place to ever take a pay cut has to be you. Make that your number-one policy. Don't let yourself be made to feel guilty either. Each individual chooses his income by his behavior.

No B.S. Ruthless Management Truth #2

Take home as much money as you can from *your* business. No nickel left behind.

There's a ton of B.S. spread around about money, including the idea that rich business owners are NOT working people. A few facts. The number of U.S. penta-millionaires (worth upward from $5 million) has more than quadrupled in the past ten years, to more than 930,000. The people in that group are mostly entrepreneurs. None got there by working in secure jobs at the post office, the department of motor vehicles, or some big corporation. Only 10% of their wealth comes from inheritance, and only 10% from passive investments; 80% comes from *earned* income. Meaning, they worked for it. Quite patiently, too, as most made their fortune in a big lump, after many years of effort, sacrifice, and risk. Most employees work 40-hour weeks; most business owners work 60- to 70-hour weeks. Should *anybody* want much greater income and financial security, there is a known, clear, present, and rather formulaic path to getting it.

Little truth is plainly and publicly spoken about this. Politicians demagogue it. I'll reach back to the magnificently coiffed, JFK wannabe, brief darling of the Left, super-rich trial lawyer John Edwards. In a speech in Cleveland on July 4, 2007, the Presidential candidate Edwards flatly stated: "No one in America should work at a full-time job and still be in poverty." This is bullshit piled high and stinking strong. It ignores the fact that lots of folks put themselves in poverty and keep themselves in poverty by birthing multiple children they can't afford to care for; by engaging in money-wasting habits they can't afford, including smoking, drinking, and gambling; and most of all by refusing to move themselves up from a lowest-paying job to a better job and again to a better job. It focuses only on societal, government, and marketplace responsibility but not at all on personal responsibility. It ignores the fact that merely raising wages is inflationary and encourages downsizing, job exporting, and automation, thereby making things worse, not better, for the lowest-skilled workers earning the lowest wages. It is shamefully disingenuous or horribly ignorant or some of each. Having said that, I happen to agree that in a country as rich as ours is— especially rich in opportunity—it is a crying shame that anyone willing to work remains in poverty. But the answers will never be found in government forcibly raising wages. It's much more complex than that. And it has to start with truth telling in place of pandering. I believe I have a lot more honest compassion for the working poor than Edwards and his ilk, because I would tell them the truth instead of perpetually waving the utterly false hope in front of them that somebody else—Edwards, Obama, Hillary, government Robin Hood—is going to ride in on a white horse and lift them up out of poverty.

We desperately need to tell everybody the blunt truth about this. We need to say: You *shouldn't* make a good living wage to support your family cleaning the toilets and sweeping the floors at the local motel. That job was never designed or intended to be your career. You should use it only as a step to the next step to the next step. And you should step as fast as you can—like somebody stepping from stone to stone, crossing a swamp. You should haul ass over to the library at night or go on the internet or find a friend to advise you or save up money and take classes to acquire additional, more valuable skills. You should beg your employer for a chance to step up and use those better skills for better income or move on to a different employer who offers a better ladder of opportunity. Maybe you should start a part-time, homebased business on the side and work toward the day you can be in business for yourself. But you shouldn't stay put in a low-value, low-wage job and somehow expect employers or the government to make your wages increase again and again.

We need to educate people that getting a certain job done has only so much value and that value does not increase by the number of years a person does it or by the person's need for income. We need to admit that our safety nets are severely flawed and porous and aren't likely to improve much, so you don't want to be dependent on them . . . but that our country offers enormous, varied, accessible opportunities. So you'd better pick one and get in gear. We need to say this as a unified voice: parents, educators, employers, civic leaders, white and black and brown and purple leaders, and politicians.

Since that's not going to happen, *you* probably need to stop watching and listening to all the politicians' and mainstream media's bleating about this. You dare not let it weaken your resolve. You need to focus on the fact that the only reason to have an employee is profit and the only kind of employee to have is a profitable one. Further, you want to use the overwhelming majority of your money available for wages to attract exceptional talent for your most important jobs and to reward truly exceptional performance. To do that, you have to be a Scrooge about paying the people who do commoditized, mundane jobs and the people providing only ordinary, barely profitable performance. You have to pay as little as you legally and possibly can for the lowest-level work, in order to, by market comparisons, grossly overpay, overincentivize, and overreward the highly profitable employees doing highly profitable work.

We Can Get Even Clearer by Dehumanizing the Equations

Fundamentally, an employee is a rented asset. It has a monthly payment to be made on it. Just like a piece of equipment. So if you are renting a hay baling machine for $300.00 a month but it breaks down all the time, makes the bales the wrong sizes, is slow, and when it's all said and done only bales about $400.00 worth of hay, what should you do with it? Turn it back in. If it costs you $300.00, it better bale $3,000.00 worth of hay. Because we are in the hay-baling business for one reason and one reason only: to make as much money as possible. And you need to remember the hay business can be good some sunny years but bad some wet years or if there are too many sunny years, and it may even be ruined altogether before long if Al Gore's right about global warming. So in the good years you have to make enough profit for those years plus more, to cover the years you make poor profits or no profits or have to reach into your pockets and put money back into the business. Your hay baler better give you a big, big return on your investment in it. If it doesn't, you may need a different hay baler. Or you may need to get out of the hay-baling business altogether, turn back in all 100 of your hay balers, and find something entirely different to do. That's why it's good to only rent the hay balers, not buy them.

So every piece of equipment—that is, every employee—must pay off at a big multiple of his cost.

Which gets us to employees' cost. Few business owners properly calculate employee cost because they leave out several very important numbers. Every CPA, MBA, and others of their ilk I've ever seen gets this wrong. Every management book I've ever read gets it wrong.

Here's how they do it: wages + taxes + benefits + overhead. So, if an employee is paid, let's say, $12.00 an hour, taxes and Social Security and workers' comp and so on add, say, 30%, that puts us at $15.60 an hour. Then add the health-care plan, the 401(k) matching contributions, the Christmas bonus, etc.—let's say that calculates out to another $1.00 an hour. Then some neglect overhead, but it belongs in there. Employees use up soap, toilet paper, steal office supplies, require heat and air conditioning, and take up space. If it costs this hypothetical business owner $2,000.00 a month for his space, utilities, and supplies, and he has four employees, that's $500.00 each divided by 160 work hours, $3.12 an hour. Now we're up to $19.72 an hour. But we are just getting started.

The REAL Costs

The first big number omitted is the do-over number. The cost of mistakes. Consider the episodically, repeatedly endangered American automakers. The most recent taxpayer-funded rescues weren't the first, and they won't be the last. This time around GM was the prime disaster into which we had to pour money, and the touting of it as a success just because the government has gotten much of its money back is a big con job. It ignores the fact that settled bankruptcy law was circumvented by President Obama, GM bondholders and shareholders had their money stolen and their rights ignored, assets obligated to them cavalierly transferred to a newly created entity in which new stock was gifted to the unions, numerous profitable dealerships summarily closed and their owners' rights ignored, and none of the core flaws in the business cured.

Among the ongoing problems guaranteeing future crises in this industry is a unionized, highly paid, grossly overpaid work force incapable of or unwilling to actually do their jobs right. Consequently these companies are awash in recalls. Hundreds of thousands of cars have to be done over. None of that cost gets taken back out of the incompetent employees' paychecks. The company just eats it. Translation: Your employees make mistakes with zero consequences or cost; you bear 100% of the burden for their screwups. And screw up they will. When I took over a terribly troubled manufacturing company, that assembly line mimicked God's for snowflakes: Every item coming off it was different. Employees can, obviously, make and ship defective goods, ship goods to the wrong place, pack goods poorly so they break, damage raw materials, waste materials, annoy and drive away customers, not answer the phone until the eighth ring instead of the third as instructed thus letting prospects you paid money for give up and hang up, and on and on and on ad infinitum. More importantly, employees not only can but *will* do these things. There is a hard cost in all this that must be factored into the employee cost in advance, because you can't go charge them for their mistakes as they happen.

Obviously, this cost varies by business, by employee, and by employer. No formula for calculating it exists that I know of. But for the sake of this hypothetical example, let's conservatively say that our pretty good hypothetical employee costs us about

$400.00 a week from waste, mistakes, and outright theft. Divide by 40 hours; add $10.00 an hour to the employee's cost. Now we're up to $29.72 an hour.

Next big number all the bean counters ignore and are ignorant of: the cost of YOUR time. With employees comes time *consumption*. In big companies, much of this is easy to see and can be cost controlled, because they employ professional baby-sitters at modest wages (called Human Resources or HRD professionals) and have layers of middle management baby-sitting each other. In a small business, however, the layers are compressed or not there at all, and you are definitely not going to pay $50,000.00 a year or so to an HRD person. So your employees are going to consume your time. They require you to take on three jobs: Leadership, Management, and Supervision. You have to hire, fire, train, coach, police. Break up knife fights (I did that with two computer programmers), listen to marital breakup stories, and this list is long. Again I know of no formula. But let's just say it's an average of two hours a week per employee.

Now, what's your time worth doing the highest-value things you do? Mine is currently worth $1,600.00 an hour and up. So if an employee sucks up two hours of my time, that's $3,200.00 divided into her 40 hours, which adds $80.00 an hour to the cost of having her. Your time is, frankly, probably less valuable than mine. To be simplistic, let's assume you're happy making $100,000.00 a year divided by roughly 2,000 work hours, which makes your time worth $50.00 an hour. If she sucks up two hours of your time this week, that's $100.00 divided into her 40 hours, adding $2.50, which brings her total cost to $32.22 an hour. If, however, you want to make $1,000,000.00 a year . . .

The final big number is the cost of her absence and replacement. I'm always amused when I'm in Washington, DC, in winter, when they announce that only the *essential* employees should brave the roads and report to work. Shouldn't only essential employees be coming in *every* day? Why is anybody employing a nonessential employee? This tells you a lot about the stupidity that blankets Washington, DC, but it's also telling about the reality of business. Any small-business owner can tell you, if the business can operate for three weeks while Mary or Billy Bob take family leave days, they aren't needed at all. But if they are needed, you have to replace them when they are absent. You do this by having other employees short and cheat their responsibilities to cover or taking your higher value time to cover or bringing in temps that cost double or triple Mary's wages. Will she be absent this year? Of course, at least 20 days, combining vacation, personal, and sick time. Then every few years, she'll quit or be fired, and you'll incur advertising, hiring, and training costs to replace her. Factor all that in. Let's guess: 20 days of your time used times your $50.00-an-hour value; $400.00 a day; $8,000.00 a year. Working backward, that comes to approximately $4.00 an hour added to her $32.22, bringing her cost to $36.22.

Well, you had no idea you were actually paying Mary $36.22 an hour, did you?

And that's my point.

I'll bet you'd require more of Mary and manage Mary differently if you did know. Now you do.

ROI

Now to ROI, return on investment. At $36.22 an hour, Mary costs you about $5,795.00 a month or $69,000.00 a year. What sort of return on that investment will be satisfactory to you? If you compare it to bank interest on CDs, then the hurdle is low. Mary need only cover her cost plus a measly $2,700.00 of profit. Of course, if you sold the business and put all the money in bank CDs, you'd never have to even see Mary or any of your other employees again. Chances are you would like something superior to bank interest just for putting up with your people and occasionally stopping by your own office. But what ROI do you want? Two-to-one, three-to-one, four-to-one? At four-to-one, Mary has to produce $276,000.00 of profit. Is she?

This, finally, gets us to the second most critical managerial decision: How will you quantify and measure the profit produced by Mary? Most business owners will tell me they need Mary and are able to tell me what Mary does, but hardly any can ever tell me how much Mary makes for them.

CHAPTER 45

Hire Slow, Fire Fast

Originally appearing as Chapter 14 from
*No B.S. Ruthless Management of
People and Profits*

I first heard "Hire Slow, Fire Fast" from Chuck Sekeres, the founder of a very successful company, Physicians Weight Loss Centers. He was attending my seminar, but when it came out of his mouth, I scribbled it down. It's at least as profound as anything Aristotle ever said. Its genius and its truth is in its being the polar opposite to what 99% of us do. (Oh, yeah, I've been guilty of this one a few times myself. And it cost me dearly.)

So, as an aside, here's the single most useful and empowering piece of success advice I have ever heard in my entire life. I've based most of what I've done in my own business life and in developing strategies for my clients on this single piece of advice. I heard this one while still a teenager, listening to a cassette tape by Earl Nightingale. Earl said that if you wanted to do something—anything—successfully and you had no instructions, no role model, no road map, no mentors, all you needed to do was look around at how the majority was doing that thing, then do the opposite—because the majority is always wrong. Whenever I teach this, there's always one twit who challenges me with our own great American democracy as his sword. After all, he'll say, our system of government is based on majority rule. Well, no, it's not. First of all, the founding fathers originally had only people paying taxes—at the time, landowners—voting, as it should be today. Second, the electoral college got stuck in to provide a last line of defense against public stupidity—in case you didn't know it, the electors aren't legally bound to vote as their state's majority has. Third, fortunately, the majority does not vote. If the majority actually, directly elected people, Kim Kardashian would be President and the guy from Duck Dynasty would be Vice President. So, no, thank our stars, our government is not majority rule. And the principle stands that the majority is always wrong, and you gain most by conforming to the majority as little as possible. (For more from me on this, visit https://MagneticMarketing.com and check out the Renegade Millionaire resources.)

Now back to this hiring and firing thing.

Most business owners fire slow. They manage like they go to the movies. Sitting through a three-hour-long movie that is rancid from 1st to 180th minute. Why? They think it has to get better. They keep hoping it will get better. Because I'm a Burt Reynolds fan, I once did this with the single worst movie ever made, *At Long Last Love* or something like that, in which Burt and Cybill Shepherd sing and dance. Bad employees do not cure themselves like ham hung in a barn. Hope isn't a sound business strategy. But that's what too many managers do. Wait and hope for a miraculous, spontaneous cure. Consequently, according to my admittedly unscientific survey of about a hundred of my clients, the average firing occurs somewhere between 6 and 18 months *after* the business owner *knew* the employee was consistently performing poorly, consistently noncompliant, poisoning the workplace, and negatively affecting others in it, or otherwise stinking up the joint. Ironically, most employees who finally get fired are mystified the axe didn't fall sooner. One told a friend of mine, "When you didn't fire me five months ago when you should have, I figured I could get away with just about anything." Some fired employees are even relieved and glad it's over; they've been visualizing the sword of Damocles overhead for months.

Being 6 to 18 months late doing anything in business is a very bad idea.

There is, sadly, one other reason the necessary firings occur so late. Sure, we're waiting and hoping for the bad movie to get good, against our best instincts and all our previous experience. But beyond that, a lot of owners delay firing people who desperately need firing because the business owner is lazy. He has permitted the bad employee to amass and control information only he knows, carried in his head or filed with his own unique code. One lawyer told me, "She's my worst employee, but I rely on her every time I go to court." Huh? And the business owner dreads the difficulty of finding and training a replacement. In this, he's like the single guy at home alone on an autumn Sunday afternoon in dirty underwear, watching football, who discovers he has no cash and his refrigerator has only a beer, a two-day-old half of a pizza, and some bologna going green around the edges. After weighing the options, he'd rather trim the green and eat the bologna and old pizza for dinner than find clothes, get dressed, go to the ATM, then go to the grocery store. Hard to have any sympathy for him when he's up half the night at the vomitorium.

Being 6 to 18 months late is inexcusable.

Next mistake: hiring fast. This is closely linked to the first mistake more often than not. Finally firing the toxic employee, you create a vacancy. It needs to be filled. You've done nothing proactive to be able to fill it until your urgent and desperate need has arisen. Thus the fact that your "best" applicant attracted from your first help-wanted posting at Monster.com has two nose rings, sports a tattoo that says "Kill the Boss," has no references, and occasionally interrupts her sentences by snarling like a dog. Hey, those phones need answering *today*.

This is the way almost everybody operates. Do the opposite.

CHAPTER 46

How to Make Every Employee's Job a Profit Center

Originally appearing as Chapter 25 from
*No B.S. Ruthless Management of
People and Profits*

S usan has to answer the phone. You have to have your phone answered. But what can Susan do while answering the phone to convert that required cost of doing business to a profitable opportunity?

She could ask a few survey questions to collect information permitting better segmentation of your list. She could tell everybody about your special of the month or direct them to your website for the article of the week. If taking orders, she can upsell and cross-sell. If taking calls from prospects, she can capture full and complete contact information for follow-up and to build your mailing list. She can do more than answer the phone.

In your hotel, the maids have to clean the rooms. But they can also place your product catalog in a very visible place (as is done in Westin® properties). She can have a scripted conversation with any guests she encounters in person, inviting them to the hotel's sports bar that night for the big game and free appetizers.

At your restaurant, the waitstaff sell food and beverages, take orders, deliver meals. But they can conversationally urge customers to join the birthday club or VIP club, get those cards filled out. (There is no more valuable asset a restaurant can own than a customer list with birthdays.)

In a dental office, dental hygienists can deliver hygiene. Or they can be taught, coached, and supervised to sell dentistry while delivering hygiene. The difference to a dental practice can be a cost of about $40,000.00 a year to a terrific profit center worth over $100,000.00 a year.

Everything I've named so far can be quantified, measured, and, if you choose, incentivized and rewarded. Which I encourage. I like to see every employee have some opportunity to earn bonus money above base pay, at least based on behavior, but at best connected to their direct contribution to profits.

One of the greatest breakthroughs that can ever occur in a business is the realization by everyone involved that everything is marketing, and that everyone ought to be involved in marketing. There's a natural inclination to separate "marketing" from "operations," which leads inevitably to viewing some jobs and the employees who perform them as costs, and as necessary evils, rather than profit centers and opportunities.

CHAPTER 47

Managing the Sales Process

Originally appearing as Chapter 33 from
*No B.S. Ruthless Management of
People and Profits*

I n most businesses, sadly, selling is an act, not a process. The mistakes made here are many. Everything is separated and isolated. Advertising. Marketing. They deliver a prospect to Sales, where, typically, the entire outcome is placed in the hands of very fallible salespeople permitted to freelance at will, committing random acts of Selling. Afterward, the customer is dumped off to Operations, where the promises made may or may not be fulfilled.

Examine just about any business with more than one person doing the selling, and you'll find each salesperson doing things differently than the others. Over in accounting, everybody's using the very same bookkeeping ledgers and 2 + 2 = 4, period. But in sales, for some crazy rationale, everybody's allowed to "wing it." If you want maximum profits, you'll figure out what the best sales presentation is, and everybody will use it. You need a program for selling that all your salespeople comply with and use.

Wrapped around the human salespeople adhering to your program, you need a complete system for selling, for moving each prospect neatly along a path—or, as the marketing wiz behind BluBlocker® and author of a terrific sales and marketing book, *Triggers*, Joe Sugarman, calls it, a "greased chute"—that connects advertising to marketing to selling, that qualifies and prepares prospects to buy before they consume the time and talent of your salespeople, and that both supports and helps control the efforts of the salespeople. One of the best quotes about all this is from a highly respected sales trainer, David Sandler, founder of the Sandler Selling System®, now with trainers and offices nationwide. David said: "If you don't have a system for selling, you are at the mercy of the customer's system for buying." I would add: and for not buying.

Such a system has to be built at the macro and micro levels.

The macro parts link all your advertising, marketing, publicity, sales, and operations pieces together with common themes, a clearly understood covenant with customers, and, as I said, a process for moving the customer smoothly along the path, from first expression of interest to completed purchase. Think of this as an exercise in control over the prospect and the process. The micro parts have to do with all of the human interaction between the prospect and receptionists, clerks, and, most of all, salespeople. Think of it as an exercise in control over the actual selling and the people doing the selling.

There's a lot of nonsense spewed about leaving salespeople to their own devices to preserve spontaneity, encourage creativity, and so on. It's all B.S. Selling is a scientific and mechanical process, not something you should make up as you go along. The person widely judged as America's number-one sales trainer, Tom

Hopkins, and I are both strong advocates of scripts. As a direct-response copywriter paid upward of $50,000.00 plus royalties to write advertisements, sales letters, and websites, I can assure you that choice of words, that is, language, matters. What I do in writing is "salesmanship in print." If it matters there, it matters in "salesmanship live," too. But "live," not only do words chosen, scripted, and used matter, so also does appearance, dress, physical movement and body language, the selling environment, the actual movement of the prospect from place to place, seating choices, props used, and much more. My colleague Sydney Biddle Barrows and I call this Sales Choreography®. We believe that everything should be choreographed, from the first step the prospect takes into the selling environment, moment by moment, movement by movement, sentence by sentence. There's quite a bit of resistance to this idea, of course, because it requires a lot of thought, discipline, and practice by the salespeople and other staff members and a lot of supervisory enforcement by management. I can assure you that, for the few who embrace it, the payoff is enormous.

Incidentally, I push my readers, newsletter subscribers, coaching members, and clients toward a "whole approach." Most of my work has to do with everything leading up to the sale. I devise the systems as well as write the copy that gets ideal prospects to raise their hands, step forward, and step onto the path constructed to then move them through qualifying and preparation, so by the time they face a salesperson or a buying decision, they view the salesperson as an expert and trusted advisor, see the company as unique, and are predisposed to do business with them. And I teach business owners how to do this for themselves. I have consultants and service providers I recommend if intense work on driving traffic online to websites or renting mailing lists or the handling of inbound calls or software systems to manage lead flow are needed. At the point that the prospect begins engaging humans and will be face-to-face with staff and salespeople, there are resources and a telecoaching program on Sales Design® that I've developed with Sydney Biddle Barrows, and Sydney does go on-site as well. Sales Design® is about mapping out step-by-step-by-step everything that is to occur with and be said to the prospect, every if-he-says-this, you-say-that movement forward toward purchase.

The Biggest Improvement You Can Make as Manager and as Sales Manager: Stop Accepting Less Than You Should Get

If you get nothing else from this book, do nothing else as a result of this book, you ought to at least take a fresh, analytical, tough-minded look at what you are getting from your people as a whole and individually for the money you are spending.

Most business owners accept shockingly poor sales results as if they make sense. In the hearing aid industry, the "close rate"—people who come to the store, get a hearing test, and get a full sales presentation—ranges from as poor as 25% to as good as 40%. Out of every 100 people, 60 to 75 who come in suffering from hearing difficulties and in need of a hearing aid do NOT buy! How can anyone managing this business accept such a thing? In the automobile business, roughly 20% of the people who come into a showroom buy a car there. That means 80 of the 100 left their homes, got in their cars, drove across town to the car dealership, braved the selling environment, looked at, asked questions about, even test-drove cars that interested them, but then were not sold a car. To me, incredible. Awful. Embarrassing. Yet car sales managers confronted about this shrug and tell me, "That's about right." No. It isn't. In a dental practice, chiropractic practice, or the like, patients coming in for consultation and exam are subsequently given a sales presentation. Here I see wildly differing results. One doctor will close 70%, another a pathetic 30%. Why the difference?

In the last comparable, completely controlled selling environment I managed myself, we brought doctors into a small meeting of several hours to group sell a product. We had one employee doing these meetings in about 25 cities a month and I did them in five a month. In three years, his close rate was never—never—below 85%. Mine hovered at 80%. Most of the time, he closed all but one person, called him the next day and closed him after the fact. I have been told by many others trying to replicate this model or with experience in this type of selling that such numbers are "impossible" and that he and I must be "freaks of nature." They're wrong. Not only are such results possible, but they should be expected, normal, and customary. We achieved them for reasons anyone *can* replicate in *any* business: at the macro level, we had a system delivering interested, qualified, prepared prospects to our selling environment; at the micro level, we had a precisely crafted presentation delivered perfectly.

If people come to buy, they ALL should buy. If that's not happening, you should be racking your brain to figure out what you are doing wrong.

The Human Factor: If You Are Going to Have Salespeople in Your Employ, Pick Carefully and Manage Tough

It's not just "Can they sell?" It's "Will they sell?" and "Will they sell here?" I learned this from a top sales management consultant, Bill Brooks, and it is profound. It's not just limited to salespeople either; it really applies to every type of employee in every type of job. Reality is, somebody who might be a good employee at Company A may be a lousy employee in the same job at Company B.

This is what makes hiring by resume so flawed.

But how can this be? After all, auto sales is auto sales, so a guy who was successful at the Cadillac dealer in Chicago ought to succeed at the Cadillac dealership in Cleveland, or the guy who was successful at the Cadillac dealership in Chicago should thrive at the Lexus dealership in Chicago. And the person who was a super receptionist at one financial planner's office will surely be just as super at another financial planner's office, right? Wrong.

Different people flourish or flunk in different environments.

Let's start back at the first question: Can he sell? If you are hiring experienced salespeople, then you can answer this question by looking at their experience to date, checking their references, seeing proof of their commissions earned. If you are hiring inexperienced people and making them into salespeople, then you might rely on much more in-depth interviews including discussing what they think is the right thing to do in different selling situations. You might utilize an aptitude test purchased from one of the many companies that provide assessment tests. And you'll be looking for nonsales experience that evidences the attitudes necessary for success in selling. For example, one client of mine with a very successful sales organization, who hires only people with no prior selling experience, asks, "Have you been successful in anything?" and "Have you struggled and found something so difficult you almost quit but then stuck with it and succeeded?"

The second question: Will he sell? Again, if recruiting experienced salespeople, you can look into their historical track record. If they had peaks and slumps and inconsistent results where they were, you'd need a good reason to believe they aren't going to import their inconsistency into your business. If they increased their sales and earnings year to year, you could hope for that same pattern in your employ. If they stagnated, you'd need good reason to expect otherwise. Sometimes just the change of scenery will revitalize a bored or complacent experienced pro, but that will usually be brief. If he got complacent there, he'll get complacent here. When considering "Will he sell?" you're trying to solve the mystery of motivation, and that's not easy. But self-motivation leaves clues. The most recent sales book he's read, most recent sales seminar he's been to, most interesting technique he's introduced to his repertoire in the past year. What he can tell you about his goals. If hiring inexperienced people for sales, again, you have no specific history to consider, but you do have nonspecific history, basically the person's whole story. Did he work two jobs to get through school or did mommy pay his way? Has he worked in any job dealing with the public, like waiting tables? Is he really interested in a sales career or settling for it because he can't find what he wants? If he's interested, he'll already be reading books, listening to CDs, and educating and preparing himself.

The third question is the trickiest. Just because he can and will sell does not mean he'll excel at selling in your employ. Your company culture may be very different than ones he's previously experienced. You may require him to present things in a way he feels is deceptive, dishonest, or unethical, or he may feel hamstrung and neutered by the ethical restraints you impose on the way he presents things. You may have a better-defined program you insist be complied with than his prior employers. He may welcome the organization and discipline, or he may chafe at it. These matters need to be explored in lengthy, frank, and detailed discussions once you get serious about a candidate. There is no point in hiring a sales professional without full disclosure of your program and how tough you are about compliance with it.

Right Sales System + Right Salespeople = Outstanding Success

Almost. The other missing link has to do with lost but viable prospects. Most systems controlling everything leading up to the sale give up on prospects too soon and too easily, or leave ongoing follow-up to the human salespeople. Doing that can be a huge mistake. Salespeople really adept at selling are usually incredibly inept and irresponsible at follow-up. They are called "salespeople," not follow-up people. Chapter 34 of *No B.S. Ruthless Management of People and Profits* talks quite a bit about plugging the leaky holes of poor follow-up. Its author is a client of mine, and I also endorse his company's unique software system. It's the one we use at GKIC™, and most of my clients use it as well. In interest of full disclosure, I am a stockholder in this company as well.

However you accomplish it, here's what's important: Once someone has raised their hand and expressed interest in your products, services, solution, or information and you put them on your path, they should be moved forward toward the sale at a prescribed yet flexible pace, with a lot of nudges by mail, email, fax, drives to different websites, teleseminars, webinars—a primary sequence but for those who fail to move at its pace, a continuing, patient sequence. Most businesses waste the lion's share of all the money spent on advertising by, first, not using it to create and capture interested prospects and then by poor or insufficient follow-up.

Beyond that, follow-up after the sale shouldn't be left in the hands of salespeople either. They will instinctively focus on their next hunt and kill, the next prospect, the next sale. But, hopefully, you are interested in creating, measuring, and maximizing long-term customer value. To do that, you have to wow 'em after the sale and continually, frequently "arrive" to keep the relationship alive.

So, finally, you have to *manage the relationships* with your prospects and your customers.

CHAPTER 48

Three Strategies for Managing Salespeople
for Maximum Results

Originally appearing as Chapter 35 from
*No B.S. Ruthless Management of
People and Profits*

T his is not an exhaustive explanation of managing salespeople. For one thing, there are many different kinds of salespeople in many different selling environments. It warrants its own book. But there are three strategies that I have used and bring into clients' companies that never fail to boost results.

Strategy #1: Proper Investment

In most businesses, the investment in salespeople is either democratized, i.e., the same for all, or weighted in an entirely unproductive way.

I have a very crude story to tell, that until now I've only told behind closed doors, most selectively. It includes a memorable image. A very successful, very rich owner of a sales organization said he had gathered his team of sales managers together for what they believed would be a daylong meeting to discuss the sagging sales in a number of areas. They were expecting a sales management master class from their fearless leader, who had once been where they were, and who had built a $50 million business from the ground up, by recruiting and managing independent salespeople. At the time, he was the youngest to achieve his status and income level, in a global organization of more than 10,000 dealers. He invited me along to watch him deliver what he called his Two-Step Sales Management Seminar. He said we'd be in and out in 20 minutes and could go somewhere and have a good breakfast.

In the room, about 15, maybe 16 anxious men were seated boardroom style around a big conference table. Most had flown in from various cities. He walked in, climbed up onto the table, and said, as best I can remember, "There are two steps to successful sales management. You are not adhering to them. I never want you to forget them." From his pocket, he took a book of matches, handed it to one of the guys, and told him to hold it back away from the table. Then he unzipped his fly, took out his penis, and urinated all over the table. Then he said: "Step 1: If and when someone shows a flicker of initiative and capability, get matches and gasoline, and invest yourself in fanning his fire. Step 2: Piss on everybody else. Most sales managers do the opposite."

He zipped up, climbed down, wiped his feet on the carpet, gestured at me to leave with him, and we went to breakfast.

Many of you won't like this story, but you probably won't forget it for a while. And you shouldn't. Most business owners and sales managers invest entirely too much time and money into trying to lift the performance of losers while leaving their winners entirely to their own devices. You will profit to a far, far greater extent by doing exactly the opposite. By supporting, working closely with, and giving more resources and opportunities to champion performers, you will get a lot more sales. If you give that same support, attention, and resources to your poor performers, you may get a little more sales. Do you want a lot or a little?

It begs the question—can you turn a poor performer into a top performer? Yes. That is what sales legend stories are made of. But it is difficult, painful, time-consuming, costly work with low odds of success. It is social work you will more likely be rewarded for in the afterlife than in this quarter's revenue. It is more certainly profitable to ruthlessly discard the weak and recruit and then facilitate the success of the strong. If you now have a sales team, you should carefully analyze who is in the top one-third of its pyramid and who is in the bottom two-thirds, fire at least half those at the bottom, and sit down with those at the top to explore and discuss what you and the company might do to aid them in being even more successful.

Strategy #2: Proper Use

Highly skilled, successful sales pros should be spending as much of their work hours as you can engineer for them—selling. Not cold prospecting, not otherwise prospecting, not stuffing envelopes, not filling out forms. *Selling.*

That means relieving them of as much of everything else as you can.

Prospecting, for example, should be replaced with marketing, and the manual labor of prospecting replaced with media. If you have a sales professional making a cold call to try and create interest from scratch, in this day and age, you are a fool. I also tell salespeople if they work for such a fool, quit and go elsewhere. Prospects can be found or created, brought forward, made to ask for information, and then to ask for a conversation or meeting with a sales pro by any number of means cheaper in net terms than hours of a sales professional's time. My book *No B.S. Direct Marketing for NON-Direct Marketing Businesses, 2nd Edition* is the primer on this. Behind it, read *No B.S. Trust-Based Marketing*. I have routinely cut the number of salespeople at a business while increasing the productivity and personal incomes of the retained ones, simultaneously increasing the business's revenue, with the methods laid out in these books.

You also want your salespeople selling to the best and highest value, highest probability prospects—not just anyone. Putting good salespeople in front of poor prospects is pretty dumb, but that's what happens when they are left on their own to prospect or when there is no management and qualifying of leads. Consider this example: A financial services firm had three representatives, each producing about $20,000.00 a month in net revenue for the firm, at little expense to the firm but commissions, for they were charged with creating their own leads and getting their own sales appointments. In my work with the firm over six months, the least effective of the three representatives was eliminated, and a new direct-marketing system costing the company about $25,000.00 a month to fund and operate was put in place; it generated 80% of the leads needed to keep the two reps fully booked with meetings and—most importantly—it put them in front of prospective clients with nearly twice the investable assets of the prospects previously dug up by the reps, and it put them in front of prospects predisposed to accept the reps as expert and trustworthy advisors. The result: each rep generated more than $60,000.00 a month in net revenue—thus the firm's number went from $60,000.00 to $120,000.00. Simplistically, if you deduct the $25,000.00 marketing cost, the firm's still ahead by $35,000.00 a month; $420,000.00 a year. There's more. By developing this kind of marketing system, a second office, it with two representatives, was possible. Better reps could be recruited and retained, because they were relieved of prospecting, could use their highest and best skill more of the time, and make more money for themselves.

Strategy #3: Proper Accountability

"If the guy meets quota and produces enough revenue, I don't care what he's doing or how he's doing it." I've heard that from business owners and sales managers a lot. Incredibly, I heard Steve Forbes utter it—on TV—about the ad reps working for *Forbes*. I respect Steve Forbes. He's smart about money. But he's dumb as a rock about this.

This is why 90% of prospects actually requesting follow-up at trade show booths never get it. This is how lead flow gets "creamed," and if the rep makes enough money to be happy by the third week of the month, he plays golf and lets unconverted leads and prospects who failed to buy at first opportunity die. You just cannot leave salespeople on their own to decide how they'll use or waste your resources and opportunities. I was largely left on my own in my first sales job, as a territory rep assigned five Midwest states, for a California-based book publisher. I excelled. I outsold all the other reps. I opened more new accounts. But I also, in a year, never went to two of those states! My success masked, and sloppy management missed noticing, that I didn't open a single account in two of my five states, and that the reorder activity in those states all came through mailed or faxed-in orders. In truth, six months in or sooner, my territory should have been cut into two, and a second sales rep assigned to half of it. Since the company advertised nationally, exhibited at national shows, and otherwise reached out to the industry on a nationwide basis, those two neglected states had a cost attached to them but nothing being done to get return on that investment. That's my answer to leaving the rep alone, with *what* he's doing.

You can't leave him alone with *how* he's doing it either. Your business's reputation and long-term sustainability and equity are all put at risk by every spoken or written or emailed or tweeted word and by every action of your representatives. Salespeople need a lot of oversight.

I work with companies that have sales speakers out on the road, delivering two- to three-hour introductory seminars in different cities, days and evenings. These speakers must record every one and send that recording in with the orders and paperwork. Obviously, every recording isn't checked. But enough are, at random, to strongly encourage every speaker stays on script. Deviations can 1) violate laws and put the company in serious trouble, 2) overpromise, setting up under-delivery, customer dissatisfaction, refunds, and online smearing, or 3) sabotage sales. The best and most profitable client I've ever had with sales reps making one-to-one, in-person presentations had a quality-control monitor who called and talked with at least one out of every eight nonbuyers, giving them a gift card for their time, to question them about what they had and hadn't been told, what they liked and didn't like about the presentation and the salesperson, and why they didn't purchase. His salary was easily covered by rescued sales, but he was worth a lot more because the salespeople knew of his meddling and knew they'd be called on anything out of order. This company's nationwide average conversion rate was double that of their industry's.

People who are given a good opportunity, who want to excel, respond reasonably well to accountability that aids them in staying on track and improving. People who resist and resent this kind of accountability are best sent packing.

PART VI

PRICING

with selections from

No B.S. Price Strategy

PRICING

In 40+ years of applying every known "plus-ing" strategy to businesses of varying types and sizes, I have found no surer or faster way to improve the owner's income than focusing on his pricing strategies. *No other.*

One reason this is so is because of "price cowardice." There is almost always more price elasticity in a business than its owner can imagine (without help) or is fully utilizing. This elasticity can be found in what is being packaged together and sold, how it is presented, the clientele targeted for it, the actual pricing, the presentation of price, and more. A lot of pricing is done as a last thought, often based on observing competitors or by "standard" industry formulas. It deserves much more thought than this, much more creativity than this.

Going on a deep exploration of price strategy possibilities and identifying applicable price elasticity opportunities for your business has never been more important than it is now. As I am writing this, in most businesses, labor costs, raw material costs, and fulfillment costs are all rising. Competition is often failing to respond sensibly—instead, watching profit margins erode and even disappear as if helpless spectators, and their fears, fragility, and fecklessness is being allowed to influence YOUR price decisions. A danger is a race to the bottom, a race where everybody is a loser. This is NOT necessary.

Rethinking Price Is Usually Overdue

I recently consulted with an owner of five offices in a health-related business, in a fiercely competitive industry, being Amazon-ed at the lowest, widest part of its price pyramid. He confessed that he along with most of his peer competitors were selling at the same prices as they were five years ago, yet all costs had risen, so they needed twice as many units of sale to produce the same net income. I said: Stop the insanity! It turned out he had *not* updated his Unique Value Proposition or modified the aim of his marketing or his presentation of price options in five years either. By doing all three, we quickly restored his net profitability. This is the nature of the information you'll find here, in these excerpts from the *No B.S. Price Strategy* book.

If you embrace all the marketing strategies shared in this "Best of" book, you will be able to sell in a competitive vacuum, where increasing and protecting your profit per unit of sale is most achievable.

To be clear, you determine your income in large part by the prices and price strategies you decide on. You write your own paycheck. If you think you are being underpaid, it is up to you to give yourself a raise!

CHAPTER 49

If and When You Discount, Get Quid Pro Quo

Originally appearing as Chapter 2 from
No B.S. Price Strategy

I am in general agreement with my co-author Jason Marrs about all the **evils of discounting**. This does not necessarily preclude my use of discounting, for my own businesses or for clients, but it makes me wary and reluctant, and motivates me to try and get something in exchange.

A simple exchange of value might be immediate response. In marketing seminars, for example, there is often an early registration discount tied to a set deadline. I will come right out and say: "If we have to keep chasing you and sending you mailing after mailing after mailing, we'll eventually get you (you know you want and need to come), but we will have spent a lot of time and money. Better to give that to you as savings in exchange for your earliest registration." This has two virtues. One, it provides a reason for the offered discount, which is some buffer against cheapening of the product or the thought that the retail price is simple fiction. Two, it has a ring of truth, because, in this case, there *is* real truth in the justification of the discount.

Years ago, when I was engaged in person-to-person, face-to-face selling of a particular product, I found myself running up against last minute price resistance. I succeeded with the strategy of "pulling the discount rabbit out of my hat"—conditional on the buyer assisting me with referrals to secure appointments with at least two friends, neighbors, or colleagues. That dates back to the 1970s, and I first learned it from Howard Bonnell, then a sales management executive with the World Book Encyclopedia Company, and from Paul J. Meyer, the founder of Success Motivation Institute, who gave a talk about perpetuating an "endless chain of referrals." Very recently, I spotted an item in *Entrepreneur* magazine about a similar strategy, referring to an electrical contractor who, after closing the sale, reveals a lower available price, if the customer will fill out referral postcards to be sent to the neighbors, right then and there.

In my consulting/copywriting practice, as of this writing, my base daily fee is $18,800.00, and copywriting project fees are calculated by multiplying that times the number of days I estimate will be required. Ten days = a fee of $188,000.00. I sometimes discount the daily consulting fee for a client booking consecutive days back to back or pre-booking multiple days spaced through the same calendar year, with reason given that I am getting value from that client in exchange for the discount; either time efficiency or the convenience of filling the calendar and not needing to worry about getting more clients. I sometimes discount the copywriting fee if I am getting several projects all related to the same product to do at the same time, with reason given: time efficiency—the same research supports all the projects, some of the copy written for one migrates to three. These are, in essence, quantity discounts, but with more elegant reason given. The one thing I never, never, never do is discount fees purely because of the client's desire to negotiate or some competitive pressure. Never, without good reason featuring some quid pro quo.

Money at a Discount

In the above example, the idea of a $188,000.00 fee for copywriting work might shock you. And if it were being paid by the client simply for a few days of copywriting work, i.e., for the time or the labor, it would be outrageous. He could hire his own copywriter as a full-time employee to be underfoot forty hours a week every week for a year for that sum. But for me, it's relatively routine because I'm not charging for time or labor; I'm charging to develop an asset the client will own, that will yield dividends over time far beyond the initial investment. For example, if, for that fee, he obtained an ad campaign driving prospects to a website where they read a sales letter and bought his products that he used for the next five years, that amortizes the fee to $37,600.00 a year. And if it sells $500,000.00 of goods each year, that's $2.5 million across its five-year life, a return on investment of almost 1,400%. Or: a discount of $2.3 million; the buying of money at a huge discount. This is what intelligent businesspeople try to accomplish anytime they pay for expertise; buy money at a good discount. And just how many times would *you* like to buy something for $188,000.00 that will yield $2.5 million over five years?

There are actually two price strategies in play in the above paragraph's explanation of my fees: first, apples to apples comparison (see the end of Chapter 52); second, selling money at a discount. The second can even lend itself to visual demonstration. For a speaker selling a moneymaking program to seminar audiences, I fashioned the exercise by calling for volunteers, picking three, bringing them up on stage, and having them bid to buy $100.00 bills—high bidder getting the $100.00 bill. Usually, some goof bid a dollar, another $20.00 or so, some wiz bid $99.00. He would give the high bidder the $100.00 bill, then pull out a giant roll of hundreds, say he would average the bids to, say, 50 and invite all who wanted in on the deal to "come on down!"—then quickly stop the madness, get everybody back in their seats, and explain that his proposition to own his system was even better, because they'd be turning a few hundred dollars into hundreds of thousands of dollars in just the next 12 months. Show of hands, how many would bid at least $1,000.00 on a briefcase containing one thousand of the $100 bills (photo shown on screen), thus paying only one dollar for each $100? **This took all the focus of the audience off his price and fixated it on the large gain to be had. The price was now *felt* as a huge discount rather than as a stiff price for the product**, which consisted of some audio CDs, manuals, and an online coaching program; the whole thing fit into a single three-ring notebook.

Back to the quid pro quo: to let somebody have a product like this, purported to be worth $100,000.00 this year and again next year and the year after that for the small price of just $1,000.00 makes no sense. Franchises sell for 50 times that much and then require even more investment, risk, and working 60 hours a week. This discount must be made rational. In this case, several reasons were given, the specifics of which are not important here, but the fact that they were given, vital.

The Something-In-Exchange Split-Test

In direct marketing, there is the all-important split-test, where just one variable is tested, "A" against "B." That might be price or the ad's headline or two different photos or any other element. Some years back, I had a regional chain of optical stores as a client.

We ran a "Sizzling Summer Sales Event," with customers getting a pair of prescription-lens sunglasses free when purchasing a regular pair of glasses, plus a family pass to a popular area water park as a free bonus. For its time, it was an extremely generous, enticing offer. I worried it might be too good to be trusted, absent some quid pro quo. So we tested one change in the advertising in one market vs. the same advertising in the other: in one, we added the requirement that the customer bring a donation of two canned food items or at least $10.00 cash for the local food banks; in the other, no such charity connection or requirement. The results were so much better with the charitable donation requirement that no argument was possible. It mattered.

As I was writing this, a popular, national menswear chain was advertising the rather preposterous offer of "buy one suit, get a second suit and a sports jacket free." I bet I could improve response by making those customers bring in a used article of clothing to donate to Goodwill. Doing so would do good, too, by the way. Why not help out a charity and let it boost your sales?

CHAPTER 50

The Nasty Cancer
of FREE

Originally appearing as Chapter 4 from
No B.S. Price Strategy

istorically, FREE has been one of the most powerful words in advertising. It still is, but it has also become the bane of existence to many of us, particularly those of us dealing in intellectual properties—like this book, home study courses and other education, or entertainment products like music, comedy, and movies. A destructive sense of entitlement in general, entitlement to free to be specific, and entitlement to free if cost of delivery is free—regardless of investment in creation—to be very specific is metastasizing through the consumer culture. It is most pervasive among young consumers rather than boomers or seniors. For example, a 2010 study by a major research firm (Piper Jaffray) revealed that only 40% of teens legally purchase music online, with 57% admitting they acquire pirated music from peer-to-peer networks and see nothing wrong with doing so. The percentage willing to pay up to 99 cents to download a song from a legal source dropped from 25% to 18% in just one year.

A must-read book about the culture of free, and its current and potential impact on various businesses, is appropriately titled *FREE*, by Chris Anderson. I do not agree with all the author's conclusions, but highly recommend thinking through all the questions he raises and the trends, evolving and predicted, he brings up as they may apply to or even mandate reinvention of your business.

Overall trends in American culture have affected and do affect both price and presentation of price. My grandparents lived in a pay-as-you-go culture. With very rare exception, they saved up to make major purchases and simply did without until they had accumulated enough money. Piggy banks, Mason jars, and coffee cans labeled with the purpose of their savings were common sights on kitchen counters—one for Vacation, another for Washing Machine, another for Back to School Clothes. Virtually every bank promoted Christmas Club accounts, to which deposits were made weekly all year long, for withdrawal only on the Friday immediately following Thanksgiving, the official start of the holiday shopping season. Most stores borrowed the idea with their own layaway plans, where you made weekly or monthly payments toward the purchase of a product in advance of getting it. Some smart merchants injected a little price strategy into that, by matching every dollar the customer put in with a dime, providing the plan was kept in force to completion and product ultimately purchased. The few things for which consumer credit was commonly used, notably homes and automobiles, were viewed by most as necessary evils and required 20% or higher down payments. And home buyers lived for the day of their backyard mortgage-burning party, with family and friends invited. This entire scene must seem a silly fiction to many reading this. But real people really lived this way. Honest. My very own father, after coming home from the Army, rode a little Briggs and Stratton motor scooter—not motorcycle, motor *scooter*—to and from work for over a year while he and mother saved up coins in a can for the big down payment on a car.

In that culture, price was very real, because it was almost always paid in cash, with money saved up over time. Even Friday night out for pizza and a movie was the result of setting aside money for a couple weeks in advance. There was a reality-based mindset about money and therefore about price. That's why your grandparents can accurately recall and report the exact price they paid for many things big and small—car or gallon of gas in a given year, while today's consumer often can't tell you

A Different Time

In 1973, the year I graduated from high school, here were the prices for the following:

Average New Home	$32,500.00
Average New Car	$3,950.00
Average Rent	$175.00/month
Harvard Tuition	$3,000.00/year
Movie Ticket	$1.75
Postage Stamp	.10
Gas	.40/gallon
Coffee	$1.00/lb.

the price paid for much of anything since it happened with a thoughtless swipe of a card, or in payments for which the total price, interest included, isn't known because it's irrelevant. Even I can tell you the prices I paid for my first three cars, in 1972, 1973, and 1975, but I can no longer recall the price of the ones I bought after that. I bought the first two for cash, the third with a hefty, saved-up down payment, a 24-month loan (the longest then possible was 36), and a co-signer. The ones after were bought much less thoughtfully or arduously, pretty much just signing my name.

My parents lived in a cultural transition from pay-as-you-go to go-now, pay-later, over time. Gradually, attitudes about credit and debt changed, and expansive use of credit not just for home and car, but furnishings, backyard pool, trips, clothes, and gifts became the fast-growing normal and accepted way of life. Marketers quickly capitalized on the opportunity to shift focus from price as reasonable or fair or competitive, to monthly payments you could afford. In a relatively short period of time, we went from very little bought on credit and debt feared and loathed to much bought on credit and debt accepted with little question or angst.

My generation went all the way. We buy everything down to our morning coffee and doughnut at the 7-Eleven with credit and think nothing of it. We wouldn't dream of delaying a washer and dryer for three years and trekking to the laundromat while saving up money for that purchase, if we have a credit card that will take the hit. Consequently, in a great many product categories, price is not much of an issue, and sometimes not even mentioned; instead only the monthly payment matters. We are now not just a society of consumers rather than producers, but we are a debt-based society rather than an ownership-based society. Given the quick obsolescence of much of what is bought on extended payments, most people actually own next to

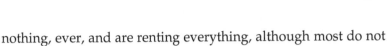

nothing, ever, and are renting everything, although most do not think of their situation in those terms.

Along the way, a parallel cultural conversion took place. My grandparents' generation subscribed to self-reliance as secular religion. Any handout was shameful. They knew there was never a free lunch. As interesting side note, the earliest attempts by marketers to offer senior citizen discounts or have seniors enroll in discount plans fell flat; seniors considered it an insult to suggest they couldn't pay their way and needed a subsidy because of their age. My parents' generation gradually embraced a less rigid allegiance to "if it is to be, it is up to me" and became more accepting of, then slowly eager for government expansion and liberal philosophy. Today, the secular religion of self-reliance is as antique as pay-as-you-go; in its place, a fast-growing, politically encouraged lust for unearned goodies, benefits, support and assistance, transfer of responsibility—to the point of entitlement.

Now, with pay-as-you-go a quaint historical footnote, go-now-and-pay-later the foundation of most consumer purchasing, the internet as a commoditizing force, and an overall cultural shift from independence to entitlement, **everything related to price is impacted, and broadly, price is under pressure.** This is more than an abstract dissertation of societal change or disintegration and political power expansion. It gets right to how Herb and Susan think about prices, payments, what they should have to pay for this or that, and what they should just be given or given access to without paying for it at all.

It's very interesting to look at media. All TV was once free. But consumers were convinced they should be willing to pay for more, more diverse, better, and "adult" TV, and cable subscriptions went from odd luxury to something most now think of as essential. Moving people from free radio to paid radio has not been nearly as successful. I say that with sorrow;

I own stock in Sirius. But even while consumers seem evermore willing to pay for TV, via cable, satellite, hulu.com TV replays, pay-per-view, they are revolting against paying for news media, particularly newspapers, prepared by real journalists with professional research; counting Tommy's blog from Mom's basement as equivalent and demanding *The New York Times* give their content free or go away altogether. Their demands—and weak-kneed publishers' acquiescence—are driving prices of books, magazines, and music into the dumpster. Even in one category like this, customers will pay for one version but insist another version should be free.

The new entitlement mentality does not stop within the borders of media and product drawn from intellectual property. A substantial percentage of people now think of health care as a right, not as products and services—so any price is viewed with hostility by many. Pensions sufficient to support oneself well throughout 30+ years of retirement, once thought of as something carrying price tags, that you bought from banks and insurance companies by saving and prudent money management, are now widely viewed as a right to which all are equally entitled regardless of what the individual has done to get educated, to advance in a career or business, to save responsibly. No less than the Ben of Ben & Jerry's Ice Cream has suggested that everybody's income be capped by law not to exceed the salary paid the President, with all the overage confiscated and redistributed according to need, to grace all with equal amounts of these basic entitlements: food, housing, health care, retirement. Thus, entire industries and professions are threatened deeply by this attitudinal trend. All are undermined to one degree or another.

Strategically, for your business, you need to use everything provided here to its maximum advantage in your situation or a better situation you choose and craft for yourself. Very candidly, you may be in a segment of a business so threatened by these trends that you should exit and apply your talents, skills, energy, and resources elsewhere. Whatever field of enterprise you are in, seeking out buyers willing to pay for value rather than those seeking value far in excess of payment or, worse, feeling entitled to value far in excess of payment, or worst, willing to steal to avoid any payment, is critical. Being able to position yourself in a category of one for certain desirable customers, critical. Creating immunity to downward price pressure, critical.

Immune systems are always multifaceted, and often combat adverse trends. Think of your physical immune system. It is strengthened or weakened by many things aside from luck-of-the-draw genetics: where you choose to live, diet, source of foods, nutrition, obtaining needed quantities of certain directly relevant vitamins and minerals, exercise, quantity and quality of sleep, personal relationships, mental attitude, faith, occupation, stress as well as many external factors, such as proximity to or exposure to toxic chemicals. Most trends are disadvantageous, and make it more difficult for you and me to maintain a strong immune system than it was for our grandparents. Our diet consists largely of processed, chemical-laden foods rather than natural foods; our physical environments more congested and polluted; our lives infinitely more complicated, hectic, and stressful. Most of us are not willing to become Amish in order to bolster our immune systems, but we can deliberately influence most of the factors I cited, and we can behave with awareness of how steep the climb, how difficult the task.

I won't belabor the point, but you could engage in the same analysis of the challenges to a healthy emotional immune system.

The same can be said about a business immune system resistant to downward pressures. You need to proactively strengthen it. Doing so involves work on more than one or two things.

CHAPTER 51

B2B Price Wars and the Way of the Warriors Who Win

Originally appearing as Chapter 9 from
No B.S. Price Strategy

Most B2B marketers succumb to the idea of competition-driven pricing. By accepting this as a fact of life, they surrender in advance and preclude other possibilities. Real warriors, of course, are disgusted by the idea of surrender, so they gravitate to the other choice: controlling the competitive environment via superior, category of one positioning, more effective marketing, and unique value propositions. In short, differentiation. When I explain this and get a stubborn business owner insisting he is in a commoditized category and has no differentiation to offer, I tell him to slit his wrists and get it over with. After all, if the brain is already dead, why keep the body alive?

Some years back, I was speaking at the national convention of the Advertising Specialty Institute and encountered a spectacularly obtuse company owner. ASI's population is comprised of all the companies that sell imprinted ballpoint pens, baseball caps, coffee mugs, and every other sort of promotional product. At the time, the internet was just beginning to exert real influence, and many—maybe most—in this field felt terrorized by price shopping made mouse-click easy. I began my speech by saying: if you believe you are in a commodities business, get out. This woman took me *very* literally. She stormed out of the room. Later, she sent her complaint letter to all parties concerned, accusing me of being ill-informed, ill-prepared, and vile, because, of course, they all *were* in a commodity business. But her facts and mine differed. No one in the promotional products and ad specialty industry needs to be in a commodity business unless they choose to, but they don't need to exit their industry either.

Keith and Travis Lee, owners of 3D (for 3-Dimensional) Mail, Inc.—who contribute their own price strategy elsewhere in *No B.S. Price Strategy*—are great examples. They sell all those products, but they specialize in selling them for use in clever direct-mail campaigns, with the copy, graphics, offer, and theme of the mailing matched to the imprinted doohickey, and they work with the client to devise the entire campaign. You can see their approach to this business at https://3DMailResults.com. Yes, you can buy most of the doodads they sell other places, but you can't buy their expertise. Further, they focus on reaching clients in clumps, as vendor-partners of marketing gurus, trainers, consultants, and coaches like me and many in different niches, from dentistry to financial planning to lawn care. They match their theme campaigns and doodads to the strategies the gurus teach, and are brought to the guru's clientele as a resource. The combination of these two positioning and marketing strategies permits the best price strategy of all: ignoring all price competition. Ironically, this has made their business so successful they can buy in big volume and buy direct from overseas manufacturers, so, often, they now also have the lowest prices. Another in the industry, who I've also coached in business as I have Keith and Travis, is B. Shawn Warren. He sells the same kind of imprinted items as part of his business, but he has specialized in serving fraternal organizations like Kiwanis, the Elks, veterans groups, and civic clubs. Another, a company called SmartPractice, created by my friends Jim and Naomi Rhode, specializes only in the dental, chiropractic, and medical fields. Their products might be commodities, but they have made sure their businesses transcend commoditization with target market specialization.

Personally, I have been in B2B my entire life, beginning in the traditional ad agency business but quickly morphing to the consulting/copywriting practice I've had for 30 years, where I've consistently charged higher fees than just about everybody else. There is, in fact, an entire directory called *Who's Charging What?* in which copywriters foolishly publish their fees—and mine (not listed there) are 4X to 100X higher. Hasn't slowed me in the least. I have also, at different times, owned a manufacturing company competing head to head with others, and been part-owner of an awards/trophy company selling to corporations, fraternal organizations, and government agencies, including the U.S. Navy, Air Force, and Marines. Never have I had these companies claim lowest prices or sell based on price, and it has generally been known that our prices were higher than competitors. In some cases, such as my consulting/copywriting practice, having very high fees is not only widely known, it's promoted as a reason to retain me if you can—if you want the best guy on the planet.

The reality of B2B commerce is that only about 20% of all purchases made by professional purchasing agents, other executives or managers, authorized department heads, and business owners are based on lowest competitive price, and

over half of that 20% occurs within the context of pre-framed competitive bidding. The other 80% of the purchases are made based on more complex criteria. That criteria ranges from the quasi-fraudulent, such as bonuses, gifts, and bribes, to simple quality of relationship to rational reasons, such as the vendor's positioning, reputation, value proposition, and added value, service, warranties, to emotional issues such as CYA for the person making the purchase or bragging rights by having the vendor. In some B2B instances "Made in the USA" once played a big role and is returning as a factor. It's new-age equivalent is "green."

Years back, a friend of mine, Pete Lillo, smartly located his print shop immediately adjacent to the area's busy post office, in a shopping center surrounded by fast-food restaurants. He knew that office employees and secretaries out for noontime errands, to the post office and to grab lunch, would drop off printing and copying work to him because of his very convenient location— without ever considering comparing his prices with other shops a few miles away, east, west, north, and south. Consequently, he quickly built and maintained a thriving, exceptionally profitable business generating approximately 300% more revenue than the national average for a shop its size, in large part thanks to prices 20% to 40% higher than other area shops. Top quality helped, but a convenient location was much more of a deciding factor in a lot of his business rather than either quality or price. For the record, accounts obtained this way, for this reason, included some very large corporations spending thousands and even tens of thousands of dollars every month on business printing.

The bottom line is: 20/80. Only 20% of the purchasing is based on competitive pricing, 80% is not. But 80% of all sellers and salespeople behave as if it was the other way around, and devote 80% of their efforts to competing on price. This is the equivalent of having a genetic predisposition for a horrible disease, being shown irrefutable, empirical evidence that 80% of the reasons people with your genetic predisposition for the disease get it have to do with eating red meat, then making 80% of your entire food intake red meat.

As comedian Ron White says: "You can't fix stupid." But ignorance is repairable, so if, until now, you just haven't known the facts and have been pricing, marketing, and selling in the false reality of competitive pricing, that's good—you can fix yourself. And fix the way you approach your market.

Why then, you might ask, does it *seem* so many B2B sales and purchases are made based on competitive pricing? Two reasons. One, because that's what you believe to be true, so you see, hear, and accept everything that verifies your belief and reject without actually seeing or hearing everything that contradicts it. Two, because 80% of the marketers and salespeople in the B2B world advertise, market, and message price despite it being a purchase determinate only 20% of the time. So the noise is much about price. And the excuse ignorant or ineffective or ignorant and ineffective manufacturers, wholesalers, vendors, professionals, and salespeople give for their failures is losing a competitive pricing battle they could not win. People love placing fault elsewhere rather than embracing personal responsibility— think overweight folks and their bad genes, big bones, low metabolism, food industry conspiracy theories.

The more important question is: Why does *any* B2B purchase get tied to competitive pricing and the lowest price? After all, buying by price alone is rather stupid. It ignores countless other factors that may be as important. Would you choose a baby-sitter for your kids by lowest price, despite the fact that he's a convicted child molester or she's a drug addict? Then why choose a computer system for your company that way?

Three key factors are responsible. One is: opportunity. The easier it is for a customer to price-shop, the more tempted he is to do so. In the consumer marketplace, a person can now stand in his local furniture store with his iPhone and check the price there against Amazon, Costco, etc. instantly, online. Sears idiotically advertises that they'll do it for you, thus boxing themselves into selling at lowest price. The B2B buyer has the internet sitting on his desk, knows how to use it, and because he can, feels he should. Price shopping goods or services has never been easier, so the temptation has never been greater, nor has the pressure from above in big companies. **Two is: the surrender in advance I'm discussing throughout this chapter, which directly links to number three: Absence of other persuasive information provided by competent marketers and sales professionals.** Few buyers really want the cheapest price; all intelligent buyers want or can be made to prefer the best value. These things are rarely the same, but in the absence of persuasive information about matters other than price, shown two apparently identical items, we'll all take the cheaper priced of the two.

As example, you want a simple navy-blue blazer. If you see two that look and feel alike, and have no brand bias, and one is $199.00 and the other $499.00, surely you're tempted to shrug and take the cheaper one—even if your Bentley is being guarded outside by your chauffer. But if somebody who is articulate explains the difference between single-stitch and double-stitch tailoring, sewn vs. glued, full vs. half lining, why one fabric will soon look shiny from dry cleaning while the other will not, odds are very good that the jacket selling for four times more is leaving that store with you.

Now let's assume you are me and you wander into a very good clothing store with top sales professionals—like I did in Las Vegas, at the Bernini store the first time I was sold a very expensive Bernini suit. There, before you even get to the product features/benefits differentiation story, you'll be engaged in different dialogue. And you may never get to the features/

benefits differentiation, as it is somewhat assumed based on the Bernini brand, and may be rendered unnecessary by the other dialogue. That dialogue began with what I did for a living and under what circumstances I might be wearing a suit? . . . Answer: professional speaking, onstage. What was my objective or what might come of such speaking? Answer: attracting a major client. And what might a client be worth? Answer: $100,000.00 and up. Hmmm. Having the best possible appearance, presenting a rich and successful appearance was therefore an important investment for me, wasn't it? As this conversation took place, I was de-jacketed, put in the suit coat, paraded in front of the mirror, oohed and aahed over, led to dressing room, swapped pants, measured and pinned, and had yet to even hear the price. In reality, what did it matter?

The B2B buyer is no different. In the absence of persuasive information about differential value, he will buy the cheapest product that meets his need, and he may very well go searching for it. As he should. The problem here is not the buyer. He's doing his job given what he has to work with—an absence of persuasive information other than price. It's the seller who's failing at his job—providing persuasive information other than price. It's you, not your customer.

Here is a million dollar fact for you. If you will hammer it into your head, it will easily be worth a million dollars during your career, probably more. **There is *no* B2B buyer of *anything* for whom some factors other than price aren't relevant and important.** Please stop, think, read it again. And again.

There is the argument, of course, that the customer is simply, purely, irredeemably a cheapskate. Really? Let's take a very thorough tour of his office as well as his home, investigate which hospital and doctor handled his bypass operation, see what car he drives, and where he stayed on vacation, etc. At his office we damn well better find the desk is nothing more than old doors secured from the city dump up on sawhorses, the bookshelves just boards on bricks, no framed pictures on walls, no brand-name copier or other equipment—all off-brand, everything bought secondhand. He better be driving a ten-year-old Yugo. His last family vacation at Motel 6 and Travelodge way, way off the beach. Not the case? Then stop with the cheapskate talk. A horse is a horse, of course, of course, unless he's Mr. Ed, but no human is a cheapskate about everything. Few are cheapskates about anything when they are provided persuasive value differential information.

If you're losing price wars, you're in the wrong war to begin with.

There are but two possible outcomes to price wars—neither one victory. The B2B price competitor either bleeds and starves to bankruptcy, slowly and painfully over time, as his profit is taken away bit by bit by bit, or he loses more skirmishes than he wins, and more importantly fails at getting good customers, obtaining only bad ones.

Many companies who let themselves get sucked into this become debt burdened, financing their present poor profitability with future obligations. The young founders of a promising software company I once advised chose this path. They were charging significant upfront fees in order to have their excellent system installed and users trained, and acquiring good, committed clients by doing so. In a paean to the gods of volume and speed, they tossed aside this model, dropped their monthly maintenance fees, and took on new accounts with no upfront financial commitment. Two calendar quarters later they expressed shock that their turnover and churn of accounts had skyrocketed, and the achievement of profitability was now stretched out many more months into the future for each month's new accounts—requiring taking on more debt. They may yet get rich, but only if a white knight arrives to buy their company.

They are gambling all on that single possibility. I suppose this is a gamble made often in the software and tech fields, and the news reports the winners, but ignores the far greater number of losers. Only you can decide for yourself, as an entrepreneur, if this is the wager you wish to make with your business. But if it isn't, then the decision to compete on price or to succumb to downward price pressure from competitors is a poor one.

CHAPTER 52

The Making of
Propositions

Originally appearing as Chapter 13 from
No B.S. Price Strategy

A customer's reaction to price is colored by the proposition attached to the price.

Let's be crude for a few minutes. This is reportedly Frank Sinatra's favorite Las Vegas joke: a middle-aged farmer and his wife from a rural area, who've rarely traveled beyond their hometown, save up for years and go to Las Vegas. When checking in, the farmer spots an extraordinarily attractive, extraordinarily well-endowed young woman in a slinky cocktail dress and impossibly high heels loitering near the elevators; he tells his wife he thinks he has spotted one of those working girls and is curious about the price. He goes over and asks her. She takes in his bib overalls, denim shirt, work shoes, and knows better, but tells him that it is $1,000.00 for an hour or $10,000.00

all night. He laughs and says "A THOUSAND dollars? Good lord and gee whiz, missy, when I was in the Navy and went on shore leave we never paid more than $50.00." He and his wife head upstairs, he telling her of this amazing situation. Morning comes, and the farmer and his wife come downstairs for the buffet breakfast—he attired as he was the night before, she in flowered, well-worn housedress, hair in curlers, no makeup. When the elevator stops on the way down, the same lady of the evening enters, gives them the once-over and says to the farmer: "See what you get for 50 bucks?"

So let's assume you are single and unencumbered, not morally opposed to prostitution, willing to pay for a sexual adventure, with sufficient discretionary income and cash in your pocket to indulge just about any whim. You're at your hotel bar one late evening when you are approached by an attractive but not, to your taste, stunning young woman, who quietly asks if you'd enjoy some company in the privacy of your room. When you inquire about price, she responds flatly: $300.00 an hour. While you're mulling it over and she visits the powder-room, let's replace her with a better salesperson, who happens also, to your taste, to be stunning. When you inquire about price, she quietly says: "For the most incredible, mind-blowing, unforgettable sexual experience of your entire life—including sex secrets passed down through generations back to the ancient Orient—$1,000.00." Which price might seem better to you? Clearly one is cheaper than the other. One is 300% higher than the other. Price may make or break this sale if you are one of those rare birds who only buys by cheapest price. But it's more likely, if the sale is made, it will be by the woman who presented the superior proposition.

And so it is in the overwhelming majority of situations. Of course, I'm not suggesting that you are the equal of a lady of the evening plying your trade at the bar, although, with Sydney

Biddle Barrows, once the infamous "Mayflower Madam," I did co-author a sales book, *Uncensored Sales Strategies*, which I suggest as an eye-opening read. But don't take offense. Take the very valuable lesson. In the above situation, price matters little. If we moved the example out onto a street corner, with street hooker and guy in a car, price might very well govern the sale. Thus, **place and buyer have an impact on both price and its impact on buying decision, so you want to present yourself in a good place to good buyers. Then, price's importance is dwarfed by proposition.** And here's the biggie: you probably can't actually control all your competition, restrict all your costs, and muster sufficient efficiencies in order to always, profitably offer the cheapest price. But you are in total control of the strength of your proposition.

Five Kinds of Propositions

There are five kinds of propositions to concern yourself with:

1. *Unique Selling Proposition (USP).* Your Unique Selling Proposition can be found in the answer to my copyright-protected

Five Propositions

1. Unique Selling Proposition (USP)

2. Unique Value Proposition (UVP)

3. Irresistible Offer

4. Unique Safety Proposition (USP)

5. Unique Experience Proposition (UEP)

question: *why should I, your prospect, choose to do business with you vs. any and every other option available?* You need a continuing USP for your business and, often, additional USPs for different products, services, offers. In a sense, this is a concise summary of your positioning. It's best if it telegraphs benefits. You can review a detailed presentation about USP in my book *The Ultimate Marketing Plan.*

Implicit in your USP, from a price strategy standpoint, should be the answer to a second question: *why should I, your prospect, choose you regardless of price, be unconcerned about price, and never consider comparison shopping based on price?*

If you have solid answers to both those questions baked in to your primary sales message, you have the foundation for aggressive pricing.

2. *Unique Value Proposition (UVP).* This includes presentation of price, and justification/minimization of price by various means, including, when bundling, the higher value of components if purchased separately; the value of the benefits to the user; money to be made or saved through ownership of the product or use of the service. The best value propositions find ways to make price a nonissue or to make the product pay for itself. An example of the latter is the new, energy-efficient windows that pay for themselves through lower electricity bills. The task is to make a *believable* case for value far in excess of price.

Remember that value encompasses intangibles as well as tangibles. If you hire a private VIP guide to escort you around at Disney World in Orlando, you still ride the same rides, see the same shows, eat in the same restaurants, buy souvenirs in the same shops as you would without the guide. There aren't two different parks. The core tangible remains the same. But the $195.00 an hour

VIP guide delivers different value to different customers. There's status, showing off, and bragging rights; there's speed and convenience, so it's less tiring and stressful, thus making the whole excursion more enjoyable; there's being able to do more in the time you're there, thus making the whole vacation more valuable. And so on. Don't leave out all the intangibles when you build your value proposition—or when you price.

3. *Irresistible Offer*. Never forget: you *aren't* doing direct-response advertising or direct marketing unless you extend a specific offer. But a bland, vanilla, ordinary offer isn't much better than no offer at all. You have to ask yourself what *your* customers will find irresistible. For example, we know from split tests that, when selling conferences to doctors, free airfare and lodging are much more persuasive than a discount of equal value. You have to know your own customers' psyche. A complete I.O. will often include discount, premiums/bonuses (plural), incentive for fast response, penalty for response after a deadline.

4. *Unique Safety Proposition*. This usually revolves around a guarantee or guarantees, warranties, providing risk reversal or risk reversal-plus (e.g., *double* your money back), and can be supported statistically—years in business, numbers served—and with social or peer proof—testimonials, client lists. The greater the skepticism, the stakes, and/or the present resistance to spending, the stronger and more reassuring the Safety Proposition needs to be. Sometimes, this can be the basis of its own profit center. I recently bought a modestly priced piece of jewelry from a catalog. The catalog copy included a 60-day "She'll Love It or Your Money Back" guarantee. When ordering on the phone, I was also given a one-year replacement warranty—if the item got

damaged, the chain broke, the jewel dislodged, the surface scarred—they would replace it free. I was upsold a two-year extension of the replacement warranty for "just $49.00 a year." I'm confident selling these $98.00 pieces of paper is more profitable than selling the $395.00 pieces of jewelry.

A lot of people are subconsciously if not consciously looking for safety, security, and certainty in an unsafe, insecure, and uncertain world. The recent years' chaos in all major institutions—government, banking, rock-of-Gibraltar companies like General Motors, the Catholic Church, etc., and in the economy, has left a lot of people feeling very anxious. Just about everybody has also had plenty of experiences where service after the sale is hard to come by, promises made before the sale forgotten. Into this environment you come with your proposition. Making it feel very, very safe to buy can be very compelling, and can support premium pricing.

I rack up some fat FedEx bills, since I send most of my work for clients and a lot of correspondence that way. I could save tens of thousands of dollars every year by using UPS, USPS Priority Mail, and other alternate carriers. Why don't I? Because the security of knowing FedEx will get it there on time is worth more to me than the difference in cost between them and lower priced competitors. Every time I fill out a FedEx airbill, I'm buying a Safety Proposition.

5. *Unique Experience Proposition (UEP).* This is the newest proposition on this list, acknowledging the reality of the New Economy as an Experience Economy, where people most willingly buy and pay premiums for complete, total, enjoyable, and unusual experiences. People want to be assured of a good experience when buying *and* from the deliverable.

Pay attention to the Experience Proposition put forth in TV commercials for Norwegian and Carnival Cruise Lines, dining at Outback Steakhouse, or marketing I've assisted with at https:// KennedysBarberClub.com. None of these are restricted to or even put primary emphasis on the core products or services: the cruise, the steak, the shave 'n haircut.

In the seminar and conference business, where I do a lot of work as a consultant, a copywriter, and occasionally as a speaker, excellent, high-value educational content has gone from the thing being sold to the minimum ante to even be in the game. To motivate attendance, a complete experience has to be offered—which may include book signings with authors, meet 'n greets and photo opportunities with celebrities, field trips to interesting sites, contests and competitions, award ceremonies, car and vacation giveaways, and more. At recent years' Glazer-Kennedy Insider's Circle™ annual Marketing and Moneymaking SuperConferences, we've featured celebrity speakers including Gene Simmons of KISS, Ivanka Trump, and Joan Rivers; actors in superhero costumes roaming the exhibit area, taking posed photos with attendees; chair-massage therapists on duty; and a VIP Lounge for a certain level of Members. A special seminar I did in conjunction with my *No B.S. Wealth Attraction in the New Economy* featured a pirate theme—pirate décor, pirate ship backdrop for photos, pirate hats and toys for attendees, plus an opportunity to be photographed with Dean Martin's Rolls-Royce (which I own), and a Night at the Races.

Ultimately, you will build a hybrid proposition, incorporating some or all of these five. For clarity's sake, you'll want to lead with the one you think serves you and fits your target market best, with the others hooked to it.

Maybe the most important thing about this for anyone inexperienced with *direct* marketing is that **you begin thinking in terms of making propositions**. Most business owners do not. Most merely advertise the existence of their business or products or services. Or its existence plus features/benefits. Or existence plus products/prices, like car dealers' or electronics stores' advertisements do. These types of marketing messages are so common they encourage commoditization and either focus on price, suggest price shopping, or fail altogether. There are very few people who care that your business exists—beyond your spouse, ex-spouse getting alimony, creditors, and possibly somebody who awakes that day with an emergent need for what you do and is in hot pursuit of it. Likewise, for the features and benefits of your products. It takes more than that to stir up interest. The making of a good proposition goes a long way.

Even in hard core, down 'n dirty direct-response advertising— the sale of a product in a two-minute TV commercial ending with "call now"—there has to be a composite of factors properly assembled for success. If you didn't see or don't remember the lessons from the TV show *PitchMen* that ran on the Discovery Channel, featuring behind-the-scenes making of the famous Billy Mays commercials, I suggest obtaining and watching the DVDs. In the first episode, you are there when the inventor of a new shoe insole arrives, a commercial is planned, script written, commercial filmed and tested. You will see Billy and his partner figure out dramatic demonstrations for the insole's shock absorption: Billy pounding his hand, protected by the insole, with a hammer; a car being driven over his hand, protected by the insole. The price is decided on, in part based on an impromptu focus group of car mechanics trying out the product and being asked what they'd pay for it, as well as competitive pricing in retail, and Billy May's experience with products on TV. The proposition is then built, to stack value far in excess of the price.

All that is then combined into a powerful, persuasive two-minute commercial that grabs attention, interests you in gel insoles even if you had zero interest in them before the commercial began, delivers a USP, suggests a UEP, and presents a UVP. A home run it is. Hundreds of thousands of pairs of the insoles have been sold since, with that commercial.

> **RESOURCE**
>
> If direct marketing is new to you, get the rules of the road and examples in every category of business in my book *No B.S. DIRECT Marketing for NON-Direct Marketing Businesses*.

Depending on what business you *think* you are in—tax preparation or taxidermy, dentistry or detailing of autos, industrial chemicals or investments—you will quickly conclude the gel insoles example has nothing to do with you. If you had a conversion here and realized you are *actually* in the business of making compelling propositions, then you would find the gel insoles example fascinating. And if you took that conversion seriously, and committed to learning all you can about making propositions, and brought that to your business, you would find that selling at higher prices and profit margins becomes infinitely easier.

Avoiding
Apples-Apples Comparisons

Two roadside vendors are situated right next to each other, both selling fresh-picked apples from their orchards. Each has good parking under shade trees. Each has good, visible signs. Each has several people there working so service is fast. Who will win the day? Sadly, probably, the one who lowers his price below wherever the other stops.

If you choose to conduct business in this kind of situation, frankly, there's little Jason or I can do to help you. Neither of us carries psychiatrist credentials.

One year, I ordered a Valentine's gift for my wife from a catalog sent to me by Calyx Flowers. Even though, at the time, I owned stock in 1-800-Flowers and have, several times, been a speaker on the same programs with 1-800-Flowers' CEO, Jim McCann, I purchased a $199.95 gift from their competitor. My reasons are very instructive. First, they sent me a catalog in the mail, while 1-800-Flowers relied on email. I do not use email and I wasn't planning to send flowers as that year's gift, so I would not have proactively gone back to 1-800-Flowers to shop. The unsolicited catalog had a chance because it arrived and snagged my attention. As Woody Allen famously said, a third of all success is showing up. Of course, email is a lot cheaper to send than full-color printed catalogs (my thoughts about the handicap of bad economics are in Chapter 16 of *No B.S. Price Strategy*).

Apples-Apples, cont.

Unique Value Proposition in Action

The gift I bought from Calyx was a "bundle" of three gifts in matching red silk boxes, delivered one per day, over three days, February 12, 13, and 14. Absent this creative offer, I might have bought one gift, and spent less. They sold three. Many might have balked at the bundle of three for $199.95 if delivered as one, but the delivery of the three gifts over three days, building up to the finale on the 14th was unique—thus a distraction from price and an added value. Ultimately, they took themselves out of clump of flowers to clump of flowers, apples to apples comparison territory altogether by changing one little element: delivery. The "bundling" of multiple items is a common way to try and boost transaction size and make direct comparison difficult, and it alone should always be considered. But Calyx went a clever step further.

Their marketing and price strategies wizards deserve applause. Unfortunately, their implementation folks got demerits. The person taking my order over the phone was ill-informed and inept, making me wish within minutes that I'd stuck with good old, reliable 1-800-Flowers. He actually said: "Gee, they just threw me on the phones and I'm not really sure of what I'm doing." It took a l-o-n-g 20 minutes to get this order done and, yes, I should have bailed out, but by then, dammit, I wanted *this* thing. Also, no attempt at an upsell. No query about a second gift for daughter, sister, mother, mistress. Sad thing is, the $199.95 thing could just as easily be $229.00, and the extra

Apples-Apples, *cont.*

money invested in better phone scripts, personnel, training, coaching, and supervision.

(Again, see Chapter 16 of *No B.S. Price Strategy*.) My advice: Don't strive to sell your stuff as cheaply as you can; strive to sell it as effectively as you can, and price to support whatever is required to do that.

By the way, I've never ordered from Calyx again—despite receiving countless catalogs. I have returned to 1-800-Flowers.

Nevertheless, Calyx's marketing and price strategy is brilliant. It perfectly illustrates the power of One Little Thing Changed, in getting you out of the apples to apples comparison territory. This must be your goal: escape apples to apples. Searching for your One Little Thing is a very big thing.

About
the Author

DAN S. KENNEDY is a made-from-scratch multimillionaire serial entrepreneur, having started, bought, built, and sold companies; an active investor including in startups, such as a now category-leading software firm; and a strategic advisor, consultant, and business coach to entrepreneurs. He is the author of over 30 business books and editor of several business and financial newsletters. He has a 40-year track record of guiding entrepreneurs to seven-figure incomes and personal wealth. As a speaker, he had nine years' tenure on the number-one seminar tour, appearing with four former U.S. Presidents including Ronald Reagan, leading celebrity entrepreneurs, and notable business speakers like Zig Ziglar, Jim Rohn, Brian Tracy, and Tom Hopkins. His own events for entrepreneurs have featured celebrity entrepreneurs like Gene Simmons, Kathy Ireland, and Joan Rivers. Dan's speaking career includes over 3,000 compensated presentations from three hours to three days in duration, in the U.S. and abroad.

Other books in the No B.S. Series by Dan Kennedy

No B.S. Business Success in the New Economy

No B.S. Grassroots Marketing with Jeff Slutsky

No B.S. Guide to Brand-Building by Direct Response

No B.S. Direct Marketing, Third Edition

No B.S. Guide to Direct Response Social Media Marketing with Kim Walsh Phillips

No B.S. Guide to Marketing to Leading-Edge Boomers & Seniors with Chip Kessler

No B.S. Guide to Maximum Referrals & Customer Retention with Shaun Buck

No B.S. Guide to Powerful Presentations with Dustin Mathews

No B.S. Trust-Based Marketing with Matt Zagula

No B.S. Price Strategy with Jason Marrs

No B.S. Ruthless Management of People & Profits, 2nd Edition

No B.S. Sales Success in the New Economy

No B.S. Time Management for Entrepreneurs, 3rd Edition

No B.S. Wealth Attraction in the New Economy

Index

Entrepreneur BOOKS

Don't miss out on the rest of
Dan S. Kennedy's books. Visit the
Entrepreneur Bookstore and use the code
below to receive 15% off any book in the
No B.S. series.

Redemption Code: NOBS15

Link to Bookstore:
https://www.entrepreneur.com/bookstore